THE GLOBAL REACH OF EUROPEAN REFUGEE LAW

Europe has the most advanced regional protection regime in the world. The predicted impact of this body of norms, including the new Common European Asylum System, has been widely identified as one that will have a 'ripple effect' beyond the EU. However, very few studies have noted the fact that this regime has already influenced the law and practice of States around the world, for some time. The purpose of this book is to gather evidence that emulation is happening (if it is), to explore the extent and identify the processes through which it is happening, and to examine the implications of these findings. Of the seven case studies examined here, all but one reveal clear evidence of emulation at some point in time. The EU protection regime, which has been most influenced by the European Court of Human Rights, is 'naturally' evolving transnationally and spreading internationally.

HÉLÈNE LAMBERT is Professor of International Law, University of Westminster, London, where she teaches refugee law, human rights law and EU law. She has been a regular consultant for the Council of Europe and the United Nations High Commissioner for Refugees (UNHCR); she also served briefly as a Protection Officer for UNHCR (1996). She has written extensively on asylum, refugees and human rights.

JANE MCADAM is Scientia Professor of Law and an Australian Research Council Future Fellow, University of New South Wales, Australia. She is also Director of the International Refugee and Migration Law project at the Gilbert + Tobin Centre of Public Law. She has undertaken consultancies for UNHCR and a number of governments on forced migration issues.

MARYELLEN FULLERTON is Professor of Law at Brooklyn Law School, New York. She has been selected twice as a Fulbright Scholar, most recently serving as the Distinguished Professor of Law at the University of Trento, Italy. In addition to publishing numerous academic works on refugee and migration law, she served as a reporter for Human Rights Watch and headed several human rights missions in Germany.

THE GLOBAL REACH
OF EUROPEAN
REFUGEE LAW

Edited by

HÉLÈNE LAMBERT

JANE McADAM

and

MARYELLEN FULLERTON

CAMBRIDGE
UNIVERSITY PRESS

CAMBRIDGE
UNIVERSITY PRESS

University Printing House, Cambridge CB2 8BS, United Kingdom

Published in the United States of America by Cambridge University Press, New York

Cambridge University Press is part of the University of Cambridge.

It furthers the University's mission by disseminating knowledge in the pursuit of education, learning, and research at the highest international levels of excellence.

www.cambridge.org
Information on this title: www.cambridge.org/9781107041752

© Cambridge University Press 2013

First published 2013

Printed in the United Kingdom by CPI Group Ltd, Croydon CRO 4YY

A catalogue record for this publication is available from the British Library

Library of Congress Cataloguing in Publication data
The global reach of European refugee law / Edited by Hélène Lambert,
Jane McAdam, and Maryellen Fullerton.
pages cm
Includes bibliographical references and index.
ISBN 978-1-107-04175-2
1. Refugees – Legal status, laws, etc. – Europe.   2. Refugees – Legal status,
laws, etc.   I. Lambert, Hélène, editor of compilation.   II. McAdam, Jane,
editor of compilation.   III. Fullerton, Maryellen, editor of compilation.
KJC6057.G56   2013
342.2408′3–dc23
2013007967

ISBN 978-1-107-04175-2 Hardback

Cambridge University Press has no responsibility for the persistence or accuracy of URLs for external or third-party internet websites referred to in this publication, and does not guarantee that any content on such websites is, or will remain, accurate or appropriate.

CONTENTS

CÉLINE BAULOZ is a research assistant on a research project on state-lessness in international law for the Programme for the Study of Global Migration at the Graduate Institute of International and Development Studies (Geneva). She is also assistant editor of the *Refugee Survey Quarterly*, and is finishing her Ph.D. thesis in international law at the Graduate Institute. She previously worked as a teaching assistant at the Geneva Academy of International Humanitarian Law and Human Rights and as a consultant for international and non-governmental organizations (including UNHCR, the International Committee of the Red Cross and the Oslo Institute for Social Research). Her areas of interest include international refugee law, international humanitarian law and international human rights law. Her present research focuses on EU and US asylum law, as well as the role of international humanitarian law in the refugee protection regime.

DAVID JAMES CANTOR (BA Hons (Cantab.), M.Sc. Dist. (London), Ph.D. (Essex)) is Director of the Refugee Law Initiative and a lecturer in international human rights law at the School of Advanced Study, University of London. His research addresses the protection of refugees and other dis-placed persons, primarily during situations of armed conflict, and he has a particular interest in refugee law, human rights law and the laws of war. Dr Cantor has carried out extensive fieldwork on displacement and armed conflict in Colombia, Ecuador, Venezuela and Panama. He has also trained and advised governments from Latin America, the Caribbean, Africa, Asia and the Pacific on international protection. He previously worked as a Legal Officer for the Refugee Legal Centre as well as for the UNHCR. His mono-graph entitled *The Return of IDPs During Armed Conflict: International Law and Its Implementation in Colombia* will be published shortly. He was recently awarded a three-year Future Research Leaders grant from the

ESCR for his project Pushing the Boundaries: New Dynamics of Forced Migration and Transnational Responses in Latin America.

VINCENT CHETAIL is Professor of Public International Law at the Graduate Institute of International and Development Studies (Geneva) and Director of the Programme for the Study of Global Migration. He is a board member of the Geneva Academy of International Humanitarian Law and Human Rights and was the Research Director of the Geneva Academy (2004–12). Professor Chetail is editor-in-chief of *Refugee Survey Quarterly*, a member of the founding editorial board of *Oxford Bibliographies in International Law*, and general editor of the series *Organisation internationale et relations internationales*. He is also Senior Research Associate at the Refugee Law Initiative (University of London), as well as a member of the Academic Network for Legal Studies on Immigration and Asylum in Europe, the Advisory Council of the Global Migration Policy Associates and the General Assembly of the International Institute of Human Rights (Strasbourg). Professor Chetail has published widely on various issues related to public international law, migration and armed conflict. He regularly serves as a consultant to governments, non-governmental organizations and international organizations and has been Visiting Professor at several universities (such as the European University Institute in Florence in 2010, the Université libre de Bruxelles since 2008 and the University of Paris XI since 2006).

JEAN-FRANÇOIS DURIEUX is a senior researcher at the Graduate Institute of International Studies Centre for the Study of Global Migration in Geneva. He is also a research associate of the Refugee Studies Centre at the University of Oxford. There he taught international human rights and refugee law (2007–09 and 2011–12), and is currently associated with its Humanitarian Innovation Project. In October 2011, he completed a thirty-year long career with the UNHCR, his last assignment being that of Director in the Division of Programme Support and Management. He served with UNHCR in Sudan, Djibouti, Canada, Mexico/Cuba/Belize, Tanzania and Myanmar. He also occupied senior positions at UNHCR headquarters in Geneva, where he was in charge of, among other things, UNHCR's contributions to the asylum harmonization debate in Europe; the development of a UNHCR research policy and service; the Convention Plus initiative; the promotion and dissemination of refugee law worldwide; and the development of performance indicators. Besides contributing to numerous UNHCR publications, he has authored or co-authored scholarly articles on a range of refugee and asylum law issues, with a major focus on legal responses to mass influxes and the implications of refugee emergencies and protracted displacement. He is a regular contributor to the *International Journal of Refugee Law* and the *Forced Migration Review*. He is a graduate of Facultés Universitaires St-Louis in Brussels, and obtained his law degree from the Catholic University of Louvain in Belgium.

MARYELLEN FULLERTON (BA, Phi Beta Kappa (Duke) JD (Antioch)) is Professor of Law at Brooklyn Law School, New York, where she teaches refugee law, immigration and nationality law, international litigation, federal courts and civil procedure. Among her most recent works are her co-authored casebooks, *Forced Migration: Law and Policy* and *Immigration and Citizenship Law: Process and Policy*, which are used by more than 100 law schools and universities throughout the US. She has been selected twice as a Fulbright Scholar, most recently serving as the Distinguished Professor of Law, Faculty of Jurisprudence, University of Trento, Italy. Earlier, she was a Fulbright Scholar in Belgium and Germany, a German Marshall Fund Fellow in Hungary, and a Visiting Scholar at the Center for Advanced Studies in Social Sciences in Spain. She has also served as editor-in-chief of the *Refugee Law Reader*, a comprehensive online resource available in English, Spanish, French and Russian for the rapidly evolving field of international refugee law. In addition to preparing numerous academic publications, she served as a rapporteur for Human Rights Watch and headed several human rights missions in Germany.

HÉLÈNE LAMBERT (Maitrise de Droit Public (Strasbourg), Ph.D. (Exeter)) is Professor of International Law in the Department of Advanced Legal Studies (School of Law, University of Westminster, London) where she teaches refugee law, human rights law and EU Law. She was previously a senior lecturer at Brunel University and a lecturer at the University of Exeter. She has been a regular consultant for the Council of Europe and the UNHCR; she also served briefly as a Protection Officer for UNHCR (1996). Professor Lambert has written extensively on asylum, refugees and human rights. Her publications include: *The Limits of Transnational Law: Refugee Law, Policy Harmonization and Judicial Dialogue in the European Union* (co-ed. with G. S. Goodwin-Gill, 2010, Cambridge University Press, paperback edn, 2013); *International Refugee Law* (ed., 2010); *International Law and International Relations* (co-authored with D. Armstrong and T. Farrell, Cambridge University Press, 2007, 2nd edn, 2012); *The Position of Aliens in Relation to the European Convention on Human Rights* (3rd edn, 2006); *Seeking Asylum: Comparative Law and Practice in Selected European Countries* (1995). She is also author of numerous articles in the *International and Comparative Law Quarterly*, the *International Journal of Refugee Law* and the *Refugee Survey Quarterly*.

JANE MCADAM (BA (Hons), LLB (Hons) (Sydney), D.Phil. (Oxford)) is Scientia Professor at the Faculty of Law, University of New South Wales, Sydney. She holds an Australian Research Council Future Fellowship and is the Director of the International Refugee and Migration Law project at the Gilbert + Tobin Centre of Public Law. She is also a non-resident senior fellow at the Brookings Institution in Washington, DC and a research associate at the University of Oxford's Refugee Studies Centre. Professor McAdam is the Co-Rapporteur of the International Law Association International Committee on International Law and Sea-level Rise; the Associate Rapporteur of the Convention Refugee Status and Subsidiary Protection Working Party for the International Association of Refugee Law Judges; a member of the Consultative Committee of the Nansen Initiative on Disaster-Induced Cross-Border Displacement; and a member of the Advisory Board of the Asia-Pacific Migration and Environment Network. She has undertaken consultancies for UNHCR and governments on forced migration issues. Professor McAdam is the author of key works on international refugee law and climate change-related movement, including: *The Refugee in International Law* (with Guy S. Goodwin-Gill, 3rd edn, 2007); *Complementary Protection in International Refugee Law* (2007); *Climate Change, Forced Migration, and International Law* (2012); *Climate Change and Australia: Warming to the Global Challenge* (with Ben Saul, Steven Sherwood, Tim Stephens and James Slezak, 2012); *Climate Change and Displacement: Multidisciplinary Perspectives* (ed., 2011); *Forced Migration, Human Rights and Security* (ed., 2008).

AUDREY MACKLIN (B.Sc. (Alberta), LLB (Toronto), LLM (Yale)) is Professor of Law at the University of Toronto. She teaches, researches and writes in the area of migration and citizenship law, gender and culture, and business and human rights. She is co-author of the Canadian text, *Immigration and Refugee Law: Cases, Materials and Commentary*, and has published articles in many peer-reviewed journals, including the *International Journal of Refugee Law*, *Georgetown Immigration Law Journal*, *Human Rights Quarterly*, *Theoretical Inquiries in Law*, *Columbia*

Journal of Law and Human Rights, European Journal of Law and Migration, Law and Social Politics and *International Migration Review*. She has also contributed to several edited book collections. Her work has explored gender-related persecution and refugee status, the securitization of citizenship and migration, the case of Omar Khadr, privatization of migration processes, the role of rights in migration law and refugee status determination. Professor Macklin was a member of Canada's Immigration and Refugee Board (1994–6), where she adjudicated refugee claims. From 2007 to the present, she has been involved in the case of Omar Khadr, a Canadian citizen detained by the US at Guantànamo Bay for ten years. In that capacity, she was an observer for Human Rights Watch (HRW) at the Military Commission proceedings in Guantànamo Bay, and represented HRW as amicus before the Supreme Court of Canada in two Khadr appeals. Professor Macklin is a founding member of the Canadian Association of Refugee Lawyers.

MARINA SHARPE (BA, LLB, BCL (McGill), M.Sc. (LSE)) is a D.Phil. candidate in the Faculty of Law at the University of Oxford, where she is also a Trudeau scholar. She was called to the bar of England and Wales in 2010 and to the New York bar in 2006, and spent almost three years in private practice at Cravath, Swaine & Moore LLP in New York and London. Prior to this, she worked as a legal adviser with the Refugee Law Project of Makerere University in Kampala, and later returned to Uganda as legal officer of the International Refugee Rights Initiative. She has also worked with AMERA-Egypt, Fahamu and the University of Oxford's Refugee Studies Centre, and regularly undertakes consultancy work for organizations including Amnesty International, the Euro-Mediterranean Human Rights Network, the EBRD and UNHCR. She co-founded and serves as a director of the US non-governmental organization Asylum Access. She has lectured at the universities of London, Oxford and Tripoli, as well as at Georgetown University's Center for Transnational Legal Studies. Her work has been published in journals including the *African Journal of International and Comparative Law*, the *International Journal of Refugee Law*, the *Journal of Refugee Studies* and the *McGill Law Journal*.

DALLAL STEVENS (LLB (Hons) (Hull), Ph.D. (Warwick), Sol. of the Supr. Court (Eng. & Wales)) is Associate Professor of Law at the University of Warwick. Her expertise is in the fields of refugee and asylum law, on which she has published widely. Much of her work has revolved around the construction of the asylum seeker within a contemporary perspective, although she has also examined the plight of the refugee in a historical context. She is author of *UK Asylum Law and Policy: Historical and Contemporary Perspectives* (2004). A particular focus of her research has been the law's treatment of asylum seekers in the UK and Europe. Her work adopts a contextual and, at times, comparative approach, and is concerned with highlighting the tension that exists between asylum law and human rights protection in this contentious area. She is currently researching asylum and refugee policies in the Middle East and has a forthcoming article in the *International Journal of Refugee Law* entitled 'Legal Status, Labelling, and Protection: The Case of Iraqi "Refugees" in Jordan'. Associate Professor Stevens has acted as an adviser to a number of national bodies, including the Home Office and Parliament. She has served as a trustee for the former immigration law advisory agency in the UK – the Immigration Advisory Service – and for the Electronic Immigration Network. She is on the editorial board of the *Immigration, Asylum and Nationality Law Journal, Law and Humanities* and, formerly, *Butterworths Immigration Law Service.*

ACKNOWLEDGEMENTS

We wish to thank our many friends and colleagues for their support for our work on this book and to express our special gratitude to Fiona Chong and to Beth Pollastro for their extraordinary assistance in preparing the manuscript for publication.

ABBREVIATIONS

AEC	African Economic Community
AsylA	Asylum Act (Switzerland)
AU	African Union
BIA	Board of Immigration Appeals
BRRA	Balanced Refugee Reform Act
CBSA	Canadian Border Services Agency
CEAS	Common European Asylum System
CEPS	Centre for European Policy Studies
CETA	Comprehensive Economic Trade Agreement
CIREFCA	Conferencia Internacional sobre Refugiados, Desplazados y Repatriados de Centro América (International Conference on Central-American Refugees, Displaced and Repatriated Persons)
CJEU	Court of Justice of the European Union
CMLR	Common Market Law Reports
COE	Council of Europe
DLR	Dominion Law Reports
EAC	East African Community
EC	European Communities
ECHR	European Convention on Human Rights
ECJ	European Court of Justice
ECOWAS	Economic Community of West African States
ECR	European Court Reports
ECRE	European Council on Refugees and Exiles
EEA	European Economic Area
ENP	European Neighbourhood Process
EU	European Union
EWCA	Court of Appeal of England and Wales
EWHC	High Court of England and Wales
EXCOM	Executive Committee
FC	Federal Court
FCA	Federal Court of Appeal
FCR	Federal Court Reports
FNA	Foreign Nationals Act (Switzerland)
IFA	internal flight alternative
Imm. LR	Immigration Law Reporter

INS	Immigration and Naturalization Service
IO	international organization
IRB	Immigration and Refugee Board
IRPA	Immigration and Refugee Protection Act
JICRA	Jurisprudence et informations de la Commission suisse de recours en matière d'asile (Jurisprudence and information of the Swiss Appeals Asylum Commission)
JO	*Journal Officiel* (France)
Mercosur	Mercado Común del Sur (Common Market of the South)
MPI	Migration Policy Institute
MS-13	Mara Salvatrucha
NGO	non-governmental organization
NR	National Reporter
NSGB	National Status Granting Body
OAS	Organization of American States
OAU	Organization of African Unity
OECD	Organisation for Economic Co-operation and Development
OJ	Official Journal of the European Union
OSAR	Organisation suisse d'aide aux réfugiés (Swiss refugees organization)
POE	port of entry
QD	Qualification Directive
REC	Subregional Economic Community
RSD	refugee status determination
SADC	Southern African Development Community
SC	Statutes of Canada
SCC	Supreme Court of Canada
SCO	safe country of origin
SCR	Supreme Court Reporter
SI	Statutory Instrument
TAF	Tribunal administratif fédéral (Swiss Federal Administrative Tribunal)
TAIEX	Technical Assistance and Information Exchange
TFEU	Treaty on the Functioning of the European Union
TPS	Temporary Protected Status
UK	United Kingdom
UN	United Nations
UNHCR	Office of the United Nations High Commissioner for Refugees
UNHRC	United Nations Human Rights Committee
UNTS	United Nations Treaty Series
US	United States
USD	United States dollars

Introduction: European refugee law and transnational emulation

HÉLÈNE LAMBERT

Europe has the most advanced regional protection regime in the world. The regime has taken shape through a series of legal undertakings on asylum, refugee law principles and human rights between Member States of the European Union (EU), aiming at an ever-greater uniformity in the law and practice of its members. The EU sought to codify a common regional system of asylum by 2012, in order to provide a single asylum procedure and a uniform protection status.[1] A regime covering twenty-four countries,[2] including some of the most developed and powerful in the world, is bound to exert considerable influence beyond Europe. The predicted impact of this body of EU norms has been widely identified in the academic literature as one that will have a 'ripple effect' beyond the EU, particularly with respect to the evolving content of international refugee law by means of changing customary law and UNHCR practice.[3] However, very few studies have noted the fact that the European protection regime has already influenced the law and practice of States

---

[1] Art. 78(2), Treaty on the Functioning of the European Union, as amended by the Treaty of Lisbon, which entered into force on 1 December 2009 (OJ 2010 No. C 83/47).

[2] Denmark opted out entirely of the asylum package; both the UK and Ireland opted out of most of the second phase (recast) of EU legislation.

[3] B. S. Chimni, 'Reforming the International Refugee Regime: A Dialogic Model' (2001) 14 *Journal of Refugee Studies* 151–68, at 157; Volker Türk and Frances Nicholson, 'Refugee Protection in International Law: An Overall Perspective', in Erika Feller, Volker Türk and Frances Nicholson (eds.), *Refugee Protection in International Law: UNHCR's Global Consultations on International Protection* (Cambridge: Cambridge University Press, 2003), p. 6; Catherine Dauvergne, *Making People Illegal* (Cambridge: Cambridge University Press, 2008), pp. 150–3; Guy S. Goodwin-Gill, 'The Search for the One, True Meaning…', in Guy S. Goodwin-Gill and Hélène Lambert (eds.), *The Limits of Transnational Law: Refugee Law, Policy Harmonization and Judicial Dialogue in the European Union* (Cambridge: Cambridge University Press, 2010), at pp. 238–9.

around the world, for some time.[4] The implications of this are great, in terms of understanding the global reach of regional systems of law, and how this shapes the relationship between international rules and standards, and national law and practice across the world when it comes to refugee protection.

This volume explores the extent to which European (or EU) legal norms of refugee protection have been emulated in other parts of the world, and assesses the implications of these trends. At times, the norms may *not* have had much discernible influence. This, too, is of interest. The aim of this volume is therefore more evaluative than speculative. We believe that now is a good time to take stock and assess the influence of European refugee law beyond the EU. This is because the first phase of the Common European Asylum System (CEAS) legislation (which codifies over twenty years of State practice) has concluded, and it is therefore a useful point in time to look both backwards and forwards. Thus, the volume examines how the European protection regime has (or has not) influenced national refugee law and protection practice in a range of States around the world. This is evaluated in two respects: first, in terms of the *extent* of influence (e.g., partial or total and the content of the norm being emulated), and second, in terms of the *processes* whereby emulation of the European protection regime has occurred (e.g., through transnational network, international or local actors). We examine the extent and processes of emulation in seven case studies: Africa, Australia, Canada, Israel, Latin America, Switzerland and the United States. The chosen cases seek to reflect a range of broad legal characteristics (e.g., diversity of civil/common law traditions) as well as characteristics more specific to refugee law (e.g., States with national refugee determination systems versus those that rely on UNHCR for this function) and EU law (e.g., States which have formal bilateral agreements with the EU versus States which do not, and therefore where diffusion may be said to be more natural). Crucially, we have selected case studies that enable us to explore the degree to which EU refugee law is emulated or eschewed, and whether this is done expressly or 'by stealth'. In this regard, for example, the case study on the United States is important in identifying and explaining the lack of transnational dialogue and emulation, thereby capturing the limits of diffusion of European refugee law. By contrast, the case studies of Switzerland, Israel, Australia, Canada, Africa and to some extent also Latin

---

[4] One such study to note this to be the case in Africa is Bonaventure Rutinwa, 'The End of Asylum: The Changing Nature of Refugee Policies in Africa' (2002) 21 *Refugee Survey Quarterly* 2–41, at 33.

America provide clear evidence of emulation, albeit in the case of Africa, this evidence is more historical than modern. Overall, the number and range of cases enables us to produce robust generalizations about the global reach of European norms in the area of international protection.

The Global Reach of European Refugee Law takes forward the research agenda first laid out by Goodwin-Gill and Lambert in *The Limits of Transnational Law: Refugee Law, Policy Harmonization and Judicial Dialogue in the European Union.*[5] Where *The Limits of Transnational law* explored the extent of transnational judicial dialogue within the EU (and explained why there was less than might be expected), *The Global Reach of European Refugee Law* examines the worldwide emulation of key norms of European refugee protection through transnational processes and actors.

Regarding terminology, the term 'law' in this volume is used in a normative sense, interchangeably with 'norm': that is, as principled beliefs about appropriate action, shared by a community, which are embedded in practice and codified in rules (i.e., law).[6] The word 'European' is used interchangeably with 'European Union (EU)' to capture the influence of the wider Europe of the Council of Europe on the EU, unless specified otherwise. 'Emulation' is understood to mean a process of diffusion. The word 'reach' in the title of the volume is used in its ordinary meaning in order to capture both the scope of the study and the capability of the emulation in terms of distance, length, degree and range. Finally, 'refugee law' in the context of this book is synonymous with the EU concept of 'international protection': it encompasses both the law under the 1951 Refugee Convention/1967 Protocol (that is, the law of 'refugee protection' *stricto sensu*), and other forms of protection under international human rights treaties. In the EU context, international protection generally translates into asylum, understood as 'the right of residence'.[7]

---

[5] Guy S. Goodwin-Gill and Hélène Lambert (eds.), *The Limits of Transnational Law: Refugee Law, Policy Harmonization and Judicial Dialogue in the European Union* (Cambridge: Cambridge University Press, 2010).

[6] Alexander Wendt, *Social Theory of International Politics* (Cambridge: Cambridge University Press, 1999); Martha Finnemore, *National Interests in International Society* (Ithaca, NY: Cornell University Press, 1996); Wayne Sandholtz and Kendall Stiles, *International Norms and Cycles of Change* (Oxford: Oxford University Press, 2009). See also Rosalyn Higgins, *Problems and Process: International Law and How We Use It* (Oxford: Clarendon Press, 1995), pp. 1–16.

[7] Arts. 13 and 18, Directive 2011/95/EU of the European Parliament and of the Council of 13 December 2011 on standards for the qualification of third-country nationals or stateless persons as beneficiaries of international protection, for a uniform status for refugees or for

A   Worldwide emulation of Europe: drivers and facilitators

A core proposition of this volume is that States worldwide have been copying, to varying degrees, European norms of refugee protection for some time. In other words, this pattern of emulation is historical, and the 1951 Refugee Convention may be seen in terms of a similar pattern of worldwide adoption of Western norms encoded in an international legal institution providing rights for refugees (see discussion in Chapter 7 on Africa).

There is a sizeable body of literature on the possible global influence of the EU within the socio-legal literature on the diffusion of law[8] and in the area of political ical sociology of the EU.[9] Up to now, most European legal scholars have taken a 'European integration' approach to European asylum law' and have focused on EU institutional development and the effects of EU law on Member States.[10] At the same time, American scholars have for some time highlighted the global promise of European legal institutions.[11] More specifically, recent work by Fullerton highlights the significance of the new EU provisions concerning war refugees on the policy debate on asylum in the United

persons eligible for subsidiary protection, and for the content of the protection granted (recast) (OJ 2011 No. L 337/9).

[8] See, e.g., William Twining, *Globalisation and Legal Theory* (Cambridge: Cambridge University Press, 2000); 'Diffusion of Law: A Global Perspective' (2004) 49 *Journal of Legal Pluralism* 1–45; 'Social Science and Diffusion of Law' (2005) 32 *Journal of Law and Society* 203–40; 'Normative and Legal Pluralism: A Global Perspective' (2010) 20 *Duke Journal of Comparative & International Law* 473–517; Gunther Teubner, 'Legal Irritants: Good Faith in British Law or How Unifying Law Ends up in New Divergences' (1998) 61 *Modern Law Review* 11–32.

[9] See, e.g., Eiko Thielemann and Nadine El-Enany, 'Refugee Protection as a Collective Action Problem: Is the EU Shirking Its Responsibilities?' (2010) 19 *European Security* 209–29; Andrew Geddes, *Immigration and European Integration: Beyond Fortress Europe?* (2nd edn, Manchester: Manchester University Press, 2008), pp. 170–85; Ian Manners, 'Normative Power Europe: A Contradiction in Terms?' (2002) 40 *Journal of Common Market Studies* 235–58.

[10] See, e.g., Elspeth Guild and Carol Harlow (eds.), *Implementing Amsterdam: Immigration and Asylum Rights in EC Law* (Oxford: Hart, 2001); Anneliese Baldaccini, Elspeth Guild and Helen Toner (eds.), *Whose Freedom, Security and Justice? EU Immigration and Asylum Law and Policy* (Oxford: Hart, 2007).

[11] Eric Stein, 'Lawyers, Judges, and the Making of a Transnational Constitution' (1981) 75 *American Journal of International Law* 1–27; Anne-Marie Burley and Walter Mattli, 'Europe Before the Court: A Political Theory of Legal Integration' (1993) 47 *International Organization* 41–76; Anne-Marie Slaughter and William Burke-White, 'The Future of International Law is Domestic (or, The European Way of Law)' (2006) 47 *Harvard International Law Journal* 327–52.

States.[12] International Relations (IR) scholars too have long been working on diffusion theories in organizational structures.[13] The empirical data reveal from the mid-twentieth century onward, growing similarity in organizational form and function within a range of specific policy areas including public healthcare, education, and managing the natural environment.[14] Such similarity constitutes a puzzle. Why is there such a degree of worldwide homogeneity in how societies organize themselves, given the great difference in local conditions and requirements?

Some sociologists predict that weaker States, often on the periphery of the world system, will emulate the policies and organizations of the post powerful and advanced States.[15] This sociological institutionalism has been criticized for offering an account of 'world culture march[ing] effortlessly and facelessly across the globe'.[16] Local conditions or 'cultural filters'[17] – policy requirements, domestic politics and national legal culture – may reasonably be expected to shape how transnational rules are received and adopted by States. Here constructivism in IR is most useful as it seeks to explain how ideas spread across borders and take effect in national policy communities. Constructivists see a world that is substantially shaped by the identities of actors and the ideas they hold about how they should organize and act (i.e., norms).[18] One such example is the norm of sovereignty, which defines the primary unit

[12] Maryellen Fullerton, 'A Tale of Two Decades: War Refugees and Asylum Policy in the European Union' (2011) 10 *Washington University Global Studies Law Review* 87–132.

[13] Emily Goldman and Leslie Eliason (eds.), *The Diffusion of Military Technology and Ideas* (Stanford: Stanford University Press, 2003); Alexander Betts (ed.), *Global Migration Governance* (Oxford: Oxford University Press, 2011); Manners, 'Normative Power Europe'.

[14] I am grateful to Theo Farrell for pointing me to this literature. John Meyer, David Frank, Ann Hironaka, Evan Schofer and Nancy Tuma, 'The Structuring of a World Environmental Regime, 1870–1990' (1997) 51 *International Organization* 623–51; Francisco Ramirez and John Meyer, 'Comparative Education: The Social Construction of the Modern World System' (1980) 6 *Annual Review of Sociology* 369–99.

[15] Paul DiMaggio and Walter Powell, 'The Iron Cage Revisited: Institutional Isomorphism and Collective Rationality', in P Powell and W. DiMaggio (eds.), *The New Institutionalism in Organizational Analysis* (Chicago: Chicago University Press, 1991), pp. 41–62.

[16] Martha Finnemore, 'Norms, Culture and World Politics: Insights from Sociology's Institutionalism' (1996) 52 *International Organization* 325–47, at 339.

[17] Manners, 'Normative Power Europe', at 245.

[18] Wendt, *Social Theory of International Politics*. See also David Armstrong, Theo Farrell and Hélène Lambert, *International Law and International Relations* (2nd edn, Cambridge: Cambridge University Press, 2012), pp. 100–10.

of political organization in the modern world, and rights and duties of that unit.[19]

Much overlap exists between these bodies of scholarship (particularly, law and IR).[20] Accordingly, this Introduction, which is written from a law perspective, draws on IR (and sociological) theory on policy and social diffusion, with the aim of identifying key pointers for chapter authors to consider in their case studies.[21]

According to Twining, 'diffusion is a pervasive, continuing phenomenon';[22] it 'refers to a vast and complex range of phenomena',[23] and raises 'questions about occasions, motives, agents, recipients, pathways, obstacles, trialability, observability, impact, and so on'.[24] Twining correctly notes that this process of diffusion is 'typically a reciprocal rather than a one-way process', hence early influences of 'Western legal traditions lose their pre-eminence'.[25] Crucially, he explains that 'processes of diffusion are nearly always mediated through local actors'.[26]

Constructivists in IR have produced numerous accounts of how norms evolve and spread. Most accounts emphasize the role of norm entrepreneurs and advocates in promoting new norms, and the role of transnational networks (professional, scientific, legal or advocacy) in diffusing norms.[27] Norm diffusion usually involves a process of socialization, where States (or policy communities within them) are pressured and/or persuaded to adopt the new norm, and internalization, where the new norm is embedded in the laws, codes and practices of the adopting

[19] Samuel Barkin and Bruce Cronin, 'The State and the Nation: Changing Norms and the Rules of Sovereignty in International Relations' (1994) 48 International Organization 107–30.
[20] See Anne-Marie Slaughter, A New World Order (Princeton: Princeton University Press, 2004).
[21] In the academic debate relating to the spread of ideas, sociologists and IR scholars have generally referred to the terminology of 'diffusion' and 'socialization', whereas lawyers have referred to 'reception' and 'transplants'. Some socio-legal scholars do however embrace the term 'diffusion'; see Twining, 'Diffusion of Law: A Global Perspective' and 'Social Science and Diffusion of Law'.
[22] Twining, 'Social Science and Diffusion of Law', 215, referring to the work of Patrick Glenn.
[23] Ibid., 240. [24] Ibid., 228. [25] Ibid., 215–16, referring to the work of Patrick Glenn.
[26] Twining, 'Diffusion of Law: A Global Perspective', 26. On the role of electoral mechanisms in shaping patterns of policy diffusion, see Katerina Linos, 'Diffusion through Democracy' (2011) 55 American Journal of Political Science 678–95.
[27] Peter Haas, 'Epistemic Communities and International Policy Coordination' (1992) 41 International Organization 1–35; Thomas Risse, 'Ideas Do Not Float Freely: Transnational Coalitions, Domestic Structures, and the End of the Cold War' (1994) 48 International Organization 165–214; Preslava Stoeva, New Norms and Knowledge in World Politics (Abingdon, Oxon.: Routledge, 2010).

community.[28] Crucially, constructivists find that specific norms are often 'localized' in the process of selective adoption by States.[29]

We may draw on this scholarship to identify the processes whereby non-EU States emulate European asylum law and protection practice. There are *two main drivers* behind the spread of norms. The first driver for emulation is new challenges and uncertainty. This emulation driver draws on rational processes and the need to succeed.[30] Where States are faced with new challenges and are uncertain about how to tackle them, then they go fishing for ideas. According to this perspective, diffusion offers a solution to a problem.[31] The second driver for emulation is normative and stems from reputation and the growing of transnational professional standards (through association or bilateral agreements with the EU, for instance). This emulation driver draws on social processes and the need to conform.[32] Here, diffusion appears more as an ideology; the underlying motivation of the diffusion is its value.[33] In law, including refugee law, a transnational professional identity, composed of expertise and norms, has developed that is shared by organizational actors the world over.[34] In the context of our study on refugee law and protection practice, the EU, as a major source of new ideas and professional standards, fulfils a leading role in this respect.

State emulation is also a process of norm diffusion. Here constructivist studies point to *three facilitating factors*. The first of these is the degree of fit between the foreign norm and local requirements, politics, laws and culture[35] – in other words, the 'context'.[36] The second, as noted already, is

[28] Martha Finnemore and Kathryn Sikkink, 'International Norm Dynamics and Political Change' (1998) 52 *International Organization* 887–917; Thomas Risse, Steven Ropp and Kathryn Sikkink, *The Power of Human Rights: International Norms and Domestic Change* (Cambridge: Cambridge University Press, 1999).

[29] Amitav Acharya, 'How Ideas Spread: Whose Norms Matter? Norm Localization and Institutional Change in Asian Regionalism' (2004) 58 *International Organization* 239–75.

[30] Paul DiMaggio and Walter Powell, 'The Iron Cage Revisited: Institutional Isomorphism and Collective Rationality', in Powell and DiMaggio (eds.), *New Institutionalism*, pp. 41–62.

[31] Twining, 'Diffusion of Law: A Global Perspective', 30.

[32] DiMaggio and Powell, 'Iron Cage Revisited'.

[33] Twining, 'Diffusion of Law: A Global Perspective', 30.

[34] Betts, *Global Migration Governance*.

[35] Jeffrey Checkel, 'Norms, Institutions, and National Identity in Contemporary Europe' (1999) 50 *International Studies Quarterly* 83–111, at 86–7; Andrew Cortell and James Davis, 'Understanding the Domestic Impact of International Norms: A Research Agenda' (2000) 2 *International Studies Review* 65–90.

[36] Twining, 'Social Science and Diffusion of Law', 211 discussing the work of Otto Kahn-Freund. See also the discussion on 'fit' and 'proximity', in Katerina Linos, 'When Do Policy Innovations Spread? Lessons for Advocates of Lesson-Drawing' (2006) 119 *Harvard Law*

the presence and role of transnational policy, legal or advocacy networks in 'transmitting' the foreign norms. The third facilitating factor is the role of advocacy groups and other stakeholders in 'pushing' for normative change from within the country in question.[37] This view of diffusion captures the more romantic view that law is embedded holistically in legal culture, and so reception can be problematic.[38]

Aside from the academic issues that result from looking at the spread and effect of European protection law worldwide, there are also important practical imperatives. Policy makers, but also legislators (in the EU and in countries around the world), want to know why the adoption of a legal rule or practice is not working, and when – and under what conditions – it will work. When faced with a choice, they also want to know how to go about choosing a particular rule or practice.[39] Domestic courts and judges want to know when it is appropriate to use foreign law.[40] Others (e.g., activists, UNHCR, human rights NGOs, etc.) want to know how to resist a restrictive rule or practice.

By examining seven case studies in detail, this book aims to remedy the lack of a sustained empirical base – identified by Twining as 'the Achilles heel of comparative law'[41] – in the area of (diffusion of) refugee law.

B   Key *trends* in European refugee law

Ever since the Single European Act (1987), issues of asylum and immigration have been part of the debate relating to the creation of an Internal

Review 1467–87. For different views on commonalities and distinctiveness between legal cultures, see, for instance, Roger Cotterrell, *Law, Culture and Society* (Aldershot: Ashgate, 2006); David Nelken, 'Puzzling Out Legal Cultures: A Comment on Blankenburg', in David Nelken (ed.), *Comparing Legal Cultures* (Aldershot: Ashgate, 1997), pp. 58–88; Pierre Legrand, 'European Legal Systems Are Not Converging' (1996) 45 *International and Comparative Law Quarterly* 52–81.

[37] Anne-Marie Clarke, *Diplomacy of Conscience: Amnesty International and Changing Human Rights Norms* (Princeton: Princeton University Press, 2002); Anne Klotz, *Norms in International Relations* (Ithaca, NY: Cornell University Press, 1995).

[38] Twining, 'Diffusion of Law: A Global Perspective', 30.

[39] *Ibid.*, 10; Twining, 'Social Science and Diffusion of Law', 217.

[40] Goodwin-Gill and Lambert, *Limits of Transnational Law.* See also Christopher McCrudden, 'A Common Law of Human Rights?: Transnational Judicial Conversations on Constitutional Rights' (2000) 20 *Oxford Journal of Legal Studies* 499–532; Sir Basil Markesinis and Jörg Fedtke, *Judicial Recourse to Foreign Law: A New Source of Inspiration?* (London: University College London and Austin: University of Texas: 2006); John Bell, 'The Argumentative Status of Foreign Legal Arguments' (2012) 8 *Utrecht Law Review* 8–19.

[41] Twining, 'Social Science and Diffusion of Law', 240.

Market and the abolition of internal borders by 1992.[42] A special group of senior civil servants (the Ad Hoc Immigration Group) was set up to reinforce external border controls and limit access into Europe. As early as 1987, this Group adopted an agreement to impose penalties on carriers responsible for bringing undocumented aliens into the European Community (EC) (1987). The Ad Hoc Group also adopted two conventions in 1990: the Convention determining the state responsible for examining the applications for asylum lodged in one of the Member States of the EC (Dublin Convention),[43] and the Convention on the gradual abolition of internal borders (Schengen Convention).[44] Both conventions contained almost identical provisions on asylum. Shortly afterwards, and clearly confirming the priorities of the EC in the field of asylum at the time (namely, internal security and external border control), the EC Immigration Ministers agreed on the text of two Resolutions and one Conclusion (1992): the Resolution on manifestly unfounded applications, the Resolution of a harmonized approach to questions concerning host third countries and the problem of readmission agreements, and the Conclusion on countries where there is generally no serious risk of persecution.[45]

The Amsterdam Treaty (1997)[46] was a major milestone in the creation of a European asylum policy through the introduction of EC competence in asylum and immigration issues in a new 'title' dealing with an area of freedom, security and justice. However, this 'title' was kept separate from the traditional provisions relating to the free movement of persons.[47] Equally important, therefore, were the Tampere European Council Conclusions, which promised a new legal objective for the development

---

[42] Art. 8A(2) Single European Act (now art. 26(2) TFEU) defines the internal market as 'an area without internal frontiers in which the free movement of goods, persons, services and capital is ensured in accordance with the provisions of this Treaty' (OJ 1987 No. L 169).

[43] Convention determining the state responsible for examining applications for asylum lodged in one of the member states of the European Communities (Dublin Convention, OJ 1997 No. C 254/1).

[44] The Schengen *acquis* – Convention implementing the Schengen Agreement of 14 June 1985 between the governments of the states of the Benelux Economic Union, the Federal Republic of Germany and the French Republic on the gradual abolition of checks at their common borders (OJ 2000 No. L 239/19).

[45] See generally Ingrid Boccardi, *Europe and Refugees: Towards an EU Asylum Policy* (Alphen aan den Rijn, the Netherlands: Kluwer Law International, 2002), pp. 27–60.

[46] OJ 1997 No. C 340.

[47] Steve Peers and Nicola Rogers (eds.), *EU Immigration and Asylum Law: Text and Commentary* (Dordrecht: Martinus Nijhoff, 2006), p. 83 (referring to Title IV as the 'ghetto' provision).

of a common asylum and immigration policy, namely, the respect of human rights. For the first time, a commitment was made to freedom based on human rights, democratic institutions and the rule of law.[48] In particular, the right to 'move freely throughout the Union … in conditions of security and justice' was affirmed.[49] This freedom was to be granted to *all*, which meant that the EU had to develop common policies on asylum and immigration.[50] The Tampere summit was a key moment in the development of common asylum and immigration policies as it was then that these policies became founded on respect for human rights, and not in the Internal Market. The Union was acquiring a new human rights dimension, and as pointed out by Boccardi, '[i]t was not coincidence that the Tampere Council also instituted the body that was going to draft the EU Charter of Fundamental Rights'.[51] That also marked the moment when it was finally acknowledged that the EU needed a Common European Asylum System (CEAS), a hugely ambitious project, and that this was to be created by 2012.

This project has so far proceeded in two stages. In stage one (1999–2005 – the Tampere Programme), a common legislative framework was adopted on the basis of international and Europe-wide standards. Six key legislative instruments were adopted during this first phase: the Asylum Procedures Directive,[52] the Qualification Directive,[53] the Dublin Regulation,[54] the Reception of Asylum Seekers Directive,[55] the Eurodac Regulation[56] and the Temporary Protection Directive.[57] Stage

---

[48] Tampere European Council, Presidency Conclusions, point 1.   [49] *Ibid.*, point 2.

[50] *Ibid.*, point 3.   [51] Boccardi, *Europe and Refugees*, p. 174.

[52] Council Directive 2005/85/EC of 1 December 2005 on minimum standards on procedures in member states for granting and withdrawing refugee status (OJ 2005 No. L 326/13).

[53] Council Directive 2004/83/EC of 29 April 2004 on minimum standards for the qualification and status of third-country nationals or stateless persons as refugees or as persons who otherwise need international protection and the content of the protection granted (OJ 2004 No. L 304/12).

[54] Council Regulation 2003/343/EC of 18 February 2003 establishing the criteria and mechanisms for determining the member state responsible for examining an asylum application lodged in one of the member states by a third-country national (OJ 2003 No. L 50/1).

[55] Council Directive 2003/9/EC of 27 January 2003 laying down minimum standards for the reception of asylum seekers (OJ 2003 No. L 31/18).

[56] Council Regulation 2000/2725/EC of 11 December 2000 concerning the establishment of 'Eurodac' for the comparison of fingerprints for the effective application of the Dublin Convention (OJ 2000 No. L 316/1).

[57] Council Directive 2001/55/EC of 20 July 2001 on minimum standards for giving temporary protection in the event of a mass influx of displaced persons and on measures promoting a balance of efforts between member states in receiving such persons and bearing the consequences thereof (OJ 2001 No. L 212/12).

two (2005–12, still ongoing – the Hague and Stockholm Programmes)[58] seeks to harmonize asylum procedures in the EU, increase cooperation between EU States on managing their external borders, and increase the standards of protection in some of the adopted common legislation (through recast instruments currently being adopted).[59]

In summary, over the past two decades, European asylum policy and law have evolved from soft law (namely, resolutions and conclusions) to hard law instruments (namely, treaty, charter, regulations and directives). Despite different legal traditions and systems, the EU has codified a regional legal framework of international protection applicable to Member States. The emerging CEAS contains a number of key, positive substantive and procedural rules, most notably, the recognition of the 'right to asylum' in the EU, which goes beyond protection from *refoulement*,[60] but also the recognition of non-State agents of persecution, gender-based persecution and the codification of subsidiary protection and temporary protection, all of which are based on State practice and/or national legislation,[61] and, finally, the recognition of basic standards of

---

[58] Communication from the Commission to the Council and the European Parliament of 10 May 2005 – The Hague Programme: ten priorities for the next five years. The Partnership for European renewal in the field of Freedom, Security and Justice (COM(2005) 184 final, OJ 2005 No. C 236). Also, European Council, the Stockholm Programme – An open and secure Europe serving and protecting citizens (OJ 2010 No. C 115/1).

[59] E.g., Directive 2011/95/EU of the European Parliament and of the Council of 13 December 2011 on standards for the qualification of third-country nationals or stateless persons as beneficiaries of international protection, for a uniform status for refugees or for persons eligible for subsidiary protection, and for the content of the protection granted (recast).

[60] Art. 18, Charter of Fundamental Rights of the European Union (OJ 2000 No. C 364/1) and Recast Qualification Directive 2011/95/EU, Recital 16. See Maria-Teresa Gil-Bazo, 'The Charter of Fundamental Rights of the European Union and the Right to be Granted Asylum in the Union's Law' (2008) 27 *Refugee Survey Quarterly* 33–52; UNHCR's written observations in CJEU Joined Cases C-411/10 and C-493/10, para. 31.

[61] Subsidiary protection refers to 'internal mechanisms adopted in order to comply with the 2004 EU Qualification Directive'. It is distinct from complementary protection, which refers to 'other forms of protection, created by national law, different from refugee status and from subsidiary protection status, conferred on persons whose return is impossible or undesirable'. See ECRE, 'Complementary Protection in Europe', July 2009, p. 4. Temporary protection on the other hand refers to 'a procedure of exceptional character to provide, in the event of a mass influx or imminent mass influx of displaced persons ... immediate and temporary protection' (art. 2(a), Council Directive 2001/55/EC on temporary protection). See generally Jane McAdam, *Complementary Protection in International Refugee Law* (Oxford: Oxford University Press, 2007).

reception (e.g., detention) for asylum seekers.[62] Yet, significant gaps and shortcomings also characterize the CEAS: a tendency towards more exceptions and derogations to established standards (e.g., limitation of the application of the Refugee Convention definition to third-country nationals,[63] the internal flight alternative concept, the safe third country, first country of asylum and safe country of origin principles, manifestly unfounded applications), restrictive access to international protection through delocalized migration control (e.g., discussions on extraterritorial processing), the Dublin rule (according to which only one Member State is responsible for determining an asylum application and corresponding transfers), increased securitization (e.g., through detention, deportation and denaturalization procedures), and a tendency, in some countries, to resort to granting subsidiary protection rather than refugee status,[64] with the former still providing fewer rights than the latter.[65] These norms and trends are further discussed below.

1   Processes of securitization

The literature on asylum in Europe generally points towards a strengthening of border controls as the EU Member States attempt to consolidate their refugee determination procedures, with the result that access to

---

[62] Council Directive 2003/9/EC of 27 January 2003 laying down minimum standards for the reception of asylum seekers. Note that the Reception Directive does not contain an upper limit on the length of detention, only the Returns Directive does (Directive 2008/115/EC of the European Parliament and of the Council of 16 December 2008 on common standards and procedures in member states for returning illegally staying third-country nationals (OJ 2008 No. L 348/98), art. 15(5),(6)).

[63] The Qualification Directive limits the scope of international protection to 'third country nationals and stateless persons' only. This led the House of Lords Select Committee on the EU to observe: 'for a major regional grouping of countries such as the Union to adopt a regime apparently limiting the scope of the Geneva Convention among themselves would set a most undesirable precedent in the wider international/global context' (*Defining Refugee Status and Those in Need of International Protection* (London: TSO, 2002), para. 54, cited in McAdam, *Complementary Protection*, p. 60).

[64] This is the case, for instance, of Bulgaria, Italy, Cyprus, Malta, Poland, Slovakia, Finland and Sweden.

[65] Directive 2011/95/EU of the European Parliament and of the Council of 13 December 2011 on standards for the qualification of third-country nationals or stateless persons as beneficiaries of international protection, for a uniform status for refugees or for persons eligible for subsidiary protection, and for the content of the protection granted. This recast Directive is a considerable improvement from the original Directive of 2004, but still today the right to residence permits (art. 24) and the right to social welfare (art. 29) remain unequally protected.

protection systems by those persons entitled to benefit from them is being denied.[66] These norms are being complemented with deteriorating reception standards, increased levels of social control, heightened policing and stricter detention policies, and the growing sophistication of expulsion procedures.[67] Any of these could potentially spread to and be adopted in countries beyond the EU (and has already occurred in some cases, as the case study chapters show).

Guild has long provided a powerful critique of the protection provided by EU Member States to refugees and of their responsibilities towards refugees.[68] She describes the protection of refugees in the EU as a process of 'deterritorialisation of protection obligations' for refugees already in, or seeking to enter, the EU.[69] The geographical EU common territory being no longer the object of sovereign responsibilities, there is now 'space for an opportunistic exclusion of protection responsibilities which are tied to sovereignty'.[70] She finds that this gap has been filled to some extent by human rights law, and the European Convention on Human Rights (ECHR) in particular. Both legal orders, the EU and the ECHR, complement each other, but they are separate. Hence, EU Member States remain accountable to the European Court of Human Rights for their protection obligations under EU law whenever these obligations involve a right or obligation under the ECHR. Recent landmark judgments clearly illustrate this point. The most notable example is *MSS* v. *Belgium and Greece*,[71] a case involving the transfer of an Afghan asylum seeker from Belgium to Greece in accordance with EU law. The European Court of Human Rights held that a presumption of safety, even where created by EU law (under the Dublin Regulation II),[72] should never be conclusive but rebuttable. Since Belgium 'knew or ought to have known' that MSS had no guarantee that his asylum

---

[66] E.g., Boccardi, *Europe and Refugees*. Elspeth Guild, *Security and Migration in the 21st Century* (Cambridge: Polity, 2009). Red Cross/EU Office, 'Position paper on the Right to Access to International Protection', Brussels, 17 November 2011.

[67] Laura Barnett, 'Global Governance and the Evolution of the International Refugee Regime' (2002) 14 *International Journal of Refugee Law* 238–62, at 253.

[68] E.g., Elspeth Guild, 'Seeking Asylum: Storm Clouds between International Commitments and EU Legislative Measures' (2004) 29 *European Law Review* 198–218

[69] Elspeth Guild, 'The Europeanisation of Europe's Asylum Policy' (2006) 18 *International Journal of Refugee Law* 630–51.

[70] *Ibid.*, 631.

[71] *MSS* v. *Belgium and Greece*, App. No. 30696/09, judgment of 21 January 2011.

[72] Council Regulation (EC) No. 343/2003 of 18 February 2003 establishing the criteria and mechanisms for determining the member state responsible for examining an asylum application lodged in one of the member states by a third-country national (OJ 2003 No. L 50/1) (Dublin II Regulation).

application would be seriously examined in Greece, and the Belgian authorities had the means to refuse to transfer him, article 3 ECHR had been
violated.[73] Belgium should have verified how the Greek authorities applied
their legislation on asylum in practice, not just assume that MSS would be
treated in conformity with the ECHR. Likewise in *Hirsi and Others* v. *Italy*, a
case involving illegal migrants from Somalia and Eritrea and their 'push-
back' to Libya (from where they came) by the Italian police, the European
Court of Human Rights held that the Italian authorities 'knew or ought to
have known' that irregular migrants would be exposed to treatment contrary to article 3 ECHR if returned to Libya;[74] and that the authorities
should have found out about the treatment to which the applicants would be
exposed after their return (in practice), and not just assume that Libya's
international commitments under human rights treaties would be respected
(in law). Thus, there can be no hiding behind notions of common territory
and loss of sovereignty before the European Court of Human Rights, which
'has pushed in the direction of a "collectivisation" of responsibility'.[75]
Gilbert, too, is critical of the EU approach towards refugee protection for
having inextricably 'fused' refugee protection and immigration control: an
immigration control mentality is driving refugee policy.[76] Consequently,
EU States will continue to choose who should be protected within the EU,
and currently this category of people is decreasing in number.[77] Another
forceful critique is provided in Chapter 9 of this volume, with Jean-François
Durieux arguing that the EU asylum system, which is based on an internal
market's logic, threatens the specificity of the Refugee Convention and
therefore the figure of the refugee.

2   Improved standards of refugee protection?

Thielemann and El-Enany argue that, until recently, EU asylum laws have
'reflect[ed] restrictive trends similar to those in other parts of the world'.[78]

---

[73] *MSS* v. *Belgium and Greece*, para. 358.
[74] *Hirsi and Others* v. *Italy*, App. No. 27765/09, judgment of 23 February 2012, para.131.
[75] Guild, 'Europeanisation', 630.
[76] Geoff Gilbert, 'Is Europe Living up to Its Obligations to Refugees?' (2004) 15 *European Journal of International Law* 963–87, at 987.
[77] *Ibid.* See also Nadine El-Enany, 'Who Is the New European Refugee?' (2008) 33 *European Law Review* 313–35.
[78] Eiko Thielemann and Nadine El-Enany, 'Beyond Fortress Europe? How European Cooperation Has Strengthened Refugee Protection', paper presented at European Union Studies Association's 11th Biennial International Conference, Los Angeles, 23–25 April 2009, p. 22.

However, looking specifically at the two most contested EU Directives, the Asylum Procedures Directive and the Returns Directive, they dismiss the claim that European cooperation is driving protection standards down, on the grounds that it is unsubstantiated by the evidence.[79] They argue instead that European cooperation in this area 'has curtailed regulatory competition and in doing so had largely halted the race to the bottom in protection standards in the EU'.[80] They further argue that these new EU protection standards are not only improved standards in relation to previous standards in the Member States, but also in relation to comparable non-EU countries of equivalent wealth and development, such as Norway, the US, Canada and Australia.[81] For instance, the highly contested concept of the 'safe third country', enshrined in the Asylum Procedures Directive and the Returns Directive, also operates in these four countries. Another instance is the use of detention practices in the context of return: restrictive detention practices currently exist in the EU under the Returns Directive, but also in Australia, the US, Canada and Switzerland (Norway being an exception, as it appears to provide better guarantees against arbitrariness).[82]

For the purpose of this volume, the relevant and important argument advanced by Thielemann and El-Enany is that EU refugee policy has not become a uniquely restrictive policy as compared with other non-EU OECD countries. Restrictive practices found in the EU asylum regime are also found in the regimes of non-EU OECD countries.[83] They do not, however, consider the issue whether this is so because of the effect of EU law on these countries (including the practice of individual EU Member States). They predict that the rights-enhancing trends noted in EU policy making are expected to continue (their argument is supported by the new round of recast Directives aimed at improving minimum standards ahead of the anticipated harmonization), while other OECD countries have leaned towards the adoption of new restrictive policies with no (regionally) agreed minimum standards to resist against such actions.[84] Some of the case study findings in this volume in fact confirm this argument (e.g., Australia, Canada, Israel and Latin America), and the implications for this will be examined further in the concluding Chapter 10.

Geddes makes a similar point, namely, that there is not necessarily anything distinct or unique about Europe when comparing responses to

[79] Thielemann and El-Enany, 'Refugee Protection as a Collective Action Problem', at 215–17.
[80] Ibid., 216. [81] Ibid., 217–20. [82] Ibid. [83] Ibid., 226–7. [84] Ibid., 219 and 226–7.

migration and asylum problems with those in the US and Australia.[85] Geddes considers 'the attempts by the EU and its Member States to influence migration from, and the migration policies of, non-EU States',[86] through various forms of dialogue and cooperation, partnerships with countries of origin and third countries, and bilateral and multilateral forums.[87] He sees value in viewing this as a process of the EU 'impos[ing] its migration and asylum priorities on non-Member States'. He asks 'what incentive is there for non-member states to agree to participate in such processes if the onus is on them to adapt to EU requirements?'[88] Geddes observes clear parallels between the exclusionary practices 'being pursued by EU states and those strategies of similar non-European States'.[89]

At this juncture, it is necessary to clarify that the purpose of this volume is less about mapping the transplantation of some of the EU refugee norms in countries with which it has formal arrangements, such as association or other bilateral agreements, as it is to look at the effects of EU refugee law by way of its more 'natural' or 'cultural' diffusion into the legal systems of non-EU countries. Indeed, even in countries with which the EU has formal arrangements, such as Switzerland and Israel, the success of diffusion is very much dependent on the facilitating factors identified above (namely, the 'fit', the 'transmitter' and the 'push') and local requirements. It may also be recalled that the aim of the book is to explore whether or not restrictive European concepts are being adopted and adapted the world over, based on the evidence found so far; in other words, it is to take stock at this point in time of what has happened, and then use this as a point of comparison for what might follow.

3   Exceptions and derogations to established international standards

Notwithstanding the arguments made by Thielemann and El-Enany, it cannot be denied that certain standards enshrined in EU asylum legislation are not in compliance with international refugee law and/or international human rights law. As strongly expressed by the European Council on Refugees and Exiles (ECRE): 'The result of the first phase of harmonization has been disappointing; the level of protection granted to asylum seekers

---

[85] Geddes, *Immigration and European Integration*, pp. 183–4.   [86] *Ibid.*, p. 170.
[87] *Ibid.*, p. 176.   [88] *Ibid.*, p. 178.   [89] *Ibid.*, p. 179.

and refugees in the EU asylum acquis is generally low.'[90] UNHCR, too, notes that the legislation adopted during the first phase of the creation of the CEAS contains or permits broad exceptions, derogations and ambiguities, which are partly responsible for the existing divergence in recognition rate and quality of asylum decision between EU Member States.[91] For instance, both UNHCR and ECRE are critical of the administrative detention of asylum seekers, which is less regulated than the detention of accused and convicted criminals. ECRE also recently observed that by allowing Member States a wide margin of discretion, the Asylum Procedures Directive fails to ensure common standards across the EU. In some countries, accelerated asylum procedures have become the rule rather than the exception. The 2009 Commission proposal to recast the Asylum Procedures Directive proposes significant improvements in EU standards with regard to some key issues, such as the right to a personal interview, training requirements for staff in asylum authorities, the right to legal assistance and representation and the right to an effective remedy. However, this proposal is meeting with resistance in the Council of the EU.[92] Furthermore, the recast proposal maintains the various safe country concepts. The 'safe country' concept has been presented as 'a new notion of *non-refoulement*', one that States were forced to create in order to deal with the emergence of 'the *potential* refugee or the asylum seeker' and the subsequent burden on asylum administrations.[93] In other words, this concept was invented to send asylum seekers back from where they had come.[94]

In summary, the substantive and procedural rules that currently form the CEAS are impaired by exceptions and derogations to existing international standards.[95] While it is true that some of these rules and practices are still evolving (through recast instruments currently being negotiated as well as through judicial interpretation), the focus of this

---

[90] ECRE Memorandum on the occasion of the Belgian Presidency of the EU (July–December 2010), p. 1.

[91] UNHCR's recommendations to Belgium for its EU Presidency July–December 2010 (June 2010) www.unhcr.org/4c2486579.html (accessed 1 December 2012).

[92] At its meeting on 5 January 2012, the Asylum Working Party examined the Council of the EU Presidency compromise suggestions on an Amended Proposal for a Directive of the European Parliament and of the Council on common procedures for granting and withdrawing international protection status (recast) (Doc. 5168/12 ASILE 4 CODEC 50).

[93] El-Enany, 'Who Is the New European Refugee?', 320.

[94] Madeline Garlick, 'The EU Discussions on Extraterritorial Processing: Solution or Conundrum?' (2006) 18 *International Journal of Refugee Law* 601–29.

[95] See Durieux's arguments on 'normative conflict' between an EU-specific 'genetic material' and the universal regime of refugee protection, in Chapter 9 of this volume.

book is on key norms of European refugee law that originated over twenty years ago in State practice and asylum policies, and which are now squarely codified in the CEAS (e.g., safe third country, safe country of origin, subsidiary protection, accelerated procedures and manifestly unfounded applications). It is notoriously difficult to trace the precise origin of a legislative rule.[96] To overcome this difficulty, this volume is interested in *trends* (e.g., a set of restrictive or liberal rules, practices or ideas), rather than specific rules.[97]

All but one (the United States) of the selected case studies in this volume provide *clear* evidence of these trends or norms having 'leaked' beyond Europe and impacted on refugee law worldwide at some point in time.

4 Europe's unique double-judicial check

It is further *predicted* that other norms likely to spread worldwide are those which the Court of Justice of the European Union (CJEU) has ruled upon, particularly, where the ruling concerns a provision of EU law that enshrines a provision of the Refugee Convention, such as cessation of refugee status[98] or exclusion from refugee status,[99] or a provision relating to subsidiary protection.[100] Indeed, once the CJEU answers a reference for a preliminary ruling in a judgment, this interpretation carries great weight as EU law – much greater weight than those provisions that have not been interpreted by the CJEU. This pioneering role by the CJEU is further amplified by the fact that while the International Court of Justice is competent, no State has ever requested its involvement and it is unlikely to ever be used in this way. While it is true that rulings of the CJEU are authoritative in respect of EU law only (in the sense of their binding legal force),[101] it is less true of their general authority

[96] Rosemary Byrne and Andrew Shacknove, 'The Safe Country Notion in European Asylum Law' (1996) 9 *Harvard Human Rights Journal* 185–228; Rosemary Byrne, Gregor Noll and Jens Vedsted-Hansen, 'Understanding Refugee Law in an Enlarged European Union' (2004) 15 *European Journal of International Law* 355–79.

[97] Twining talks about 'patterns relating to law' ('Diffusion of Law: A Global Perspective', 5).

[98] ECJ, Joined Cases C-175, 176, 178, 179/08, *Salahadin Abdulla and Others* v. *Germany*, ECR [2009] I-1493.

[99] CJEU, Joined Cases C-57/09 and C-101/09, *Bundesrepublik Deutschland* v. *B and D*, judgment of 9 November 2010.

[100] ECJ, Case C-465/07, *Mr and Mrs Elgafaji* v. *Staatssecretaris van Justitie* (*Dutch Secretary of State for Justice*), judgment of 17 February 2009.

[101] As commented by Advocate General Eleanor Sharpston in her Opinion of 4 March 2010 in the Case C-31/09 *Bolbol* v. *Bevándorlási es Állampolgársági Hivatal* (*Hungarian Office for Immigration and Citizenship*).

(persuasive or not) as rulings from the first ever supranational court to have interpreted provisions of the Refugee Convention. These rulings will carry enormous weight in generally influencing the interpretation of the Refugee Convention – that is, in promoting an interpretation of what is 'normal' interpretation in 26 of the 144 countries signatories to the Refugee Convention/Protocol. The idea behind this ability to shape conceptions as 'normal' has been identified as constitutive of Europe's normative power.[102] In sum, we can *predict* a 'jurisprudential glow' of the CJEU's judgments outside the EU.[103] In the context of this volume, this prediction is based on the suggested influence of the CJEU's judgment in the landmark case *Mr and Mrs Elgafaji* v. *the Dutch Secretary of State for Justice*, on the US Board of Immigration Appeals, hence this case is introduced here. *Elgafaji* was the first judgment to be given by the CJEU (which was then called the ECJ). The Court was asked to answer two questions referred by the Raad van State (Dutch Council of State) relating to the scope of subsidiary protection granted by article 15(c) Qualification Directive:[104] Does article 15(c) offer supplementary or merely equivalent protection to article 3 ECHR? If supplementary, what are the criteria for eligibility to protection under article 15(c)? Following the opinion of Advocate General Maduro,[105] the CJEU ruled that article 15(c) Qualification Directive is different in content from article 3 ECHR (enshrined in article 15(b) Qualification Directive), hence the interpretation of these provisions must be carried out independently.[106] While article 15(a) and article 15(b) 'cover situations in which the applicant for subsidiary protection is specifically exposed to the risk of a particular type of harm', namely the death penalty, torture, inhuman or degrading treatment or punishment, article 15(c) 'covers a

---

[102] Manners, 'Normative Power Europe', 240. This is discussed further in Chapter 10 of this volume.

[103] Dauvergne, *Making People Illegal*, p. 150.

[104] Chapter V – Qualification for Subsidiary Protection

    Article 15 – Serious harm
    Serious harm consists of:

    (a) death penalty or execution; or
    (b) torture or inhuman or degrading treatment or punishment of an applicant in the country of origin; or
    (c) serious and individual threat to a civilian's life or person by reason of indiscriminate violence in situation of international or internal armed conflict.

[105] Delivered on 9 September 2008.   [106] *Elgafaji*, para. 28.

more general risk of harm', namely a 'threat ... to a civilian's life or person'.[107] It added that the threat in question 'is inherent in a general situation of "international or internal armed conflict" and the reference to "indiscriminate" violence implies that this term "may extend to people irrespective of their personal circumstances"'.[108]

> The Court ruled that the existence of a serious and individual threat to the life or person of an applicant for subsidiary protection is not subject to the condition that that applicant adduce evidence that he is specifically targeted by reason of factors particular to his personal circumstances; the existence of such a threat can exceptionally be considered to be established where the degree of indiscriminate violence characterising the armed conflict taking place ... reaches such a high level that substantial grounds are shown for believing that a civilian, returned to the relevant country or, as the case may be, to the relevant region, would, solely on account of his presence in the territory of that country or region, face a real risk of being subject to that threat.[109]

It further related the 'level of indiscriminate violence' with the 'level of individualization' as regards the standard of proof – they are inversely proportional: 'the more the applicant is able to show that he is specifically affected by reason of factors particular to his personal circumstances, the lower the level of indiscriminate violence required for him to be eligible for subsidiary protection'.[110]

In sum, the interpretation provided by the CJEU of the word 'individual' in article 15(c) Qualification Directive means that there is no need for the applicant to demonstrate that s/he is individually or 'specifically' targeted in order to enjoy the protection of article 15(c). Rather, the importance of article 15(c) is its ability to provide protection from serious risks that are *situational*, rather than individual. This interpretation, which rejects a high degree of individualization, must be praised for it is in full compliance with both international refugee law[111] and international human rights law,[112] and echoes the views of the UNHCR,

---

[107] *Ibid.*, paras. 32–4.   [108] *Ibid.*, para. 34.   [109] *Ibid.*, para. 45; see also para. 35.
[110] *Ibid.*, para. 39.
[111] Although not necessarily state practice, which often requires that the asylum seeker be 'deliberately targeted' (e.g., *R* v. *SSHD, ex parte Adan and Aitseguer*, House of Lords, judgment of 19 December 2000).
[112] Since its judgment in *Salah Sheek* v. *the Netherlands*, App. No. 1948/04, judgment of 11 January 2007, the European Court of Human Rights no longer requires an individual to be singled out or targeted. See also *NA* v. *United Kingdom*, App. No. 25904/07, judgment of 17 July 2008; and *Sufi and Elmi* v. *United Kingdom*, App. Nos. 8319/07 and 11449/07, judgment of 28 June 2011.

which recommended that the EU legislator delete the term 'individual' in article 15(c) Qualification Directive.[113]

This case clearly illustrates the CJEU's awareness of the conflicting dimensions of EU asylum policy.[114] From a human rights (and refugee protection) perspective, the interpretation given by the CJEU in *Elgafaji* makes absolute sense: subsidiary protection is made effective by interpreting article 15(c) as offering something more than article 15(b) (or 3 ECHR), and international protection is to be granted where a risk of harm to human rights is likely to arise without requiring that an individual be personally targeted. This interpretation is in harmony with the case law of the European Court of Human Rights in Strasbourg. The latter indeed recognized that cases could arise where a general situation of violence in a country of destination is of 'a sufficient level of intensity' that removal to it would *necessarily* breach article 3 ECHR.[115] From a security (or control of the external borders of the EU) viewpoint, this ruling too makes perfect sense: the CJEU 'entrusted the [national authorities] with a key aspect of article 15(c), namely [the assessment of the level of indiscriminate violence,] the turning point at which indiscriminate violence becomes an exceptional situation'.[116]

The ECHR and the case law of the European Court of Human Rights further influence the interpretation of the principle of *non-refoulement* in EU refugee law.[117] This is the case in particular when provisions of the EU Charter of Fundamental Rights or of CEAS law overlap with provisions of the

---

[113] UNHCR also recommended that this term be deleted from Recital (26), according to which: 'Risks to which a population of a country or a section of the population is generally exposed do normally not create in themselves an individual threat which would qualify as serious harm.' Note that article 15 (as well as Recital 26, now Recital 35) has been left untouched in the Recast Directive 2011/95/EU of 13 December 2011.

[114] Koen Lenaerts, 'The Contribution of the European Court of Justice to the Area of Freedom, Security and Justice' (2010) 59 *International and Comparative Law Quarterly* 255–301, at 296.

[115] European Court of Human Rights, *NA* v. *United Kingdom*, App. No. 25904/07, judgment of 17 July 2008, para.115. And now for an application of this finding to Mogadishu (Somalia), see European Court of Human Rights, *Sufi and Elmi* v. *United Kingdom*.

[116] Lenaerts, 'Contribution of the European Court of Justice', at 297.

[117] This is a two-way process. In *MSS* v. *Belgium and Greece*, the Grand Chamber of the European Court of Human Rights referred to EU legislation as an express source of law for its judgment; this is novel but not unexpected because the European Court of Human Rights often looks at consensus or near consensus, or for international norms reflecting a high degree of agreement.

ECHR. With respect to the Charter,[118] the CJEU recently granted special significance to article 3 ECHR and its case law[119] when interpreting the corresponding article 4 of the Charter.[120] It regarded article 4 of the Charter as imposing the same level of protection as article 3 ECHR.[121] Regarding CEAS law, particularly the Qualification Directive, the CJEU accepted that protection under article 3 ECHR is squarely provided by article 15(b) Qualification Directive,[122] and that the latter should be interpreted with due regard to the ECHR.[123] However, divergence in views between Luxembourg and Strasbourg prevails when comparing article 3 ECHR with article 15(c) Qualification Directive. The view from the CJEU (see discussion above) is that article 15(c) has something more to offer than article 15(b) (which is equivalent to article 3 ECHR) in terms of protection[124] – although what this 'something more' is remains unclear. In contrast, the view from the European Court of Human Rights is that article 3 ECHR offers 'comparable protection' to that afforded under article 15(c) Qualification Directive, since both courts impose an 'exceptionality requirement' when the risk to a person arises in a situation of general violence.[125] Notwithstanding these differences, it is unquestionable that in Europe, the ECHR offers very real added

---

[118] The EU Charter of Fundamental Rights was approved in 2000 at the Nice summit; it became binding law following the entry into force of the Lisbon Treaty in 2009 (OJ 2007 No. C 306).

[119] Particularly *MSS v. Belgium and Greece*.

[120] *NS v. Secretary of State for the Home Department* and *ME and Others v. Refugee Applications Commissioner and Minister for Justice, Equality and Law Reform*, Joined Cases C-411/10 and C-493/10 [2011] ECR I-0000, paras. 89 and 91. The case involved asylum seekers from Afghanistan, Iran and Algeria who had arrived in Greece prior to travelling in the UK and Ireland, and so raised very similar issues to the case *MSS v. Belgium and Greece*. See Advocate General Trstenjak's statement that 'particular significance and high importance are to be attached to the case-law of the European Court of Human Rights in connection with the interpretation of the Charter of Fundamental Rights, with the result that it must be taken into consideration in interpreting the Charter' (para. 146).

[121] *NS v. Secretary of State for the Home Department* and *ME and Others v. Refugee Applications Commissioner and Minister for Justice, Equality and Law Reform* (para. 94). Both art. 3 ECHR and art. 4 EU Charter provide: 'No one shall be subjected to torture or to inhuman or degrading treatment or punishment'.

[122] Art. 15(b) Qualification Directive defines serious harm as 'torture or inhuman or degrading treatment or punishment of an applicant in the country of origin'.

[123] ECJ, case C-465/07, *Elgafaji v. Staatssecretaris van Justitie*, 17 February 2009 (OJ 2009, No. C 90/4, para. 28).

[124] *Ibid*. This view is shared by the UK Upper Tribunal: see *AMM and Others (conflict; humanitarian crisis; returnees; FGM) Somalia v. Secretary of State for the Home Department*, CG [2011] UKUT 00445 (IAC).

[125] European Court of Human Rights, *Sufi and Elmi v. United Kingdom*, para. 226, and ECJ, *Elgafaji*, paras. 37–8. To read more on this, see Hélène Lambert, 'The

protection against *refoulement* to victims of armed conflicts who meet neither the requirement of the refugee definition (article 1A(2) Refugee Convention), nor article 15(c) Qualification Directive. This is not necessarily the case in other regions.[126] However, where EU law may be better equipped than ECHR law is on the issue of the right to asylum (and a legal status) following a finding of violation of *refoulement*.[127] Indeed, the European Court of Human Rights has so far failed to recognize any further duties (beyond *non-refoulement*) on the part of Contracting States, such as to allow access to an asylum procedure or to grant a particular protection status to persons protected against *refoulement*. For the European Court of Human Rights, these remain matters for individual Member States.[128] All that the Strasbourg Court has acknowledged is that asylum seekers constitute a category of particularly vulnerable people.[129] Thus, it may be argued that the right to asylum by way of guaranteeing access to the asylum procedure and of granting refugee status is a key element of EU law (as well as the Refugee Convention)[130] but not of ECHR law, which continues to see the right to asylum purely in terms of protection against *refoulement*.[131]

C   Structure of the book

The volume is divided into ten chapters. This chapter (Chapter 1) introduces the conceptual framework for the book and the necessary tools for testing the hypothesis that European refugee law is being emulated in non-EU countries around the world. It identifies two key drivers and

---

Next Frontier: Expanding Protection in Europe for Victims of Armed Conflict and Indiscriminate Violence', forthcoming in (2013) *International Journal of Refugee Law.*
[126] I thank Jane McAdam for this point.
[127] Note that for persons coming from another EU Member State, the right to asylum is subject to the rules on responsibility sharing, rebuttable presumption and transfer provided in Council Regulation (EC) No. 343/2003 of 18 February 2003. This situation is discussed fully in Chapter 9 of this volume.
[128] In *Hirsi et al.* v. *Italy*, App. No. 27765/09, judgment of 23 February 2012, paras. 208–11, the European Court of Human Rights, having found that the transfer of the applicants exposed them to the risk of being subjected to ill-treatment in Libya and of being arbitrarily repatriated to Somalia and Eritrea, held that 'the Italian Government must take all possible steps to obtain assurances from the Libyan authorities that the applicants will not be subjected to treatment incompatible with article 3 of the Convention or arbitrarily repatriated'. See Violeta Moreno-Lax, '*Hirsi Jamaa and Others* v. *Italy* or the Strasbourg Court versus Extraterritorial Migration Control?' (2012) 12 *Human Rights Law Review* 574–98.
[129] *MSS* v. *Belgium and Greece.*
[130] UNHCR's written observations in CJEU Joined Cases C-411/10 and C-493/10, paras. 12–32, and UNHCR's oral submissions in the same joined cases, para. 12.
[131] This issue is further discussed in Chapter 9 of this volume, pp. 244–55.

three facilitating factors behind the emulation of European protection norms. The two drivers are new challenges and uncertainty, and reputation and growing transnational professional standards. The three facilitating factors are the local context (fit), transnational networks (transmitter) and advocacy groups (push for change). It further examines basic norms or trends in European refugee law – namely, restrictive norms, such as the safe third-country rule and accelerated procedures, and liberal norms, such as subsidiary protection – for the case study chapters to consider, and presents Europe's unique judicial safety mechanisms.

Chapters 2 to 8 cover seven case studies. In each of the chapters, the primary research question was to explore the effect of European refugee law in the selected country. To the extent that evidence of emulation was found to have taken place, the authors were asked to analyse this evidence by paying particular attention to the key drivers and facilitators elaborated in Chapter 1, as well as the 'context' or local requirements. The chapters are ordered based on the strength of the evidence found of emulation, starting with Australia, Latin America and Canada where clear evidence of 'natural' emulation is found. These chapters are followed by the cases of Israel and Switzerland where strong evidence of 'formal' emulation is found. Africa follows with clear evidence of past (but not of present) emulation, and, finally, the United States where no explicit evidence is found.

Chapter 9 provides a cautionary tale of diffusion of European law by challenging some of our assumptions about EU asylum law (and ECHR law). It warns against a system (the CEAS) that is based on the logic of an internal market (namely, mutual trust and free movement) and a European human rights framework that too often sees protection against *refoulement* as an end in and of itself. Durieux argues that these (the CEAS and the ECHR) must not allow the specificity of refugee protection (and of the refugee) to be dislodged in this region.

Drawing on the findings in each of the case studies, Chapter 10 provides some conclusions about the emulation of European refugee law around the world. Thus, it consolidates and summarizes the analysis of the evidence produced through the various case studies, and it considers the theoretical implications of this evidence, for international, EU and domestic refugee law.

Through this methodology, we believe that an accurate examination and evaluation of the global reach of European law in the area of international protection is possible. It is hoped that through the assessment of the evidence obtained, and the theoretical implications, this volume will make a significant contribution to the debates about the diffusion of law and the role of the EU as a normative power.

2

Migrating laws? The 'plagiaristic dialogue' between Europe and Australia

JANE McADAM

A   Introduction

There has long been a conversation of sorts between national governments seeking to 'domesticate' their obligations under international law.
In the asylum space, there is no doubt that States cast an eye around to
see what others are doing – or can get away with – when it comes to
tightening the rules on entry, entitlements and border security. The
policies and practices of Australia and the European Union (EU)
undoubtedly assert mutual influence, although pinpointing the deriva-
tion of specific ideas can be very difficult, not least because it is rarely
formally documented.

In a common law country like Australia, the EU is not a traditional
comparative jurisdiction. While it is not uncommon for Australian
courts to examine the approach of other countries in interpreting the
meaning of key concepts in refugee law,[1] especially in the absence of
domestic precedent, the natural reference points are the United
Kingdom (UK),[2] New Zealand and Canada. Courts engage with this
jurisprudence to explore approaches to treaty interpretation, and frequently to affirm their own reasoning or explain why they think an
approach taken elsewhere is incorrect. The use of foreign law often

Thank you to Fiona Chong for her extensive research assistance, and to Matthew Albert and
Naomi Hart for additional research tasks. I am grateful to Professor Rosalind Dixon for her
helpful reading suggestions on diffusion theory.
[1] See Jane McAdam, 'Interpretation of the 1951 Convention', in Andreas Zimmermann
(ed.), *The 1951 Convention relating to the Status of Refugees and Its 1967 Protocol: A
Commentary* (Oxford: Oxford University Press, 2011).
[2] Interestingly, since the UK now reflects EU law, there may be an indirect influence on
Australian interpretation in this way. On this point, see, e.g., *Minister for Immigration
and Multicultural Affairs* v. *Kabail* [1999] FCA 344, at para. 14.

'seems to be about the protection of judges themselves in that it provides a form of reassurance and checks on their own power'.[3]

By contrast, there is a marked absence of transnational judicial dialogue about refugee law in the EU. As Lambert and Goodwin-Gill's edited collection about the use of foreign law by the national courts within Europe demonstrates, there is little cross-fertilization of national jurisprudence there, even though States are interpreting the same European directives.[4] One might therefore anticipate even less cross-fertilization in jurisdictions that are not bound by the same instruments.

In Australian refugee jurisprudence, there is little direct reference to EU law. As a general principle of interpretation, the High Court of Australia has observed that:

> Australian courts will endeavour to adopt a construction of the [Migration] Act and the Regulations, if that construction is available, which conforms to the [Refugee] Convention. And this Court would seek to adopt, if it were available, a construction of the definition in Art 1A of the Convention that conformed with any generally accepted construction in other countries subscribing to the Convention, as it would with any provision of an international instrument to which Australia is a party and which has been received into its domestic law ... But despite these respects in which the Convention may be used in construing the Act, it is the words of the Act which govern.[5]

In the same case, Kirby J. stated that in cases involving the Refugee Convention,[6] 'national courts are exercising a species of international jurisdiction', since they 'play an important role in expressing the

---

[3] Hélène Lambert, 'Transnational Judicial Dialogue, Harmonization and the Common European Asylum System' (2009) 58 *International and Comparative Law Quarterly* 519–43, at 530, referring to Cherie Booth's remarks at a one-day conference at the British Institute of International and Comparative Law entitled 'European Influences on Public Law: 5 Years of the HRA 1998 in English Law and Recent Developments in France' (October 2005).

[4] See Hélène Lambert and Guy S. Goodwin-Gill (eds.), *The Limits of Transnational Law: Refugee Law, Policy Harmonization and Judicial Dialogue in the European Union* (Cambridge: Cambridge University Press, 2010).

[5] *Minister for Immigration and Multicultural and Indigenous Affairs* v. *QAAH of 2004* (2006) 231 CLR 1, at para. 34 (citation omitted) (Gummow ACJ, Callinan, Heydon and Crennan JJ.). Kirby J. argued that courts should have 'appropriate regard to the fact that the definition of "refugee" originates in an international treaty' and needs to be interpreted in the context and for the purpose in which it was devised (*Applicant A* v. *Minister for Immigration and Ethnic Affairs* (1997) 190 CLR 225, at 292).

[6] Convention Relating to the Status of Refugees, Geneva, 28 July 1951, in force 22 April 1954 (189 UNTS 137), read in conjunction with the Protocol Relating to the Status of Refugees, New York, adopted 31 January 1967, in force 4 October 1967 (606 UNTS 267) (together, Refugee Convention).

meaning of the Convention and deciding the application of such treaty law'.[7] He therefore saw it as imperative that this conversation be properly situated within an international context because:

> in the absence of established State practice on the interpretation of Art 1C(5) of the Convention, the decision of this Court has the potential to influence the interpretation of the Convention beyond Australian law. Experience demonstrates that courts in many countries, including Australia, pay close regard to court decisions in other countries grappling with the meaning and application of the Convention.[8]

This argument is even more potent when it comes to the influence that the Common European Asylum System (CEAS) may have, given the large number of States involved in it and the jurisprudence and State practice being generated. As Kirby J. observed, 'it is desirable, so far as possible, to observe common approaches to the interpretation and application of an international treaty',[9] and consideration of comparative domestic case law can assist in achieving this. While courts would be 'well advised to draw upon the international jurisprudence which has collected around a crucial provision', Kirby J. nonetheless emphasized the need for caution in assessing foreign jurisprudence, since national statutory or constitutional influences may affect the approach taken.[10] Indeed, the High Court of Australia has rejected comparative law arguments where the particular interpretation of the Refugee Convention asserted has been influenced by national human rights instruments, such as the Canadian Charter of Rights and Freedoms, which has no parallel in Australia.[11] Similarly, 'safe third country' cases have been distinguished from UK cases on the basis of different statutory regimes.[12]

It is likely that the CEAS will start to exert a greater influence on Australian refugee law in the coming years. This may happen indirectly, through examination of UK cases and legislation which give effect to certain European directives, and more directly, as Australian legislation starts to

---

[7] *QAAH*, para. 78 (Kirby J.), referring to *Al-Kateb* v. *Godwin* [2004] HCA 37 (2004) 219 CLR 562, at para. 168, citing Ian Brownlie, *Principles of Public International Law* (5th edn, Oxford: Oxford University Press, 1998), p. 584.

[8] *Ibid.*, para. 54 (Kirby J.).

[9] *Minister for Immigration and Multicultural Affairs* v. *Respondents S152/2003* (2004) 222 CLR 1, at para. 111 (Kirby J.). See the use of comparative jurisprudence by McHugh J., at paras. 54ff.

[10] *Applicant A*, p. 296 (Kirby J.), referring to *Ram* v. *Minister for Immigration and Ethnic Affairs* (1995) 57 FCR 565, at 567.

[11] *Ibid.*, p. 247 (Dawson J.).

[12] *Minister for Immigration and Multicultural Affairs* v. *Kabail* [1999] FCA 344, at para. 13.

adopt concepts that are well developed in the CEAS. An example of the latter is complementary protection (known as 'subsidiary protection' in the EU), which became part of Australian law in 2011 and took effect on 24 March 2012 as a ground on which a protection visa could be granted.

While it is apparent that European developments in asylum law have influenced Australia's legislative and policy responses, charting precisely how this has occurred is complicated. Formal records describing such influence are rare. Rather, as this chapter shows, influence stems from personal interactions between the Immigration Minister and his or her counterparts in EU Member States; from research by the Department of Immigration and Citizenship (Immigration Department) into comparative practices when formulating policy; from the interventions of academics and non-governmental organizations (NGOs) in parliamentary inquiries, and more generally through their advocacy and scholarly writings; and through consideration of European jurisprudence by the courts.

This chapter explores each of these elements to gauge the extent to which EU practices have historically influenced Australian refugee law and policy, and to assess the degree to which they may continue to do so in the future. The first part of the chapter does this through an examination of three substantive areas: the importation of the 'safe third country' concept into Australia in the 1990s; the (unspoken) influence of the UK's proposal on Regional Processing Centres (in the early 2000s) on Australia's regional processing proposals; and the influence of the Qualification Directive on the creation of codified grounds for complementary protection in Australian law.[13] The second part of the chapter examines the processes by which EU practices may exert influence on Australian law and policy, alluded to above.

B   Safe third countries

One of the first occasions on which EU law influenced Australian refugee law was in the mid-1990s in relation to the 'safe third country' concept.

---

[13] Council Directive 2004/83/EC of 29 April 2004 on minimum standards for the qualification and status of third-country nationals or stateless persons as refugees or as persons who otherwise need international protection and the content of the protection granted (OJ 2004 No. L304/12) (Qualification Directive). See also Directive 2011/95/EU of the European Parliament and of the Council of 13 December 2011 on standards for the qualification of third-country nationals or stateless persons as beneficiaries of international protection, for a uniform status for refugees or for persons eligible for subsidiary protection, and for the content of the protection granted (recast) (OJ 2011 No. L337/9).

The concept originated in Switzerland in 1979, spreading slowly to a handful of other European countries in the 1980s before being adopted more widely during the 1990s.[14] It was formally incorporated into EU law through the Dublin Convention in 1990,[15] which was replaced in 2003 by the Dublin Regulation.[16]

The 'safe third country' notion has been described as a 'basic ingredient in the transformation of European asylum law and policy' because it 'challenges core principles enshrined in the 1951 Geneva Convention and in long-settled administrative law doctrine'.[17] In its European origins, it was used to preclude asylum seekers who had travelled through States believed to respect human rights from entering refugee status determination procedures in other countries.[18] It has subsequently been developed and expanded in the EU through the Procedures Directive, which also incorporates the notion of a 'super safe' European country.[19]

[14] Chetail and Bauloz, Chapter 6 of this volume; E. W. Vierdag, 'The Country of "First Asylum": Some European Aspects', in David A. Martin (ed.), *The New Asylum Seekers: Refugee Law in the 1980s* (Dordrecht: Martinus Nijhoff, 1988), p. 76; Gregor Noll, 'Visions of the Exceptional: Legal and Theoretical Issues Raised by Transit Processing Centres and Protection Zones' (2003) 5 *European Journal of Migration and Law* 303–41, at 310.

[15] Convention determining the State responsible for examining applications for asylum lodged in one of the member states of the European Communities, 15 June 1990 (OJ 1997 No. C254/1) (Dublin Convention). See generally Rosemary Byrne and Andrew Shacknove, 'The Safe Country Notion in European Asylum Law' (1996) 9 *Harvard Human Rights Journal* 185–228 (origins of 'safe third country'/'safe country of asylum'/'first country of asylum' discussed from p. 189); Eva Kjaergaard, 'Opinion: The Concept of "Safe Third Country" in Contemporary European Refugee Law' (1994) 6 *International Journal of Refugee Law* 649–55 (discussion of Dublin Convention as the first formal instrument to define terms related to 'safe third country' notion from p. 651); Morten Kjaerum, 'The Concept of Country of First Asylum' (1992) 4 *International Journal of Refugee Law* 514–30 (discussion of development of 'safe third country' concept in Europe from p. 515); Stephen Legomsky, 'Secondary Refugee Movements and the Return of Asylum Seekers to Third Countries: The Meaning of Effective Protection' (2003) 15 *International Journal of Refugee Law* 567–677 (discussion of Western European origins from p. 575).

[16] Council Regulation (EC) No. 343/2003 of 18 February 2003 establishing the criteria and mechanisms for determining the Member State responsible for examining an asylum application lodged in one of the Member States by a third-country national (OJ 2003 No. L50/1) (Dublin Regulation).

[17] Byrne and Shacknove, 'Safe Country', 186.   [18] *Ibid.*, 188.

[19] Council Directive 2005/85/EC of 1 December 2005 on minimum standards on procedures in Member States for granting and withdrawing refugee status (OJ 2005 No. L236/13), art. 36(2) (Procedures Directive) (art. 39 in the recast version: European Commission, Amended Proposal for a Directive of the European Parliament and of the Council on common procedures for granting and withdrawing international protection status (recast), COM (2011) 319 final, 1 June 2011). The fallacy of this concept was made clear in *MSS* v. *Belgium*

1   Legislative framework

The 'safe third country' notion was first introduced into Australian refugee practice in 1994. On 24 May of that year, the Immigration Minister, Senator Nick Bolkus, issued guidelines 'to provide a framework for recommending the grant of stay in Australia to persons of human-itarian concern who do not meet the requirements for refugee status but who face hardship if returned to their country of origin which would evoke strong concern in the Australian public'.[20] In them, he introduced the concept of a 'safe third country' for the first time. The guidelines provided that there was no public interest in providing residence on humanitarian grounds to a person who had a 'safe third country in which to reside [where that] country would accept that person'.[21] There was no reference to Europe, either in the guidelines or the accompanying media release.

The first reference to the term 'safe third country' in the Australian Parliament was on 21 September 1994 during the second reading speech of the Migration Amendment Bill (No. 4) 1994 (Cth).[22] This bill was introduced in response to the arrival in Australia of two boats of Vietnamese asylum seekers (forty-eight people in total) in 1994. Their refugee claims had already been rejected in Indonesia, pursuant to the Comprehensive Plan of Action (CPA), and Australian law at the time required their protection applications to be assessed *de novo*. The pur-pose of the bill was '[t]o provide that entrants who have previously been assessed overseas for refugee status will not be required to be reassessed by Australian authorities',[23] a position supported by the United Nations

---

and Greece (European Court of Human Rights, Grand Chamber, App. No. 30696/09, 21 January 2011).

[20] Minister for Immigration and Ethnic Affairs, *Guidelines for Stay in Australia on Humanitarian Grounds* (24 May 1994), at para. 1 http://parlinfo.aph.gov.au/parlInfo/download/media/pressrel/IMAA6/upload_binary/imaa63.pdf;fileType=application/pdf (accessed 28 February 2012).

[21] 'Grant of residence on humanitarian grounds must be limited to exceptional cases, where the applicant's fears are well founded and based on serious grounds presenting threat to personal security, intense personal hardship or abuse of human rights. The provision is not intended to address cases where the applicant ... has a safe third country in which to reside and that country would accept the person' (*ibid.*, para. 6).

[22] Hansard, Senate, p. 1066, 21 September 1994 (Senator Crowley). For the first reference to 'safe third country' in the House of Representatives, see Hansard, House of Representatives, p. 2831, 8 November 1994 (Mrs Crosio).

[23] Department of Parliamentary Services (Cth), *Bills Digest: Migration Laws Amendment Bill (No. 4) 1994*, No. 151 of 1994, 23 September 1994, p. 1.

High Commissioner for Refugees (UNHCR).[24] The rationale was that if Australia were to redetermine claims, this could

> encourage more people who have been refused refugee status in other CPA countries to try for 'another chance' of refugee status by coming to Australia. With the alternative of forced repatriation it can be expected that many people would be willing to undertake this course of action. Another difficulty is the impression that may be given that the CPA countries operate under different criteria or rules (which may or may not be true – refer to the Remarks section) and the possibility that it may encourage other countries to think that their assessment is not conclusive so that the arrivals may as well be directed to Australia rather than assessed.[25]

The bill inserted subdivision AI into the Migration Act 1958 (Cth), providing that certain non-citizens were unable to apply for certain visas, including those 'covered by CPA or an agreement with a pre-scribed safe third country'. Section 91D defined a 'safe third country' as a prescribed country ('in relation to the non-citizen, or in relation to a class of persons of which the non-citizen is a member') with which the non-citizen 'has a prescribed connection', such as being present in that country at a particular time, or having a right to enter and reside in that country. Further, in relation to each safe third country, the Immigration Minister was required to table in Parliament a statement about:

(a) the compliance by the country, or each of the countries, with relevant international law concerning the protection of persons seeking asylum; and

(b) the meeting by the country, or each of the countries, of relevant human rights standards for the persons in relation to whom the country is prescribed as a safe third country; and

(c) the willingness of the country, or each of the countries, to allow any person in relation to whom the country is prescribed as a safe third country:

    (i) to go to the country; and

    (ii) to remain in the country during the period in which any claim by the person for asylum is determined; and

---

[24] Ibid., p. 3.

[25] Ibid. See also Migration Act 1958 (Cth), s. 91A: 'the Parliament considers that certain non-citizens who are covered by the CPA, or in relation to whom there is a safe third country, should not be allowed to apply for a protection visa or, in some cases, any other visa. Any such non-citizen who is an unlawful non-citizen will be subject to removal under Division 8'.

(iii) if the person is determined to be a refugee while in the country –
to remain in the country until a durable solution relating to the
permanent settlement of the person is found.[26]

The CPA refers to the Comprehensive Plan of Action approved by the
International Conference on Indo-Chinese Refugees in June 1989. This
was a regional arrangement designed to assist displaced persons from
Vietnam and Laos following the conflict in Indo-China. In conjunction
with UNHCR, countries of first asylum determined whether such people
were 'refugees', and, if found to be so, they were resettled in countries
including Australia. A media release issued in August 1994 had foreshadowed that the CPA was the basis on which the 'safe third country'
provision would be introduced.[27] However, it seems that the introduction of the notion of 'safe third country' (separately from the CPA) was
almost singularly focused on the movement of Vietnamese people from
China. Pursuant to section 91D(3), the Australian government designated China as a safe third country on 27 January 1995.[28]

Although the 'safe third country' concept was by this time well
established in Europe, there was no mention of European practice during
the bill's second reading speech in the House of Representatives or in the
Explanatory Memoranda.[29] However, during parliamentary debate,
there were a number of references to the use of the 'safe third country'
concept in the European context. When the bill was read for a second
time in the Senate, Senator Short stated:

> In general, the safe third country concept states that someone who has had
> access to the system of protection in a safe third country will be denied access
> to Australia's onshore refugee determination processes and will be returned
> to that safe third country. Countries such as Austria, Canada, Denmark,

---

[26] Migration Act, s. 91D(3). Sections (c)(i) and (ii) were inserted in response to suggestions
by UNHCR. UNHCR also proposed an additional ground which was not included:
'whether the non-citizen has strong links to Australia or [there are] other compelling
humanitarian reasons for the person not to be returned to the safe third country'. See
discussion by Senator Ellison: Hansard, Senate, p. 1913, 18 October 1994, referring to
the submission by Mr Fontaine, UNHCR.

[27] Nick Bolkus, 'Refugee Decisions for 17 Boat People' (Media Release, 29 August 1994).

[28] Migration Amendment Regulations 2004 (No. 4).

[29] See Hansard, House of Representatives, pp. 2830–33, 8 November 1994 (Mrs Crosio);
Explanatory Memorandum, Migration Legislation Amendment Bill (No. 4) 1994 (Cth);
Supplementary Explanatory Memorandum, Migration Legislation Amendment Bill (No. 4)
1994 (Cth); Revised Explanatory Memorandum, Migration Legislation Amendment Bill
(No. 4) 1994 (Cth).

Finland, France, Germany, Greece, Italy, the Netherlands, Sweden and the UK have adopted the safe third country concept in one form or another.

The system which most closely resembles the one proposed in this bill is that of Canada ... The British define an STC [safe third country] as one in which the life or freedom of an asylum applicant would not be threatened within the meaning of article 33 of the UN convention, and the government of which would not send the applicant elsewhere in a manner contrary to the principles of the 1951 convention and 1967 protocol. The provisions under which a country will be a designated safe third country in relation to a non-citizen in the Australian context are set out in the bill.[30]

These remarks were repeated almost verbatim in the House of Representatives by the Opposition spokesman on immigration, Philip Ruddock, who also noted that the safe third-country concept 'was subjected to some examination by the parliamentary committee' which examined the bill, and '[a] number of us were very strongly of the view that these matters that are specifically sanctioned within the international covenants to which we are a party ought to form part of the system here'.[31] Indeed, as noted by Senator Ellison, a member of that Committee, of the 'number of concerns ... expressed in relation to the legislation', 'the greatest concern was in relation to the term "safe third country"'.[32]

The Committee's report noted that '[s]ome witnesses pointed out that other jurisdictions, principally Canada and the European Community, had enacted legislation providing for the prescribing of safe third countries',[33] referring in particular to the fact that:

The member states of the European Union have arrangements for a safe third country procedure following the Dublin Convention of June 1990, which has been signed by all 12 member states but ratified by only six so far (Denmark, Greece, Italy, Luxembourg, Portugal and the UK). This is supplemented by the Schengen Agreement of 19 June 1990 which is open only to EC countries.[34]

The Committee also referred to submissions by the Immigration Department about the UK's use of the safe third-country concept and the numbers of asylum seekers removed pursuant to it.[35]

---

[30] Hansard, Senate, p. 1906, 18 October 1994 (Senator Short).
[31] Hansard, House of Representatives, p. 2835, 8 November 1994 (Mr Ruddock).
[32] Hansard, Senate, p. 1913, 18 October 1994 (Senator Ellison).
[33] Senate Standing Committee on Legal and Constitutional Affairs, *Migration Legislation Amendment Bill (No. 4) 1994: Report by the Senate Standing Committee on Legal and Constitutional Affairs* (October 1994), at para. 1.25.
[34] *Ibid.*, para. 1.28.   [35] *Ibid.*, para. 1.29.

In early 1995, Parliament introduced the Migration Legislation Amendment Bill (No. 2) 1995, 'to enable the recently enacted safe third country provisions of the Migration Act 1958 to cover Vietnamese refugees who had already been successfully resettled in the People's Republic of China but who lodged claims for a protection visa in Australia after 30 December 1994'.[36] During debate, it was noted that the 'safe third country' concept

> has only been around for the last couple of years. To that extent, only two years ago when I went to Europe I had an opportunity to scrutinise the safe third country concept and to discuss it with the UNHCR and others in both Geneva and elsewhere. It can be said that Australia has moved as quickly as is practically and desirably possible to introduce this concept into our legislation.[37]

Mr Ferguson observed that Australia's practice was 'not an isolated circumstance; it is part of an international pattern. What we are doing today in Australia is paralleled in Canada, the United Kingdom, Germany, Finland and France. At the moment the United States is considering similar measures. Europe is getting towards a situation where there is an understanding as to which country has primary responsibility for particular cases.'[38]

This suggests that some international consensus – however small – may help to justify the adoption of a practice or a rule.

2 Judicial consideration

European safe third-country practices have been mentioned on a number of occasions in Australian case law. In *NAEN* v. *Minister for Immigration and Multicultural and Indigenous Affairs*, the Dublin Convention was raised by counsel 'to support the proposition that a safe country in international law is one with which the refugee has a prior

---

[36] Hansard, House of Representatives, p. 877, 9 February 1995 (Mrs Crosio).
[37] Hansard, Senate, pp. 808–9, 9 February 1995 (Senator Bolkus).
[38] Hansard, House of Representatives, p. 884, 9 February 1995 (Mr Ferguson). 'The purpose of the Migration Legislation Amendment Bill (No. 2) 1995 is to enable the recently enacted safe third country provisions of the Migration Act 1958 to cover Vietnamese refugees who had already been successfully resettled in the People's Republic of China but who lodged claims for a protection visa in Australia after 30 December 1994. More generally, the bill is also to enable the safe third country provisions of the act to have effect from a specified date preceding the date of commencement of any future agreements and relevant regulations' (Hansard, House of Representatives, p. 877, 9 February 1995 (Mrs Crosio)).

association, whether by way of citizenship or physical connection'.[39] In *Minister for Immigration and Multicultural Affairs* v. *Thiyagarajah*, the court examined the concept in light of academic commentary and the comparative practices of the UK and Canada to conclude 'that international law does not preclude a Contracting State from taking this course where it is proposed to return the asylum seeker to a third country which has already recognized that person's status as a refugee, and has accorded that person effective protection, including a right to reside, enter and re-enter that country'.[40] In *Minister for Immigration and Multicultural Affairs* v. *Kabail*, the court distinguished the English case of *R* v. *Secretary of State for the Home Department, ex parte Abdi* – in which asylum seekers were removed to Spain without any consideration of the merits of their claims – on the basis that there was no comparable legislative scheme in Australian law which would authorize such removal.[41] Nicholson J. noted that:

> In the case of the United Kingdom and of any countries which are members of the European Economic Community there is the question of the degree to which such decisions are influenced by or are the product of the development of the European Economic Community and generally the development of closer relations within European countries.[42]

The incorporation of the 'safe third country' concept in Australian law provides a neat illustration of a number of 'emulation drivers' identified by Lambert in Chapter 1 of this volume. In particular, European law provided a source for responding to new challenges in Australia, and its characterization in parliamentary debate as part of a growing international consensus helped to 'legitimize' the development of similar Australian legislation.

---

[39] *NAEN* v. *Minister for Immigration and Multicultural and Indigenous Affairs* [2003] FCA 216, at para. 55.

[40] *Minister for Immigration and Multicultural Affairs* v. *Thiyagarajah* (1997) 80 FCR 543 at 562. See also discussion by Lee J. in *Al-Rahal* v. *Minister for Immigration and Multicultural Affairs* [2001] FCA 1141, at paras. 30–2; *Patto* v. *Minister for Immigration and Multicultural Affairs* [2000] FCA 1554 at para. 32; *Minister for Immigration and Multicultural Affairs* v. *Gnanapiragasam* (1998) 88 FCR 1, at 13; *NAGV and NAGW of 2002* v. *Minister for Immigration and Multicultural and Indigenous Affairs* [2005] HCA 6 (2005) 222 CLR 161 (mentioned by six judges but no discussion of its history; Kirby J. refers to the scholarship of Kay Hailbronner but does not otherwise refer to law or practice in Europe).

[41] *Kabail*, para. 13, distinguishing *R* v. *Secretary of State for the Home Department, ex parte Abdi* [1996] 1 WLR 298.

[42] *Kabail*, para. 14.

C   Regional protection and offshore processing

The safe third-country concept underpins asylum transfer schemes
(such as the Dublin Regulation and the failed 2011 Australia–Malaysia
Arrangement) and proposals to establish regional processing centres
(such as those suggested by the UK and Australia). Indeed, these exemplify
what Guild foreshadowed as 'the sophistication of the safe third country and
safe country of origin principles'.[43] Both operate within a policy framework
of deterrence and seek to facilitate the 'deterritorialisation of protection
obligations' for refugees and asylum seekers.[44]

1   Regional processing centres

In early 2011, the Australian government announced its intention to
establish a regional processing centre for asylum seekers in East Timor.
Since the proposal was publicized before the East Timorese government
had agreed to it, details were scant, but it was premised on the idea that
asylum seekers in the region would be transferred safely to East Timor
to have their protection claims determined, rather than spontaneously
undertaking dangerous boat voyages from transit hubs such as Indonesia
and Malaysia. Commentators expressed significant concerns about the
ability of a poor, developing country such as East Timor to operate such a
facility. In particular, many viewed it as an attempt by Australia to use
the country as a dumping ground for people it had a responsibility to
process and protect.[45]

The East Timor plan was reminiscent of a failed UK proposal,
announced in March 2003, to establish 'transit processing centres' outside the EU to which asylum seekers entering the EU would be returned

---

[43] Elspeth Guild, 'The Europeanisation of Europe's Asylum Policy' (2006) 18 *International
Journal of Refugee Law* 630–51, at 637.

[44] *Ibid.*, p. 632. As a deterrence strategy, see generally Angus Francis, 'Bringing Protection
Home: Healing the Schism between International Obligations and National Safeguards
Created by Extraterritorial Processing' (2008) 20 *International Journal of Refugee Law*
273–313. On the blurry distinction in 'regionalism' between deterrence and contain-
ment, see Karin Fathimath Afeef, 'The Politics of Extraterritorial Processing: Offshore
Asylum Policies in Europe and the Pacific', RSC Working Paper No. 36 (October 2006).

[45] See generally Tamara Wood and Jane McAdam, 'Australian Asylum Policy All at Sea:
An Analysis of *Plaintiff M70/2011* v. *Minister for Immigration and Citizenship* and the
Australia–Malaysia Arrangement' (2012) 61 *International and Comparative Law
Quarterly* 274–300 and references cited therein.

to have their protection claims determined.[46] Those found to be in need of international protection were to be resettled in an EU Member State in accordance with burden-sharing policies, or granted temporary asylum.[47] Denmark and the Netherlands strongly supported this approach, having collaborated with the UK to develop the ideas underpinning it in the context of the Intergovernmental Consultations (IGC) on Migration, Asylum and Refugees.[48] Indeed, when the Danish government had assumed power in 2001, it had promoted discussion on 'reception in the region' – a topic it also advocated during its presidency of the EU in 2002. It drew on precedents such as the United States' (US) policy of processing Haitian and Cuban asylum seekers at Guantánamo Bay and Australia's Pacific Solution.[49] Italy and Spain also signalled their approval of the UK proposal.[50]

However, following in-depth discussions with EU Member States, acceding States and representatives of relevant international organizations and NGOs, the European Commission said that further research was needed before a formal position could be taken. Such discussions had revealed concerns about where such centres would be located (within or outside the EU); whether they would be compatible with 'EU legislation, national legislation, the legislation of the envisaged countries hosting such centres or zones, and the European Convention

---

[46] Secretary of State for the Home Department, 'Statement on Zones of Protection' (Media Release, Stat010/2003, 27 March 2003), to which was appended the UK's proposal 'New International Approaches to Asylum Processing and Protection', contained in House of Lords European Union Committee, *Handling EU Asylum Claims: New Approaches Examined* (HL Paper 74, 11th Report of Session 2003–04), Appendix 5; European Commission, Communication from the European Commission to the Council and the European Parliament: Towards more accessible, equitable and managed asylum systems (COM(2003) 315 final, 3 June 2003). See generally Alexander Betts, 'The International Relations of the "New" Extraterritorial Approaches to Refugee Protection: Explaining the Policy Initiatives of the UK Government and UNHCR' (2004) 22 *Refuge* 58–70; Madeline Garlick, 'The EU Discussions on Extraterritorial Processing: Solution or Conundrum?' (2006) 18 *International Journal of Refugee Law* 601–29.

[47] See further Guy S. Goodwin-Gill and Jane McAdam, *The Refugee in International Law* (3rd edn, Oxford: Oxford University Press, 2007), pp. 409–12.

[48] Parliamentary Assembly of the Council of Europe, *Assessment of Transit and Processing Centres as a Response to Mixed Flows of Migrants and Asylum Seekers*, Doc. 11304 (Committee on Migration, Refugees and Population, 15 June 2007), at para. 20; see also the 2004 proposals by the German Interior Minister, Otto Schily, for the creation of 'safe zones' in North Africa, to be funded by the EU: paras. 23–4; Noll, 'Visions', 306.

[49] See Noll, 'Visions', 303–4.

[50] Agence Europe, Bulletin Quotidien Europe, 28 March 2003 (cited *ibid.*, 306).

on Human Rights'; which procedural rules (EU or national) would
govern such centres; and the extent to which it would be possible to
transfer asylum seekers to such centres if they had not transited through
or otherwise stayed in the countries in which they were located.[51]
The European Commission presented its report at the Thessaloniki
European Council in June 2003, where a number of States vigorously
opposed the UK proposal.[52] The UK government ultimately decided
not to pursue it.[53] Had the proposal been adopted, however, it would
have 'gear[ed] the Common European Asylum System towards processing and protecting in the region of origin rather than within the
Union, thus introducing a paradigm shift in EU asylum and migration
policies'.[54]

Interestingly, there is evidence that Australia's Pacific Solution, created in 2001, was a clear source of inspiration for the UK and Danish
proposals.[55] Indeed, Australia's Immigration Minister at the time, Philip
Ruddock, welcomed the UK's proposal by noting its 'remarkable
similarity' to the Pacific Solution.[56] Yet, the Pacific Solution was itself
reminiscent of the US' offshore processing of Cuban and Haitian asylum
seekers at Guantánamo Bay in the 1990s.[57] The bill's digest, prepared by
the Department of the Parliamentary Library, alerted politicians to this

[51] European Commission, Towards more accessible, equitable and managed asylum systems, p. 6.
[52] House of Lords European Union Committee, *Handling EU Asylum Claims*, at para. 57.
See further Noll, 'Visions'.
[53] *Ibid.*   [54] Noll, 'Visions', 307.
[55] *Ibid.*, 304, 313, 328 (referring to the Danish Memorandum). See also Refugee Council
(UK), 'Unsafe Havens, Unworkable Solutions' (Position Paper, June 2003), at para. 5.5.1,
noting the similarities between the policies; Kim Ward, 'Navigation Guide: Regional
Protection Zones and Transit Processing Centres' (Information Centre about Asylum
and Refugees in the UK, November 2004), p. 27, arguing that the UK government was
'directly inspired by the Australian government's "Pacific solution" for refugees and
asylum seekers'. Amnesty International suggested that the Pacific Solution 'set the scene
for a new phase in state responses to the demands of their voluntarily assumed international legal obligations' ('UK/EU/UNHCR: Unlawful and Unworkable: Amnesty
International's Views on Proposals for Extraterritorial Processing of Asylum Claims',
AI Index: IOR 61/004/2003, 17 June 2003, p. 18); UK Government, 'New Vision for
Refugees' (Summary), 7 March 2003, p. 4 www.proasyl.de/texte/mappe/2003/76/3.pdf
(accessed 29 November 2012), noting that Australia might work with the UK as a
partner given that it had 'to some extent piloted this approach'.
[56] Minister for Immigration, Multicultural and Indigenous Affairs, 'UK Asylum Proposals
Worth Consideration' (Media Release, MPS 21/2003, 3 April 2003).
[57] Azadeh Dastyari, 'Refugees on Guantanamo Bay: A Blue Print for Australia's "Pacific
Solution"?' (2007) 79 *Australian Quarterly* 4–8, at 6.

precedent.[58] It was not discussed, however, in parliamentary debates on the proposed legislation.[59]

According to Noll, both the Pacific Solution and the US model were discussed at a mini-IGC meeting on 23 April 2003, involving Denmark, the Netherlands, the UK, the European Commission, IGC, the International Organization for Migration and UNHCR.[60] However, what was omitted was consideration of extensive analysis by the IGC in 1994–5 about regional processing, in which the US model was critiqued.[61]

Furthermore, as Noll points out, as early as 1986, Denmark had proposed a resolution in the General Assembly to create regional UN processing centres to administer resettlement,[62] and similar ideas were raised again in Europe during the 1990s:

> these ideas have a relatively long history. They have been discussed well in advance of the Pacific Solution policy of Australia. Back in the mid 1990s the Netherlands, for example, proposed this idea before the inter-governmental consultation on refugees and exiles, and the idea was debated then and thought to be, both legally and practically, infeasible. But then the idea was raised again by Jack Straw when he was Home Secretary in the late 1990s, so although the Australian policy has had some influence, it has a long history.[63]

2 Transfer arrangements

In 2011, following the failure of the East Timor proposal and considerable political embarrassment, the Australian government looked for other options within the Asia-Pacific region.[64] Malaysia emerged as a

[58] Department of Parliamentary Services (Cth), *Bills Digest: Border Protection (Validation and Enforcement Powers) Bill 2001*, No. 62 of 2001–02, 20 September 2001, pp. 14–16. While bills digests are not official parliamentary or government documents, but are written by the research division of the Parliamentary Library, they are 'prepared for general distribution to Senators and Members of the Australian Parliament' to inform them about legal or policy issues 'for use in parliamentary debate and for related parliamentary purposes' (see disclaimer at the beginning of the Bills Digest).

[59] Border Protection (Validation and Enforcement Powers) Act 2001 (Cth); Migration Amendment (Excision from Migration Zone) Act 2001 (Cth); Migration Amendment (Excision from Migration Zone) (Consequential Provisions) Act 2001 (Cth).

[60] See Noll, 'Visions', 307.   [61] *Ibid.*, 313–14.

[62] 'International Procedures for the Protection of Refugees', UNGA draft resolution (12 November 1986) (UN Doc A/C.3/41/L.51), cited in Noll, 'Visions', 311.

[63] Gil Loescher interviewed in 'Migration Experts Discuss the Global Dilemma of an Estimated 22 Million Refugees', *Breakfast*, ABC Radio (21 May 2003).

[64] For a fuller examination of this, see Wood and McAdam, 'Australian Asylum Policy'.

potential new partner. On 25 July 2011, the governments of Australia and Malaysia announced that they had entered into an 'Arrangement' for the transfer of asylum seekers.[65] Its purpose was to deter asylum seekers from travelling by boat to Australia, and it accordingly provided that the next 800 asylum seekers to arrive unlawfully in Australia would be transferred to Malaysia, in exchange for the resettlement in Australia of 4,000 UNHCR-approved refugees in Malaysia.[66] The joint media release by the Australian Prime Minister and Minister for Immigration stated that the Arrangement showed 'the resolve of Australia and Malaysia to break the people smugglers' business model, stop them profiting from human misery, and stop people risking their lives at sea'.[67] The Australian government also emphasized that asylum seekers transferred to Malaysia would 'go to the back of the queue'.[68]

Whereas the Australian government saw the Arrangement as a 'true burden-sharing arrangement in line with the principles of collective responsibility and cooperation',[69] legal experts were concerned about its compliance with Australia's international obligations under human rights and refugee law,[70] especially in light of Malaysia's extensive record of ill-treatment of

---

[65] Arrangement between the Government of Australia and the Government of Malaysia on Transfer and Resettlement (25 July 2011) (Australia–Malaysia Arrangement).

[66] Prime Minister and Minister for Immigration and Citizenship, 'Transcript of Joint Press Conference' (12 September 2011) www.pm.gov.au/press-office/transcript-joint-press-conference-canberra-15 (accessed 3 November 2011).

[67] Prime Minister and Minister for Immigration and Citizenship, 'Australia and Malaysia Sign Transfer Deal' (Media Release, 25 July 2011) www.pm.gov.au/press-office/aus tralia-and-malaysia-sign-transfer-deal (accessed 3 November 2011).

[68] 'Gillard Reaches Asylum Agreement with Malaysia', Q&A, 7 May 2011 www.abc.net.au/news/ stories/2011/05/07/3210503.htm?site=qanda (accessed 16 November 2011). This is in stark contrast to the UK proposal for transit processing centres, which considered the deterrence factor to be *removal* to such centres, from which refugees would be resettled in EU countries: see 'New International Approaches to Asylum Processing and Protection'.

[69] Prime Minister and Minister for Immigration and Citizenship, 'Transcript of Joint Press Conference'.

[70] See, e.g., Australian Refugee Law Academics, Submission No. 25 to Senate Legal and Constitutional Affairs References Committee, *Inquiry into Australia's Agreement with Malaysia in Relation to Asylum Seekers* (15 September 2011); 'Refugee expert says Australia/Malaysia swap illegal', *ABC News*, 10 June 2011 www.abc.net.au/worldtoday/ content/2011/s3240886.htm (accessed 3 November 2011); Jane McAdam, 'Explainer: The Facts about the Malaysian Solution and Australia's International Obligations', *Conversation*, 16 June 2011 http://theconversation.edu.au/explainer-the-facts-about-the-malaysian-solution-and-australias-international-obligations-1861 (accessed 3 November 2011); Savitri Taylor, 'Regional Cooperation and the Malaysian Solution' *Inside Story*, 9 May 2011 http://inside.org.au/regional-cooperation-and-the-malaysian-solution (accessed 3 November 2011).

asylum seekers and refugees, including arbitrary detention, deprivation of basic services and their lack of status under Malaysian law.[71]

The High Court of Australia found that the Arrangement was unlawful under the Migration Act.[72] A central part of the High Court's analysis was that 'effective protection' could not be guaranteed in Malaysia (although the court tried to disguise that it was making any formal determination as to conditions in Malaysia).[73] Since the creation of the Pacific Solution, the executive had reserved the power to designate particular countries as ones to which asylum seekers could be removed (Nauru and Papua New Guinea). The High Court held that the Immigration Minister could not validly find that Malaysia was safe for the applicants because it:

> first, does not recognise the status of refugee in its domestic law and does not undertake any activities related to the reception, registration, documentation and status determination of asylum seekers and refugees; second, is not party to the Refugees Convention or the Refugees Protocol; and, third, has made no legally binding arrangement with Australia obliging it to accord the protections required by those instruments.[74]

Although neither has drawn on the other, recent Australian and European authority have both affirmed that the safety of a third country is to be ascertained not merely on the basis of which international treaties it has ratified, but must also be assessed according to actual practice.[75] Where

---

[71] See, e.g., Human Rights Watch, 'World Report 2011: Malaysia' (January 2011) www.hrw. org/world-report-2011/malaysia (accessed 3 November 2011); Amnesty International, 'Abused and Abandoned: Refugees Denied Rights in Malaysia' (June 2010) www.amnesty. org/en/library/asset/ASA28/010/2010/en/2791c659-7e4d-4922-87e0-940faf54b92c/asa2801 02010en.pdf (accessed 3 November 2011); Amnesty International, 'Malaysia: Human Rights at Risk in Mass Deportation of Undocumented Migrants' (December 2004) www.amnesty. org/en/library/asset/ASA28/008/2004/en/a4e9ce8d-d57c-11dd-bb24-1fb85fe8fa05/asa280 082004en.html (accessed 3 November 2011); UNHRC, *Report of the Working Group on Arbitrary Detention: Mission to Malaysia*, 8 February 2011 (UN Doc. A/HRC/16/47/ Add.2).

[72] *Plaintiff M70/2011 and Plaintiff M106/2011* v. *Minister for Immigration and Citizenship* [2011] HCA 32 (31 August 2011) (2011) 280 ALR 18.

[73] *Ibid.*, para. 114 (Gummow, Hayne, Crennan and Bell JJ.). Any determination by Australia that Malaysia was 'safe' was akin to article 27(2)(b) of the Procedures Directive (art. 38(2)(b) in the recast version), which permits 'national designation of countries considered to be generally safe'.

[74] *M70*, para. 135; see also paras. 117ff.

[75] *Ibid.*, para. 67 (French CJ); para. 245 (Kiefel J.); MSS in *Hirsi* v. *Italy* (European Court of Human Rights, Grand Chamber, App. No. 27765/09, 23 February 2012), at paras. 153–4, the European Court of Human Rights stated that the presence of UNHCR in Libya was insufficient to ensure that a person would be protected from *refoulement*.

such practice does not meet the standards set by those formal obligations, removal of asylum seekers to those territories will be unlawful.

A departmental document entitled 'Onshore Protection Interim Procedures Advice on Assessing International Obligations and Protection/ Non-Refoulement Guidance for Pre-Removal Assessment Officers', prepared in anticipation of the Agreement taking effect, directed Australian immigration officials *not* to assess whether the person was a refugee. Rather, they were asked to determine whether Malaysia was a 'safe third country',[76] and in that respect were referred expressly to the EU Procedures Directive.[77] It is significant that a CEAS instrument has been referenced in such a direct way in Australian asylum policy. Given that this is an internal departmental document, it is not possible to ascertain how commonly other such documents draw on existing EU law in directing immigration officials how to carry out their assessments. However, this shows the potential reach of CEAS principles into non-EU States – especially since they are incorporated at the first level of the decision-making process and thus something to which every asylum seeker would be exposed.

3   A regional legal framework: transplanting the EU model?

A problem with transplanting European notions such as the 'safe third country' and related concepts such as regional processing is that Australia finds itself in a radically different region. Very few States in the Asia-Pacific region are parties to the major international human rights treaties, and only thirteen are signatories to the Refugee Convention or its Protocol.[78] Of the two signatory States with comprehensive refugee status determination systems in place – Australia and New Zealand – Australia does not have a domestic bill of rights.

Nevertheless, both major political parties in Australia view the cooperation of other countries in the region as essential to managing asylum arrivals to Australia, either through a revamped Pacific Solution

---

[76] The presumption was that the country was safe, but 'the whole point of having this individuated analysis is obviously to separate out cases to identify those exceptional cases where the removal may not be able to occur' (submissions of the Solicitor-General in *M70* [2011] HCATrans. 224 (23 August 2011)).

[77] This is mentioned in *M70* at para. 38 (French CJ).

[78] Among the States of the Asia-Pacific, only the following are parties to the Refugee Convention or its Protocol: Australia, Cambodia, China, Fiji, Japan, Nauru, New Zealand, Papua New Guinea, Philippines, Republic of Korea, Samoa, Solomon Islands and Timor-Leste and Tuvalu.

(operational since August 2012) or through some form of regional processing or transfer scheme (which the government is still pursuing). Both parties frame asylum as a form of migration that can be managed through tighter border controls, rather than as a humanitarian issue, although the government's catchphrase that the aim of its policies is to 'save lives at sea' has proved to be a popular 'humane' rationale.

In its submission to the Senate inquiry into the Australia–Malaysia Arrangement, the Immigration Department situated the proposed transfer agreement within a broader global context, noting that '[i]n recent times the responses of other States to displacement have involved the development of long term regional frameworks'.[79] The CEAS was expressly referred to, as was the Mexico Plan of Action of 2004 and the 2009 Convention for the Protection and Assistance of Internally Displaced Persons in Africa, as being 'indicative of the broader recognition of the need for, and value of, regional approaches to displacement'.[80] Although UNHCR and leading refugee NGOs generally support greater regional cooperation, it is on the basis that any new framework must genuinely foster better protection within the region as a whole and not deflect Australia's responsibilities onto other States.[81]

There are many challenges in creating a truly regional approach to asylum in the Asia-Pacific region, and an Asia-Pacific CEAS is but a distant dream. Whereas there are well-developed regional human rights systems in Europe, Africa and the Americas, there is a notable gap in the

---

[79] Department of Immigration and Citizenship, Submission No. 31 to Legal and Constitutional Affairs References Committee, *Inquiry into Australia's Arrangement with Malaysia in relation to Asylum Seekers* (September 2011), at para. 20.

[80] *Ibid.*

[81] Refugee Council of Australia, '2010 High Priorities List: Asylum Policy Issues' (20 October 2010) www.refugeecouncil.org.au/docs/current/2010_Asylum_priorities.pdf (accessed 30 October 2011). See also 'A Regional Refugee Protection Framework: A Joint Statement by Australian Non-Government Organisations' (1 August 2010) www.refugeecouncil.org.au/docs/releases/2010/100801_Regional_Protection_Framework.pdf (accessed 3 November 2011). UNHCR presented the original proposal for a Regional Cooperation Framework to the November 2010 Ad Hoc Workshop on Regional Cooperation in Manila: UNHCR, 'Regional Cooperative Approach to Address Refugees, Asylum-Seekers and Irregular Movement' (Manila, 22–23 November 2010) www.baliprocess.net/files/Regional%20Cooperation%20Approach%20Discussion%20document%20-%20final.pdf (accessed 30 October 2011); Submission by seventeen refugee law academics to the Expert Panel on Asylum Seekers (July 2012) www.gtcentre.unsw.edu.au/sites/gtcentre.unsw.edu.au/files/expert_panel_11_7_12.pdf (accessed 29 November 2012).

Asia-Pacific region. There is no regional human rights treaty, much less any supervisory or institutional framework.[82] This is coupled with the fact that there is undoubtedly a perception among a number of countries in the region that Australia's preoccupation with boat arrivals is a 'non'-issue compared to the serious socio-economic issues many of them face. For some States, such as Malaysia, the protection space is barely recognized: even UNHCR-recognized refugees are considered to be 'illegal immigrants' under domestic law and subject to imprisonment or removal.[83]

The 2011 decision of the High Court of Australia in *M70* made clear that any regional cooperation involving asylum seekers in which Australia is involved must be underscored by minimum human rights protections, including respect for the principle of *non-refoulement*, access to courts of law,[84] freedom from discrimination[85] and treatment as least as favourable as that accorded to its nationals with respect to employment,[86] education[87] and religious freedoms.[88] Very few countries within the Asia-Pacific region guarantee such rights to asylum seekers. The considerable legal and institutional differences between the Asia-Pacific region and the EU have been noted on a number of occasions in Parliament.[89]

Even within the EU – a region where all States are parties to the same human rights instruments – the CEAS has been far from perfect. Cases such as *MSS* v. *Belgium and Greece* provide a stark illustration of the considerable variability between Member States' policies and practices relating to reception conditions and procedural protections for asylum seekers in different EU Member States, despite all States being bound by the same regional laws.[90] As UNHCR has observed, although the

---

[82] See, e.g., Andrea Durbach, Catherine Renshaw and Andrew Byrnes, '"A Tongue But No Teeth?": The Emergence of a Regional Human Rights Mechanism in the Asia Pacific Region' (2009) 31 *Sydney Law Review* 211–38.

[83] See *M70*, paras. 32–3 (French CJ).   [84] Refugee Convention, art. 16(1).

[85] *Ibid.*, art. 3.   [86] *Ibid.*, art. 17(1).   [87] *Ibid.*, art. 22(1).   [88] *Ibid.*, art. 4.

[89] See, e.g., Hansard, House of Representatives, p. 1636, 11 October 1994 (Mr Ferguson); Hansard, House of Representatives, p. 1321, 14 March 2002 (Mr Ferguson): 'Part of the problem we have in this country is that, unlike Europe, the countries around Australia are not signatories. Do we see much government activity to try and get them to sign? No, we do not.'

[90] For the difficulties in doing so even within the EU, where States are parties to the same human rights instruments, see House of Lords European Union Committee, *Handling EU Asylum Claims*, p. 81.

objective of the CEAS is for all EU Member States to provide the same level of protection to asylum seekers, 'a lack of consistency remains a key challenge'.[91] The 'interpretation and application of the asylum instruments continue to differ, often producing sharply divergent outcomes in terms of international protection'.[92] In the absence of a regional human rights legal or institutional culture, the creation of a workable system in the Asia-Pacific region therefore seems like a very distant goal.

D Eurodac

Another area in which EU practices have been raised is in relation to the collection, storage and use of biometric data belonging to 'unauthorized' non-citizens entering or leaving Australia. In debating the Migration Legislation Amendment (Identification and Authentication) Bill 2003, attention was drawn to the Eurodac system. It was alluded to in the Explanatory Memorandum[93] and discussed in submissions to the Legal and Constitutional Legislation Committee,[94] the Committee's report on the bill,[95] and in parliamentary debate.[96]

---

[91] UNHCR, '2013 Country Operations Profile: Europe' www.unhcr.org/pages/4a02d9346. html (accessed 17 February 2012).

[92] UNHCR, 'UNHCR's Recommendations to Poland for Its EU Presidency, July–December 2011', p. 5 www.unhcr.org/4df8d00f9.html (accessed 17 February 2012): 'In 2010, looking only at countries that adjudicated significant numbers of applications, protection rates for Afghans seeking asylum ranged from 0% in one country to 91% in another – in the same sub-region. For Iraqis, the overall protection rates ranged from 14% to 79% and for Somalis, from 33% to 93%.'

[93] Explanatory Memorandum, Migration Legislation Amendment (Identification and Authentication) Bill 2003, at para. 4.

[94] See, e.g., Victorian Bar, Submission No. 4 to Senate Legal and Constitutional Legislation Committee, *Inquiry into the Provisions of the Migration Legislation Amendment (Identification and Authentication) Bill 2003* (3 September 2003), at paras. 1.23–1.25; Public Interest Advocacy Centre, Submission No. 2 to Senate Legal and Constitutional Legislation Committee, *Inquiry into the Provisions of the Migration Legislation Amendment (Identification and Authentication) Bill 2003* (1 September 2003). See also the extensive discussion by the Committee in questioning Mr John Gibson (Victorian Bar and Refugee Council of Australia): Hansard, Senate Legal and Constitutional Legislation Committee, pp. 4, 6, 8–9, 8 September 2003.

[95] Legal and Constitutional Legislation Committee, *Provisions of the Migration Legislation Amendment (Identification and Authentication) Bill 2003* (Cth of Australia, 2003), at paras. 3.21–3.26.

[96] Second reading debates: Hansard, Senate, p. 19,509, 10 February 2004 (Senator Sherry); Hansard, Senate, p. 19,513, 10 February 2004 (Senator Ludwig); Hansard, Senate, p. 19,595, 10 February 2004 (Senator Vanstone); Hansard, House of Representatives, p. 20,472, 18 September 2003 (Mr Organ).

The Liberal Immigration Minister, Philip Ruddock, drew on comparative State practice to argue for the introduction of the bill:

> Other countries are responding in a similar fashion and are introducing
> identification testing measures for exactly the same reasons that we are –
> to combat identity fraud. The European Union member states have
> established Eurodac, which is a centralised system for comparing finger-
> prints of asylum seekers. The United States will soon require all travel
> and entry documents to include a biometric identifier. In the United
> Kingdom there is provision for developing regulations to require non-
> citizens to provide external physical characteristics data as well as iris
> scans. So this bill is consistent with what is happening internationally.[97]

Interestingly, a Labor MP, Ms Roxon, implicitly queried the relevance of
EU practices for Australia compared to the practices in Australia's
immediate region:

> We understand that Europe is trialling a fingerprint database called
> Eurodac – for the purpose of ensuring that asylum seeker claims are
> processed in the first European country where a claim has been made and
> to combat forum shopping within Europe – but other such systems are
> yet to be established or used according to agreed guidelines. Clearly this
> is of great relevance to us. For the introduction of these measures to have
> any real security impact for Australia, our data would presumably need
> to be able to be compared against some sort of international database.
> When countries that Australia may need to deal with regularly on these
> security issues have not implemented, or even proposed to implement,
> complementary systems it does seem that we might be getting ahead of
> ourselves.[98]

The Committee recommended in its report that:

> based on evidence that the Eurodac system achieves a more appropriate
> balance between individual rights, privacy considerations and identifi-
> cation testing measures, the Bill be amended so that the storage, secur-
> ity, retention and destruction procedures of the Eurodac system provide
> the framework for the legislative regime in relation to all personal
> identifiers.[99]

This is one of the only occasions when EU practices have been expressly
recommended as a model for Australian legislative change.

[97] Hansard, House of Representatives, p. 20,489, 18 September 2003 (Mr Ruddock).
[98] *Ibid.*, p. 20,451, 18 September 2003 (Ms Roxon).
[99] Legal and Constitutional Legislation Committee, *Provisions*, Recommendation 2.

E Complementary protection

The policy area in which there has been the most sustained influence and invocation of EU law is in the codification of complementary protection in the Migration Act. In 2011, the Migration Amendment (Complementary Protection) Act 2011 (Cth) created new grounds for a protection visa. Section 36(2) of the Migration Act now provides that a protection visa in Australia must be granted to a non-citizen with respect to whom:

> the Minister is satisfied Australia has protection obligations because the Minister has substantial grounds for believing that, as a necessary and foreseeable consequence of the non-citizen being removed from Australia to a receiving country, there is a real risk that the non-citizen will suffer significant harm.

Section 36(2A) provides that a non-citizen will suffer 'significant harm' if:

(a) the non-citizen will be arbitrarily deprived of his or her life; or
(b) the death penalty will be carried out on the non-citizen; or
(c) the non-citizen will be subjected to torture; or
(d) the non-citizen will be subjected to cruel or inhuman treatment or punishment; or
(e) the non-citizen will be subjected to degrading treatment or punishment.[100]

Exceptions are contained in section 36(2B) and exclusion clauses are contained in section 36(2C).

Prior to 2012, although Australia had ratified all the international human rights treaties from which *non-refoulement* obligations derive, asylum seekers could not found a protection claim on these obligations because they were not reflected in domestic law.

As someone closely involved in advocating for the introduction of complementary protection legislation in Australia, it is clear to me that EU law and practice had considerable influence and persuasive value – certainly behind the scenes, if less obviously in official records. As the region with the most extensive jurisprudence on States' *non-refoulement* obligations under human rights law (from the European Court of Human Rights) and the 2004 codification of these obligations in the Qualification Directive, the EU provided an instructive model. Those drafting the legislation were certainly aware of it.

---

[100] For a detailed overview, see Jane McAdam, 'Australian Complementary Protection: A Step-By-Step Approach' (2011) 33 *Sydney Law Review* 687–734.

When the first government bill on complementary protection was introduced in 2009, the Parliamentary Secretary for Multicultural Affairs and Settlement Services, Mr Ferguson, noted:

> Australia is almost alone among modern Western democracies in not having a formal system of complementary protection in place. Many European and North American countries already have established complementary protection arrangements. The New Zealand government already has a bill before their parliament to introduce complementary protection. This bill brings Australia into line with what is now recognised as international best practice in meeting core human rights obligations.[101]

When a slightly revised bill was introduced in 2011, the Immigration Minister, Mr Bowen, stated: 'The bill also brings Australia into line with many like-minded countries, including New Zealand, Canada, the United States of America and many European countries.'[102]

These statements are the most explicit examples in the asylum field of EU and other foreign State practice influencing Australian legislative change.

The resultant Australian legislation bears some similarities to the Qualification Directive, particularly in the way the threshold test and grounds of 'significant harm' are set out, but it is by no means identical. Legislators were willing only to reflect Australia's *non-refoulement* obligations deriving from specific treaty provisions, rather than incorporating obligations stemming from customary international law. For this reason, there is no equivalent to article 15(c) Qualification Directive. Australia provides an identical status to Convention refugees and beneficiaries of complementary protection, whereas the EU regime contemplates (now only slightly) different statuses.[103] Although, like the

---

[101] Hansard, House of Representatives, p. 8989, 9 September 2009 (Mr Ferguson).

[102] *Ibid.*, p. 1357, 24 February 2011 (Mr Bowen, Minister for Immigration and Citizenship).

[103] The original Qualification Directive contained 'subsidiary protection' for persons with a protection need based on an instrument other than the Refugee Convention. The recast version removes most of the differences between refugee status and the status granted to beneficiaries of subsidiary protection: see Recital 39, and the title of the directive itself, which refers to a 'uniform status' for both groups. However, distinctions are still permitted in art. 24 (residence permits may be of a lesser duration for beneficiaries of subsidiary protection) and art. 29(2) (social welfare may be limited to core benefits for beneficiaries of subsidiary protection).

Qualification Directive, there is a general risk exception, it is less convoluted than the test contained there (in Recital 35).

Expanded exclusion grounds exist for beneficiaries of complementary protection, as in the EU.[104] However, whereas asylum seekers in the EU Member States have the protection of article 3 ECHR (from torture or inhuman or degrading treatment or punishment), no equivalent protection exists in Australian law. Accordingly, it is unclear what the status of excluded persons will be,[105] and it is possible that they will be held in indefinite immigration detention.[106] Such an outcome would not be lawful in the EU.[107] This signals the danger of transposing rules from one regime to another, where the underlying legal protections are not the same.[108]

Since Australia's complementary protection provisions only took effect from 24 March 2012, it is still unclear how influential jurisprudence stemming from EU Member States will be in interpreting the meaning of Australia's complementary protection provisions.[109] If New Zealand provides any indication, they will be particularly useful in the early stages of creating a domestic body of case law.[110] However, while it is likely that there will be an 'Australianization' of complementary protection concepts within a short time-frame, if Australia is to give full effect to the international obligations on which its domestic law is based,[111] it is important that decision makers are mindful of the well-developed jurisprudence elsewhere on the same concepts. One of the

---

[104] Qualification Directive, art. 13; Migration Act, s. 36(2C).

[105] See Explanatory Memorandum, Migration Amendment (Complementary Protection) Bill 2011 (Cth), at para. 90.

[106] See *Al-Kateb* v. *Godwin*.

[107] Convention for the Protection of Human Rights and Fundamental Freedoms, Rome, 4 November 1950, in force 3 September 1953 (213 UNTS 221) (European Convention on Human Rights, as amended) (ECHR), art. 5 and related cases.

[108] See Chapter 9 of this volume.

[109] For a list of all published complementary protection decisions to date, see www.gtcentre. unsw.edu.au/resources/international-refugee-and-migration-law-project (accessed 1 May 2012).

[110] New Zealand adopted complementary protection provisions in its Immigration Act 2009, ss. 130–1. For cases drawing on European jurisprudence, see, e.g., *AC (Syria)* [2011] NZIPT 800035, at paras. 59ff; *BG (Fiji)* [2012] NZIPT 800091, at paras. 142ff. See also the earlier discussion of the Qualification Directive in the context of the internal relocation alternative: *Refugee Appeal No. 76044* (11 September 2008), at paras. 114ff. Judges may be more aware of comparative case law if they are involved in the work of the International Association of Refugee Law Judges.

[111] See Explanatory Memorandum, Migration Amendment (Complementary Protection) Bill 2011 (Cth).

richest sources of that jurisprudence is the European Court of Human
Rights, and latterly the Court of Justice of the EU, as well as the case law
from EU Member States.[112]

F   Processes of influence

This section examines the processes by which EU asylum law and policy
may influence developments in Australia. As noted above, even where
Australia has adopted European practices in domestic law, there is little
formal documentation of this. However, an examination of a wider
variety of sources suggests that European practices are sometimes used
as reference points in distinguishing Australian practices, or invoked as
models of good practice when arguing for legislative change. This section
examines the extent to which: (a) judges import European concepts in
Australian refugee law cases; (b) the Immigration Department considers
EU law in advising on Australian policy; and (c) academics, NGOs and
the personal observations/connections of parliamentarians drawing on
European practices influence the development of legislation and policy
in Australia.[113]

1   Case law

In common law jurisdictions like Australia, there is already considerable
consideration of foreign case law concerning the interpretation of the
Refugee Convention.[114] Courts typically engage with such jurisprudence

---

[112] Given the lack of comparable detail in UNHRC cases considering the prohibition on
cruel, inhuman or degrading treatment in art. 7 International Covenant on Civil and
Political Rights, New York, adopted 16 December 1966, in force 23 March 1976 (999
UNTS 171), the jurisprudence of the European Court of Human Rights is a particularly
useful source.

[113] Anne-Marie Slaughter's work on global government networks provides an interesting
theoretical perspective on these influences: see, e.g., 'Global Government Networks,
Global Information Agencies, and Disaggregated Democracy' (2003) 24 *Michigan
Journal of International Law* 1041–75; 'Sovereignty and Power in a Networked World
Order' (2004) 40 *Stanford Journal of International Law* 283–327; Anne-Marie
Slaughter and William Burke-White, 'The Future of International Law Is Domestic
(or, the European Way of Law)' (2006) 47 *Harvard International Law Journal* 327–52.
See also Katerina Linos, 'Diffusion through Democracy' (2011) 55 *American Journal of
Political Science* 678–95; Katerina Linos, 'When Do Policy Innovations Spread? Lessons
for Advocates of Lesson-Drawing' (2006) 119 *Harvard Law Review* 1467–87.

[114] See generally McAdam, 'Interpretation'.

to explore approaches to treaty interpretation in other countries, as well as to affirm their own approach or explain why they think an approach taken elsewhere is incorrect.[115]

It is entirely appropriate for courts and tribunals to look to other jurisdictions in applying concepts that derive from international human rights instruments – especially when such concepts are new to that domestic context. The House of Lords has said that comparative refugee case law is 'of importance' precisely because there is no supranational court with the authority to issue determinative rulings on the meaning of the Refugee Convention.[116] To implement international obligations effectively and in accordance with their contemporary understanding in international law, such openness in approach is essential.

> To the extent that this Court cuts itself off from insights expressed in the UNHCR Guidelines, the Handbook and expert views, about the meaning and purposes of the Convention, it reduces its own capacity for accurate decision making. It limits the value that its decisions may have for other countries that will have no such inhibitions. It risks adopting interpretations of the Convention that put it at odds with the courts of other State parties engaged in the interpretation of the treaty. And it reveals a degree of parochialism that, unless clearly warranted by the peculiarities of domestic law, is inappropriate to the legal task of interpreting, and giving effect to, the provisions of an international treaty which Australia has opted to ratify and which it has incorporated by reference into its federal law.[117]

It is also important that the dialogue remains open so that concepts are revisited over time and their fundamental human rights bases developed and upheld. For this reason, decision makers need to be aware of the idiosyncrasies of foreign regimes – such as the CEAS – to ensure that their own interpretation of the underlying international obligations from

---

[115] Lambert, 'Transnational Judicial Dialogue', 530.

[116] *Secretary of State for the Home Department* v. *K* [2006] UKHL 46, at para. 10 (Lord Bingham). Obviously, the weight given to a decision depends on the status of the court from which it comes, including the place of the court in the curial hierarchy.

[117] *QAAH*, para. 81, referring to *Adan* v. *Secretary of State for the Home Department* [1999] 1 AC 293, at 297–8 as an example of a court with 'no such inhibitions'. See also Anthony M. North and Joyce Chia, 'Towards Convergence in the Interpretation of the Refugee Convention: A Proposal for the Establishment of an International Judicial Commission for Refugees', in Jane McAdam (ed.), *Forced Migration, Human Rights and Security* (Oxford: Hart, 2008), p. 228, who propose the creation of an international judicial commission to 'encourage convergence of interpretation by exposing differences in interpretation of the Convention, and expounding and explaining the preferable construction'.

which they are drawn are not diluted by narrow regional or domestic exceptions.[118]

For example, article 15(b) Qualification Directive restricts subsidiary protection based on article 3 ECHR to cases where an individual faces a real risk of torture or inhuman or degrading treatment in his or her *country of origin*. This limitation does not mean that a person fearing removal contrary to article 3 to any *other* country can be lawfully deported, but simply that he or she is not eligible for subsidiary protection under the Qualification Directive. Furthermore, the Qualification Directive as a whole applies only to 'third country nationals', thereby precluding the consideration of a refugee or subsidiary protection claim by an EU national under that instrument. This does not absolve Member States of their more extensive obligations under the Refugee Convention, which extend to *any* refugee (without geographical limitation). As the House of Lords Select Committee on the EU noted, 'for a major regional grouping of countries such as the Union to adopt a regime apparently limiting the scope of the Geneva Convention among themselves would set a most undesirable precedent in the wider international/global context'.[119] If foreign decision makers are not aware of the broader context, then they may inadvertently apply narrower concepts and circumscribe the application of non-return to inhuman or degrading treatment in their own jurisdiction in a manner that is contrary to international law.

The courts have also relied heavily on academic scholarship in adopting principles drawn from the practice of other countries.[120] Counsel, too, has a role to play in continuing to take arguments based on comparative practices to the courts.[121]

---

[118] See, e.g., *Applicant A*, p. 296, where Kirby J., referring to *Ram*, p. 567, stressed the importance of caution in assessing foreign jurisprudence, since national statutory or constitutional influences may affect the approach taken.

[119] House of Lords Select Committee on the EU, *Defining Refugee Status and Those in Need of International Protection* (HL Paper 156, 28th Report of Session 2001–02), at para. 54. See also Jane McAdam, *Complementary Protection in International Refugee Law* (Oxford: Oxford University Press, 2007), pp. 60–1; Chapter 9 of this volume.

[120] For discussion, see, e.g., Hugo Storey, 'The Advanced Refugee Law Workshop Experience: An IARLJ Perspective' (2003) 15 *International Journal of Refugee Law* 422–9; McAdam, 'Interpretation'.

[121] See, e.g., *K's case*, para. 9 (Lord Bingham). For an example of a scathing response to submissions seeking to rely on case law of the European Court of Human Rights, however, see Hill J. in *Lorenzo v. Minister for Immigration and Multicultural and Indigenous Affairs and Commonwealth of Australia* [2004] FCA 435, at paras. 57–60. A search on 'European Court of Human Rights'/'ECHR' as at 2 March 2012 revealed references to decisions of the

2   Immigration Department

Responses by the Immigration Department to parliamentary questions on notice confirm my own observations of the way in which that entity develops policy and legislation. Depending on the issue, there may be quite considerable analysis of comparative law and policy in the preparatory stages. This is especially so in areas where Australia is proposing the introduction of a practice that is already well established elsewhere (e.g. complementary protection); indeed, the existence of the foreign practice may be a reason why its introduction is mooted in the first place. The use of comparative material in this way is what Lambert describes as

European Court of Human Rights in the following Australian refugee cases: Federal Court: *Minister for Immigration and Ethnic Affairs and Refugee Review Tribunal* v. *Singh* [1997] FCA 354 (7 May 1997) (*Chahal* v. *United Kingdom* (1996) 23 EHRR 413); *Ovcharuk* v. *Minister for Immigration and Multicultural Affairs* [1998] FCA 1314 (16 October 1998) (cited *Applicant A*, in which High Court cited *Golder* v. *United Kingdom* (1975) 1 EHRR 524); *Thiyagarajah* (cited *Applicant A*, in which the High Court cited *Golder*); *Applicants M160/2003* v. *Minister for Immigration and Multicultural and Indigenous Affairs* [2005] FCA 195 (8 March 2005) (*Osman* v. *United Kingdom* (1998) 29 EHRR 245); *Applicant M38/2002* v. *Minister for Immigration and Multicultural and Indigenous Affairs* [2003] FCA 458 (15 May 2003) (*Chahal*); *SBZD* v. *Minister for Immigration and Citizenship* [2008] FCA 1236 (14 August 2008) (cited *S152/2003*, in which HCA cited *Osman*); *Singh* v. *Minister for Immigration and Multicultural Affairs* [1998] FCA 619 (9 June 1998) (*Chahal*); *VRAW* v. *Minister for Immigration and Multicultural and Indigenous Affairs* [2004] FCA 1133 (3 September 2004) (*Osman*); *MZ RAJ* v. *Minister for Immigration and Multicultural and Indigenous Affairs* [2004] FCA 1261 (29 September 2004) (*Osman*); *Ruddock* v. *Vadarlis* [2001] FCA 1329 (18 September 2001) (*Amuur* v. *France* (1992) 22 EHRR 533); *Applicant S100 of 2004* v. *Minister for Immigration and Multicultural and Indigenous Affairs* [2004] FCA 1364 (26 October 2004) (cited *S152/2003*, in which the High Court cited *Osman*); Full Federal Court: *SHKB* v. *Minister for Immigration and Multicultural and Indigenous Affairs* [2005] FCAFC 11 (18 February 2005) (cited *S152/2003*, in which the High Court cited *Osman*); *Minister for Immigration and Multicultural and Indigenous Affairs* v. *Al Masri* [2003] FCAFC 70 (15 April 2003) (*Chahal*); *SZBBP* v. *Minister for Immigration and Multicultural and Indigenous Affairs* [2005] FCAFC 167 (19 August 2005) (cited *S152/2003*, in which the High Court cited *Osman*); High Court of Australia: *A* v. *Minister for Immigration and Ethnic Affairs* (1997) 190 CLR 225 (*Golder*); *Minister for Immigration and Multicultural Affairs* v. *Haji Ibrahim* (2000) 204 CLR 1 (*Golder*); *Re Minister for Immigration and Multicultural Affairs, ex parte Epeabaka* (2001) 206 CLR 128 (*Huber* v. *Switzerland*, European Court of Human Rights, 23 October 1990, Ser. A, No. 188); *Minister for Immigration and Multicultural Affairs* v. *Respondents S152/2003* (2004) 222 CLR 1 (*Osman*); *NABD of 2002* v. *Minister for Immigration and Multicultural and Indigenous Affairs* (2005) 216 ALR 1 (*Kokkinakis* v. *Greece* (1993) 17 EHRR 397); *NAIS* v. *Minister for Immigration and Multicultural and Indigenous Affairs* (2005) 228 CLR 470 (*Silva Pontes* v. *Portugal* (1994) 18 EHRR 156; *Hornsby* v. *Greece* (1997) 24 EHRR 250; *Frydlender* v. *France* (2001) 31 EHRR 52).

'fishing for ideas'.[122] Such research is used in order to: (a) evaluate how Australia's position on the issue relates to practice elsewhere; and (b) determine how practices elsewhere might inform the shaping of Australian law on the issue. It is rare for the detail of this to be reflected in the formal record.

Committee discussions in Parliament reveal how foreign practices may be applied in Australia. In one exchange, Senator Ludwig stated:

> You mentioned that the definition in relation to serious harm and systematic and discriminatory conduct is drawn from elsewhere … Can you point me to the area it comes from or the legislation that it may be based on – where you have actually got it from, unless you have constructed it independently of that – or is it modelled on overseas experiences? In addition, if there are overseas models that you have based it on, are there decisions in those various jurisdictions which go to explain or define, as far as the courts are concerned, its operation?

Ms Bedlington from the Immigration Department provided the following response:

> There is no one single source. When we were looking at this, we canvassed overseas case law as well as our own case law, we looked at what was then proposed legislation from the US and Canada and the current state of jurisprudence in Australia, and we pulled it all together. The proposal is a result of that extensive examination. It is not based on a single particular model.[123]

In 2000, the Senate Legal and Constitutional References Committee recommended that the Immigration Department 'maintain an up-to-date comparative database of international refugee determination systems in a number of countries which are State parties to the relevant international conventions … in a format that is easily accessible'.[124] In response, the government stated that:

> The International Section of DIMA [Department of Immigration and Multicultural Affairs] has information on refugee determination systems of a number of other countries. A principal source of information is the

---

[122] Chapter 1 of this volume, p. 7.

[123] Hansard, Senate Legal and Constitutional References Committee, p. 16, 21 September 2001.

[124] Senate Legal and Constitutional Affairs References Committee, *A Sanctuary under Review: An Examination of Australia's Refugee and Humanitarian Determination Processes* (Cth of Australia, 2000), p. xviii, Recommendation 6.1.

Inter-Governmental Consultations on Asylum Refugee and Migration Policies in Europe, North America and Australia (IGC) of which Australia is an active member and which produces regular comparative reports and data on refugee matters. Most of this IGC information is publicly available. Since countries adopt different legislative and policy approaches to their refugee determination systems, data collected by countries are not always strictly compatible.[125]

Elsewhere, the Immigration Department further explained that:

The department monitors developments in a range of comparison countries and has noted the various arrangements in place, or planned, in some countries to provide for some form of complementary protection. Such arrangements are not uniform between countries, and in particular differing approaches are taken in the extent to which issues of providing protection against refoulement under international instruments are differentiated from arrangements which provide continued residence for broader public interest or personal interest grounds such as family links to the country. There is no consistent international approach on these issues. The various forms of complementary protection/humanitarian stay, contemplated in some countries do not necessarily deliver the same residence entitlements and benefits as are conferred on persons found to be refugees.[126]

3   Development of legislation and policy

A search of Australian parliamentary Hansard, including Committee hearings, reveals some degree of awareness of comparative practices in Europe and North America.[127] Given the considerable amount of time spent debating asylum policy in the Australian Parliament, however, the attention given to foreign practices is relatively scant. Nevertheless, there are some interesting trends.

---

[125] Hansard, Senate, p. 21,747, 8 February 2001 (Government response to Recommendation 6.1).

[126] Response to Question taken on Notice, Senate Legal and Constitutional References Committee (11 October 2005), Immigration and Multicultural and Indigenous Affairs Portfolio, referring also to Department of Immigration, Multicultural and Indigenous Affairs, 'Complementary Protection and Australian Practice' in UNHCR Regional Office for Australia, New Zealand, Papua New Guinea and the South Pacific, *Discussion Paper: Complementary Protection* (No. 2, 2005), pp. 7–8.

[127] A search was done on the terms 'migration' (a term included in any refugee bill) and 'Europe'/'EU'.

In virtually all cases, the information derives from submissions by
NGOs,[128] UNHCR[129] or academics.[130] Comparative asylum policies are

[128] See, e.g., Senate Legal and Constitutional Legislation Committee, *Provisions of the
Migration Amendment (Judicial Review) Bill 2004* (Cth of Australia, 2004), at para.
3.85 (referring to submissions by the Law Council of Australia); Senate Legal and
Constitutional Legislation Committee, *Migration Legislation Amendment (Judicial
Review) Bill 1998* (Cth of Australia, 1999), at paras. 3.1, 3.33–35 (referring to submis-
sions by National Legal Aid); Senate Legal and Constitutional Affairs References
Committee, *A Sanctuary under Review*, paras. 1.81, 1.86, 1.101 (referring to submis-
sions by the Refugee Council of Australia), paras. 2.45, 5.30, 5.34 (referring to sub-
missions by the Australian Law Reform Commission, Law Council of Australia and
Amnesty International); Senate Select Committee on Ministerial Discretion in
Migration Matters, *Report* (Cth of Australia, 2004), at paras. 8.55, 8.70 (referring to
submissions by the Human Rights and Equal Opportunity Commission, Amnesty
International and the Refugee Council of Australia) and Additional Comments by
Senator Andrew Bartlett of the Australian Democrats, pp. 194, 197–8 (referring to
submissions by UNHCR, Amnesty International, the Refugee Council of Australia,
CCJDP and the Uniting Church of Australia); Joint Standing Committee on Migration,
Immigration Detention in Australia: Community-Based Alternatives to Detention (Cth
of Australia, 2009), at paras. 2.95ff (referring to a variety of sources); Joint Standing
Committee on Migration, *Immigration Detention in Australia: Facilities, Services and
Transparency* (Cth of Australia, 2009), at para. 1.3 (referring to submissions by the
International Detention Coalition); Hansard, Joint Standing Committee on Migration,
pp. 39, 41–2, 45, 21 March 2003 (Ms Engelhart, Amnesty International Australia, oral
evidence); Refugee Council of Australia, Submission No. 12 to the Senate Legal and
Constitutional Legislation Committee, *Inquiry into the Provisions of the Migration
Legislation Amendment (Procedural Fairness) Bill 2002* (April 2002), p. 4.
[129] See, e.g., discussion in oral evidence by UNHCR to the Committee about the proposed
refugee definition in the Qualification Directive, and discussion about the creation of
the CEAS: Hansard, Legal and Constitutional References Committee, pp. 22–3, 32, 21
September 2001 (UNHCR, oral evidence); Hansard, Select Committee on Ministerial
Discretion in Migration Matters, pp. 23, 25, 18 November 2003 (UNHCR, oral evidence); UNHCR, Submission No. 20 to the Senate Standing Committee on Legal and
Constitutional Affairs, *Inquiry into the Migration Amendment (Complementary
Protection) Bill 2009* (30 September 2009) (Qualification Directive).
[130] See, e.g., Senate Legal and Constitutional Affairs References Committee, *Australia's
Arrangement with Malaysia in relation to Asylum Seekers* (Cth of Australia, October 2011),
at para. 3.7 (referring to submissions by Ben Saul); Senate Select Committee on Ministerial
Discretion in Migration Matters, *Report* (Cth of Australia, 2004), at paras. 8.56–57, 8.61–62
(referring to submissions by Jane McAdam); Joint Standing Committee on Migration,
Immigration Detention in Australia: Community-Based Alternatives to Detention (Cth of
Australia, 2009), at paras. 2.140–42 (referring to submissions by Howard Adelman);
Hansard, Legal and Constitutional References Committee, pp. 182–3, 186, 21 August 2002
(Penelope Mathew, oral evidence); Hansard, Legal and Constitutional Legislation
Committee, pp. 39, 44, 13 April 2005 (Ben Saul, oral evidence); Hansard, Joint Standing
Committee on Migration, pp. 3, 9, 25 February 2009 (Howard Adelman, oral evidence);
Penelope Mathew, Submission No. 34 to Senate Legal and Constitutional Committee, *Inquiry
into the Migration Legislation Amendment (Further Border Protection Measures) Bill 2002*,

rarely raised by parliamentarians themselves.[131] The general exception is when foreign practices are invoked to support the introduction of restrictive measures.[132] For example, one government senator sought to counter claims by the former Human Rights Commissioner that Australia's Pacific Solution was inhumane by drawing on practices from other countries to justify Australia's policy of processing asylum seekers in Nauru and Papua New Guinea:

> Illegal immigrants from Cuba who are intercepted offshore by the United States, are now being processed in Guantanamo, in the Mariana Islands and in Midway, and they're given asylum in a Latin American country or returned to Cuba. In Europe there are similar procedures. Germany is now returning third country asylum seekers to the Czech Republic or Poland.[133]

Similarly, in seeking to justify the extension of safe third-country provisions to Vietnamese refugees who had resettled in China but subsequently claimed asylum in Australia, a government MP explained that:

> This is not an isolated circumstance; it is part of an international pattern. What we are doing today in Australia is paralleled in Canada, the United Kingdom, Germany, Finland and France. At the moment the United States is considering similar measures. Europe is getting towards a situation where there is an understanding as to which country has primary responsibility for particular cases.[134]

pp. 4–5 (Dublin Convention); Jane McAdam, Submission No. 35 to Senate Select Committee, *Inquiry into Ministerial Discretion in Migration Matters* (23 September 2003); Penelope Mathew and ANU Law Students for Social Justice Society, Submission No. 204 to Senate Legal and Constitutional Committee, *Inquiry into the Administration and Operation of the Migration Act 1958* (9 August 2005), pp. 18–19 (complementary protection; EU Temporary Protection Directive) www.aph.gov.au/Parliamentary_Business/Commit tees/Senate_Committees?url=legcon_ctte/completed_inquiries/2004-07/migration/sub missions/sub204.pdf (accessed 21 March 2012); Jane McAdam, Submission No. 21 to Senate Standing Committee on Legal and Constitutional Affairs, *Inquiry into the Migration Amendment (Complementary Protection) Bill 2009* (28 September 2009) (Qualification Directive); Michelle Foster and Jason Pobjoy, Submission No. 9 to Senate Standing Committee on Legal and Constitutional Affairs, *Inquiry into the Migration Amendment (Complementary Protection) Bill 2009* (28 September 2009), pp. 7, 13–14 (Qualification Directive).

[131] Although note the invocation of foreign practice by government MPs as a rationale for introducing complementary protection, discussed above, which is very rare.

[132] See further below.

[133] Senator Helen Coonan, interview on *Breakfast*, ABC Radio (2 October 2001).

[134] Discussion of Migration Legislation Amendment Bill (No. 2) 1995, Hansard, House of Representatives, p. 884, 9 February 1995 (Mr Ferguson).

In adopting extended exclusion clauses for beneficiaries of complementary protection, the Immigration Minister stated:

> By incorporating these exclusion provisions into the Migration Act, Australia will be following general international practice, particularly in the European Union, where similar clauses have been incorporated into most countries' respective legislative versions of complementary protection.[135]

In relation to proposed provisions on the collection and storage of biodata, the Explanatory Memorandum to the Migration Legislation Amendment (Identification and Authentication) Bill 2003 noted:

> The proposed measures will align Australian identification powers with similar measures in place in Canada, the United Kingdom, the United States of America and the European Union, thereby creating important opportunities for information exchange in relation to counter terrorism and forum shopping.[136]

Suggestions that equally harsh, if not harsher, policies are in place in Europe or North America are often invoked to support restrictive legislation in Australia:

> Few nations lack detention policies and the interest groups would be unimpressed by sterner European and US practices for turning around claimants at sea. The same people who cited very limited, rare US parole practices diverted their attention from the almost universal trend in Europe. Whether it be Sweden, the UK, France or Germany, the action is towards more trenchant measures to counter perceived manipulation of their previously liberal refugee admission policies.[137]

> People talk to us about Europe. I will not specify the many problems with processing and the many human rights abuses in Sweden, Ireland or Spain, to give three good examples.[138]

> Other countries are responding in a similar fashion and are introducing identification testing measures for exactly the same reasons that we are – to combat identity fraud. The European Union member states have established Eurodac, which is a centralised system for comparing fingerprints of asylum seekers. The United States will soon require all travel

---

[135] Hansard, House of Representatives, p. 1359 (Mr Bowen, Minister for Immigration and Citizenship), during second reading speech of Migration Amendment (Complementary Protection) Bill 2011. See also Hansard, House of Representatives, p. 8991, 9 September 2009 (Mr Ferguson) (second reading speech of Migration Amendment (Complementary Protection) Bill 2009).

[136] Explanatory Memorandum, Migration Legislation Amendment (Identification and Authentication) Bill 2003, at para. 4.

[137] Hansard, House of Representatives, p. 1679, 3 March 1994 (Mr Ferguson).

[138] *Ibid.*, p. 4416, 26 June 2002 (Mr Ferguson).

and entry documents to include a biometric identifier. In the United Kingdom there is provision for developing regulations to require non-citizens to provide external physical characteristics data as well as iris scans. So this bill is consistent with what is happening internationally.[139]

More enhanced identification powers to match those in place in Canada, the European Union, the UK and the US will provide opportunities for information exchange to combat the movement of illegal migrants, terrorists and transnational crime into Australia. This will help to ensure that we can identify noncitizens who exploit refugee and immigration provisions by assuming false identities and those who attempt to conceal the fact that they have effective protection in another country – that is, their first country of asylum, to which they will be returned.[140]

Sometimes, politicians seek to undermine the credentials of those offering comparative material:

People might say that the systems of appeal in those [European] countries are better because 200,000 or 100,000 people are running around those countries and are no longer part of the processing system. People might say that that is great and that we should copy those countries because, basically, they allow people freedom. The people saying these things do not mind that these people might have totally fraudulent claims.[141]

Such conclusions are commonly based on personal observations from MPs' study trips abroad, with information gleaned from conversations with foreign counterparts or anecdotes.[142] Very often, such comparative assessment is used to portray Australia as a model for other jurisdictions:[143]

---

[139] *Ibid.*, p. 20,489, 18 September 2003 (Mr Ruddock).

[140] *Ibid.*, p. 20,467, 18 September 2003 (Mr Prosser); see also Hansard, House of Representatives, p. 20,461, 18 September 2003 (Mr Hatton); Hansard, House of Representatives, pp. 20,449–50, 18 September 2003 (Ms Roxon).

[141] *Ibid.*, p. 4416, 26 June 2002 (Mr Ferguson).

[142] See, e.g., Hansard, Senate, p. 7481, 9 December 2002 (Senator Bartlett); Hansard, Senate, p. 808, 9 February 1995 (Senator Bolkus); Hansard, House of Representatives, p. 26, 9 August 2006 (Mr Randall).

[143] See also Hansard, Senate, p. 19,595, 10 February 2004 (Senator Vanstone); Hansard, Senate, p. 7484, 9 December 2002 (Senator Scullion): 'The intergovernmental consultations on asylum in Europe, North America and Australia are leadership roles. We are showing the world the way in regard to these matters'; interview with Foreign Minister Alexander Downer, 'Foreign Minister discusses withdrawal of migration bill and response from Indonesia', *Lateline* (ABC television, 14 August 2006): 'To be honest with you, particularly in Europe but in other parts of the world, developed countries are asking themselves whether they shouldn't have had a stronger approach to this ... Now I think other countries – and it's what they say to me privately – they admire the way we do it.'

When I had a study trip to Europe some years ago I was able to go to the
various migration agencies. I went to London House and to the House of
Commons and I spoke to people in migration because that is an interest of
mine. I am the chair of the Joint Standing Committee on Migration and I am
chair of the government members' committee on migration. I learned that
the British are in awe of our migration tracking system. In fact, they say to us,
'We would love to have the ability that you have to track people who come in
and out of your country because, quite frankly, we've really got no idea.'[144]

This problem of rorting is not unique to Australia. Recently I visited Europe,
basically to look at the question of refugees but also at migration legislation as
it applies in countries in Europe, given the problems in Europe at the moment.
I went to people in England, Germany, Switzerland, Czechoslovakia, Greece
and Italy. The interesting thing in those countries was that they have one thing
in common: they admire the migration law of this country. In three examples
they have sought a full briefing by our Government on Australia's entry
arrangements. These countries do not really have any laws that can be applied,
and people wander through that region at will ... They want to look at our
system because it, by comparison, is a Rolls-Royce system. We will be happy
to brief some of those European countries on our system.[145]

The rest of the world – especially Europe, that multicultural melting pot –
looks to us and says, 'How do you get it so right?' So this is about making
it better. We do get it right mostly, and we are an inspiration for the
UNHCR about how to get it right.[146]

Occasionally, MPs have compared Australian and European practices to
acknowledge how disproportionate Australia's restrictive asylum policy
is in light of the relatively small numbers involved:

In the winter recess I spent 21 days in Europe and Scandinavia. I visited
eight countries looking at reception and detention centres and talking
to officials ... I visited Denmark, Sweden, Britain, France, Holland,
Germany, Italy and Switzerland. Each and every one of those countries
handles the situation with asylum seekers much better than does
Australia, and they are dealing with so many more people than does
Australia. It is such a joke when people talk about the number of people
coming to this country. Sweden deals with 18,000 asylum seekers a year;
Holland deals with 40,000 a year; Germany deals with 70,000 a year; and
Britain deals with over 100,000 a year. Each and every one of those
countries handles those numbers without the trauma that we have in

[144] Hansard, House of Representatives, p. 39, 27 March 2007 (Mr Randall).
[145] Ibid., p. 2689, 7 November 1991 (Gerry Hand, Minister for Immigration).
[146] Ibid., p. 7077, 24 June 2009 (Mr Perrett), during second reading debate of Migration
Amendment (Abolishing Detention Debt) Bill 2009.

Australia. Each of those countries has a detention centre, but the difference between us and them is that, whereas we lock up everyone immediately upon arrival, they – I must admit that they are tough detention centres – lock them up only when they are about to be deported.[147]

Moreover, seen from the perspective and context of Europe, the arrival of 4,000 people in these boats in the beginning of 2000 was not something to be hysterical about anyhow. I recently met with the deputy chair of the German Bundestag in parliament house, and he asked me to describe the nature of the problem. After hearing of those small numbers of arrivals in 2000, the deputy chair responded in a very surprised tone, saying, 'Mr Danby, we received 350,000 from Yugoslavia in that one year.' So you have to see this in context.[148]

Otherwise, only members of minor parties (Greens, Democrats, independents) have raised more liberal foreign practices as reasons why Australian policy should be softened:[149]

It is about time we looked at how other countries approach the issue of unauthorised arrivals of asylum seekers, particularly some of the models in Europe. Sweden is one particularly good example. People there are allowed out into the community after initial assessment. Obviously, you have to assess security and health concerns, but then you have people out in the community in a monitored sense and you provide them with ongoing assistance and information about what is actually going on, what their rights are and what their future might hold. That system, I believe, has proven to be quite successful, not just in terms of people who are judged to be refugees but also those whose applications are refused and are then deported.[150]

This is not a system that is new and untested. In fact Complementary Protection has a long history in most other western countries, including the United Kingdom, Canada and the United States of America. The European Union is moving to adopt a consistent form of Complementary Protection as part of its process to harmonise asylum law.[151]

The Immigration Department occasionally raises European practices in its own submissions to parliamentary inquiries which can lead to quite extensive discussions about how they compare or relate to Australian

---

[147] *Ibid.*, p. 30,135, 23 August 2001 (Mr Hollis).

[148] *Ibid.*, p. 12,276, 2 December 2008 (Mr Danby, Migration Committee Report Speech).

[149] Hansard, Senate, p. 26,822, 28 August 2001 (Senator Brown); Hansard, Senate, p. 22,330, 30 March 2004 (Senator Bartlett); Hansard, House of Representatives, p. 47, 9 August 2006 (Mr Andren); Hansard, Senate, p. 1458, 20 March 2008 (Senator Nettle); Hansard, Senate, p. 27,706, 24 September 2011 (Senator Stott Despoja).

[150] Hansard, Senate, p. 26,845, 29 August 2001 (Senator Bartlett).

[151] *Ibid.*, p. 85, 13 September 2006 (Senator Bartlett).

policy.[152] Despite considering foreign practices, its approach is probably best encapsulated by the remark: 'I think we need to design a process that meets the requirements of Australia and not necessarily be driven by the difficult politics around the EU.'[153]

This is in marked contrast to the use of foreign material by academics, UNHCR and NGOs.[154] They typically raise examples of more liberal European practices as a means of advocating for policy change which would bring Australia into line with such approaches, and in turn with its obligations under international human rights law. Such interventions have been particularly pronounced in relation to mandatory detention,[155] complementary protection[156] and identity checks.[157]

The area in which the most extensive comparative analysis has been made with Europe is complementary protection.[158] This is also the only

---

[152] See discussion of other European countries' practices in relation to the interpretation of the refugee definition in Hansard, Senate Legal and Constitutional References Committee, pp. 7, 16, 32-7, 21 September 2001 (Ms Bedlington, Immigration Department, oral evidence); discussion of Eurodac, noting that problems relating to identity fraud 'are problems Australia is not facing alone' (Hansard, Senate Legal and Constitutional Legislation Committee, p. 15, 8 September 2003 (Mr McMahon, Immigration Department, oral evidence)); Hansard, Senate Select Committee on Ministerial Discretion in Migration Matters, p. 65, 5 September 2003 (Mr Rizvi, Immigration Department, oral evidence), suggesting a lack of public confidence in migration management in Europe.

[153] Hansard, Senate Legal and Constitutional Legislation Committee, p. 29, 8 September 2003 (Vincent McMahon, Immigration Department, oral evidence).

[154] See above nn. 128-30.

[155] See, e.g., NSW Young Lawyers, *Submission No. 198 to Senate Legal and Constitutional Committee, Inquiry into the Administration and Operation of the Migration Act 1958* (9 August 2005), p. 10: 'The outsourcing of the management of detention facilities is part of a general trend that the YLHRC observes in Europe and the United States. It also comes at a time when Public Private Partnerships gain greater use in the provision of public services'; Hansard, Joint Standing Committee on Migration, p. 62, 24 October 2008 (Ms Curr, Asylum Seeker Resource Centre): 'Mandatory detention has to go. There is no reason for it. Other countries do not do it. Look at the rest of the world. Nobody does it. In the UK, Europe, Denmark – run down the list – there is no mandatory detention. I ask you to please consider this, when making your recommendations' (Hansard, Joint Standing Committee on Migration, pp. 6-10, 22 January 2009 (Mr Mitchell, International Detention Coalition, oral evidence)).

[156] See, e.g., Hansard, Select Committee on Ministerial Discretion in Migration Matters, pp. 3, 6, 13, 23 September 2003 (Mr Gee, oral evidence); Hansard, Legal and Constitutional References Committee, pp. 6-7, 26 September 2005 (Ms Clark, Law Society of South Australia, oral evidence); Hansard, Legal and Constitutional References Committee, p. 58, 27 September 2005 (Mr Ball, Commission for Christian World Service, National Council of Churches in Australia); Hansard, Legal and Constitutional References Committee, p. 55, 28 September 2005 (Sister Britt, Edmund Rice Centre, oral evidence). See also above nn. 128-30.

[157] See discussion of Eurodac in Part D above.   [158] See also above nn. 101-2.

issue on which European practices have been expressly invoked by government MPs in support of legislative change:[159]

> most Western democracies have a formal system of complementary protection in place. This is hardly controversial territory. The European Union, Canada and the United States have already established complementary protection arrangements and we know that New Zealand has recently introduced complementary protection legislation. Once again, in a matter which is entirely rational and which is being reflected in legislatures right round the world in developed countries, we see that the opposition lags behind and that it simply sees these matters, which are of significant national and international importance and which go to our level of compassion as a community, as an opportunity to grandstand and secure political points.[160]
>
> Passing this bill brings us in line with the United States of America, Canada, the United Kingdom and nations across Europe, and also our neighbours across the ditch.[161]

Apart from a Committee recommendation that Australia follow certain aspects of Eurodac,[162] complementary protection is also the only topic which has resulted in a Committee expressly relying on the European experience in making recommendations for Australia. In the Senate Select Committee's inquiry into Ministerial Discretion in Migration Matters in 2003, the Committee's attention was drawn to the (then draft) EU Qualification Directive through submissions by the present author.[163] It went on to find the following:

> In the light of these developments, the Committee is concerned that Australia is one of the few countries in the developed world that does not have a system of complementary protection. The Committee is left in no doubt that the current Australian practice of relying solely on ministerial discretion places it at odds with emerging international trends.[164]
>
> While the Committee finds that support for the concept of complementary protection is widespread amongst Australia's peak non-governmental

---

[159] See also Department of Parliamentary Services (Cth), *Bills Digest: Migration Amendment (Complementary Protection) Bill 2009*, No. 70 of 2009–10, 24 November 2009, p. 13; Department of Parliamentary Services (Cth), *Bills Digest: Migration Amendment (Complementary Protection) Bill 2011*, No. 79 of 2010–11, 11 March 2011, p. 13.

[160] Hansard, House of Representatives, p. 3832, 12 May 2011 (Ms Smyth).

[161] *Ibid.*, p. 3825, 12 May 2011 (Mr Hayes).

[162] Legal and Constitutional Legislation Committee, *Provisions of the Migration Amendment (Judicial Review) Bill 2004* (Cth of Australia, 2004), Recommendation 2.

[163] Senate Select Committee on Ministerial Discretion in Migration Matters, *Report* (Cth of Australia, 2004), at paras. 8.61–62.

[164] *Ibid.*, para. 8.80.

bodies concerned with refugee and asylum seeker issues, it is reluctant to recommend any particular system of complementary protection for Australia. *The Committee's view stems from the varied experience with complementary protection in Europe and Australia's past experience with the section 6A(1)(e) process.*[165]

The Committee takes seriously the practical and policy challenges being experienced by European countries which have implemented complementary protection. These challenges are readily acknowledged by even the most ardent supporters of complementary protection, but they are not considered to be insurmountable. *Having said that, the Committee does not wish to overstate the relevance to Australia of the European experience.*[166]

Another area in which there has been considerable analysis of European law and policy is in relation to immigration detention (and alternatives to it). In that context, one finds an express reference to the Reception Conditions Directive, although in discussion rather than a formal recommendation.[167]

What this suggests is that parliamentary committees are heavily reliant on academics and others drawing attention to relevant comparative practices in other countries. It would be imprudent to assume that this global positioning otherwise automatically occurs. The development of complementary protection in Australia shows that if evidence is put before committees and policy makers, then it may be taken into account. The point is to ensure that it is put before them in the first place, and this is where UNHCR, academics and NGOs have an important role to play.

Indeed, the great utility of comparative State practice was noted by the Senate Legal and Constitutional Affairs References Committee in its recommendation that the Immigration Department maintain a comparative database of international refugee determination systems.[168]

---

[165] *Ibid.*, para. 8.92 (emphasis added).
[166] *Ibid.*, para. 8.93 (emphasis added, citation omitted).
[167] Joint Standing Committee on Migration, *Immigration Detention in Australia: Community-Based Alternatives to Detention* (Cth of Australia, 2009), p. 63, figure 3.1, referring to Council Directive 2003/9/EC of 27 January 2003 laying down minimum standards for the reception of asylum seekers (OJ 2003 No. L31/18) (Reception Conditions Directive).
[168] Senate Legal and Constitutional Affairs References Committee, *A Sanctuary under Review*, p. xviii (Recommendation 6.1). It noted that the department had already compiled comparative material on the UK, the US, Canada, New Zealand, Germany and the Netherlands. Elsewhere in that report, the practices of those countries, as well as Sweden, were discussed in relation to the suspensive effect of asylum appeals and Australian policy (para. 10.8).

4   Personal connections/observations

Finally, influence may come through individual connections. For example, Lynton Crosby, the former political strategist and campaign director for Prime Minister John Howard, subsequently worked for Conservative politician, Michael Howard, during the 2005 UK election campaign. He is said to have 'inspired' the Conservative party's decision to make refugees a defining campaign issue.[169]

Philip Ruddock – who was to become Australia's longest-serving Immigration Minister, from 11 March 1996 to 7 October 2003 – relied on extensive meetings with his European counterparts and others working in the refugee field to inform his understanding of the implementation of refugee law in those countries, and to position Australia's own policies in a global context. He frequently sought to characterize Australia as the 'world leader' on some of the most restrictive asylum practices in contrast to Europe's 'failed' approaches:

> I regularly talk to the British ministers who have had responsibility for this area. Jack Straw was the minister for Home Affairs, and his successor, David Blunkett, are both British ministers who I have talked regularly to about these issues, and they acknowledge that if you are going to have effective immigration controls, if you are going to be able to assist those refugees who have the greatest need for protection and who are in vulnerable situations, you need to be able to regulate your borders to be able to manage migration flows and to be able to deal with refugee resettlement ... I've said if you wanted to adopt failed policy you would look at what they've been doing up until now in Europe and you would implement it. You would essentially open up the detention centres, let everybody loose, and you would see the result.[170]

In one of the most brazen examples of this, Ruddock presented his department's contributions to UNHCR's Global Consultations process (2001–02) at UNHCR's Executive Committee meeting in 2002.[171]

---

[169] Nicholas Watt, 'The Guardian profile: Lynton Crosby', *Guardian*, 28 January 2005 www.guardian.co.uk/politics/2005/jan/28/uk.conservatives (accessed 28 February 2012).

[170] Philip Ruddock, 'Meet the Press' (*Channel 10*, 23 June 2002). See also Philip Ruddock, Minister for Immigration and Multicultural and Indigenous Affairs, 'Managed Migration: Who Does the Managing?' (Presentation to Senior Government Officials and Academics, Australia House, London, 16 August 2002).

[171] See Philip Ruddock, 'Address to UNHCR Executive Committee Meeting' (Speech delivered at UNHCR Executive Committee Meeting, Geneva, 30 September 2002) http://parlinfo. aph.gov.au/parlInfo/download/media/pressrel/ZHJ76/upload_binary/zhj764.pdf;fileType= application/pdf (accessed 7 March 2012).

Entitled *Interpreting the Refugees Convention: An Australian Contribution*, the volume was described by Ruddock as representing 'part of my department's intellectual contribution' to 'international discussion and debate' on the interpretation of the Refugee Convention, 'reflect[ing] a rigorous analysis of current international law and Australia's considered position on interpretation of some of the important provisions of the Convention'.[172] The general approach was summarized in the Introduction:

> Australia is firmly committed to meeting is obligations under the Refugees Convention and contributing to the international protection system. However, the Australian Government is concerned that community support for refugees and Australia's capacity to participate in international burden sharing may be undermined by an expanded interpretation of the Convention and the extent of abuse by non-bona fide asylum-seekers of its provisions ... In the Australian Government's view, the original intentions of the Convention's drafters should be given primacy in a contemporary examination of interpretation and application of the Refugees Convention, leaving it up to States to determine to what extent and in what manner they choose to augment the Convention's provisions.[173]

Compared to his successors, Minister Ruddock travelled very extensively, including numerous trips to Europe.[174] In 2002, for example, he travelled to Belgium for the annual Australian–European Commission

---

[172] Department of Immigration and Multicultural and Indigenous Affairs, *Interpreting the Refugees Convention: An Australian Contribution* (Cth of Australia, 2002), Foreword by Minister Ruddock.

[173] *Ibid.*, pp. 3–4.

[174] Travel schedules can be accessed from the profiles of Immigration Ministers on the Parliament of Australia website and the purpose of travel can be seen in accounts of entitlements paid to Minsters by Department of Finance: www.finance.gov.au/publications/parliamentarians-reporting/index.html (accessed 20 March 2012). The following details are compiled from both sources. Immigration Minister Chris Bowen (Labor): US (July 2010); Timor-Leste, Indonesia and Malaysia (October 2010); Malaysia and Switzerland (December 2010); Indonesia (March 2011); Malaysia (April 2011 and June–July 2011) www.aph.gov.au/Senators_and_Members/Parliamentarian?MPID=DZS#conferences (accessed 5 October 2012); Immigration Minister Chris Evans (Labor): Indonesia (January 2008); Indonesia, Malaysia, Thailand and Singapore (August 2008); Vietnam (January 2009); Indonesia (March and April 2009); India and Sri Lanka (July 2009); China (November 2010) http://aph.gov.au/Senators_and_Members/Parliamentarian?MPID=AX5 (accessed 5 October 2012); Immigration Minister Kevin Andrews (Liberal): Indonesia (during the first half of 2007; official report not available to the public); Immigration Minister Amanda Vanstone (Liberal): Thailand, China and Vietnam (April–May 2004); Papua New Guinea (December 2004); Indonesia (February–March 2005); US and Canada (April–May 2005); Hong Kong, Italy, Switzerland, UK and China (October 2005); Bangladesh, India and Sri Lanka (March

Ministerial Consultations, visited the UK and France to discuss border protection, and went to Sweden, Denmark, Norway and Finland to discuss resettlement issues and offshore processing arrangements.[175] By comparison, Labor's Immigration Ministers have had far fewer overseas trips, most of which have been within the region and none to any EU Member State.

G Conclusion

It is very difficult to identify precisely where ideas originate in asylum practices and how they cross-pollinate. The extent to which the CEAS specifically has had an impact on Australian law and policy to date is hard to ascertain. However, there exists what might be termed a 'plagiaristic dialogue', in that States borrow heavily from each other

2006); Thailand and Indonesia (June 2006); New Zealand (July 2006); US (September 2006) http://parlinfo.aph.gov.au/parlInfo/search/display/display.w3p;query=%28Id:handbook/ allmps/7e4%29;rec=0 (accessed 5 October 2012); Immigration Minister Philip Ruddock (Liberal): Indonesia (April 1996); China (August 1996); UK, Switzerland and the Middle East (September–October 1996); UK, Austria and Republics of former Yugoslavia, Turkey and Greece (July 1997); Indonesia, Malaysia, China and the Philippines (September 1997); Former Yugoslav Republic of Macedonia, Greece and Turkey (April–May 1998); South Africa, Kenya, Rwanda, Egypt and UK (January 1999); Thailand (April 1999); US, Canada, New Zealand and South America (June–July 1999); China (November 1999); Jordan, Syria, Turkey, Iran, Pakistan, South and East Africa and Europe (January 2000); Indonesia (January–February 2000); Switzerland, UK, Germany, Belgium, the Netherlands and Italy (March–April 2000); New Zealand (April 2000); Singapore, Malaysia, Thailand, India and France (July 2000); Switzerland and Papua New Guinea (September–October 2000); Iran, Jordan, Lebanon, United Arab Emirates, Sweden, Switzerland and UK (January 2001); Indonesia, Thailand and Vietnam (June 2001); Indonesia (September 2001); UK, Switzerland and Spain (December 2001); Manus Island, Papua New Guinea and Nauru (February 2002); Indonesia, Japan, Cambodia and Laos (February–March 2002); China, UK, Belgium, France, Sweden, Denmark, Norway, Finland and Pakistan (April–May 2002); Iran and Afghanistan (May 2002); South Africa, Greece, Yugoslavia, Czech Republic, Austria and UK (August 2002); Switzerland, Canada, Malaysia, the Philippines and Republic of Korea (September–October 2002); Papua New Guinea (November 2002); Indonesia (March and April 2003); UK, Bangladesh, Sri Lanka and Pakistan (July 2003); Republic of Armenia, Switzerland and Iran (September–October 2003) www.aph.gov.au/Senators_and_Members/Parliamentar ian?MPID=0J4#conferences (accessed 5 October 2012). It is interesting to note that the purpose of many of Philip Ruddock's regional meetings was described as combating illegal immigration and people smuggling, rather than international protection.

[175] Department of Finance and Administration, *Parliamentarians' Travel Paid by the Department of Finance and Administration: January to June 2002* (December 2002), p. 144.

but typically without any clear acknowledgement.[176] In Noll's view, this is not accidental: 'the selective approach to precedents and the avoidance of a broad and transparent debate reflects a desire to skip the burden of connecting to earlier arguments and problematic experiences',[177] a strategy that 'prefers the gesture of decision to the ratio of discourse'.[178]

The broad themes of securitization and immigration control identified in Chapter 1 of this book are certainly borne out in Australian refugee law and practice. Indeed, in the absence of national or regional human rights guarantees, Australia has developed some of the most draconian asylum policies in the industrialized world. Both the EU and Australia seem to have conflated 'asylum' with 'immigration'. Whereas the former is about providing international protection to those at risk of persecution or other forms of serious harm, the latter is about controlling entry to territory and in accordance with the 'national interest' of the State.[179] The extent to which Australia has deliberately mimicked a 'Fortress Europe'-style approach is difficult to demonstrate, but its approach clearly follows the trend in industrialized States of limiting protection options and characterizing asylum seekers as part of an 'illegal' wave of immigrants, failing to distinguish between those who have a protection need and those who do not.

The absence of a domestic bill of rights or regional human rights treaty in the Asia-Pacific has facilitated the creation of relatively extreme deterrence policies in Australia, which would be unlawful in the EU. For example, in the absence of a provision equivalent to article 5 ECHR, which constrains the use of detention, Australia continues a practice of mandatory detention for asylum seekers who arrive without a valid visa.[180] Section 196 of the Migration Act provides that detention continues until a non-citizen is either removed from Australia or

---

[176] As Maarten den Heijer observes, '[c]urrent European policies are to a considerable extent based on experiences of traditional immigration countries, such as the United States, Canada and Australia' ('Europe Beyond Its Borders: Refugee and Human Rights Protection in Extraterritorial Immigration Control', in Bernard Ryan and Valsamis Mitsilegas (eds.), *Extraterritorial Immigration Control: Legal Challenges* (Leiden and Boston: Martinus Nijhoff, 2010), p. 171).

[177] Noll, 'Visions', 314.   [178] *Ibid.*

[179] See, e.g., Geoff Gilbert, 'Is Europe Living Up to Its Obligations to Refugees?' (2004) 15 *European Journal of International Law* 963–87, at 968.

[180] Mandatory detention was introduced by the Migration Amendment Act 1992 (Cth), which commenced on 1 September 1994.

granted a visa, and the High Court of Australia confirmed in *Al-Kateb* that this means it is indefinite and may last for the term of a person's life.[181]

Australian law has no equivalent of article 3 ECHR (the prohibition on torture or inhuman or degrading treatment or punishment). A claim such as that against Greece in *MSS* v. *Belgium and Greece* could not be brought in Australia (unless it were under the law of negligence, rather than human rights law). Until the passage of the Migration Amendment (Complementary Protection) Act 2011 (Cth), there was no codified basis on which an asylum seeker could claim protection on the basis of arbitrary deprivation of life, the death penalty, torture, or cruel, inhuman or degrading treatment or punishment.

Australia has implemented offshore processing regimes which, though mooted in the European context, have not taken hold systemically. Indeed, EU Member States have questioned their legality in light of the ECHR and international treaty obligations.[182]

International human rights obligations are only justiciable in Australian courts to the extent that they are reflected in national law. With very few such protections in place, there is little in the substantive law that provides a basis for reviewing practices such as those described above. Australia also relies heavily on ministerial discretion, which means that in certain circumstances, there is no legislative guarantee that international protection claims will be considered in accordance with Australia's obligations under international law.[183] The challenges

---

[181] *Al-Kateb* v. *Godwin*; cf. *A* v. *Secretary of State for the Home Department* [2004] UKHL 56 (known as the '*Belmarsh Prison* case'). The issue of indefinite detention is again before the High Court of Australia in *Plaintiff S138/2012* v. *Director General of Security*.

[182] European Commission, Towards more accessible, equitable and managed asylum systems, p. 6.

[183] For example, pursuant to s. 46A Migration Act, all asylum seekers who are 'offshore entry persons' (namely boat arrivals) are barred from applying for a protection visa, unless the Minister considers it to be in the public interest to permit them to do so. Although this discretion is always exercised in practice, it remains the case that it is not a right at law. Further, prior to 24 March 2012 when the complementary protection criteria in s. 36 Migration Act took effect, asylum seekers could not lodge a protection claim on the basis of fear of return to arbitrary deprivation of life, torture, cruel, inhuman or degrading treatment or punishment. Rather, consideration of such criteria was dependent on the asylum seeker first lodging a refugee claim, having that claim rejected by the immigration official and the Refugee Review Tribunal, and then lodging an application to the minister pursuant to s. 417 Migration Act, requesting the minister to exercise his or her personal discretion to (a) consider the claim on public interest grounds, and (b) grant a visa to enable the person to remain in Australia.

that have succeeded in the courts have been largely on the basis of technical or procedural points or questions of statutory interpretation.[184] In light of all this, there remains a risk, therefore, that even the most restrictive EU practices could be interpreted even more restrictively in the Australian context.

---

[184] See, e.g., *Plaintiff M61/2010E* v. *Commonwealth of Australia* [2010] HCA 41 (2010) 243 CLR 319; *M70*.

3

European influence on asylum practices in Latin America: accelerated procedures in Colombia, Ecuador, Panama and Venezuela

DAVID J. CANTOR

This chapter explores the impact of European practices on contemporary refugee law in Latin America. The topic is one that has generated relatively little academic attention, reflecting a broader lack of scholarly interest in refugee law in the global South, and particularly in Latin America. Even within the circumscribed body of literature on refugee law in Latin America, analysis has concentrated on those protection-related developments that appear to possess a strong local flavour. These have included the elaborate regional system of political asylum,[1] the extended refugee definition adopted in the 1984 Cartagena Declaration[2] and refugee resettlement schemes.[3] The present chapter complements these existing studies by examining European influence on the practice of international protection by Latin American States.

A major development within Latin American refugee law has been the appearance of procedures for dealing with 'manifestly unfounded' and 'clearly abusive' claims in the asylum systems of certain States. The adoption of these procedures represents one area in which refugee law

---

[1] See, e.g., the collection by Leonardo Franco (ed.), *El asilo y la protección internacional de los refugiados en América Latina* (San José: Editorama, 2004).

[2] Cartagena Declaration on Refugees, adopted by the Colloquium on the International Protection of Refugees in Central America, Mexico, and Panama, 22 November 1984, in 'Annual Report of the Inter-American Commission on Human Rights' (1984–5) OAS Doc. OEA/Ser.L/V/II.66/doc.10, rev. 1, 190–3 (Cartagena Declaration). See the collected essays in UNHCR, *Memoria del Vigésimo Aniversario de la Declaración de Cartagena sobre los Refugiados 1984–2004* (San José: Editorama, 2005).

[3] For a recent example, see Liliana Lyra Jubilut and Wellington Pereira Carneiro, 'Resettlement in Solidarity: A New Regional Approach Towards a More Humane Durable Solution' (2011) 30 *Refugee Survey Quarterly* 63–86.

practice in Europe – originating in regional initiatives by the Council of
Europe and later taken up by the Common European Asylum System
(CEAS) created by the European Union (EU)[4] – has had a notable
impact on Latin American States. The tendency appears particularly
accentuated in the territories that bridge the Andean and Central
American subregions, particularly those States most affected by the
current dynamics of refugee protection in Latin America: Colombia,
Ecuador, Panama and Venezuela.[5] This runs counter to suggestions in
earlier scholarship that States in the Common Market of the South
(Mercosur) would be the principal imitators of asylum developments
in Europe.[6] Instead, this chapter contends that it is in the adoption of
these accelerated procedures at the other end of the continent where
European asylum practices are currently having their greatest impact.

   The chapter opens by tracing the historical engagement by Latin
American States with European concepts of asylum. This provides the
context for pursuing a more detailed examination of recent developments in the region; in particular, the accelerated procedures adopted in
recent years by Colombia, Ecuador, Panama and Venezuela for dealing
with 'manifestly unfounded' or 'clearly abusive' claims.[7] The chapter
then analyses how Latin American States – through the mediation of the
United Nations High Commissioner for Refugees (UNHCR) – have
emulated a European set of standards for identifying such claims.
Similarly, it is argued that European practices driven by the processes
leading to the formation of the CEAS have inspired, in turn, the use of
these procedures by Latin American States as a means of screening

---

[4] See Part B below.
[5] Accelerated procedures have also been adopted in recent years by other Latin American
    States, such as Costa Rica (Decree 36831-G of 28 September 2011, arts. 139–140) and El
    Salvador (Decree 79/05 of 7 September 2005, art. 15). Their accelerated procedures
    broadly follow the tendencies described in this chapter.
[6] Frances Nicholson, 'Challenges to Forging a Common European Asylum System in Line
    with International Obligations', in Steve Peers and Nicola Rogers (eds.), *EU Immigration
    and Asylum Law: Text and Commentary* (Leiden and Boston: Martinus Nijhoff, 2006),
    p. 533. Mercosur is a subregional organization comprising Argentina, Brazil, Paraguay
    and Uruguay (full members), as well as Bolivia, Chile, Colombia, Ecuador and Peru
    (associate members).
[7] The data on which this analysis rests were gathered in part through fieldwork undertaken
    by the author in the relevant countries between March and May 2011 as part of a wider
    project funded by UNHCR. The author conducted 145 semi-structured interviews with
    190 subjects, including government officials, humanitarian workers and displaced per-
    sons. Relevant interviews are listed in the Appendix at the end of the chapter and
    anonymized at the request of the subjects.

admissibility to substantive refugee status determination procedures. By applying the theoretical framework from Chapter 1, the analysis not only identifies the drivers behind these changes but also the factors responsible for facilitating the inter-regional transmission of the concepts themselves. This chapter concludes by exploring the wider implications of the emulation of European asylum practices by Latin American States.

A   European influence on Latin America

European influence on the institution of asylum in Latin America is not a new phenomenon. This opening section traces the broad history of Latin American engagement with European concepts of asylum in order to provide a wider regional context for understanding contemporary developments in the Andean–Central American 'bridge'. Two distinct factors will assume importance as the argument develops in this chapter: first, the enduring significance of political asylum as a trope that frames Latin American attitudes towards refugee law; and, second, the importance of UNHCR as a channel for facilitating the transmission of concepts in refugee law.

1   European antecedents to political asylum in Latin America

International refugee law may have been forged as a response to refugee flows in twentieth-century Europe, but its historical roots lie in earlier practices of political asylum. Yet the concept of political asylum has retained most prominence in Latin America, where it has been developed through regional treaties and, perhaps, custom.[8] Indeed, the historical response by Latin American States to 'European' refugee law cannot be understood in isolation from the dominance of the political asylum paradigm in this region. Nonetheless, ideas of political asylum ultimately had their origin in Europe, representing the original instance of European influence on international protection in Latin America.

In spite of the proud standing of the institution of political asylum in Latin America, its origins are clearly European. Asylum in Europe was initially conceded on religious grounds, being the main reason for seeking foreign refuge during the seventeenth century. The shift from religious to political asylum became apparent in the aftermath of the French

---

[8] However, see the analysis of the International Court of Justice in respect of the non-existence of a regional custom of diplomatic political asylum in Latin America: *Asylum Case (Colombia v. Peru)* (1950) ICJ Rep 266.

Revolution.[9] Subsequently, the European practice of political asylum during the early nineteenth century – particularly by Spain – formed the basis for the framework of treaties and custom that became a feature of international relations between the newly independent Latin American States in the nineteenth and twentieth centuries.[10] Even as diplomatic and territorial political asylum continued on its own trajectory in Europe from the late nineteenth century onwards, it served as the formative inspiration for the Latin American institution of asylum.

It is paradoxical, then, that for much of the twentieth century the dominance of political asylum in Latin America functioned to limit engagement by States in the region with the new 'refugee' law being created as a response to mass population outflows in Europe between the two world wars. During that period, Latin American States participated relatively little in the pertinent international conferences.[11] Instead, they proposed strengthening the Latin American institution of territorial political asylum and extending it to Europe in order to resolve the refugee problem. This proposal was largely ignored by European States, but found some favour within Latin America, leading to the conclusion of the 1939 Montevideo Treaty on Political Asylum and Refuge.[12] In part this provided a means of extending territorial political asylum to those persons seeking refuge in Latin America from the Spanish Civil War.[13]

Latin American States' investment in the concept of political asylum also contributed to the distanced attitude that this region displayed towards the modern refugee regime in the post-Second World War period. Mass movements of such 'refugees' were largely seen as a European problem, unlike the small-scale movements of well-heeled Latin American political leaders that were familiar to States in this region. During the negotiations leading to the conclusion of the 1951 Convention relating to the Status of

---

[9] Atle Grahl-Madsen, 'The European Tradition of Asylum and the Development of Refugee Law' (1966) 3 *Journal of Peace Research* 278–89.

[10] Cecilia Imaz, 'El asilo diplomático en la política exterior de México' (1993) 40–1 *Revista Mexicana de Política Exterior* 53–71, at 53.

[11] There was almost no participation by Latin American States in refugee conferences during this period, except in the United States-led 1938 Evian Conference: see Claudena Skran, *Refugees in Inter-War Europe: The Emergence of a Regime* (Oxford: Oxford University Press, 1995), tables 8 and 17.

[12] Montevideo Treaty on Political Asylum and Refuge, adopted 4 August 1939; reprinted in Manley O. Hudson (ed.), *International Legislation* (Washington, DC: Carnegie Endowment for International Peace, 1949), vol. VIII, p. 404.

[13] Jaime Esponda Fernández, 'La tradición latinoamericana de asilo y la protección internacional de los refugiados', in Franco, *El asilo*, pp. 93–4.

Refugees,[14] Latin American States therefore endorsed a narrow framing of the refugee definition with temporal and geographical limitations restricted to the refugee situation in inter-war Europe. Moreover, consistent with the Latin American understanding of political asylum, they emphasized that the granting of asylum was a discretionary right of States rather than a duty.[15] Political asylum thus continued to be the paradigm through which refugee law was understood.

This stance persisted in the decade following the adoption of the Refugee Convention. Latin American States were slow to ratify the new treaty,[16] and the few that did maintained geographical reservations restricting its application to European refugees.[17] In parallel, and partly in reaction to those European war refugees who were resettled in Latin America, the Organization of American States (OAS) negotiated new treaties to further extend the framework of political asylum, particularly through the 1954 Convention on Territorial Asylum.[18] Though few States ratified this treaty,[19] it provided a regional device that could be used to manage the impact of European refugee problems in Latin America. Until the 1960s, therefore, the ultimately European institution of political asylum remained the basis for granting refuge on the territories of Latin American States and helped buttress their rejection of 'European' refugee law.

2   Latin America's reaction to 'European' refugee law

Increased Latin American engagement with refugee law from the 1960s onwards was driven by States' perceptions of new regional asylum challenges that approximated more closely to those that led to the

---

[14] Convention relating to the Status of Refugees, Geneva, 28 July 1951, in force 22 April 1954 (189 UNTS 137) (Refugee Convention).

[15] Flávia Piovesan and Liliana Lyra Jubilut, 'Regional Developments: Americas', in A. Zimmermann (ed.), *The 1951 Convention relating to the Status of Refugees and Its 1967 Protocol: A Commentary* (Oxford: Oxford University Press, 2011), pp. 210–12.

[16] Only five States were parties to the 1951 Refugee Convention prior to 1967, most ratifying the treaty during the 1960s: Ecuador (1955); Brazil (1960); Colombia and Argentina (1961); Peru (1964). See UN Treaty Collection website: http://treaties.un. org (accessed 1 October 2012).

[17] Leonardo Franco, 'El derecho internacional de los refugiados y su aplicación en América Latina', in *Anuario Jurídico Interamericano 1982* (Washington, DC: Organización de Estados Americanos, 1983).

[18] Convention on Territorial Asylum, Caracas, 28 March 1954, in force 29 December 1954, *OAS Treaty Series* No. 18.

[19] See OAS, 'Multilateral Treaties' www.oas.org/DIL/treaties.htm (accessed 1 October 2012).

development of refugee law in Europe. As a result, States began to reconfigure their relationship with this perceived 'European' body of law, especially in light of UNHCR-led efforts to expand its relevance to refugee problems in other parts of the world. The practical support afforded by UNHCR to States responding to these new large-scale displacements on the South American continent provided a basis for it to facilitate the future development of refugee law in the region.

The mass population movements from Cuba and Haiti in the early 1960s, combined with local integration difficulties for the destitute displaced persons, led to the adequacy of the political asylum model being questioned. In 1965, the OAS began drafting an Inter-American Refugee Convention, which incorporated elements of both regional asylum law (1954 Convention on Territorial Asylum and Refuge) and 'European' refugee law (Refugee Convention).[20] The project appears to have been abandoned in favour of the framework offered by the simultaneous UNCHR-led drafting of the 1967 Protocol.[21] However, Latin American States initially showed relatively little interest in ratifying the Protocol even though some had participated in the drafting process.[22]

The main catalyst for adhesion to international refugee law standards by Latin American States was instead the large-scale refugee flows produced by the Southern Cone dictatorships of the 1970s and, later, the Central American crises of the 1980s. Indeed, the ratification of the 1967 Protocol by all five Southern Cone States (and Ecuador) by the early 1970s formed the basis for a growing regional acceptance of the utility of the international refugee framework. Simultaneously, UNHCR established a presence and a reputation in the region as a crucial provider of technical, material and political support to States in responding to these new displacement crises.[23] Ratification of the 1967 Protocol by most Central American and Andean States followed in response to the massive refugee flows in and from Central America during the 1980s, thereby

---

[20] OAS, *Informe anual de la Comisión Interamericana de Derechos Humanos 1981–1982* (San José: OAS, 1982) OEA/Ser.L/V/II.57, Doc.6, rev.1, ch. VI.B.

[21] Protocol relating to the Status of Refugees, New York, adopted 31 January 1967, in force 4 October 1967 (606 UNTS 267).

[22] See UNHCR, *Proposed Measures to Extend the Personal Scope of the Convention relating to the Status of Refugees of 28 July 1951*, 12 October 1966 (UN Doc. A/AC.96/346), Annex I.

[23] For a summary of UNHCR activities in this crisis, see Gil Loescher, *The UNHCR and World Politics: A Perilous Path* (Oxford: Oxford University Press, 2001), pp. 168–76.

further consolidating formal acceptance of the refugee law framework within the region.[24]

The high point of intra-regional Latin American cooperation on refugee protection was achieved during the Central American crises of the 1980s, particularly through the Cartagena (1984) and CIREFCA (1989) processes.[25] UNHCR was the crucial external factor in facilitating and promoting these processes of local refugee law development, reflecting its position as an increasingly vital point of reference on refugee protection for States in the region.[26] The agency has since attempted to build upon this framework to further promote refugee law in Latin America, such as through the San José (1994) and Mexico (2004) colloquia[27] and other regional meetings.[28] Its continuing potential for facilitating the transmission of refugee law concepts through local networks should not be underestimated.

Overall, the influence of European refugee law on Latin America during this period appears to have been relatively small. In general terms, perhaps the most that can be said is that the adhesion to refugee law treaties by Latin American States shows an overcoming of their previous resistance to this 'European' body of law. On the details of the law, the external influences appear to have been more squarely African. Thus, the 1967 Protocol was itself largely a response to new groups of refugees in Africa,[29] and the innovative standards of the 1984 Cartagena Declaration were inspired more by the 1969 OAU Refugee Convention

---

[24] The following States ratified the Protocol: Dominican Republic, Costa Rica, Panama and Peru (1978); Colombia and Nicaragua (1980); Bolivia (1982); El Salvador and Guatemala (1983); Haiti (1984); Venezuela (1986). Honduras and Mexico only ratified the Protocol in 1992 and 2000 respectively. See UN Treaty Collection website: http://treaties.un.org (accessed 1 October 2012).

[25] Conference documents can be found at UNHCR, *Documentos y conclusiones de Reuniones Regionales* www.acnur.org/paginas/index.php?id_pag=3170 (accessed 1 October 2012).

[26] For a detailed analysis of the Cartagena process, see Leonardo Franco and Jorge Santistevan de Noriega, 'La contribución del proceso de Cartagena al desarrollo del derecho internacional de refugiados en América Latina', in UNHCR, *Memoria del Vigésimo Aniversario de la Declaración de Cartagena*.

[27] See Declaración de San José sobre refugiados y personas desplazadas (San José, 5–7 December 1994); 'Mexico Declaration and Plan of Action to Strengthen the International Protection of Refugees in Latin America' (2005) 17 *International Journal of Refugee Law* 802–17.

[28] See Declaración de Brasilia sobre la protección de personas refugiadas y Apátridas en el continente americano (Brazil, 11 November 2010).

[29] Terje Einarsen, 'Drafting History of the 1951 Convention and the 1967 Protocol', in Zimmermann, *1951 Convention*, pp. 70–1.

than by European practices.[30] By contrast, and in spite of its proximity, the impact of the protection practices of the United States of America (US) on these developments was much less significant. UNHCR played a crucial role both in promoting the local development of refugee law in Latin America and channelling refugee concepts that had been developed in or for other parts of the world.

3   Spain as a model for refugee status determination procedures in Latin America

One significant task in which UNHCR has been engaged since its arrival in Latin America has been helping States to build and develop their asylum systems. In outlining the form commonly taken by refugee status determination procedures in Latin America – including Colombia, Ecuador, Panama and Venezuela – this section lays the groundwork for the chapter's core argument: that the accelerated status determination procedures recently adopted by certain Latin American States emulate European standards.[31] Two main features of the Inter-Ministerial Commissions used for refugee status determination by most Latin American States are highlighted here. First, the form of these procedures bears a family resemblance to practice on the European continent, specifically by Spain, which may facilitate further emulation. Second, these refugee status determination procedures reflect an approach that continues to be rooted in the localized concept of political asylum in Latin America.

Most Latin American States conduct refugee status determination through Inter-Ministerial Commissions, sometimes referred to as 'institutional collegiate commissions'.[32] Such commissions are usually composed of delegates from designated government ministries, often the Interior Ministry, the Foreign Ministry and the Ministry of Defence. These meet in session periodically to consider and vote upon the claims

---

[30] For instance, the expanded refugee definition in Conclusion 3 of the Cartagena Declaration appears to have been inspired by that in art. 1(1) Organization of African Unity Convention Governing the Specific Aspects of Refugee Problems in Africa, Addis Ababa, 10 September 1969, in force 20 June 1974 (1001 UNTS 45): Roberto Cuéllar *et al.*, 'Refugee and Related Developments in Latin America: Challenges Ahead' (1991) 3 *International Journal of Refugee Law* 482–98, at 484.

[31] See Part C below.

[32] At present, only Honduras does not employ the Inter-Ministerial Commission structure for refugee status determination. See further, Juan Carlos Murillo González, 'El derecho de asilo y la protección de refugiados en el continente americano', in UNHCR, *La protección internacional de refugiados en las Américas* (Quito: Mantis, 2011), p. 59.

for asylum received and documented by administrative officials. In most States, UNHCR has the right to participate in these commission sessions as a non-voting observer. The outcome of the commission's voting takes the form of a non-binding recommendation about whether to recognize an applicant's refugee status, which is then sent to the minister designated to take the ultimate decision.

There are strong similarities between this procedure and that pioneered by Spain in 1984.[33] The relevant Spanish law established an Inter-Ministerial Commission, which formulated recommendations to the Minister of the Interior, who took the ultimate decision on the granting of asylum. It also required an invitation to be extended to UNHCR to participate in Commission sessions dealing with refugee status.[34] The present Spanish asylum system – adopted through its 2009 law on asylum[35] – continues to be based upon this essential structure. The Spanish Inter-Ministerial Commission structure may thus be the inspiration for the subsequent decrees through which this structure was adopted in the pertinent Latin American States. The shared language and high degree of fit between the legal and administrative systems of Spain and some Latin America States may be viewed as important facilitating factors. Over the past fifteen years, the adoption of this form of status determination procedure has been consistently commended to States in the region by UNHCR.[36]

However, a crucial difference exists concerning the review of negative decisions. The 1984 Spanish legislation expressly provided for judicial review of negative decisions,[37] which is echoed by the Venezuelan legislation.[38] By contrast, the rules in Colombia,[39] Ecuador[40] and Panama[41] provide at most for reconsideration by the national authority

---

[33] Law 5/1984 (26 March 1984). Note that the framework was later amended by Law 9/1994 (19 May 1994).

[34] Law 5/1984, arts. 6–7, 23–24.   [35] Law 12/2009 (30 October 2009).

[36] Email correspondence from Regional Legal Unit, Americas Bureau, UNHCR, 2 April 2012, on file with author.

[37] Law 5/1984, art. 24.

[38] Organic Law on Refugees and Asylees (3 October 2001), arts. 20–21; Decree 2491/03 (28 July 2003), arts. 14–16.

[39] Originally through Decree 2817/84 (20 November 1984), art. 7; presently by Decree 4503/09 (19 November 2009), art. 16.

[40] Originally through Decree 3293/87 (30 September 1987), arts. 15–17; then by Decree 3301/92 (6 May 1992), arts. 24–25. This has been maintained by the more recent Decree 1182/12 (30 May 2012), arts. 47–48.

[41] Decree 23/98 (10 February 1998), art. 46.

that made the original decision. Some attempts by asylum applicants to challenge negative decisions have been made through existing judicial avenues for the protection of fundamental rights (e.g. *amparo* or *tutela* mechanisms). However, the reported judgments show that the higher courts refuse to consider whether the procedures established by domestic law are sufficient to protect the individual rights that may be violated by *refoulement*. Rather, judicial intervention will take place only when these procedures are not followed, with orders limited to requiring the relevant minister to remake the decision in line with the established procedure.[42]

Within refugee status determination procedures, this pronounced emphasis on State discretion echoes the tenets of the political asylum framework – with the granting of asylum ultimately conceived as a right of States rather than of individuals. Interviewees stressed the discretionary aspect of these administrative structures in practice.[43] For instance, in Colombia, the 'diplomatic and political' logic resulting from locating the national refugee authorities in the Ministry of Foreign Affairs was highlighted by practitioners.[44] Similarly, in Ecuador the decision to routinely deny asylum to Cubans, even those with strong claims, appears to reflect the contemporary political sympathies between Cuba and Ecuador.[45] The continued influence of the 'political asylum' trope may also be seen in the reported higher court judgments that privilege State discretion to choose the form of asylum procedures over the substantive protection of refugee rights.[46]

One result of this approach is that national jurisprudence contains no significant interpretation of the refugee definition, which is instead undertaken within the relevant administrative refugee authority. Interviews in these countries showed that UNHCR constitutes the principal external source of interpretative guidance. Its policy statements – particularly the UNHCR Handbook and UNHCR's Guidelines on International Protection – form the bedrock for officials' legal interpretation of the refugee definition and they are sometimes even treated as a source of binding legal authority.[47] UNHCR is also the principal source

---

[42] See, e.g., *Sentencia T-704/03, Reza Pirhadi v. Ministerio de Relaciones Exteriores y el Departamento Administrativo de Seguridad DAS*, Constitutional Court of Colombia, 14 August 2003; *Case No. 0106-2005-RA*, Constitutional Tribunal of Ecuador, 11 May 2006. In practice, this approach appears to have been followed also by the Venezuelan lower courts upon receiving *tutela* applications from asylum seekers (Interview 99).
[43] Interviews 3, 14, 61, 81.   [44] Interview 3.   [45] Interviews 14, 16.
[46] See text to n. 42 above.   [47] Interviews 3, 14, 16, 54, 56, 60, 82, 89, 107, 143.

of country of origin information.[48] Thus, regarding UNHCR country-specific positions, a Colombian practitioner noted that 'the fact of being from UNHCR makes [them] valid' for government decision makers.[49] As such, UNHCR's guiding influence in these States extends to the interpretation of refugee law concepts by government decision makers as well as advising on wider systemic issues.

Whether other external legal sources are used by administrative officials to guide their interpretation of refugee law – and, if so, which ones – varies considerably. A few cite refugee law jurisprudence from the US, UK or Australia,[50] or the gender-related jurisprudence of the Inter-American Court of Human Rights,[51] sometimes reflecting the citations in the written briefs submitted by asylum practitioners.[52] In short, aside from the possible European basis for any specific set of UNHCR guidelines, the degree of European influence on the interpretation of refugee law in Latin America appears to be minimal.

B   Accelerated procedures and Europe

In the last fifteen years, Colombia, Ecuador, Panama and Venezuela have all adopted special procedures for dealing with 'manifestly unfounded' and 'clearly abusive' asylum claims. In order to place these Latin American developments in context, the present section describes the wider standards on accelerated procedures on which the Latin American legal frameworks are modelled. It shows that these standards were developed by UNHCR during the 1980s as a response to the phenomenon of mixed migration flows experienced in Europe and other industrialized countries. It argues that Europe not only provided the initial inspiration for the drafting of these UNHCR standards, but also represents the continent where these standards have received their greatest subsequent elaboration.

1   The global framework of the UNHCR Executive Committee

UNHCR Executive Committee Conclusion No. 30 (1983) sets out guidelines for dealing with 'manifestly unfounded or abusive' asylum applications in order to address the 'serious problem' that such applications represent for States, both as a burden for affected countries and as

---

[48] Interviews 1, 3, 96.   [49] Interview 3.   [50] Interviews 14, 60.
[51] Interviews 16, 60, 143.   [52] Interview 3.

detrimental to applicants with good grounds for seeking recognition as refugees.[53] The terms 'manifestly unfounded' and 'clearly abusive' are defined, as are the minimum standards applicable to accelerated procedures for determining such claims.[54] It is important to set out these standards in some detail in order to demonstrate not only the debt that they owe to Europe, but also the degree to which they inform the accelerated procedures recently adopted by Latin American States.

Conclusion No. 30 represented an evolution in thinking for UNHCR's Executive Committee. In 1977, the initial Executive Committee position on 'clearly abusive' claims suggested that these might constitute an exception to the principle that asylum applicants should be permitted to remain in the country of asylum pending an *initial* decision on the asylum claim.[55] However, the Executive Committee revisited this position in 1982, prompted both by the 'proliferation [of such applications] in a number of countries' and UNHCR's concerns about whether adequate safeguards existed in the 'far-reaching' range of reactive measures adopted by these governments.[56] Its resulting Conclusion No. 28 (1982) directed that the issue be examined further and recommended basic procedural criteria, that were reflected in Conclusion No. 30.[57]

The conceptual starting point for the minimum standards agreed by the Executive Committee in Conclusion No. 30 was its recognition that the national procedures for refugee status determination

> may usefully include special provision for dealing in an expeditious manner with applications which are considered to be so obviously without foundation as not to merit full examination at every level of the procedure.[58]

Conclusion No. 30 thus followed Conclusion No. 28 in identifying accelerated procedures as the appropriate response to such applications, rather than implementing visa requirements for certain nationalities, limiting the right to work of asylum seekers or dispensing with essential procedural safeguards.[59]

---

[53] UNHCR Executive Committee, Conclusion No. 30 (XXXIV) (20 October 1983), para. c.
[54] *Ibid.*, paras. d–f.
[55] UNHCR Executive Committee, Conclusion No. 8 (XXVIII) (12 October 1977), para. e(vii).
[56] UNHCR, *Follow-up on Earlier Conclusions of the Sub-Committee on the Determination of Refugee Status, inter alia, with reference to the Role of UNHCR in National Refugee Status Determination Procedure*, 3 September 1982 (UN Doc. EC/SCP/22/Rev.1), paras. 25–7.
[57] UNHCR Executive Committee, Conclusion No. 28 (XXXIII) (20 October 1982), para. d.
[58] Executive Committee, Conclusion No. 30, para. d.
[59] UNHCR, *Follow-up on Earlier Conclusions*, 3 September 1982, para. 26.

Conclusion No. 30 also defined the scope of applications amenable to resolution through such accelerated procedures in line with Conclusion No. 28. Often termed 'clearly abusive' or 'manifestly unfounded' claims, these are framed relatively narrowly in order to encompass only those applications which are 'clearly fraudulent or not related to the criteria for the granting of refugee status laid down in [the Refugee Convention] nor to any other criteria justifying the granting of asylum'.[60]

Moreover, in view of the grave consequences of an erroneous asylum determination, Conclusion No. 30 reiterated the minimum guarantees for such accelerated procedures recommended by Conclusion No. 28. These included 'a complete personal interview' by, wherever possible, an official of the authority competent to determine refugee status, and the opportunity 'to have a negative decision reviewed', albeit through more simplified procedures than those applied in normal circumstances.[61] Since the adoption of these guidelines in 1983, the Executive Committee has frequently called upon States to ensure that such procedures have no detrimental effect upon international protection, even as it expresses its concern at the 'growing abuse' of the institution of asylum.[62]

2   European practice as the basis for the UNHCR framework

Europe is not only the continent that has elaborated UNHCR's standards on accelerated asylum procedures to the greatest extent, but also the region that provided the original inspiration for these general standards. Nonetheless, these two developments have their locus in different European institutions. This section shows that, while the EU has expanded the remit and role of such procedures, the standards were originally within the framework of the Council of Europe. Both of these developments ultimately responded to the new challenges perceived by European States as a result of increased mixed migration flows in their territories beginning in the 1980s.[63]

---

[60] Executive Committee, Conclusion No. 30, para. d.   [61] Ibid., para. e.

[62] See, inter alia, UNHCR Executive Committee, Conclusion No. 46 (XXVIII) (12 October 1987), para. j; UNHCR Executive Committee, Conclusion No. 65 (XLII) (11 October 1991), para. n; UNHCR Executive Committee, Conclusion No. 79 (XLVII) (11 October 1996), para. l; UNHCR Executive Committee, Conclusion No. 85 (XLIX) (9 October 1998), para. s; UNHCR Executive Committee, Conclusion No. 87(L) (8 October 1999), para. k.

[63] See, e.g., David A. Martin (ed.), The New Asylum-Seekers: Refugee Law in the 1980s (Leiden: Martinus Nijohff, 1988).

The European genesis of these standards is expressly recognized in the UNHCR background study to Conclusion No. 30. That study confirmed that the increase in unfounded asylum claims was a trend that affected 'a number of industrialized States',[64] before expressly acknowledging the wording of the adopted 'manifestly unfounded' or 'clearly abusive' definition as based upon 1981 Recommendation R(81) 16 of the Council of Europe Committee of Ministers to Member States.[65] There, the Council of Europe defined the 'abusive applications' referred to by UNHCR in Conclusion No. 8 as ones in which the claim 'is fraudulent or is related neither to the criteria for the granting of refugee status laid down in Article 1.A(2) of the [Refugee Convention] nor to other criteria justifying the granting of asylum'.[66]

The European influence on the general standards on accelerated procedures adopted by UNHCR is thus clearly demonstrated. Nonetheless, this soft law recommendation, entitled 'Harmonisation of national procedures relating to asylum', was itself an elaboration of the minimum procedural standards for refugee status determination expressed by Executive Committee Conclusion No. 8.[67]

Europe is also the continent where the general standards on accelerated procedures disseminated by UNHCR have subsequently received the greatest elaboration in the context of the harmonization of asylum procedures by the EU (in its various incarnations). This began with the resolution adopted in 1992 by the Ministers of Member States of the European Communities (EC) on 'manifestly unfounded applications for asylum', which specifically acknowledged the Executive Committee Conclusion No. 30 as its inspiration.[68] The adaptation process was continued by the Council of the EU in its 1995 resolution on 'minimum guarantees for asylum procedures'.[69] At the time of writing,

---

[64] UNHCR, *Follow-up on Earlier Conclusions of the Sub-Committee on the Determination of Refugee Status with Regard to the Problem of Manifestly Unfounded or Abusive Applications*, 26 August 1983 (UN Doc. EC/SCP/29), para. 3.

[65] *Ibid.*, para. 10.

[66] Council of Europe, Recommendation No. R (81) 16 of the Committee of Ministers to Member States on the harmonisation of national procedures relating to asylum, 5 November 1981, para. 4.

[67] *Ibid.*, preamble.

[68] Council of the European Union, Council Resolution of 30 November 1992 on manifestly unfounded applications for asylum, preamble.

[69] Council of the European Union, Council Resolution of 20 June 1995 on minimum guarantees for asylum procedures (OJ 1996 No. C274/13). For a detailed commentary on

the 2005 Council of the EU Procedures Directive represents the state of the art on accelerated procedures in Europe,[70] although proposals to recast this instrument are under discussion.[71] The five clusters of claim types currently outlined as examples of those suitable for accelerated procedures in the EU framework extend far beyond the range of scenarios deemed appropriate by Conclusion No. 30.[72]

C   Latin American emulation of European accelerated procedures

This section builds upon the preceding argument to show how the ultimately European standards on accelerated procedures disseminated by UNHCR have been emulated by the national asylum systems of Colombia, Ecuador, Panama and Venezuela. This emulation has been partial in that most of these States use accelerated procedures as a form of admissibility screening to prevent access by asylum seekers to the substantive refugee status determination process. Nonetheless, as in Europe, the challenges perceived as arising from new flows of displaced persons are the driving force behind the adoption of the procedures in Latin America. The section concludes by arguing that, while UNHCR guidelines may facilitate transmission of the technical framework developed in Europe, States' use of these procedures as a form of admissibility screening was directly inspired by European practice.

---

this and the 1992 Resolution, see Ingrid Boccardi, *Europe and Refugees: Towards an EU Asylum Policy* (London: Kluwer, 2002), pp. 75–8, 104–5.

[70] Council Directive 2005/85/EC of 13 December 2005 on minimum standards on procedures in Member States for granting and withdrawing refugee status (OJ 2005 No. L326/13), arts. 23(3)–(4), 28.

[71] European Commission, Amended Proposal for a Directive of the European Parliament and of the Council on common procedures for granting and withdrawing international protection status (recast) (COM(2011) 319 final), 1 June 2011.

[72] Above and beyond fraudulent claims and those not disclosing relevant grounds for asylum, the EU Procedures Directive provisions on accelerated procedures also encompass claims to which safe third-country or country of origin arrangements apply, where the applicant is a danger to the national security or public order of the Member State, and vexatious applications: Hemme Battjes, *European Asylum Law and International Law* (Leiden and Boston: Martinus Nijhoff, 2006), p. 335. An even greater range of grounds was put forward in the 1992 Resolution, but these were effectively disowned by the Commission in 1997: Maria-Teresa Gil-Bazo, 'Accelerated Procedures in European Union Law', in Ashley Terlouw (ed.), *Binnen 48 uur. Zorgvuldige behandeling van asielverzoeken?* (Nijmegen: Wolf Legal Publishers, 2003), pp. 268–70.

1   Accelerated procedures in the Andes and Central America

Unlike European States, those in Latin America have not developed a regional harmonized position on accelerated procedures.[73] Rather, such procedures have been adopted in a piecemeal fashion by Colombia, Ecuador, Panama and Venezuela, as neighbouring States in the Andean–Central American subregions. Like the wider national asylum systems in most of these States,[74] their accelerated procedures have been created by the exercise of discretionary rule-making powers either by the president of the Republic (Colombia, Ecuador and Panama) or the national Inter-Ministerial Commission (Venezuela), rather than by laws passed by the legislature.

The pattern of adoption of these accelerated procedures is also intriguing. Although they were adopted by Panama in 1998 through a presidential decree that created its present asylum system,[75] other States adopted them over a decade later. This happened next in Ecuador through a 2009 presidential decree that amended parts of the existing asylum system.[76] However, the provisions on accelerated procedures caused such an outcry from UNHCR and civil society representatives that Ecuador delayed making them operational until early 2011.[77] In Colombia, accelerated procedures formed part of a 2009 presidential decree that replaced the entire existing asylum system *de novo*.[78] The relevant Venezuelan provisions were adopted in the 2010 Regulations of the national refugee authority.[79] The clustering of these developments over the past three years, and the outlier of Panama, raise interesting questions regarding the driving factors at play in these neighbouring States. Nevertheless, it is clear that the procedures adopted directly emulate Executive Committee Conclusion No. 30.

---

[73] Wider Latin American processes of refugee law harmonization differ sharply from those undertaken in Europe. For a description, see José H. Fischel de Andrade, 'Regional Policy Approaches and Harmonization: A Latin American Perspective' (1998) 10 *International Journal of Refugee Law* 389–409.

[74] With the exception of Venezuela, the general asylum system of each of the other three States was itself established by presidential decree rather than by organic law.

[75] Decree 23/98, arts. 40–41.   [76] Decree 1635/09 (25 March 2009), art. 3.

[77] Interviews 16, 17. The implementing instrument was Ministerial Accord 003 (11 January 2011) signed by the Minister for External Relations, Trade and Integration, unpublished, on file with the author. The following year, Decree 1182/12 was adopted to replace the earlier Ecuadorian instruments. It further formalized the use of accelerated procedures (arts. 24–26 and 31–33).

[78] Decree 4503/09, arts. 11–12.

[79] Internal Regulations of the National Refugee Commission (28 January 2010), arts. 24–25.

Most of the relevant national instruments expressly acknowledge this UNHCR influence. The 1998 Panamanian Decree explicitly recognizes Executive Committee Conclusions as 'documents for consultation',[80] reflecting UNHCR participation in the drafting process.[81] The 2009 Colombian Decree proclaims the conformity of its accelerated procedures to 'the guidelines stipulated by the Executive Committee of UNHCR'.[82] The 2011 Ecuadorian Ministerial Accord – implementing the accelerated procedures in the 2009 Decree – is even more explicit in its preamble. This declares that Executive Committee recommendations must be complied with and reproduces text from Conclusion No. 30 to affirm (incorrectly) that the Executive Committee has proclaimed the incorporation of accelerated procedures in national asylum systems as a duty upon States.[83]

The national instruments follow Conclusion No. 30 in considering that accelerated procedures may be applied only to claims that are 'manifestly unfounded' or 'clearly abusive'. Their conception of these two notions is also close to the definitions provided by the Executive Committee. They uniformly consider that claims bearing no relation to the criteria for asylum are 'manifestly unfounded', although the 2009 Colombian Decree defines this rather widely.[84] Similarly, they characterize 'clearly abusive' claims as based on fraudulent behaviour, although the precise definition varies to encompass 'fraudulent' claims (Panama), claims where the 'falsity of the grounds alleged' is observed (Venezuela), and claims where asylum is invoked 'to avoid justice or compliance with the law' or evidencing 'manipulation of the process and/or deception to obtain personal or collective benefits' (Ecuador).[85] The 2009 Colombian Decree identifies as 'clearly abusive' claims where 'the principal motivation consists in misleading or deceiving

---

[80] Decree 23/98, art. 77.   [81] Interview 89.   [82] Decree 4503/09, art. 11.

[83] The preamble does so by changing the wording of the paragraph quoted above as text to n. 58 from 'may usefully include' to 'must include' accelerated procedures.

[84] Decree 4503/09, art. 11, para. 1 states that this refers to claims which 'do not show the existence of a well-founded fear of persecution' or in which the reasons for leaving the country of origin 'clearly fall outside' those for refugee status.

[85] Ministerial Accord 003, art. 2(d). Article 3 states that the first category of 'abusive' applications is inadmissible since these circumstances do not fall within the competence of the Ministry of External Relations, as the institutional locus for receiving applications for asylum. The new framework adopted by Ecuador in 2012 largely mirrors the earlier provisions on manifestly unfounded and clearly abusive claims (see Decree 1182/12, arts. 24–25). It also creates a novel category of 'illegitimate' claims (art. 26) subject to even more severe procedural strictures (art. 33, para. 3). This concept applies when there are serious reasons to believe that a claimant has committed, on Ecuadorian territory, acts that would merit exclusion from refugee status pursuant to art. 10 of the same decree.

the [RSD authorities]' and provides a lengthy list of examples of such behaviour.[86] In practice, Colombia also tends to use its time limit for claiming asylum as an admissibility device.[87]

The technical aspects of these accelerated procedures are clearly based upon Conclusion No. 30. However, these standards have also been adapted to local requirements. As will become evident in the discussion of the new migration challenges that have driven this change, the clearest example of local adaptation is one of the 'clearly abusive' behaviours listed in the 2009 Colombian Decree: '[T]he applicant has been intercepted by immigration authorities in the process of leaving [Colombia]'.[88]

In general, however, the national frameworks for accelerated procedures in all four of these States emulate the standards set out by the Council of Europe and disseminated by UNHCR. Moreover, these States have not been influenced by the definitional elaboration of these concepts undertaken by the EU, nor by its extension of such procedures to a wider range of grounds. Some terminology that accords closely with that found in the EC 1992 Resolution and EU 2005 Procedures Directive among the additional Colombian examples of 'clearly abusive' behaviour is the exception in this regard.[89]

There is one important way in which contemporary asylum practices of European States, particularly Spain,[90] have inspired the implementation of this framework. This is the tendency of Latin American States to treat accelerated procedures as a form of screening prior to an asylum seeker's admission to the substantive refugee status determination process, rather than an accelerated form of the normal process. This is explicit in the Ecuadorian framework, which describes the procedure

---

[86] Decree 4503/09, art. 11, para. 2.

[87] The Colombian framework (like that of some of the other neighbouring States) has long stipulated the time period within which asylum applications must be lodged: Decree 2817, art. 3 gave 30 days; Decree 4503/09, art. 5 now gives 60 days. Although persons submitting an application outside this time limit are required by the provisions to explain their lack of compliance, the legal effects of the non-compliance are not specified. In practice, however, it appears that Colombia treats this as another ground for inadmissibility: Interviews 1, 143.

[88] Decree 4503/09, art. 11, para. 2(a).

[89] In Decree 4503/09, the art. 11, para. 2 grounds that '[i]t is proved that documentation has been destroyed [by the applicant] with the intention of deceiving the authorities about her personal data or identity' and '[f]alse or doctored documentation is presented and their authenticity is insisted upon [by the applicant]' are similar to grounds listed in the 1992 EC Resolution of the Council of Immigration Ministers at para. 9(a) and (c). The art. 11, para. 2 ground that the '[authority] verifies the repeated presentation of applications by the same person that do not identify new elements in justification' is similar to the 2005 Procedures Directive, art. 23(4)(h).

[90] See Part 3(a) below.

as one of admissibility.[91] While the Colombian and Panamanian instruments describe the procedures as a rapid route to rejection of the substantive claim,[92] in practice both treat them as a form of admissibility proceeding.[93] In these States, the percentage of asylum claims rejected without substantive consideration as a result of being declared inadmissible is worryingly high[94] as a result of the legal concepts of 'manifestly unfounded' and 'clearly abusive' being applied in an arbitrary fashion.[95] Practitioners argue that this admissibility issue is currently the most serious refugee protection problem in these States.[96]

The problem is further exacerbated by the structure of the accelerated procedures. It is true that all States at least provide for an interview with the national refugee authority as recommended by Conclusion No. 30. However, Panama – and formerly Ecuador – departs from the terms of Conclusion No. 30 by denying any possibility of challenging negative decisions on admissibility.[97] In Colombia and Venezuela, challenges to negative decisions on admissibility are permitted through an application for reconsideration,[98] which is decided at the discretion of the national administrative authority that made the original decision. The inherent emphasis on unfettered State discretion in granting asylum demonstrates the continuing force of the trope of political asylum in Latin American refugee law. Combined with the use of accelerated procedures as a form of admissibility, it raises serious questions about the compatibility of these procedures with the obligation under international law to determine claims for refugee status fairly.[99]

---

[91] Ministerial Accord 003, art. 7; now replaced by Decree 1182/12, arts. 31–33. This is also the case for the El Salvadorian framework established by Decree 79/05.

[92] Decree 4503/09 (Colombia), art. 12; Decree 23/98 (Panama), art. 41.

[93] Interviews 1, 61.

[94] Precise figures were not available at the time of fieldwork. Nonetheless, it was reported that in Ecuador even among Colombian claims some 30 per cent were rejected as inadmissible (Interview 16), while in Panama only 6 per cent of cases actually reached consideration by the Commission, many of the remaining 94 per cent having been rejected as inadmissible (Interview 62).

[95] Interviews 1, 3, 16, 61, 96, 143.   [96] Interview 62.

[97] Decree 23/98 (Panama), art. 41. Ministerial Accord 003 (Ecuador), art. 7, para. 3 denied the possibility of appeal. This has now apparently been changed by art. 33 of Decree 1182/12 (Ecuador), which gives claimants a period of 'up to 3 days' to challenge the decision on administrative grounds.

[98] Decree 4503/09 (Colombia), art. 12(3); 2010 Regulations (Venezuela), art. 25(4).

[99] For more on the scope of this obligation, see Guy S. Goodwin-Gill and Jane McAdam, *The Refugee in International Law* (3rd edn, Oxford: Oxford University Press, 2007), pp. 528–37.

2   Drivers for change

States' adoption of accelerated procedures responds to new challenges and uncertainty perceived in the pressures placed on the national asylum systems by particular refugee flows. The fact that Colombia, Ecuador, Panama and Venezuela have emulated these ultimately European devices is no accident. Indeed, these States have been among the most affected by two of the major flows of refugees to impact on Latin America in the past fifteen years. In each State, the change has been prompted by one or both of the following factors: first, the significant outflow of Colombians in need of international protection to neighbouring countries since the mid-1990s; and, second, the increasing number of so-called 'extracontinentales' (migrants from outside the Americas) claiming asylum in their territories from 2008 onwards.

(a)   Upsurge in Colombian refugees

One factor driving the adoption of accelerated procedures has been the increased number of Colombians seeking asylum in the territories of neighbouring States since the mid-1990s, particularly in the more lawless border regions.[100] The approach adopted by Ecuador, Panama and Venezuela towards this still largely 'invisible' population is heavily influenced by their shifting international relations with Colombia.[101] Nonetheless, all three countries tend to view the spillover of the Colombian conflict and refugees as presenting threats that need to be addressed within the framework of national security.

Panama tends to view refugees as a national security issue,[102] and accelerated procedures were introduced as part of the creation of a modern asylum system by a 1998 presidential decree that responded to displacement effects of the intensification of the armed conflict in such neighbouring

---

[100] As at the end of 2010, it was estimated that Ecuador, Panama and Venezuela collectively hosted 337,302 of a global total of 395,600 Colombian refugees and persons in a refugee-like situation and 55,655 of a global total of 59,954 Colombian asylum seekers: UNHCR, *2010 Global Trends* (June 2011), Annex, tables 5 and 12.

[101] See Martin Gottwald, 'Protecting Colombian Refugees in the Andean Region: The Fight against Invisibility' (2004) 16 *International Journal of Refugee Law* 517–46 and, more recently, David J. Cantor, 'Restitution, Compensation, Satisfaction: Transnational Reparations and Colombia's Victims' Law' (UNHCR, New Issues in Refugee Research, Research Paper No. 215, August 2011).

[102] Interview 61.

regions of Colombia as the Chocó.[103] Similarly, Ecuador implemented accelerated procedures in 2011 as part of a backlash against the system of 'expanded registration' (registro ampliado) that it had devised in consultation with UNHCR.[104] This ran parallel to the normal asylum process and recognized 27,740 Colombian refugees during its one year of operation between 2009 and 2010.[105] There was a strong perception in official circles that this system had been too open to abuse by economic migrants and criminal elements from Colombia and was therefore responsible for increased insecurity in Ecuador.[106] Although officials initially signalled that the accelerated procedures would be applied only to extracontinentales, they are also applied to Colombian asylum claims.[107] In both States, therefore, security risks perceived in the Colombian refugee dynamic contributed to the implementation of accelerated procedures.

(b)   Flows of extracontinentales

The second, and arguably most significant, driver in the emulation of accelerated procedures is the challenges felt most acutely by this group of States as a result of the dramatic increase in asylum claims from extracontinentales since the second half of 2008. The majority of these extracontinentales are irregular migrants from Africa (particularly the Horn of Africa) and Asia (particularly South-East Asia).[108] While the arrival of these nationalities in Latin America is not new, and the absolute numbers remain small,[109] the increase in asylum claims by extracontinentales

---

[103] Indeed, a sustained increase can be charted in the numbers of refugees – predominantly Colombians – arriving in Panama in the two years preceding its adoption: UNHCR, Refugees and Others of Concern to UNHCR: 1998 Statistical Overview (July 2000), table I.4.

[104] It was based on similar experimental procedures developed by UNCHR in Malaysia and for Iraqis in Jordan, Syria and Lebanon: Dirección General de Refugiados, Política del Ecuador en materia de refugio (Quito: Ministerio de Relaciones Exteriores, Comercio e Integracíon, 2008), p. 37.

[105] It also registered 1,169 persons as asylum seekers for more in-depth investigation of their claims for asylum: Johanna Roldán León, 'El registro ampliado de refugiados en la frontera norte del Ecuador: un proyecto pionero en la protección internacional de refugiados en la región', in UNHCR, La protección internacional de refugiados, p. 83.

[106] Interviews 10, 11, 16, 54.   [107] Interviews 16, 51.

[108] Araceli Azuara, 'Panorama general de la migración extracontinental en las Américas', in OAS Comisión Especial de Asuntos Migratorios, Memoria: Migración extracontinental en las Américas (6 April 2010), pp. 3–6.

[109] For instance, UNHCR reported that in 2008–09, the number of asylum applications by extracontinentales in the whole of Latin America still only numbered around 2,500: cited in International Organization for Migration (IOM), Informe preliminar a la XI Conferencia Sudamericana sobre Migraciones: Migrantes extracontinentales en Sudamérica (August 2011), p. 0.

year on year since 2008 is significant. Recent figures suggest that *extracontinentales* account for up to 40 per cent of asylum claims lodged in some Latin American States.[110] Indeed, it has been estimated that the number of *extracontinentales* claiming asylum in Colombia quadrupled in just one year.[111]

There are several features of this increased migration pattern to Latin America that have prompted concern among States in the Andean and Central American zones. First, the *extracontinentales* are generally groups of young men of working age whose arrival in Latin America is facilitated through international trafficking networks.[112] Second, their ultimate destination is usually the US or Canada, with Latin American States being simply transit countries in this new migratory route towards the global North.[113] Thus, most *extracontinentales* enter the region through either Ecuador or Brazil and then continue their journey northwards through Latin America by land and/or sea.[114] Indeed, the upsurge in the number of *extracontinentales* corresponds closely to Ecuador's elimination of visa requirements for most nationalities in 2008 as part of the 'universal citizenship' agenda of its president.[115] Latin American States, however, argue that the use of new migratory routes through the region also results from Europe's recent 'strengthening [of] border controls' in an attempt to dissuade irregular migration.[116] As such, while European practice offers a model for responding to new migratory flows, it is also perceived as a cause of these new uncertainties in Latin America.

The means and source of this migration is cited by these States as a national security concern, both in terms of the criminality of the

---

[110] UNHCR, 'Africans and Asians Attracted to Latin America as a Migration Route', 10 November 2010 www.unhcr.org/refworld/docid/4cdba5f82.html (accessed 1 October 2012).

[111] Interview 1.

[112] There are, however, cases of single women, unaccompanied minors and a few families: see Facultad Latinoamericana de Ciencias Sociales (Costa Rica), *Diagnóstico sobre la situación actual, tendencias y necesidades de protección y asistencia de las personas migrantes y refugiadas extracontinentales en México y América Central* (2011).

[113] While in Brazil and Argentina some of the refugees settle permanently, this tendency is less notable in the Andes and Central America: Juan Carlos Murillo González, 'Principios básicos y posibles respuesta programáticas', in OAS Comisión Especial de Asuntos Migratorios, *Memoria: Migración extracontinental en la Américas* (6 April 2010), pp. 19, 22.

[114] IOM, *Informe preliminar*, pp. 10–11.

[115] Interview 3. The concept of 'universal citizenship' is given expression in the 2008 Political Constitution of Ecuador, art. 416(6).

[116] Azuara, 'Panorama general', 3.

trafficking networks and the fear that, because many come from countries in conflict, the migrants themselves 'could be linked to illegal groups'.[117] For example, Ecuador detained over sixty mostly South Asian migrants in March 2011.[118] Those who claimed asylum had their claims treated as inadmissible.[119] While most were eventually deported, a few were rapidly and summarily rendered to Guantánamo Bay as suspected terrorists, apparently at the request of the US.[120] Yet, more generally, all States cited as a serious abuse of their asylum systems the fact that many *extracontinentales* only claimed asylum when detected by the authorities, and then abandoned the territory to travel northwards without waiting for the final decision, or even after having been recognized as refugees.[121] These concerns about abuse of the institution of asylum have led to regional debate in Latin American forums on the issue of *extracontinentales*.[122] At the national level, however, the typical response is simply to utilize accelerated procedures to reject the asylum claims of *extracontinentales* as inadmissible.[123]

3   Factors facilitating emulation of Europe

The argument thus far has endeavoured to show that new perceived asylum challenges have driven the emulation by certain Latin American States of an accelerated procedures framework developed in Europe. This section argues that the process of emulation has been facilitated by two distinct factors. The first is the example that the use of accelerated procedures as a form of admissibility proceeding by European States,

---

[117] *Ibid.*, 8.

[118] Interview 12. See also the reports of these events in the *El Comercio* newspaper of Ecuador, e.g., '3 paquistaníes detenidos en Quito aceptan vínculos con terrorismo' (14 September 2011).

[119] Interview 14.   [120] Interview 12.   [121] Murillo González, 'Principios básicos', 20.

[122] To date, the issue has been debated by States, UNHCR and other organizations in the 2009 UNHCR Regional Conference in San José (UNHCR, *Summary Report: Regional Conference on Refugee Protection and International Migration in the Americas – Protection Considerations in the Context of Mixed Migration* (San José, Costa Rica, 19–20 November 2009), pp. 14–15), the 2010 OAS Special Commission on Migration Matters (OAS Comisión Especial de Asuntos Migratorios, *Memoria: Migración extracontinental en la Américas* (6 April 2010)), and the 2010 Meeting of the Regional Consultation Group on Migration and 2011 XI Conference of the Regional Migration Conference (Puebla Process) (see, e.g., Conclusiones de la Reunión del Grupo Regional de Consulta sobre Migración de la Conferencia Regional sobre Migración (Querétaro, Mexico, 16–18 November 2010); IOM, *Informe Preliminar*).

[123] Interviews 1, 14, 17, 62.

such as Spain, represents for other parts of the world in addressing mixed migration challenges. The second is the profile of UNHCR and its role within the region, which has facilitated the use of UNHCR standards as a basis for the technical framework of accelerated procedures.

(a)   Spain as a European model of deterrence

A common language (Spanish) and a similar administrative and legal system make Spain an accessible example of European asylum practice for Latin American States. Although few of the Latin American accelerated procedures provisions are modelled directly on Spanish law, Spain has provided a strong source of inspiration for the use of admissibility proceedings as a form of deterrence.[124] This practice was introduced into Spanish law in 1994 through amendments to its previously generous asylum system that allowed accelerated procedures to be employed on the wide range of grounds outlined in the 1992 EC Resolution.[125] Ostensibly 'to avoid the fraudulent use of the system ... by economic migrants',[126] these changes were required by its entry into the European Communities and Schengen Area.[127] By the early 2000s, it was estimated that over 70 per cent of asylum claims in Spain were denied access to substantive consideration through this mechanism.[128]

Spain has certainly served as a direct inspiration for the adoption of admissibility procedures by Latin American States. For instance, Colombian officials have referred to practices by European countries, including Spain, as a justification for their use of national provisions to declare as inadmissible any asylum application lodged later than sixty days after arrival in the country.[129] Spanish practice is also clearly the inspiration for the admissibility procedures adopted by Ecuador. Indeed, immediately

---

[124] EU-influenced Spanish legislation has also provided a partial template for more positive developments in Latin America in the form of instruments that provide for 'complementary protection' status alongside refugee status (for example, the recent Mexican Law on Refugees and Complementary Protection (27 January 2011), art. 28).

[125] Law 5/1984 (as amended by Law 9/1994), art. 5(6).   [126] Law 9/1994, preamble.

[127] Maria-Teresa Gil-Bazo, 'The Role of Spain as a Gateway to the Schengen Area: Changes in Asylum Law and their Implications for Human Rights' (1998) 10 *International Journal of Refugee Law* 214–29, at 216.

[128] Maryellen Fullerton, 'Inadmissible in Iberia: The Fate of Asylum Seekers in Spain and Portugal' (2005) 17 *International Journal of Refugee Law* 659–87, at 669. These procedures were reformulated in 2009 along with the rest of the asylum system by a national law in light, *inter alia*, of the requirements of the 2005 EU Procedures Directive (see Law 12/2009, art. 25).

[129] Interview 143.

prior to drafting the decree that provided for procedures to deal with manifestly unfounded claims, Ecuadorian officials expressed a strong interest in how Spain used inadmissibility procedures and requested substantial information regarding the relevant Spanish laws.[130] This information appears to have been channelled to the Ecuadorian authorities through UNHCR. The broader point here is that these Latin American States are drawn to emulate European practice – and not, for example, that of the US or Australia – through the accessible and powerful model of deterrence offered by Spain.

(b)   UNHCR as a mediating agency

While European practice appears to have inspired interest among Latin American States in using accelerated procedures as a form of admissibility screening, Latin American procedures themselves are directly based upon the terminology of UNHCR Executive Committee Conclusion No. 30. This particular guidance is rooted directly in the concepts developed by the Council of Europe, which have been further elaborated under the CEAS.[131] Europe is thus the originator of the concepts expressed by Conclusion No. 30.

UNHCR's role as the crucial point of external reference on refugee protection for most Latin American States has helped to facilitate their reference to Conclusion No. 30 as a technical model for national regulations. However, even though UNHCR offices in Colombia, Ecuador, Panama and Venezuela provide advice and assistance to the national governments on legal and policy development, the agency's satisfaction with the final outcome is far from assured. In Colombia and Ecuador, for instance, proposals on the form of accelerated procedures being developed by UNHCR in partnership with the State and civil society organizations were ultimately ignored in favour of a more stringent framework.[132] Across these States, UNHCR has been critical also of the use of admissibility procedures to prevent access to the minimum procedural guarantees provided for in the substantive refugee status determination process.[133]

The fact that Conclusion No. 30 is itself based upon the standards developed by the Council of Europe in 1981 brings into focus a wider question raised by this study. Clearly, UNHCR's non-binding standards in any area of refugee protection are themselves drafted in a sufficiently

---

[130] Interview 16.   [131] See Part B above.   [132] Interviews 1, 16, 17.
[133] Interviews 14, 62, 143.

broad manner so as to facilitate their 'fit' with the variety of different legal and administrative systems that are employed around the world, and hence their adoption by States. Nonetheless, the background 'problem' that prompts the drafting of such standards, as well as the detail of the standards themselves, will often result from some particular refugee crisis affecting one or more States or groups of States. Particularly in regions such as Latin America where UNHCR has played a prominent role in the promotion and development of refugee law at the national and regional levels, a broader question may instead be formulated: to what extent are UNHCR policy standards generally influenced or inspired by developments in Europe (or any other region of the world)?

D   Conclusion: future prospects

This chapter has established a history of partial emulation of European asylum practices by Latin American States, starting with the acceptance of the Old World concept of political asylum and ending with the recent adoption of European accelerated refugee status determination procedures by certain Andean and Central American States. In general, it has shown that such emulation is driven by uncertainty arising from the identification of new kinds of forced displacement within the region, and is facilitated by the compatibility between Latin American and Spanish legal systems, as well as by the presence of UNHCR. The aim here is not to underplay local innovation in Latin American refugee law, the significance of which has been documented elsewhere. Rather, this important understanding must be complemented by the acknowledgement of the powerful example that Europe offers for the development of refugee law in other parts of the world.

The adoption by States in the Andean–Central American 'bridge' of special procedural devices for dealing with 'manifestly unfounded' or 'clearly abusive' asylum applications constitutes one contemporary example of this phenomenon. This emulation has been accompanied by the utilization of other 'European' asylum practices in these Latin American States during the past few years. Thus, since 2008, there has been a notable increase in the use of administrative detention for illegal entry, as well as interception at sea and in transit countries.[134] Deportations and expulsions of asylum seekers – especially *extracontinentales* – have also increased dramatically in

---

[134] Murillo González, 'Principios básicos', 20.

this part of the world.[135] Ad hoc practices involving readmission of asylum seekers and refugees registered by one State but later detected on the territory of a second State, have also been observed.[136] While the US, Australia and other parts of the world may make use of similar measures, the coherence and power of the combined European framework invests them with a particular appeal and authority, not least among those States with colonial or linguistic ties to one or more of the former European powers.

One question for the future is whether this latest round of emulation is temporary. A dominant factor driving the adoption of such measures has been the increase in the number of arrivals of *extracontinentales* following the abolition of many visa requirements to enter Ecuador. During interviews, officials and practitioners in various States expressed the hope that Ecuador's reintroduction of visa requirements for the ten main nationalities of *extracontinentales* in late 2010 would help to resolve the problem.[137] At the time of writing, it is not clear whether this has resulted in a sustainable drop in numbers or simply a reorienting of the migration routes on the part of the traffickers.[138] If the latter, the question is whether this might lead newly affected Latin American States to consider introducing similar admissibility procedures as those adopted by the States studied here. In any event, the data raise the wider question whether Latin America may one day follow the European path of instituting regional procedures for dealing with secondary movements and other 'troublesome' aspects of asylum.

Finally, the Latin American dynamics described in this chapter raise a set of questions about the wider global consequences of present restrictive approaches to asylum in Europe. Even if Latin American States have been vociferous in their objections to elements of EU migration policy, it is clear that the measures these same States have adopted to deal with the asylum–migration nexus are inspired by the same source. European asylum policies may serve not to contain migratory flows but rather to channel them to other parts of the world. If other regional blocs follow the same restrictive set of practices towards asylum as those presently dominant in Europe, this raises the possibility of any diverted irregular migration routes simply reorienting themselves once again towards Europe. In short, Europe's construction of an 'asylum' fortress can

---

[135] This is the case in Colombia: see IOM, *Informe preliminar*, p. 15.
[136] Murillo González, 'Principios básicos', 21.   [137] Interviews 3, 17.
[138] Interviews 3, 62.

maintain its logic only at the expense of pushing these issues towards other less well-resourced States. Its implications for the long-standing principle of international cooperation and burden-sharing of the refugee 'problem' are significant.

APPENDIX   INTERVIEW LIST

Colombia

1. Project head, humanitarian organization, Colombia, 31 March 2011
3. Lawyer, university law clinic, 1 April 2011
143. Official, humanitarian organization, Colombia, 9 May 2011

Ecuador

10. Director, governmental body, Ecuador, 4 April 2011
11, 12, 17. Official, humanitarian organization, Ecuador, 3–5 April 2011
14. Lawyer, humanitarian organization, Ecuador, 5 April 2011
16. Official, humanitarian organization, Ecuador, 5 April 2011
51. Head, humanitarian organization, Ecuador, 14 April 2011
54. Director, governmental body, Ecuador, 14 April 2011
56. Three lawyers, governmental body, Ecuador, 15 April 2011
60. Official, governmental body, 15 April 2011

Panama

61. Director and three other lawyers, humanitarian organization, Panama, 18 April 2011
62. Head, humanitarian organization, Panama, 18 April 2011
81. Director, humanitarian organization, Panama, 25 April 2011
82. Official, governmental body, Panama, 25 April 2011
89. Lawyer, independent, Panama, 25 April 2011
96. Official, governmental body, Panama, 26 April 2011

Venezuela

99. Head and other lawyer, humanitarian organization, Venezuela, 28 April 2011
107. President, governmental body, Venezuela, 28 April 2011

4

A safe country to emulate? Canada and the European refugee

AUDREY MACKLIN

A Introduction

Asylum policies seem to migrate across borders with notably greater ease than asylum seekers themselves. Many – though not all – of these 'mobile' asylum policy instruments aim to securitize, deter, deflect and reject asylum seekers. The easy circulation and morphing of ideas between Canada, the US, Australia, the EU Member States and the EU itself can make it difficult to identify sources or label any particular iteration as an instance of emulation.

Canada is both sending and receiving country for this policy migration: in the 1980s, Canada pioneered techniques of deterritorialized border control by posting Canadian immigration officers at airports overseas to scrutinize documents of embarking passengers bound for Canada. It also imposed penalties on air and sea carriers who transported undocumented or improperly documented migrants. Jurisprudence from the Canadian courts, especially in the early 1990s, advanced the recognition of non-State actors as agents of persecution, and civilian victims of civil war violence as potential refugees. Canada's Immigration and Refugee Board introduced the precedential gender–persecution guidelines in 1993,[1] which were explicitly commended and adapted transnationally and globally. In the early 1990s, Canada unsuccessfully attempted to import the safe third-country model of the Dublin

---

Special thanks to Krista Stout for her excellent research assistance, as well as to the Social Sciences and Humanities Research Council of Canada for its financial support.
[1] Immigration and Refugee Board, 'Women Refugee Claimants Fearing Gender-Related Persecution: Guidelines Issued by the Chairperson Pursuant to Section 65(3) of the Immigration Act' (effective 13 November 1996) www.irb-cisr.gc.ca/eng/brdcom/referen ces/pol/guidir/pages/women.aspx (accessed 11 October 2012).

Convention (later Regulation)[2] as a means of deflecting the 40 per cent of asylum seekers who arrived via the US–Canada border. However, the impact of 9/11 on Canada–US border management created a political context within which Canada could negotiate the Canada–US Safe Third Country Agreement.[3]

In mid-2012, the Canadian government passed Bill C-31, Protecting Canada's Immigration System Act (Bill C31), which amended the existing Immigration and Refugee Protection Act (IRPA) regarding asylums seekers in several respects: Bill C-31 expands executive powers to detain asylum seekers, bars access to permanent residence and family reunification for five years for certain refugees, truncates the refugee determination process, and extracts and shares biometric data about asylum seekers.[4]

The asylum policies of Canada and each of its 'peer' jurisdictions coalesce around an intractable paradox:[5] every asylum seeker who reaches the frontier of a State Party simultaneously embodies that State's international protection obligation under the Refugee Convention, and the failure of that State's border control apparatus to prevent the asylum seeker's arrival. And each State, including Canada, strives to perfect border control, usually at the expense of protection.

The 2012 revisions to Canadian refugee law include a new safe country of origin (SCO) provision. The Minister of Citizenship and Immigration

[2] Convention determining the State responsible for examining applications for asylum lodged in one of the Member States of the European Communities, 15 June 1990 (OJ 1997 No. C245/1); Council Regulation (EC) No. 343/2003 of 18 February 2003 establishing the criteria and mechanisms for determining the member state responsible for examining an asylum application lodged in one of the member states by a third-country national (OJ 2003 No. L50/1).
[3] Agreement between the Government of Canada and the Government of the United States of America for Cooperation in the Examination of Refugee Status Claims from Nationals of Third Countries, 29 December 2004 www.cic.gc.ca/english/department/laws-policy/safe-third.asp (accessed 11 October 2012). See Audrey Macklin, 'Disappearing Refugees: Reflections on the Canada–US Safe Third Country Agreement' (2005) 36 *Columbia Human Rights Law Review* 365–426. See also *Canadian Council for Refugees* v. *Canada* (2007), 2007 FC 1262, reversed (2008), 2008 FCA 229, leave to appeal to SCC refused (5 February 2009), 395 NR 387n.
[4] Bill C-31, Protecting Canada's Immigration System Act, 1st Sess., 41st Parl., 2012 (assented to 28 June 2012), SC 2012, c. 17. Bill C-31 amends the Immigration and Refugee Protection Act (IRPA), SC 2001, c. 27, as well as the Balanced Refugee Reform Act (BRRA), SC 2010, c. 8, a bill that was passed in June 2010 but whose provisions did not come into force prior to Bill-31.
[5] Convention relating to the Status of Refugees, Geneva, 28 July 1951, in force 22 April 1954 (189 UNTS 137), read in conjunction with the Protocol relating to the Status of Refugees, New York, adopted 31 January 1967, in force 4 October 1967 (606 UNTS 267).

is authorized to designate certain countries of origin of asylum seekers as 'safe',[6] with the consequence that the protection claims of asylum seekers from those States will be subject to comparatively inferior refugee determination process and reception conditions. The political context of the SCO provision is the disproportionate representation of Hungarian Roma among asylum seekers in Canadian refugee statistics, and the government's targeting of Roma as 'bogus' asylum seekers bent on abusing Canada's asylum and social welfare system.[7] In effect, the SCO concept was imported by Canada from European States in order to repel European asylum seekers from Canada.

Draft regulations under the new law propose to cut by half the time available to SCO asylum seekers from the initial referral of an asylum claim to the hearing date.[8] They will also be denied access to an administrative appeal on the merits.[9] Although they may apply for judicial review of their rejection, removal orders will not be stayed pending an application, meaning that State authorities may deport asylum seekers before a court decides to hear their case.[10]

With respect to reception conditions, an SCO asylum seeker is prohibited from seeking a work permit for six months.[11] An Executive Order dealing with healthcare strips asylum seekers from SCOs of access

[6] IRPA, s. 109.1 (as amended by Bill C-31, SC 2012, c. 17, s. 58) (not yet in force). The provision technically uses the term 'Designated Country of Origin' (DCO) under the amended IRPA, but will be referred to in this chapter as SCO.

[7] See, e.g., Kathryn Blaze Carlson, 'Record number of Hungarian asylum-seekers landing on Canada's doorstep', National Post, 4 November 2011 http://news.nationalpost.com/2011/11/04/record-number-of-hungarian-asylum-seekers-landing-on-canadas-doorstep/ (accessed 15 October 2012); 'Tories sweeping immigration reforms target influx of claims from Roma gypsies', National Post, 16 February 2012 http://news.nationalpost.com/2012/02/16/conserva tives-to-announce-further-barriers-to-deter-bogus-refugee-claimants-report/ (accessed 11 October 2012); Will Campbell, 'Federal government considers detaining Roma refugee claimants, report suggests', Globe and Mail, 18 August 2012 www.theglobeandmail.com/news/politics/federal-government-considers-detaining-roma-refugee-claimants-report-suggests/article4487855/ (accessed 15 October 2012). The other target group of the SCO was Mexicans.

[8] IRPA, subs. 111.1(2) (as amended by Bill C-31 2012, c. 17, s. 59) (not yet in force); IRPA, s. 113.1 (as amended by Bill C-31 2012, c. 17, s. 40) (not yet in force); Proposed Regulations Amending the Immigration and Refugee Protection Regulations, SC 2012, c. 17, s. 59, subs. 159(9) (not yet in force) www.gazette.gc.ca/rp-pr/p1/2012/2012-08-04/html/reg1-eng.html (accessed 5 October 2012) ('Proposed Regulations'): the time limit for claimants from SCOs is 30 or 45 days, whereas it is 60 days for those from non-SCOs.

[9] IRPA, subs. 110(2)(d.1) (as amended by Bill C-31 2012, c. 17, s. 84) (not yet in force).

[10] Ibid., subs. 48(2) (as amended by Bill C-31, 2012, c. 17, s. 20) (not yet in force); ibid., subs. 49(1)(a) (in force).

[11] Proposed Regulations, s. 206 (not yet in force).

to public healthcare unless they pose a risk to public health or safety.[12] Emergency care will be denied unless the failure to treat puts at risk the welfare of Canadians who might come into contact with them.[13] Here, then, is what appears to be a textbook case of Canada emulating Europe: the SCO principle is directly traceable to 'white lists' of safe countries introduced by several European States in the 1990s, including Canada's imperial progenitor, the UK.[14] Indeed, the Canadian government explicitly invoked the UK, Ireland, France, Germany, the Netherlands, Norway, Switzerland and Finland as precedents for its own SCO provision.[15] The EU Qualification Directive authorizes Member States to use SCO lists in their national asylum regimes, and also contemplates the adoption of a common EU-level list of safe countries to which all Member States would subscribe.[16] The logic animating SCO lists is that asylum seekers from designated States are opportunistic migrants exploiting the refugee system (including its slow pace) to circumvent more restrictive admissions regimes for non-citizens. Therefore, the pursuit of efficiency,

[12] Order Respecting the Interim Federal Health Program, 2012, in force 30 June 2012, SI 2012–26, Canada Gazette Vol. 146(9) 2012, repealing Order in Council PC 157-11/848 of June 20, 1957, as amended by Order Amending the Order Respecting the Interim Federal Health Program, 2012, in force 18 July 2012, SI 2012–49, Canada Gazette Vol. 146(15) 2012.

[13] The revision to the Interim Federal Health Program slashed access to public healthcare for all asylum seekers and privately sponsored refugees. It replaced a basket of healthcare services and access to basic prescription, dental and optical services that approximated what indigent Canadians received. However, the cuts were more draconian for some categories than others. Asylum seekers from non-designated countries remain eligible for essential or emergency medical care. See Citizenship and Immigration Canada, 'Interim Federal Health Program: Summary of Benefits' (n.d.) www.cic.gc.ca/english/refugees/outside/summary-ifhp.asp (accessed 9 October 2012). For background and analysis of the changes and their projected impact, see Steve Barnes, 'The Real Cost of Cutting Refugee Health Benefits', Wellesley Institute, 23 May 2012 www.wellesleyinstitute.com/publication/the-real-cost-of-cutting-refugee-health-benefits (accessed 11 October 2012).

[14] See Cathryn Costello, 'The Asylum Procedures Directive and the Proliferation of Safe Country Practices: Deterrence, Deflection and the Dismantling of International Protection?' (2005) 7 European Journal of Migration and Law 35–69, at 50–1; Michael John-Hopkins, 'The Emperor's New Safe Country Concepts: A UK Perspective on Sacrificing Fairness on the Altar of Efficiency' (2009) 21 International Journal of Refugee Law 218–55.

[15] Citizenship and Immigration Canada, 'Backgrounder: Designated Countries of Origin' (n.d.) www.cic.gc.ca/english/department/media/backgrounders/2012/2012–06–29a.asp (accessed 11 October 2012).

[16] Directive 2011/95/EU of the European Parliament and of the Council of 13 December 2011 on standards for the qualification of third-country nationals or stateless persons as beneficiaries of international content of the protection granted (recast) (OJ 2011 No. L337/9) (Recast Qualification Directive).

securitization, border control and deterrence of asylum seekers ostensibly justifies harsher, peremptory mechanisms to expedite the likely rejection and swift removal of these SCO asylum seekers.

The danger, of course, is that SCO lists make the prediction of rejection self-fulfilling in two ways. First, the 'safe country' badge of approval signals to first-level decision makers the executive's prejudgement of the merits of individual cases, thereby weakening the appearance (if not reality) of adjudicative independence. Second, the truncated timelines and restricted access to appeal, review and stays of removal mean that asylum seekers may lack adequate time to secure legal counsel and properly prepare their claim prior to the hearing. These deficiencies heighten the risk of false negative determinations which cannot be rectified because refused claimants will also be deprived de jure of the right to internal appeal, and de facto of access to judicial review.

Cast in terms of 'emulation drivers' and 'facilitating factors' described in the Introduction, one might portray the driver for Canada's adoption of an SCO provision as the challenge of deterring Roma asylum seekers. Canada's recognition of the EU as the supranational aggregate of some of the 'most advanced and powerful States in the world system'[17] assures a context of affinity and receptiveness to EU norms. The existence of established intergovernmental networks facilitates norm transmission between Canada and EU Member States and the EU itself. The shared common law tradition of Canada and the UK, where the general SCO concept has withstood judicial scrutiny (if not each application), could offer Canadian policy makers some reassurance that the policy was legally sturdy.[18]

This chapter sets out to complicate this hypothesis, at least to the extent that emulation connotes a valorization of the source (Europe) that exerts an influence distinct from the perceived merits of the actual policy. The Canadian SCO policy was doubtless inspired by the precedent of individual EU Member States (especially the UK). But I contend that Canada's posture towards the EU was less about emulation than appeasement. I suggest that the EU's stature as supranational political and economic power *did* spur the adoption of the SCO, but not because the European imprimatur made the SCO concept intrinsically enticing.

---

[17] Lambert, Chapter 1 of this volume, pp. 1 and 7–8.

[18] *Husan v. Secretary of State for the Home Department* (UK) [2005] EWHC 189 (Admin.); *R v. Secretary of State for the Home Department v. Javed* (UK) [2001] EWCA Civ. 789 (Court of Appeal, Civ. Div.).

Instead, I identify two motives driving Canada's adoption of an SCO provision: first, placating EU irritation about visa requirements; and, second, facilitating the conclusion of the Canada–EU Comprehensive Economic Trade Agreement.

The remainder of this chapter describes the initial resort to visas to preclude the arrival of Roma asylum seekers, followed by the search for alternative strategies to deter European asylum seekers. I explain a political economy account of why Canada adopted an SCO provision in 2012, more than two decades after the introduction of analogous provisions by various European States. I then explain the functional differences between the Canadian SCO and its transatlantic cousins. Finally, I speculate that the normative subtext of Canada's SCO provision may owe as much to another EU instrument, the 1999 Aznar Protocol to the Treaty of Amsterdam[19] (which denies access to asylum in the EU by EU citizens), as it does to the SCO concept (which governs third-country nationals seeking asylum in the EU).

B   Roma asylum seekers in Canada

Since the fall of the Berlin Wall in 1989 and the demise of communism in Central and Eastern Europe, a steady trickle of asylum seekers have made their way to Canada. These have included Central and East European Roma. Indeed, the political liberalization associated with the end of autocratic rule had the perverse effect of unleashing dormant (or at least suppressed) manifestations of anti-Roma sentiment. Then, as now, Roma asylum claims were typically based on fear of persecution in the form of persistent, systemic and severe acts of harassment, discrimination and violence on account of their Roma identity. Agents of persecution included both the State (especially police, local officials and education authorities) and non-State actors, including right-wing and neo-Nazi political groups and private citizens. Even where the State was not the primary agent of persecution, Roma claimants asserted that the State was unwilling or unable to protect them from the abuse, threats, harassment and discrimination by non-State actors.

---

[19] EU, Protocol on Asylum for Nationals of Member States, 16 December 2004 (OJ 2004 No. C310/362), to the Treaty of Amsterdam amending the Treaty on European Union, the Treaties Establishing the European Communities and Related Acts, 2 October 2007 (OJ 1997 No. C340/1) (Aznar Protocol).

Under Canadian refugee law, all asylum seekers who fear persecution by non-State actors must surmount an evidentiary presumption of State protection. Independent of any SCO concept, Canadian refugee law requires asylum seekers to discharge an evidentiary burden of adducing 'clear and convincing evidence' that the State of nationality is unable or unwilling to fulfil its duty to adequately protect asylum seekers from persecution by non-State actors. The normative premise is that States have the primary duty to protect their nationals. Refugee status is a form of surrogate protection that is triggered only if and when States fail to execute their duty.[20] In the Supreme Court of Canada's 1993 *Ward* v. *Canada (Minister of Employment and Immigration)*[21] judgment, the Court explained that

> [N]ations should be presumed capable of protecting their citizens. Security of nationals is, after all, the essence of sovereignty. Absent a situation of complete breakdown of state apparatus ... it should be assumed that the state is capable of protecting a claimant.
>
> ...
>
> In the case of a nondemocratic State, contrary evidence might be readily forthcoming, but in relation to a democracy like the United States contrary evidence might have to go to the extent of substantially impeaching, for example, the jury selection process in the relevant part of the country, or the independence or fair-mindedness of the judiciary itself.
>
> Although this presumption increases the burden on the claimant, it does not render illusory Canada's provision of a haven for refugees. The presumption serves to reinforce the underlying rationale of international protection as a surrogate, coming into play where no alternative remains to the claimant.[22]

While the presumption of State protection applies to virtually all countries that are not embroiled in civil war or bear the label 'failed States', it is also the case that the presumption is, in principle, rebuttable with respect to any State.[23]

As Central and East European countries were transitioning from communism to post-communism, and then to some version of capitalist democracy, Canada acknowledged their ostensible progress by removing

---

[20] See generally James Hathaway, *The Law of Refugee Status* (Toronto: Butterworths, 1991).

[21] (1993) 20 Imm. LR (2d) 85; 103 DLR (4th) 1.   [22] *Ibid.*, paras. 57–8.

[23] Notably, Patrick Ward was a dual citizen of the Republic of Ireland and Great Britain, both of which are generally regarded as democratic, rights respecting States. Ireland conceded its inability to protect Ward, who was targeted for reprisal by the Irish National Liberation Army for disloyalty (*ibid.*, paras. 2–6, 53, 97).

the visa requirement for visitors from those States. The visa requirement is a standard and effective technique for preventing potential refugees from reaching Canada by air. It works by requiring all nationals to apply for and obtain a visa prior to visiting Canada. Canadian embassy officials will deny a visa to anyone whom they believe might seek refugee status in Canada. Travellers without the requisite visa will be barred from a Canada-bound flight. The visa is also a blunt instrument that generates diplomatic friction, offends the sensibility of targeted States and strains trade, economic and political relationships with those States.

C   Keeping Roma out, take 1: the institutional response

In October 1994, Canada rescinded its long-standing visa requirement for Hungary, and did the same for the Czech Republic in April 1996. The number of Czech asylum seekers spiked in the summer of 1996, when several hundred Roma asylum seekers claimed refugee status in Canada. Within a year, the number of refugee claimants went from fewer than 200 to over 1,500. By October 1997, the visa was reinstituted for the Czech Republic, and the number of Czech refugee claimants in Canada was negligible. Ever since, the Czech Republic has made it a point of honour to impose a retaliatory visa on Canadians whenever Canada imposes a visa on the Czech Republic. Meanwhile, Canada opted not to reimpose the visa on Hungary, a country with a larger population, more dynamic economy and stronger diasporic presence in Canada.

Instead, the response to Hungarian asylum seekers emanated from the Immigration and Refugee Board (IRB), the quasi-judicial tribunal tasked with determining refugee claims. The IRB was established in 1989, and is formally independent of government.[24] In 1998, the IRB launched a 'lead case' initiative. The stated purpose of the initiative was to encourage consistent, expeditious and informed decision making among the large and dispersed body of IRB decision makers without compromising the adjudicative autonomy of any individual adjudicator. IRB management would identify an asylum claim that was more or less typical in its facts, and where asylum claims from that country displayed a pattern of

---

[24] Decision makers are appointed for fixed and renewable terms, and enjoy security of tenure for the duration of their terms of appointment. The subjective experience of independence is compromised by the fact that initial appointment and reappointments are decided by Cabinet (the executive), on the advice of the Minister of Citizenship and Immigration. Recent legislative amendment will replace the decision makers with public servants.

inconsistent outcomes. The IRB would marshal expert witnesses and extensive evidence, and the decision in that case would serve as a persuasive (though formally non-binding) precedent for future cases.[25] The stated goal of the lead case initiative was to encourage consistency, not to produce a particular outcome. The IRB selected a Hungarian Roma asylum claim as its first – and, as it turned out, only – lead case.

At the time the plan to develop a lead case for Hungarian Roma was formulated, it was not apparent that any problem of inconsistency in decision making actually existed. Only sixty-five Hungarian refugee claims had been decided in the previous eight months, and most were positive.[26] However, email exchanges between senior IRB management in mid-1998 adverted to Citizenship and Immigration Canada's criticism of the IRB's relatively high acceptance rate of Czech Roma, the growing intake of Hungarian Roma and the (unfounded) speculation that 'there are 15,000 (yes, fifteen thousand) Hungarian Roma on their way to Canada'.[27]

In the autumn of 1998, the IRB conducted the lead case hearing into a Hungarian Roma family's refugee claims. The hearing lasted several days and heard from many witnesses. The IRB rejected each claimant, and articulated what have become standard reasons for denial of Roma asylum claims in virtually all subsequent decisions: the claimants lacked credibility and exaggerated past incidents of abuse, including racist attacks directed against them.[28] Moreover, 'the acts of discrimination, which the claimants did undeniably suffer in Hungary, do not amount to persecution, individually nor cumulatively'.[29] Finally, the claimants failed to rebut the presumption that Hungary, a democratic State, was able and willing to provide adequate State protection from non-State agents of persecution.[30]

Days before the decision was released in Canada in January 1999, Canadian government officials alerted the Hungarian media that they were forthcoming. The actual lead case decision was also leaked to Hungarian media outlets, and the largest circulation Hungarian newspaper ran the story under the banner headline 'Canada does not grant asylum to Hungarian Roma'.[31]

---

[25] Geza v. Canada (Minister of Citizenship and Immigration) [2006] 4 FCR 377; 2006 FCA 124, reversing Geza v. Canada (Minister of Citizenship and Immigration) [2005] 3 FCR 3; 2004 FC 1039 (Federal Court), at paras. 7–8 (Geza (FCA)).
[26] Ibid., para. 18.   [27] As cited in ibid., para. 15.
[28] Geza v. Canada (Minister of Citizenship and Immigration) [2005] 3 FCR 3; 2004 FC 1039 (Federal Court), at para. 9.
[29] Ibid., para. 10.   [30] Ibid.   [31] Geza (FCA), para. 36.

In December 1998, the Canadian acceptance rate for Hungarian Roma cases decided that year was 71 per cent. By June 1999, the acceptance rate plummeted to 9 per cent.[32] The claimants in the lead case challenged the decision before the Federal Court of Canada on the basis that the circumstances of its deployment disclosed a reasonable apprehension of bias towards a negative outcome. The first-level Federal Court rejected the bias argument, but the Federal Court of Appeal accepted it and set aside the original lead case decision. The Federal Court of Appeal acknowledged that it could not point to a 'smoking gun' that demonstrated an illegitimate motive. Nevertheless, it found that the cumulative effect of the evidence presented by the appellants sufficed to raise a reasonable apprehension 'that the lead case strategy was not only designed to bring consistency to future decisions and to increase their accuracy, but also to reduce the number of positive decisions that otherwise might be rendered in favour of the 15,000 Hungarian Roma claimants expected to arrive in 1998, and to reduce the number of potential claimants'.[33] As such, it interfered with the autonomy of decision makers to determine asylum claims based on the evidence specific to the individual claimant.

The Federal Court of Appeal's decision was rendered in 2006, and the government did not appeal to the Supreme Court of Canada. This meant that the lead case on Hungarian Roma was mired in litigation for seven years, and ultimately invalidated. But this did not mean that cases decided in the intervening period in conformity with the lead case were reversed.[34] Although the recognition rate for Hungarian Roma remained low in the ensuing years, the number of arrivals continued to rise until 2001, when over 4,000 Hungarians claimed refugee status. Then, in December 2001, the Canadian government reimposed a visa requirement on Hungary. By 2002, the number of Hungarian asylum seekers dropped to 223, and by 2007, only 23 Hungarians made asylum claims in Canada.

D   Keeping Roma out, take 2: jurisprudential imagination

On 1 May 2004, Hungary and the Czech Republic, along with eight other Central European States, acceded to the European Union.[35] As 'EU citizens', Hungarian and Czech citizens enjoyed new mobility rights

---

[32] *Ibid.*, para. 39.   [33] *Ibid.*, paras. 60–1.   [34] *Ibid.*, para. 72.
[35] The other EU-10 States were Estonia, Cyprus, Latvia, Lithuania, Malta, Poland, Slovenia and Slovakia. Bulgaria and Romania joined the EU on 1 January 2007.

within the enlarged EU. Several among the original EU Member States elected to temporarily withhold from these new Member States the full suite of residence and employment rights available to the original EU-15 citizens, albeit the delayed implementation would expire in 2011.

Canada lifted the visa requirement on the Czech Republic and Hungary in October 2007.[36] History repeated itself: asylum flows from both countries resumed and accelerated.[37] In July 2009, Canada reimposed the visa requirement on the Czech Republic but not Hungary.[38] Czech refugee claims shrivelled from over 1,500 in 2009 to 32 in 2010,[39] but the reimposition of the visa triggered consternation from both the Czech Republic and the EU.[40] Meanwhile, the stream of Hungarian asylum seekers did not abate.

In 2009, I was contacted by a refugee lawyer about notes by a Canadian border official that were disclosed to his client prior to the hearing. When asylum seekers present themselves at a Canadian port of entry (POE), a Canadian Border Services Agency (CBSA) officer questions the person to determine whether he or she is eligible to make a refugee claim in Canada. CBSA officers are neither qualified nor authorized to determine whether a person is a refugee. Nevertheless, in the course of gathering information relevant to eligibility, the CBSA officer typically inquires into the substance of the person's asylum claim. These notes are frequently introduced into refugee hearings to impugn the credibility of a

---

[36] Citizenship and Immigration Canada, 'Backgrounder: The Visa Requirement for the Czech Republic' (13 July 2009) www.cic.gc.ca/english/department/media/background ers/2009/2009-07-13a.asp (accessed 11 October 2012).

[37] The number of refugee claims from the Czech Republic rose from a handful in 2007, to 845 in 2008 and 1,846 in the first four months of 2009 (*ibid.*).

[38] Canada also imposed a visa requirement on Mexico at the same time, also because of the rise in Mexican asylum claims.

[39] Citizenship and Immigration Canada, 'Canada: Total Entries of Refugee Claimants by Top Source Countries' (n.d.) www.cic.gc.ca/english/resources/statistics/facts2010/tem porary/25.asp (accessed 11 October 2012).

[40] Mark B. Salter and Can E. Mutlu, 'The "Next Generation" Visa: Belt And Braces or the Emperor's New Clothes?' (October 2011) Centre for European Policy Studies (CEPS) Paper on Liberty and Security in Europe; Alejandro Eggenschwiler, 'The Canada–Czech Republic Visa Affair: A Test for Visa Reciprocity and Fundamental Rights in the European Union' (November 2010) CEPS Paper on Liberty and Security in Europe; Sergio Carrera, Elspeth Guild and Massimo Merlino, 'The Canada–Czech Republic Visa Dispute Two Years on: Implications for the EU's Migration and Asylum Policies' (October 2011) CEPS Paper on Liberty and Security in Europe; Judit Tóth, 'The Incomprehensible Flow of Roma Asylum-Seekers from the Czech Republic and Hungary to Canada' (November 2010) CEPS Paper on Liberty and Security in Europe. All papers are accessible at www.ceps.eu (accessed 11 October 2012).

refugee claimant, in the event of perceived inconsistency between the port-of-entry notes and subsequent evidence from the asylum seeker.

The POE notes by this particular CBSA officer contained the following entry:

> I will, however, be seeking the Minister's intervention in your case as it is my opinion that your claim for protection lacks any basis. First of all, you failed to avail yourself of your own country's protection by not reporting XXXX to the Hungarian police ... As a Hungarian citizen, you have the right to establish residence in any of the countries of the European Union. Under the 'Charter of the Fundamental Rights of the European Union', Chapter 5, Article 45, Paragraph 1, 'Every citizen of the Union has the right to move and reside freely in the territory of the member states'. I want to make sure that whoever has to decide on your application for protection is aware that if you felt persecuted in Hungary ... you could have gone to live in any of the other [] countries of Europe. To grant you refugee status without you showing proof that you have a well founded fear of persecution in all of the twenty-seven countries of the European Union, would be a gross abuse of our refugee protection system.[41]

I initially dismissed the CBSA officer's notes as the exasperated ramblings of a frustrated border official who happened to latch onto a nugget of legal knowledge about the EU. However, I subsequently learned (anecdotally) that this CBSA officer was not alone: some IRB decision makers were raising the same queries in hearings, and a few US lawyers were preparing to meet similar arguments in US asylum proceedings.

There is no basis in international refugee law for a requirement that an asylum seeker from an EU Member State who makes a claim for refugee protection in Canada (or anywhere outside the EU) must demonstrate a well-founded fear of persecution against each EU Member State. The proposition trades on an inchoate analogy of the EU to a notional 'United States of Europe' (where each Member State is a sub-federal unit of the greater whole), or perhaps a depiction of EU citizenship as tantamount to nationality. From a legal perspective, either analogy is specious.

A refugee claim is lodged against a State, such as Hungary, not the EU as such. No other State is 'internal' to Hungary. No Member State can be an internal protection alternative to an asylum seeker from another Member State. Of course, the UK, Germany, Greece, Portugal and Hungary are all internal to the EU. But the EU, *qua* supranational entity,

---

[41] Notes by CBSA officer provided by refugee lawyer (redacted), September 2009, on file with author.

is neither subject nor object of the Refugee Convention. One cannot seek refugee status *from* the EU in either sense of the word. In order to construct twenty-seven Nation-States as subordinate units of a greater territorial whole, one must reimagine the EU as an undifferentiated political federation. This feat of political isomorphism collides with the current self-understanding of the States that comprise the EU.

One might be tempted by the notion that mobility rights furnish EU citizens with a form of secure denizenship status in other Member States, which in turn triggers the application of exclusion under article 1E Refugee Convention. Article 1E provides that the Convention does not apply to a person 'who is recognized by the competent authorities of the country in which he has taken residence as having the rights and obligations which are attached to the possession of the nationality of that country'. Of course, it is apparent from the text of article 1E that the provision does not apply to an asylum seeker who has not actually taken up residence in another State prior to seeking asylum in a third State.

More significantly, the depiction of EU citizenship as quasi-nationality rests on the common but mistaken belief that EU citizens enjoy unfettered mobility and residence rights throughout the EU. The right to enter and the right to remain in a State classically accrue only to nationals, and are regarded as the singularly novel entitlements of EU citizenship.

But the free mobility and residence rights of EU citizens tend to be overstated as a matter of law, and unevenly respected in practice. The European Parliament and Council's Free Movement Directive guarantees EU citizens and family members visa-free entry to other Member States.[42] Leaving aside the incomplete phasing-in of full employment rights for Romanians and Bulgarians in various EU States, the EU citizen's residence rights are contingent, not unconditional. EU citizens may remain in another EU Member State for three months, after which continued residence depends on being (or being a family member of) one of the following: employed or self-employed; endowed with sufficient resources and private health insurance to preclude recourse to public social assistance; or enrolled in post-secondary education and possessing sufficient financial resources and insurance.[43] Failure to meet

---

[42] Directive 2004/38/EC of the European Parliament and of the Council of 29 April 2004 on the right of citizens of the Union and their family members to move and reside freely within the territory of the Member States (OJ 2004 No. L158/77) (Free Movement Directive).

[43] *Ibid.*, art. 7, pp. 93–5. Pursuant to art. 8(4), pp. 96–7, 'sufficient resources' must be individually calibrated, and in any case cannot be higher than the minimum threshold for social assistance eligibility.

the threshold of economic self-sufficiency leads to loss or non-renewal of EU residence rights.[44]

Finally, even if one provisionally accepts that EU mobility and residence rights are sufficient to attract article 1E exclusion, recent State practices towards Roma who do exercise their mobility rights in the EU suggest that realization of the norm of equal EU citizenship is compromised by Roma's unequal citizenship at the domestic level. First, the very marginalization that leads people to flee their country of nationality may also impede their access to labour markets in other EU Member States.[45] Second, EU Member States, most notably France and Italy, have recently come under harsh criticism in the Council of Europe's Commissioner for Human Rights report, 'Human Rights of Roma and Travellers in Europe', for harassment, evictions and collective expulsion of Roma, all in contravention of the Free Movement Directive.[46] In the summer of 2010 and again in 2012, the French government launched an aggressive deportation campaign against Roma from other Member States.[47] There is no small irony in the fact that in a political space consecrated to the principle of free movement, a despised minority stereotyped as intrinsically itinerant confront reconstituted barriers to their movement within that space.

---

[44] *Ibid.*, art. 6, p. 92. Note also that permanent resident status is a discrete and more secure form of legal status for which EU citizens may apply after a minimum of five years of residence *qua* EU citizen (*ibid.*, Chapter IV, at 105ff.). The category of permanent resident status further underscores the fact that the residence rights appertaining to EU citizenship are not tantamount to permanent resident status, much less national citizenship, in a Member State.

[45] See, e.g., Council of Europe, Commissioner for Human Rights, 'Human Rights of Roma and Travellers in Europe' (February 2012), at 157–67 www.coe.int/t/commissioner/source/prems/prems79611_GBR_CouvHumanRightsOfRoma_WEB.pdf (accessed 17 June 2012) (Commissioner for Human Rights, 'Human Rights of Roma'). See, generally, Helen O'Nions, 'Slippery Citizenship', working draft (September 2012), on file with author.

[46] Council of Europe, Commissioner for Human Rights, 'Human Rights of Roma and Travellers in Europe'.

[47] The European Commission threatened in October 2010 to initiate infringement proceedings against France for non-compliance with the Free Movement Directive. In response, France pledged to legislate the transposition of the directive into French law (Law No. 2011–672 of 16 June 2011 on Immigration, Integration and Nationality, JO No. 0139 of 17 June 2011, p. 10290). Human Rights Watch subsequently issued a report indicating persistent French contravention of the Free Movement Directive: Human Rights Watch, 'France's Compliance with the European Free Movement Directive and the Removal of Ethnic Roma EU Citizens', a briefing paper submitted to the European Commission in July 2011 (28 September 2011) www.hrw.org/news/2011/09/28/france-s-compliance-european-free-movement-directive-and-removal-ethnic-roma-eu-citi (accessed 11 October 2012). See also Human Rights Watch, 'France: One Year On, New Abuses against Roma' (29 September 2011) www.hrw.org/news/2011/09/29/france-one-year-new-abuses-against-roma (accessed 17 October 2012).

In short, the feasibility of persecuted Roma relocating to another EU Member State is enhanced by the principle of freedom of movement, and diminished by the contingency of residence and employment rights, as well as the pervasively denigrated status of Roma in Europe.

Irrespective of the limited legal and practical relevance of EU citizenship for Roma asylum seekers, the mobility rights of EU citizens figures prominently in the rhetoric deployed to discredit than. In the course of justifying the reimposition of a visa requirement on the Czech Republic in mid-2009, Citizenship and Immigration Minister Jason Kenney declared that 'the refugee claims from Czechs make no sense because they could easily move to the twenty-six other Western democracies in the European Union'.[48] Since then, Minister Kenney has subsequently repeated the same argument with respect to Hungarian Roma.[49] In 2011, the Canadian Border Services Agency intelligence branch launched 'Project SARA' to investigate the trajectory, motivations and alleged criminal activity of Hungarian Roma asylum seekers, with a view to proposing policies to more effectively deter and expel them. In its January 2012 report 'Project SARA: International and Domestic Activities Final Report',[50] the CBSA succinctly stated the case for rejecting Hungarian Roma asylum claims based on EU mobility rights: 'Hungary's membership in the European Union ... does allow its citizens to travel freely within the European Union, which should facilitate their escape from any immediate danger, and negate their need to travel to Canada'.[51]

E Keeping Roma out, take 3: safe country of origin

Canada's array of deflection and deterrence strategies, along with its relative geographic isolation, largely succeed in repelling asylum seekers. By 2011, the number of asylum seekers reaching Canada from any single

---

[48] 'Kenney defends visa rules for Czech nationals', *CTV News*, 15 July 2009 www.ctv.ca/ CTVNews/TopStories/20090714/visas_immigration_090714/ (accessed 11 October 2012).

[49] See Rick Westhead, 'Why the Roma are fleeing Hungary and why Canada is shunning them', *The Star.com*, 13 October 2012 www.thestar.com/news/world/article/1270 708–roma-in-hungary-feel-persecuted-but-they-have-nowhere-to-turn (accessed 13 October 2012): 'Kenney has said Hungarian Roma ought to consider moving to other countries if they feel endangered. For instance, he says Roma have freedom of movement within the European Union.'

[50] Canada Border Services Agency (Intelligence, GTA Region – Analytical Unit), 'Project SARA: International and Domestic Activities Final Report', 31 January 2012 https://www.document cloud.org/documents/470868-cbsa-project-sara.html (accessed 19 October 2012).

[51] *Ibid.*, 54.

State in the Global South was reduced to a dribble. Hungary emerged as the top source country (4,423), followed by China (1,913). No other State was a source of more than 1,000 asylum seekers. Apart from China, none of the top-ten source countries for asylum claims in Canada figured on the top-ten list of source countries for refugees worldwide.[52] Hungarian refugee claims comprised about one-quarter of all refugee claims referred to the IRB in 2011 (see Table).

The acceptance rate among Hungarian Roma in Canada was low in most years, and an unusually high number of claimants formally

Claims referred, finalized and decided: Hungary[53] 2005–11

	Referred	Accepted	Rejected	Abandoned	Withdrawn	% Accepted of total finalized	% Accepted of total decided
2005	60	51	268	41	25	13%	16%
2006	46	67	41	7	12	53%	62%
2007	34	16	15	1	6	42%	51%
2008	285	22	13	9	39	27%	63%
2009	2,418	3	5	47	204	1%	60%
2010	2,296	22	72	107	970	2%	23%
2011	4,423	165	738	249	838	8%	18%

Note:
1 Claims finalized and decided in a given year may have been referred in a previous year.
2 Total finalized = (accepted + rejected + withdrawn + abandoned).
3 Total decided = (accepted + rejected).

---

[52] In 2011, 1,913 Chinese nationals made refugee claims in Canada. Of the remaining top-ten source countries for refugee claims in Canada, the arrivals per country of origin ranged from 632 to 904. See Human Rights Research and Education Centre, University of Ottawa, 'IRB Refugee Status Determinations (1989–2011 Calendar Years)' (n.d.) www.cdp-hrc.uottawa.ca/projects/refugee-forum/projects/documents/REFUGEESTAT SCOMPREHENSIVE1999–2011.pdf (accessed 28 September 2012). None of the top-ten source countries for refugees globally are on the top-ten-list of source countries for refugee claimants in Canada, except China (which is tenth on the global list). See UNHCR, 'A Year of Crises: UNHCR Global Trends 2011', 18 June 2012 www.unhcr. org/4fd6f87f9.html, at 14, table 5 (accessed 11 October 2012).

[53] IRB, Refugee Protection Division, 'Claims Referred and Finalized: Hungary' (n.d.), on file with author.

withdrew their refugee claims or abandoned them by not showing up for the hearing.[54] The Minister of Citizenship and Immigration frequently cited the 2010 statistics, in which over 90 per cent of total finalized claims consisted of withdrawn or abandoned claims.

Two features of the statistics bear noting: first, the IRB conducted only 94 Hungarian hearings in 2010, even though the inventory of Hungarian claims (based on referrals in the previous year) numbered over 2,000. The small number of cases decided on the merits provides a partial explanation of why abandoned and withdrawn claims comprised such a large proportion of the total number of finalized claims. In 2011, more hearings were conducted, and the proportion of abandoned claims (25 per cent) and withdrawn claims (30 per cent) dropped to 55 per cent.

The second statistical anomaly is that the data publicized by the IRB in 2011 lumps abandoned and withdrawn claims together with rejected claims and labels all as negative determinations in the 'total finalized', thereby inflating the number of 'refused' claims and shrinking the recognition rate.[55] Standard practice of the United Nations High Commissioner for Refugees (UNHCR) and the EU is to calculate recognition rates based only on claims decided on the merits, and to segregate files closed for administrative reasons (including abandonment and withdrawal) where no decision is rendered on the merits. If the statistics are recalculated based only on claims actually decided, the recognition rate for Hungarian claims is significantly higher.[56]

Since 2011, two important developments helped to shape legislative reforms affecting claimants from EU Member States. In June 2011, the

[54] Refugee claimants are issued a conditional removal order when they make a refugee claim. If a final claim is rejected, or withdrawn or abandoned, the conditional removal order becomes effective.

[55] See above n. 53. The statistics publicized by the IRB only provided recognition rates based on claims finalized, not claims decided.

[56] The reasons for the high abandonment and withdrawal rates are unclear and probably variable. Rumours abounded of a few incompetent and/or corrupt counsel and consultants providing false and misleading information to Roma in Hungary and bad legal advice to Roma in Canada. Some claimants may have deduced that their claims – rightly or wrongly, fairly or unfairly – were doomed to fail anyway. Some who abandoned their claims may have opted to try their luck living 'underground' or simply returned to Hungary on their own initiative. Those who withdrew, however, were not evading the system. By taking the affirmative step of terminating the refugee determination process, they intentionally triggered the departure process and made themselves available for removal from Canada. Whatever the motives and meaning behind the abandonment and withdrawal rates, Minister of Citizenship and Immigration Jason Kenney incessantly and effectively equated 'abandoned' and 'withdrawn' with 'bogus'.

Conservative party won a majority of seats in Parliament. This unshackled the Conservatives from the restraints that tempered them as a minority government. Borrowing from familiar populist rhetoric across the global North (and especially Australia), the government unleashed a public relations campaign of demonization of asylum seekers in order to prepare the ground for harsher policies of detention, accelerated determination procedures, immizeration, intensified precarity and family separation of asylum seekers and refugees.

Along with Sri Lankan Tamils, the government targeted Hungarian Roma asylum seekers for particular vilification. The former were framed as smuggled migrants and potential security threats (Tamil Tigers or sympathizers).[57] Hungarian Roma were cast as the consummate 'bogus' refugees who chose to migrate to Canada for the purpose of exploiting Canada's social welfare system.[58] A typical media story in early 2012 related the following:

> 'Our government is very concerned about the recent increase in refugee claims from democratic countries that respect human rights', Kenney told reporters in Ottawa after introducing the bill in the House of Commons on Thursday.
>
> 'The growing number of bogus claims from European Union democracies is only exacerbating the problem', he said.
>
> Kenney said that while many Roma face difficulties at home, they are not persecuted by the state. He said many came to Canada to abuse its 'generous' welfare system.
>
> 'To be perfectly honest with you, we have people showing up at . . . the airport where they make their asylum claim, asking where they can get their cheque from, their welfare cheque', he said, referring to the growing Roma population.
>
> . . .
>
> 'Canada's asylum system is broken', Kenney said. 'Requirements are needed to ensure the quicker removal of bogus claimants.'[59]

---

[57] See, e.g., Douglas Quan, 'Experts say security reasons may keep Tamils in detention', *Vancouver Sun*, 6 September 2012 www.vancouversun.com/news/Experts+security+reasons+keep+Tamils+detention/3486992/story.html (accessed 15 October 2012).

[58] Income assistance (welfare) is provided at the provincial level. The federal government does not control these expenditures.

[59] 'Tories sweeping immigration reforms'. Minister Kenney also sponsored an information campaign in Hungary to discourage Roma from seeking asylum in Canada, including an appearance on a right-wing television station in Hungary in 2011, and an official visit in 2012. See MTI, 'Canada vows to continue deporting Hungarian asylum seekers', *Politics. hu*, 15 October 2012 www.politics.hu/20121015/canada-vows-to-continue-deporting-hungarian-asylum-seekers (accessed 15 October 2012).

In spring 2012, the government introduced the Protecting Canada's Immigration System Act (Bill C-31).[60] This bill amended the IRPA by clawing back earlier compromise legislation (the Balanced Refugee Reform Act)[61] passed when the government was in a minority position. It revived provisions of two bills that had been earlier rejected by opposition parties as draconian and unconstitutional.[62] It also ushered in the SCO provision described in the introductory section.

As part of the legislative process, Bill C-31 was examined by the multiparty Parliamentary Standing Committee on Citizenship and Immigration before submission to Parliament for a final vote. Among the witnesses appearing before the Committee was the EU Ambassador to Canada, Bernhard Brinkmann, as well as embassy officials from Hungary and Germany.

Ambassador Brinkmann and his EU colleagues had little to say to Canadian parliamentarians about the SCO principle. Despite repeated invitations from government committee members,[63] EU representatives declined to pronounce on the legality of the UK's SCO provisions under EU or international law.[64] For his part, the German representative emphasized that German law neither mandated nor permitted accelerated hearing procedures for asylum seekers on the German SCO list.[65] Indeed, the fact that the government invited testimony from the EU ambassador but not the UK High Commissioner suggests that Canadian parliamentarians may have lacked a clear understanding of the existing scope of the Common European Asylum System, or the respective roles of Member States and the EU in asylum determination.

On the other hand, several EU witnesses reiterated the mobility rights of EU citizens, including Roma. The EU Ambassador also referred

---

[60] See above n. 4.   [61] BRRA.

[62] While in a minority government, the Conservatives also tried and failed to advance two bills that, *inter alia*, purported to combat human smuggling by imposing automatic, unreviewable, warrantless, one-year detention on allegedly smuggled migrants (including asylum seekers).

[63] Standing Committee on Citizenship and Immigration, 41st Parl., 1st Sess., CIMM-40, 7 May 2012 (Standing Committee, 7 May 2012). EU witnesses declined repeated invitations to endorse the domestic SCO regimes of various Member States. See, e.g., exchange between Ms Roxanne James and Ms Ioana Patrascu, at p. 22. The government members were especially interested in the UK SCO process, which contemplates hearings within days of arrival (*ibid.*).

[64] *Ibid.* See statement by Ms Ioana Patrascu, p. 22, in response to a question on the UK SCO timelines: 'I'm not in a position to comment on specific practices of member states without first checking, but these can vary.' See John-Hopkins, 'Emperor's New Safe Country', 238–44, for a description of the new UK timelines (as of 2007).

[65] Standing Committee, 7 May 2012, above n. 63, pp. 27–8.

obliquely to the Aznar Protocol, which renders citizens of EU Member States ineligible for asylum in another EU Member State:

> Between member states, we don't accept asylum seekers from one member state who is going to another member state. The treaty itself says that because we have democracies based on the rule of law, and we have oversight of this rule of law and the principles of asylum and so on by the European Commission and the European Court of Justice and so on, an asylum seeker from a member state is inadmissible in another member state he or she goes to.[66]

Another EU witness tacitly bolstered the inference that EU mobility rights obviated the need for asylum when she remarked that 'there are legal provisions concerning Roma who are EU citizens. They are EU citizens; therefore, they benefit from the regime of freedom of movement, and they are outside the scope of the EU asylum instruments.'[67]

The EU Ambassador and his Hungarian counterpart generally concurred with the government's depiction of Roma asylum seekers as economic migrants seeking to exploit Canada's social welfare system.[68] But the EU Ambassador also reiterated EU dismay with the ongoing visa requirements for the Czech Republic, Bulgaria and Romania:

> Citizens from three of our member states – Romania, Bulgaria, and the Czech Republic – still require visas to come to Canada, whereas Canadian citizens have visa-free travel within the entire European Union. For the countries concerned, but also for the European Union as a whole, it's a serious issue because of matters of principle. Our visa policy is based on the principle of reciprocity. If you grant visa-free access to one country, then that country should also grant you visa-free access to its territory. It's also because of solidarity among member states. This is a problem, especially the reintroduction of the visa for the Czech Republic.[69]

---

[66] *Ibid.*, p. 21 (Mr Bernhard Brinkmann). Other EU officials attempted, however, to provide greater nuance. See, e.g., statement by Ms Angela Martini: 'on the first part of your question regarding whether any country, even Canada, could be producing refugees who are persecuted, in a way, yes, I could agree. At the same time, in the European Union we have the presumption that each country is a safe country of origin. It doesn't prevent . . . a member state from examining a claim. It's not obliged to refuse it' (*ibid.*, p. 24). See also statement by Ms Anja Kabundt: 'You can't say that applicants who are Roma are generally not admitted as asylum seekers, so you have to check each case. If you check the circumstances of each case, it might be that even a Roma coming from another European country may be accepted as an asylum seeker' (*ibid.*, p. 27.)

[67] *Ibid.*, p. 26 (Ms Ioana Patrascu).

[68] *Ibid.*, p. 27 (Mr Bernhard Brinkmann); Standing Committee on Citizenship and Immigration, 41st Parl., 1st Sess., CIMM-37, 2 May 2012, pp. 6–7 (Mr Imre Helyes).

[69] Standing Committee, 7 May 2012, above n. 63, p. 20 (Mr Bernhard Brinkmann).

Despite the EU's diffidence regarding visa reciprocity – the EU had not, in fact, imposed a retaliatory visa on Canada – Bulgaria, Romania and the Czech Republic possessed considerable leverage in another EU domain, namely trade relations. Canadian Prime Minister Stephen Harper was anxious to finalize the Canada–EU Comprehensive Economic Trade Agreement (CETA). The CETA requires not only the consent of the European Parliament, but ratification by each of the EU's twenty-seven Member States. In response to media inquiry, the EU Ambassador bluntly reminded Canadian reporters that Romania, Bulgaria and the Czech Republic took umbrage at the Canadian visa requirement: 'These three member states, will they give approval to a [trade] agreement if they still need visas? Probably not.'[70]

If a visa requirement injures the pride of targeted States, designation as an SCO placates the national ego. At the time of writing, it is widely anticipated that the Minister of Citizenship and Immigration will designate at least Hungary, the Czech Republic, Bulgaria and Romania as SCOs. Alternatively, the minister could simply declare all Member States of the EU to be SCOs.[71] For Hungary's part, Tamás Király, Hungarian Deputy Head of Mission in Canada, welcomed the prospect of SCO status: 'We sincerely hope that Hungary will be a designated "safe" country of origin. This would largely reduce the incentives for economic migrants to come to Canada as asylum seekers.'[72]

Notably, at the very moment that the government was defending its SCO provisions by deriding 'bogus' Hungarian claims, the Federal Court of Canada remonstrated an IRB decision maker for adopting an unreasonable approach to State protection in the context of a Hungarian Roma claim:

> It is not enough to say that steps are being taken that some day may result in adequate state protection. It is what state protection is *actually provided* at the *present time* that is relevant. **In the present case, the evidence**

---

[70] Campbell Clark, 'Visa feud clouds Harper's free-trade dream with Europe', *Globe and Mail*, 26 April 2012 www.theglobeandmail.com/news/politics/.../article4102974/ (accessed 11 October 2012).

[71] Mexico is another likely object of ministerial designation. As noted earlier, Mexico was irritated by the visa imposition in 2009, especially since it is a party (along with Canada and the US) to the North American Free Trade Agreement.

[72] Daniel Proussalidis, 'Tories push through crackdown on refugees', *Toronto Sun*, 24 April 2012 www.torontosun.com/2012/04/24/tories-push-through-crackdown-on-refugees (accessed 11 October 2012).

is overwhelming that Hungary is unable presently to provide adequate
protection to its Roma citizens.[73]

Meanwhile, European human rights bodies, civil society and the media
continue to report on the deterioration of the Hungarian political situation, the ascending power of the anti-Roma, anti-Semitic, Jobbik
party, the slide towards authoritarian rule and the intensification of
anti-Roma harassment, hate speech and orchestrated violence.[74]

F   Safe country of origin: Canada and the Procedures Directive compared

The EU Asylum Procedures Directive (Procedures Directive) stipulates
minimum standards for national SCO lists, and also enumerates the
criteria for an EU-level SCO list.[75] Unlike article 31 Procedures
Directive's SCO provision, the Canadian SCO provision does not label
SCO claims 'manifestly unfounded', or place a specific onus on the SCO
claimant to demonstrate 'serious grounds for considering the country
not to be an SCO in his/her particular circumstances'.[76] But in the
Canadian context, such a requirement would be doctrinally redundant
anyway. The Supreme Court of Canada's *Ward* decision already presumes that States are able and willing to adequately protect their nationals, and places the burden on the asylum seeker to adduce 'clear and
convincing evidence' to the contrary.[77] This leaves little jurisprudential
space for an SCO principle to do substantive work in Canadian refugee
law. Therefore, the formal legal consequences of a Canadian SCO designation relate solely to the procedure of refugee determination and to
reception conditions.

The Canadian SCO scheme tracks article 23(4)(c)(i) Procedures
Directive in so far as the Canadian provision mandates, and the EU

---

[73] *Hercegi* v. *Canada (Minister of Citizenship and Immigration)* [2012], 2012 FC 250 (Federal Court), at para. 5 [emphasis added]. See also *Rezmuves* v. *Canada (Minister of Citizenship and Immigration)* [2012], 2012 FC 334.

[74] Westhead, 'Why the Roma are fleeing'.

[75] Directive 2005/85/EC of the European Council of 1 December 2005 on minimum standards on procedures in Member States for granting and withdrawing refugee status (OJ 2005 No. L236/13), arts. 29, 30 and 36(2) (Procedures Directive).

[76] *Ibid.*, art. 31(2) (applications from SCOs are deemed unfounded); art. 31(1) (an SCO for a particular applicant may only be considered as 'safe' where the applicant has not submitted any serious grounds for considering the country unsafe in his or her partic-ular circumstances).

[77] *Ward* v. *Canada (Minister of Employment and Immigration)*, paras. 57–8.

provision permits, accelerated determination procedures for asylum seekers from designated SCOs. However, the EU Asylum Reception Directive prohibits discrimination in access to basic healthcare, and explicitly forbids denial of emergency treatment to asylum seekers.[78] In contrast, the Canadian regime withholds coverage for emergency, life-saving treatment of any SCO asylum seeker.[79]

Bill C-31 establishes both a quantitative and a qualitative route to designation as an SCO. Designation is at the sole, subjective discretion of the minister. Section 109.1(2)(a) of the amended IRPA, grants the Minister of Citizenship and Immigration authority to identify an SCO according to the following method:

1. The minister picks a number.[80]
2. The number of refugee claimants from a given country equals or exceeds that number.
3. The minister may designate that country as safe if
   (a) the percentage of rejected claimants (refused on the merits + abandoned/withdrawn, divided by total claims determined) meets or exceeds a percentage to be determined by the minister,[81] or
   (b) the percentage of abandoned or withdrawn claims meets or exceeds a percentage to be determined by the minister.

The quantitative method for designating a country as safe is endogenous, meaning that it originates from within the refugee determination system itself. The provision provides no time-frame for the calculation of the minimum number of claims or percentages of rejected or abandoned/ withdrawn claims. A background document released by Citizenship and Immigration suggested that the minister is considering a minimum rejection rate of 75 per cent (in which abandoned and withdrawn claims are counted as rejections), or an abandonment/withdrawal rate of at least 60 per cent.[82] The obverse is that any country with a recognition rate

---

[78] Directive 2003/9/EC of the European Council of 27 January 2003 laying down minimum standards for the reception of asylum seekers (OJ 2003 No. L31/18).
[79] Order Respecting the Interim Federal Health Program, 2012, above n. 12.
[80] IRPA, s. 109.1(3) (not yet in force) provides that 'The Minister may, by order, provide for the number, period or percentages referred to in subsection (2).'
[81] *Ibid.*
[82] Citizenship and Immigration Canada, 'Backgrounder: Summary of Changes to Canada's Refugee System in Protecting Canada's Immigration System Act' (n.d.) www.cic.gc.ca/ english/department/media/backgrounders/2012/2012-02-16f.asp (accessed 11 October 2012).

below 25 per cent can be designated as safe. This is disturbing, given that the overall refugee claim recognition rate in Canada in 2010 and 2011 was only 38 per cent (of total decided), the lowest in IRB history.[83]

Relying on these quantitative indicators as proxies for the actual safety of the country of origin either presumes or is indifferent to the integrity of the decision-making process, including tacit or explicit political interference in the decision-making process. Abandonment and withdrawal count as negative decisions for purposes of calculating refusal rates, and also count on their own as a discrete basis for designation. High refusal rates, or high abandonment/withdrawal rates, constitute reasons for designation as an SCO. This means that the minister's inference that those who withdraw or abandon their asylum claims are 'bogus' is held against those asylum seekers who do not, in fact, withdraw or abandon their claims.

The judgment of the English High Court in *Husan v. Secretary of State*[84] addresses the logical flaw in relying on endogenous factors as proof that a country or origin is safe.[85] As Justice Wilson remarks 'it does not necessarily follow that the number of invalid claims suggests an absence of serious risk of persecution in Bangladesh'. At most, it indicates that many of the asylum seekers who appear before the tribunal do not meet the definition of a refugee. It does not, however, prove the 'acceptability under the Conventions of the likely treatment, if returned to Bangladesh, of honest applicants with at any rate genuine fears'.[86]

Unlike the practice of individual EU Member States, the Procedures Directive does not provide a quantitative formula for safe country designation. The reason is obvious: the EU does not conduct asylum determination. Each EU Member State operates its own asylum determination apparatus. Wide disparities in recognition rates between EU Member States, especially in relation to the same countries of origin, refute the reliability of asylum recognition rates as proof that a given country of origin is safe. For example, the UNHCR 2011 Global Trends report noted that in 2010, the total recognition rate for Afghan asylum

---

[83] Human Rights Research and Education Centre, University of Ottawa, 'By the Numbers: Refugee Statistics' (n.d.) www.cdp-hrc.uottawa.ca/projects/refugee-forum/projects/Statistics.php (accessed 11 October 2012).

[84] *Husan v. Secretary of State for the Home Department* (UK).

[85] The rejection rates relied on in that case did not include files closed for administrative reasons, such as abandonment or withdrawal.

[86] *Husan v. Secretary of State for the Home Department* (UK), paras. 56–7.

seekers ranged from 11 per cent (Greece), to 32 per cent (UK), to 58 per cent (Belgium) to 73 per cent (Sweden).[87]

Given the weak correlation between asylum refusal rates and country of origin conditions, it seems unsurprising that the separate SCO lists maintained by EU Member States also vary significantly in the number and identity of designated countries of origin.[88] Since EU Member States' SCO lists overlap so little with one another, it is equally unsurprising that EU Member States have failed to reach consensus under the Procedures Directive on a harmonized SCO list.[89]

Ultimately, inter-State comparison of asylum rejection rates also subverts the rationality of any national scheme that purports to rely on its own recognition rate as the basis for SCO designation. Just as States diverge in recognition rates, so too will individual decision makers or regional offices within a State display inconsistency. For instance, while the average Canadian recognition rate for Hungarian claimants in 2011 was 18.3 per cent (of total decided), the rate among Canadian decision makers varied from 0 per cent to 80 per cent among adjudicators who determined ten or more claims.[90]

Under the amended IRPA, the alternative method for designating a country as safe is qualitative and exogenous. It applies where the total number of refugee claims from a given country does not equal or exceed the number picked by the minister. The minister can use the qualitative method, for instance, to designate any EU Member State as a safe country, even if Canada receives no (or virtually no) asylum seekers

---

[87] UNHCR, 'A Year of Crises', p. 28: the total recognition rate captures both refugee and subsidiary or complementary protection.

[88] See Commission of the European Communities, 'Impact Assessment', annex to the Commission staff working document accompanying the proposal of the European Parliament and of the Council on minimum standards on procedures in Member States for granting and withdrawing international protection, SEC (2009) 1376 (Part II), Annex 12 (10 October 2009), at 38 www.europarl.europa.eu/registre/docs_autres_institutions/commission_europeenne/sec/2009/1376/COM_SEC(2009)1376_EN.pdf (accessed 11 October 2012).

[89] The Court of Justice of the EU ultimately annulled art. 29 Procedures Directive (authorizing a common list) on grounds related to EU institutional process: Case C-133/06, *Parliament* v. *Council* [2008] ECR I-3189; [2008] 2 CMLR 54.

[90] For data on variation in recognition rates within the Canadian IRB, see Sean Rehaag, '2011 Refugee Claim Data and IRB Member Recognition Rates: Outcomes by Country and Board Member' (4.table_.xls) (12 March 2012) http://ccrweb.ca/en/2011-refugee-claim-data (accessed 25 June 2012): the average recognition rate for Hungarian refugee claimants in 2011 was 18.3 per cent, but among decision makers who determined ten or more claims, the rate varied from 0 per cent to 80 per cent.

from that country. Section 109.1(2) authorizes the minister to designate
a safe country

> if the Minister is of the opinion that in the country in question
>
> (i)   there is an independent judicial system,
> (ii) basic democratic rights and freedoms are recognized and mechanisms
>   for redress are available if those rights or freedoms are infringed, and
> (iii) civil society organizations exist.

These formal indicators of country conditions do not require the minister to consider the actual human rights record of the country at issue.
The existence of an independent judicial system says little about genuine
access to justice. No metric for assessing 'recognition' of basic human
rights, or the effectiveness of redress, is set out. The relevance of civil
society organizations' mere existence is unexplained. Civil society organizations dedicated to investigating, publicizing and protesting human
rights abuses do not necessarily prove that a country is safe; indeed, their
existence may demonstrate the opposite.

In determining that a country is safe, the minister need not consult
individuals, organizations or institutions with expertise in evaluating the
political and human rights context of individual countries. The minister
need only hold the subjective opinion that the conditions are met for
designation. The possible review or delisting of an SCO appears not to
have occurred to the drafters. The mechanisms for designating a country
as safe are unaccompanied by any process for revising or reversing the
decision in light of new evidence.

The Canadian SCO provisions compare unfavourably in this regard to
the Procedures Directive. Annex II to the Procedures Directive focuses
the SCO inquiry beyond formal adherence to human rights instruments
or the existence of judicial institutions, and directs attention to the actual
occurrence of persecution, torture, inhuman or degrading treatment or
indiscriminate violence.[91]

The assessment must take account of, *inter alia*, the extent to which
protection is provided against persecution or mistreatment by:

> (a) the relevant laws and regulations of the country and the manner in
>   which they are applied;
> (b) observance of the rights and freedoms laid down in the European
>   Convention for the Protection of Human Rights and Fundamental

---

[91] Procedures Directive, Annex II, designation of safe countries of origin for the purposes
of arts. 29 and 30(1), p. 33.

Freedoms and/or the International Covenant for Civil and Political Rights and/or the Convention against Torture, in particular the rights from which derogation cannot be made under Article 15(2) of the said European Convention;

(c) respect of the *non-refoulement* principle according to the Geneva Convention;

(d) provision for a system of effective remedies against violations of these rights and freedoms.[92]

Annex II incorporates by reference the definition of persecution contained in article 9 Recast Qualification Directive.[93] This definition of persecution encompasses the cumulative, severe effect of discriminatory laws, enforcement practices and access to judicial remedies, as well as conduct by non-State actors where the State is unable or unwilling to provide protection.[94] In the result, the Procedures Directive precludes listing a State that engages in, or fails to adequately protect against, severe discrimination, harassment and violence that cumulatively amount to persecution.

Whereas the Canadian Minister of Citizenship and Immigration has unfettered discretion to designate a country as safe, the Procedures Directive requires that listing decisions be made with due regard to information provided by 'the UNHCR, the Council of Europe, and other relevant international organizations'.[95] The inclusion of the Council of Europe as a source of information about country conditions is particularly significant in the context of European Roma. The UNHCR, other United Nations bodies,[96] and civil society organizations[97] have each documented the condition of Roma in Europe. Among public institutions, the Human Rights Commissioner for the Council of Europe has gathered some of the most detailed, comprehensive, regular and credible evidence of pervasive, ongoing anti-Roma

---

[92] *Ibid.* [93] Recast Qualification Directive. [94] *Ibid.* art. 9, pp. 15–16.

[95] Procedures Directive, arts. 29(3), pp. 26–7 and 30(5), p. 27.

[96] See UNHRC, *Report of the Special Rapporteur on Contemporary Forms of Racism, Racial Discrimination, Xenophobia and Related Intolerance, Githu Muigai*, 19 May 2009 (A/HRC/11/36).

[97] See, e.g., Human Rights Watch, *Everyday Intolerance: Racist and Xenophobic Violence in Italy* (New York: HRW, 2011); Amnesty International, 'Mind the Legal Gap: Roma and the Right to Housing in Romania', AI Index: EUR 39/004/2011, 23 June 2011; European Roma Rights Centre, 'Roma Under Attack: Violence against Roma Surges in Central and Eastern Europe' (27 September 2012) www.errc.org/article/roma-under-attack-vio lence-against-roma-surges-in-central-and-eastern-europe/4059 (accessed 17 October 2012).

discrimination, policies, harassment and violence committed, condoned or tolerated by State and non-State actors.[98] Whether Hungary would qualify as an SCO under the Procedures Directive is a moot question, however, because the Aznar Protocol deems any State that meets the criteria for membership in the EU as an SCO and disqualifies a citizen of one EU State for asylum in any other EU State. In effect, the Aznar Protocol conclusively presumes all EU Member States are SCOs. The EU Common European Asylum System is already harmonized around the principle that only third countries produce refugees.[99]

The Aznar Protocol begins with a lengthy recital that summarizes the various pre-accession conditions that States must meet to gain admission to the EU. It identifies the judicial and political measures available to European institutions to respond to alleged failures of Member States to adhere to their human rights obligations. It cites the principle of freedom of movement and residence for all EU citizens within the EU (eventually enshrined in the Free Movement Directive), and expresses the wish 'to prevent the institution of asylum being resorted to for purposes alien to those for which it is intended'. This preamble culminates in a lone article which creates a virtually irrebuttable presumption of safety: 'Given the level of protection of fundamental rights and freedoms by the Member States of the European Union, Member States shall be regarded as constituting safe countries of origin in respect of each other for all legal and practical purposes in relation to asylum matters.' Absent very exceptional circumstances, no 'application for asylum made by a national for a Member State may be taken into consideration or declared admissible for processing by another Member State'.[100]

---

[98] See Commissioner for Human Rights, 'Human Rights of Roma'; Council of Europe (COE), Commissioner for Human Rights, and Organization for Security and Co-operation in Europe, High Commissioner on National Minorities, 'Recent Migration of Roma in Europe' (2nd edn, 10 October 2010) https://wcd.coe.int/com.instranet.InstraServlet?com mand=com.instranet.CmdBlobGet&InstranetImage=1672771&SecMode=1&DocId=163 9906&Usage=2 (accessed 17 October 2012); COE, Commissioner for Human Rights, 'Human Rights in Europe: No Grounds for Complacency' (April 2011) www.coe.int/t/commissioner/Viewpoints/ISBN2011_en.pdf (accessed 17 October 2012).

[99] Recast Qualification Directive, arts. 1 and 2(d).

[100] Aznar Protocol, sole art. The Aznar Protocol grew out of a dispute between Spain and Belgium regarding the extradition of a Basque fugitive to Spain, and was animated by Spain's concern that Basque citizens might claim asylum in other European States. While the Aznar Protocol carves out exceptional circumstances where a Member State may adjudicate an asylum claim made by a citizen of another Member State, the

If the Aznar Protocol did not deem EU Member States to be safe, it is not self-evident that Hungary (among other EU Member States) would meet the Procedures Directive's own standards for designating an SCO. The irony that one European institution deems all Member States safe, while another European institution contradicts it, was not lost on Council of Europe Human Rights Commissioner Thomas Hammarberg. In his 2010 note on the breach of the free movement rights of Roma in the EU, Hammarberg remarked:

> In general, European governments seem not to accept that Roma could have protection needs. In the European Union the policy is that all EU member states shall be considered 'safe countries of origin' in respect of each other in asylum matters. Consequently, a citizen of one EU member state may not be granted international protection in another EU member state.
> It may be sobering to learn that whereas Roma from Hungary have been refused asylum in France, for instance, Roma individuals from the same country – and from the Czech Republic – have sought and been granted asylum in Canada.[101]

In comparison to the Procedures Directive's SCO provisions, Canada's qualitative criteria and process for SCO designation appear minimalist and formal. In this regard, it is arguable that Canada's SCO criteria owe more to the Aznar Protocol: Canadian law permits the minister to permanently deem a country as safe based on his opinion that an independent judiciary, civil society and recognition of basic democratic rights exist. The Aznar Protocol's preamble does something similar. It lists the prerequisites that States must meet to earn accession to the EU; recites the various human rights instruments binding upon EU

exceptions are very narrow and require that any claim accepted for processing be presumed 'manifestly unfounded'. In practice, no State except Belgium appears to have invoked the exceptions. As of 2007, Belgium processed a single case from an EU citizen (a Finnish national), which it ultimately rejected.
[101] Thomas Hammarberg, Council of Europe, 'European Migration Policies Discriminate against Roma' (22 February 2010) www.coe.int/t/commissioner/Viewpoints/100222_en.asp (accessed 25 May 2012). The European Council on Refugees and Exiles (ECRE) has also drawn attention to the fact that 'EU Member states themselves cannot be considered safe countries of origin as a number of EU citizens have been recognized as refugees outside the EU' ('Comments from the European Council on Refugees and Exiles on the European Commission Proposal to Recast the Asylum Procedures Directive' (May 2010), at 40 www.ecre.org/topics/areas-of-work/protection-in-europe/162.html (accessed 25 May 2012)). See also ECRE, 'Comments from the European Council on Refugees and Exiles on the Amended Commission Proposal to Recast the Asylum Procedures Directive' COM (2011) 319 final (1 September 2011) www.ecre.org/component/content/article/57-policy-papers/248-ecrecommentsrecastapd2011.html (accessed 15 July 2012). See also Carrera, 'Canada–Czech Republic visa dispute'.

Members; notes the authority of the EU to take measures against Member States who are non-compliant with EU treaty obligations; affirms the jurisdiction of the European Court of Justice as a mechanism of redress – and highlights the mobility rights of EU citizens. These are the formal criteria that, to quote the opening word of the Protocol's sole article, make the safety of EU countries an irrevocable *given*.

While Thomas Hammarberg uses the acceptance of Roma asylum seekers in Canada to invite a critique of the Aznar Protocol, the Canadian Border Services Agency uses the same facts to demonstrate Canada's gullibility in recognizing European Roma as refugees.

G   Conclusion

Since the initial arrival of Roma asylum seekers in the mid-1990s, the Canadian government's goal has been to repel them. The optimal legal instrument for achieving that objective was, and remains, a visa. Exploring the genesis of the SCO concept as visa alternative affirms that the power and influence of the EU *qua* supranational polity mattered considerably to the outcome, but not in the way the emulation thesis might predict. That the SCO happened to be an invention of European States emerges as more an opportunistic coincidence than an instance of deliberate emulation. The specific contribution of EU-level legal instruments – notably the Procedures Directive – seems tenuous. Certain functional aspects of European States' SCO provisions could not be transplanted directly in Canadian refugee law, partly due to variation in jurisprudential soil conditions.

Yet, the quest for a visa substitute was motivated precisely by the political power of the EU. Canada could not conclude a free-trade agreement with its 'second-largest trading partner' and the 'world's largest integrated economy' absent the consent of each EU Member State.[102] And no Member State will ratify a free-trade agreement as long as Canada imposes a visa on its nationals. This political calculus led the Canadian government to seek inspiration from the national asylum regimes of European States as resources for a second-best option, the SCO.[103]

---

[102] Foreign Affairs and International Trade Canada, 'EU Ambassadors Show Support for Canada–EU Economic and Trade Agreement' (Media Release, 2 October 2012) www.international.gc.ca/media_commerce/release_photo_distribution/2012/10/02b.aspx?lang=eng&view=d (accessed 11 October 2012).

[103] According to media accounts, the government also considered automatically detaining all Roma asylum seekers as a deterrent measure: 'Federal government mulls detaining

Having said that, discursive traces of the EU's normative influence become more visible if one shifts the lens away from the SCO (as European device for deterring third-country nationals), and towards the Aznar Protocol (as European device for effacing the European refugee).

Here, it is noteworthy that while the Canadian Minister of Citizenship and Immigration's vilification campaign unmistakably targets Hungarian Roma, he increasingly codes them as 'European', rather than Hungarian, and leaves it to others to explicitly name them as Roma. The actual country conditions prevailing in Hungary, and the specificity of Roma as disadvantaged minority, fade from view. They are replaced by the reconstituted European asylum seeker, whose fraudulence is demonstrated by the fact of seeking refuge from the 'democratic European Union':

> [W]e've seen a troubling growth in fake asylum claims coming particularly from the democratic European Union ... and almost none of those European asylum claims turn out to be well-founded or in need of Canada's protection ... That's why in Bill C-31, we've streamlined the process for the designation of certain countries of origin from which claims will receive accelerated treatment.[104]

Just as the Aznar Protocol has evicted citizens of EU Member States from the legal terrain of the EU asylum regime, so too does Canada's introduction of the European-inspired SCO provision begin to efface them from Canadian asylum law, as prelude to repelling them from Canadian territory. And it does so by portraying Europe as Europe chooses to portray itself. As the Canadian Border Security Agency stated in its 2012 intelligence report ('Project Sara') on Hungarian Roma asylum seekers:

> Every European Union (EU) state recognizes that a European state, in order to join the EU, must meet the Union's stringent human rights standards and undertake to protect their own nationals and nationals of other countries within their borders from human rights abuses and persecution. Therefore, nationals of any EU state cannot make refugee claims in another EU state. This is in accordance with Protocol 29 (the '[Aznar] Protocol') of the EU's Amsterdam Treaty which limits asylum in EU states to 'third country nationals', i.e. people who are not citizens of the EU. No EU country will entertain refugee claims by Hungarian Roma,

Roma refugee claimants', *CBCNews*, 18 August 2012 www.cbc.ca/news/canada/story/2012/08/18/canada-roma-detain.html (accessed 11 October 2012).
[104] 'Speaking Notes for the Honourable Jason Kenney, PC, MP, Minister of Citizenship, Immigration and Multiculturalism at a News Conference to Announce Royal Assent of the Protecting Canada's Immigration System Act' (29 June 2012) www.cic.gc.ca/english/department/media/speeches/2012/2012-06-29.asp (accessed 11 October 2012).

since Hungary has in place the institutional framework to ensure that
Hungarian nationals are not persecuted in their homeland.[105]

The ultimate emulation by Canada of the EU lies less in the adoption of a
particular legal instrument (safe country of origin) and more in the
normative move of subscribing to the erasure of the European refugee
as legal subject.

H   Postscript

On 15 November 2012, a Federal Court judge set aside and remitted a
negative decision concerning Hungarian Roma asylum seekers, in which
the initial rejection was predicated on the availability of State protection.
The Federal Court noted that the documentary evidence from the 2010
US Department of State Human Rights Report for Hungary (upon which
the IRB purported to rely) indicated that 'the level of democracy is at an
all time low' and that the report 'explicitly contradicts' the IRB's finding
that 'Roma can expect state authorities to protect them'.[106]

   Exactly one month later, on 15 December 2012, Minister of
Citizenship and Immigration Jason Kenney issued the orders bringing
the safe country of origin regime into force. The quantitative thresholds
apply to any country that generated thirty or more asylum claims in any
twelve month period in the previous three years. As predicted, designation is triggered by an acceptance rate lower than 25 per cent (where
abandonment and withdrawal count as rejection) or a withdrawal or
abandonment rate higher than 60 per cent. In principle, a country could
be designated as safe where, three years earlier, the acceptance was lower
than 25 per cent, even if civil war erupted thereafter and the acceptance
jumped to 80 per cent.

   The minister named twenty-seven States to his safe country list and
added another eight (including Mexico) in February 2013.[107] Fourteen
are designated according to one of the two quantitative thresholds, while

---

[105] CBSA, 'Project SARA', p. 25.

[106] *Katinszki v. Canada* (Minister of Citizenship and Immigration) [2012] 2012 FC 1326
   (Federal Court), para. 17.

[107] Department of Citizenship and Immigration, Order Establishing Quantitative
   Thresholds for the Designation of Countries of Origin; Order Designating Countries
   of Origin, Canada Gazette, Part I, Vol. 146, No. 50, 15 December 2012, 3378–80 www.
   gazette.gc.ca/rp-pr/p1/2012/2012-12-15/html/index-eng.html (accessed 14 December
   2012); Department of Citizenship and Immigration, Order Designating Countries of
   Origin, Canada Gazette, Part I, Vol. 147, No. 8, 23 February 2013, 317–18 www.gazette.

thirteen are designated on the basis of the qualitative criteria. All EU Member States except Romania and Bulgaria, along with the United States and Croatia, appear on the safe country list. Hungary and the Czech Republic are designated on the basis of acceptance and/or abandonment rates. Each of the thirteen States designated according to qualitative criteria are EU Member States that generated fewer than thirty (and often zero) asylum claims in Canada over the last three years.

In announcing the safe country list, Immigration Minister Jason Kenney carefully avoided naming any individual State from which asylum seekers claim refugee protection, and instead focused his prepared remarks exclusively on the European Union as polity: 'It is remarkable that the European Union – with its democratic tradition of freedom, respect for human rights, and an independent judiciary – has been the top source region for asylum claims made in Canada.'[108]

In the Canadian legal imagination, Europe is now a country, and it is safe.

gc.ca/rp-pr/p1/2013/2013-02-23/html/notice-avis-eng.html#dl05 (accessed 11 May 2013).
[108] Citizenship and Immigration Canada, News Release: Making Canada's Asylum System Faster and Fairer, 14 December 2012 www.cic.gc.ca/english/department/media/releases/2012/2012-12-14.asp?utm_source=media-centre-email&utm_medium=email-eng&utm_campaign=generic (accessed 14 December 2012).

5

Between East and West: the case of Israel

DALLAL STEVENS

A Introduction

Israel provides an interesting case study for examining the global reach of European asylum and refugee law, situated as it is between East and West, and in view of its long association with the European Union (EU). The legal basis for the EU's relationship with Israel arises from the Euro-Mediterranean Agreement (also known as the Association Agreement) signed in 1995. Mainly focused on political dialogue and economic cooperation, the Agreement makes a passing but crucial reference to human rights, stressing that:

> [r]elations between the Parties, as well as all the provisions of the Agreement itself, shall be based on respect for human rights and demo-cratic principles, which guides their internal and international policy and constitutes an essential element of this Agreement.[1]

This promises much, but, in so far as refugee protection is concerned, the Agreement is silent. Rather, it focuses on cooperation on immigration and 'illegal migratory flows'.[2] It was therefore left to other initiatives to develop collaboration in the asylum field, as well as on broader migration issues. In particular, such can be found in the Barcelona Process, launched in 1995 between the EU and fourteen Mediterranean partners,

---

[1] Euro-Mediterranean Agreement establishing an association between the European Communities and their Member States, of the one part, and the State of Israel, of the other part, 21 June 2000 (OJ 2000 No. L147/3), art. 2.

[2] *Ibid.*, art. 57: 'The Parties shall co-operate with a view in particular to:
  - defining areas of mutual interest concerning policies on immigration,
  - increasing the effectiveness of measures aimed at preventing or curbing illegal migra-tory flows.'

including Israel,[3] and in the European Neighbourhood Policy (ENP), established in 2004 'with the objective of avoiding emergence of new dividing lines between the enlarged EU and [its] neighbours and instead strengthening the prosperity, stability and security of all'.[4] An ENP Action Plan was jointly endorsed in December 2004, advancing cooperation on certain areas of interest to Israel and the EU, including justice, home affairs and migration.[5] The Plan, like the Association Agreement, once more stresses that 'Israel and the EU are committed to achieve closer political co-operation and dialogue on the basis of their common values: the respect for human rights and fundamental freedoms, democracy, good governance and international humanitarian law'.[6] Yet this reflection of rights and fundamental freedoms is not always apparent in the migration context, where concerns with criminality come to the fore. For example, included in 'Priorities for Action' is the need to 'strengthen co-operation on migration-related issues, fight against organized crime, including trafficking in human beings and police and judicial co-operation'.[7] Asylum gets a poor mention in the various objectives to encourage 'effective management of migration flows';[8] we are simply informed that there will be an exchange of information and practices in the field of asylum policy.[9] Importantly, though, there is talk of identifying 'the scope for Israel to participate in relevant EU programmes and . . . the scope for legislative approximation'.[10] In this sense, it would appear that, among the many countries considered in this book, Israel is one of the most likely candidates to be influenced by European asylum law and protection practices.

Israel has consulted the EU about asylum policy at a time when it was confronting an expansion of asylum applications, and was considering improving its asylum law and policy. In June 2008, for example, under the European Commission's Technical Assistance and Information

---

[3] Barcelona Declaration adopted at the Euro-Mediterranean Conference (27–28 November 1995) http://trade.ec.europa.eu/doclib/docs/2005/july/tradoc_124236.pdf (accessed 23 November 2012). It aims to create a common area of peace and stability, establish a free-trade area and promote intercultural dialogue.

[4] European Commission, 'European Neighbourhood Policy' (30 October 2010) http://ec. europa.eu/world/enp/policy_en.htm (accessed 23 November 2012).

[5] EU/Israel Action Plan: http://ec.europa.eu/world/enp/pdf/action_plans/israel_enp_ap_ final_en.pdf (accessed 23 November 2012).

[6] Ibid., para. 2.1.   [7] Ibid., p. 3.

[8] The focus of the Action Plan is to combat terrorism and fighting organized crime, including trafficking in human beings: EU/Israel Action Plan, para. 2.4.

[9] Ibid., p. 15.   [10] Ibid.

Exchange (TAIEX) initiative, a seminar was organized in Jerusalem entitled 'Legal and Illegal Immigration and Asylum: The Example of the EU'. The meeting included judges, legal advisers and police from the EU, Member States and Israel, and the United Nations High Commissioner for Refugees (UNHCR). It was clearly an opportunity to share information and practice, and covered both the then current migration and asylum context in Israel and the EU *acquis*, Member State practices, illegal immigration and family reunification.[11] Further meetings were held in 2008,[12] and, in December 2009, a second seminar was arranged in Israel, to which experts from EU Member States were, once more, invited, with a view to discussing experience and policy options.[13] A third initiative, comprising the Euro-Med Migration Projects,[14] aims to strengthen 'cooperation in the management of migration so as to build up the Mediterranean partners' capacity to provide an effective, targeted and comprehensive solution to the various forms of migration'.[15] While the earlier projects included legislative convergence in migration law,[16] the latest, Euro-Med Migration III (2012–14), has moved away from the focus on legal convergence and is concerned with legal migration, migration and development, and illegal migration.

The extent to which the ENP Action Plan, TAIEX discussions and seminars, and the Euro-Med Projects have influenced the development of Israeli policy on asylum is difficult to assess. But it is clear that the EU has imparted its own perception of asylum and its approach to managing migration: that is, notwithstanding its articulated pro-protection stance, the tendency to conflate asylum with (illegal) immigration, and to discuss asylum within the context of criminality, terrorism and trafficking. The inevitable effect is to undermine protection and overemphasize the importance of citizenship and security. It would appear that Israel has read these signals well.

[11] The Agenda and copies of some PowerPoint presentations are available on the TAIEX website: http://ec.europa.eu/enlargement/taiex/dyn/taiex-events/library/detail_en.jsp? EventID=30343 (accessed 23 November 2012).
[12] Commission of the European Communities, *Implementation of the European Neighbourhood Policy in 2008: Progress Report Israel*, 23 April 2009 (SEC(2009) 516/2), p. 11.
[13] European Commission, *Implementation of the European Neighbourhood Policy in 2009: Progress Report Israel*, 12 May 2010 (SEC(2010) 520), p. 11.
[14] Euro-Med I (2004–07), Euro-Med II (2008–11) and Euro-Med III (2012–14).
[15] See, e.g., objectives of Euro-Med Migration III: www.enpi- nfo.eu/mainmed.php? id=391&id_type=10 (accessed 23 November 2012).
[16] In addition to labour migration, they include the fight against illegal immigration and the relationship between migration and development.

B   Background to Israel's asylum regime

Until recently, Israel did not face the same challenges as the EU in relation to inward migration and refugee flows. Asylum seekers generally numbered in the hundreds: for example, some 250 Vietnamese in the 1970s; 100 Bosnians in 1993; 112 Albanian Muslims in 1999.[17] The one exception was in 2000 when over 6,000 asylum applications were made, the majority from members of the South Lebanese Army and their families following the withdrawal of Israel from Lebanon;[18] the numbers actually granted refugee status in Israel were also equally low.[19] However, from about 2006, this began to change, initially as a conse- quence of Egypt's treatment of African asylum seekers (coming mainly from the African countries of Eritrea, Ethiopia, Somalia, Kenya, Sudan, Côte d'Ivoire and Chad) in 2005. Since the 1990s, Southern Sudanese and other sub-Saharan Africans had made their way to Egypt and had been assessed by UNHCR for refugee status. This was because Egypt, though a signatory to the 1951 Refugee Convention and its 1967 Protocol,[20] had not established its own asylum determination procedure or institutional framework. In June 2004, UNHCR suspended refugee status determination for Sudanese asylum seekers, as a result of the cessation of armed conflict in Southern Sudan, and replaced it with an asylum seeker registration card. This carried a (renewable) entitlement to a six-monthly residence permit. However, Sudanese asylum seekers objected and commenced a peaceful demonstration outside UNHCR's Cairo offices. They were protesting in the main about the lack of status and opportunity for resettlement, as well as their very poor living con- ditions in Egypt. The sit-in, in the end involving some 3,000 people, was violently broken up by the Egyptian police in December 2005, and at

[17] Anat Ben-Dor and Rami Adut, *Israel: A Safe Haven? Problems in the Treatment Offered by the State of Israel to Refugees and Asylum Seekers* (Report and Position Paper, Tel Aviv University, Buchmann Faculty of Law, Public Interest Law Resource Centre, and Physicians for Human Rights, September 2003), pp. 21–3.

[18] *Ibid.*, p. 22. The relevant figures for 1999 to 2005 are: 540 (1999); 6,148 (2000); 456 (2001); 355 (2002); [none provided for 2003]; 922 (2004); 909 (2005). UNHCR, *2005 UNHCR Statistical Yearbook: Israel* www.unhcr.org/4641be5d0.html (accessed 23 November 2012).

[19] The relevant figures for 1999 to 2005 are: 128 (1999); 4,075 (2000); 4,168 (2001); 4,179 (2002); 4,179 (2003); 574 (2004); 609 (2005) (*ibid.*).

[20] Convention relating to the Status of Refugees, Geneva, 28 July 1951, in force 22 April 1954 (189 UNTS 137), read in conjunction with the Protocol relating to the Status of Refugees, New York, adopted 31 January 1967, in force 4 October 1967 (606 UNTS 267) (together Refugee Convention).

least twenty eight people died and a considerable number were detained. Rather than return to their countries, often afflicted with ongoing internecine warfare, many Africans chose instead to take the hazardous journey across the Sinai desert into Israel.[21] As a consequence, Israel faced a sudden increase in both asylum applications[22] and economic migrants, which continues today. There is great concern that smugglers are heavily involved in assisting would-be migrants to access Israel, and this has influenced recent changes in the law and attitudes to new arrivals. Current estimates are that there are some 45,000 Africans in Israel.[23] The Israeli government considers that 98 per cent are seeking work,[24] but at the same time does not deport many. Rather, they are detained for a few weeks following arrival and then released.[25] Somewhat unusually, Eritreans and Sudanese are not permitted to apply for asylum, but are treated on a group basis.

C   Israeli asylum determination

Although it is one of the few countries in the region to have signed the Refugee Convention,[26] Israel has not incorporated it into national law.[27] Until recently, it had not felt the need to establish a national asylum

---

[21] See Yonathan Paz, 'Ordered Disorder: African Asylum Seekers in Israel and Discursive Challenges to an Emerging Refugee Regime' (UNHCR, New Issues in Refugee Research, Research Paper No. 205, March 2011), p. 3.

[22] The relevant figures for 2006 to 2010 are: 1,348 (2006); 5,382 (2007); 8,373 (2008); 809 (2009); 1,448 (2010). Compiled from UNHCR, UNHCR Statistical Yearbooks, available at www.unhcr.org/pages/4a02afce6.html (accessed 23 November 2012).

[23] As is often the case where mixed migration patterns are involved, and where entry may be irregular or via smuggling routes, it is very difficult to gauge the exact number of new arrivals. In 2012, one report suggested that approximately 2,000 people were entering Israel per month: Dallia Moniem, 'Torture in Egyptian desert', Africa Review, 2 March 2012 www.africareview.com/Special+Reports/Torture+in+the+desert/-/979182/1357834/-/fnqhl3/-/index.html (accessed 23 November 2012). UNHCR, meanwhile, suggests that some 1,000 persons per month are crossing the Egypt–Israel Sinai border: UNHCR, '2012 Regional Operation Profile: Middle East' www.unhcr.org/cgi-bin/texis/vtx/page?page=49e4864b6&submit=GO (accessed 23 November 2012).

[24] Amnon Ben Ami, Director of the Population and Immigration Borders Authority, as cited in Omri Efraim, 'Who are the Sinai infiltrators?', Ynetnews.com, 12 December 2011 www.ynetnews.com/articles/0,7340,L-4160678,00.html (accessed 23 November 2012).

[25] Amnesty International, 'Israel: New Detention Law Violates Rights of Asylum Seekers', 11 January 2012 www.amnesty.org/en/news/new-israeli-detention-law-violates-asylum-seekers-rights-2012-01-10 (accessed 23 November 2012).

[26] Egypt, Iran, Turkey and Yemen are also signatories.

[27] Israel has entered reservations: arts. 8 and 12 do not apply; art. 28 applies with the limitations resulting from s. 6 Passports Law, 5712–1952.

regime either. The generally low number of applications since Israel's accession to the Refugee Convention, and, as is the case with its Arab neighbours, an association of refugee policy with the Palestinian issue, acted as disincentives.[28]

From the early 1980s to 2002, the UNHCR representative in Israel received applications from asylum seekers, prepared the files and then passed them to UNHCR's Geneva headquarters, where refugee status determination was carried out.[29] The average time for a decision was two years,[30] and the Israeli government generally accepted UNHCR's decision.[31] In 2001, the Minister of the Interior promulgated an internal directive entitled Regulations regarding the Treatment of Asylum Seekers in Israel, in which a basic asylum process was set out, partly transferring responsibility for asylum decision making to the State of Israel. Applications were still to be made to the UNHCR representative in Israel, who conducted initial screening and the substantive interview before forwarding the information to the Ministry of the Interior, and its Advisory Committee for a final decision.[32] This confirmed Israel as the first Middle Eastern country to establish its own refugee status determination mechanism.[33] This system applied from 2002–09, with the National Status Granting Body (NSGB) assuming the role of the Advisory Committee and formulating the recommendation to the Minister of the Interior, who made the final decision.[34] On 1 July 2009, full transfer to the Ministry of the Interior of the responsibility for refugee status determination commenced, and, in January 2011, the 2001 Regulations were revised in a document entitled Procedure for Handling Political Asylum Seekers in Israel.[35] This provides a much more detailed refugee determination system, introducing further stringent measures, an ability to reject applicants without full consideration of their claim,

[28] See UNHCR, 'Q&A: Growing Caseload of Asylum Seekers for UNHCR Officers in Israel', 13 July 2007 www.unhcr.org/469797404.html (accessed 23 November 2012).

[29] Ben-Dor and Adut, Israel, p. 26.   [30] Ibid.

[31] UNHCR, 'Q&A: Growing Caseload of Asylum Seekers'.

[32] The Regulations are contained in Ben-Dor and Adut, Israel, Annex A.

[33] Michael Kagan and Anat Ben-Dor, Nowhere to Run: Gay Palestinian Asylum Seekers in Israel (Tel Aviv University, Buchmann Faculty of Law, Public Interest Law Program, April 2008), p. 23.

[34] See Anat Ben-Dor and Michael Kagan, 'The Refugee from My Enemy Is My Enemy: The Detention and Exclusion of Sudanese Refugees in Israel' (Minerva Center for Human Rights, Working Paper, 19 November 2006).

[35] Ministry of Interior, Population Immigration and Border Authority, Procedure for Handling Political Asylum Seekers in Israel, entered into force 2 January 2011 http://piba.gov.il/Regulations/Procedure%20for%20Handling%20Political%20Asylum%20Seekers%20in%20Israel-en.pdf (accessed 23 November 2012).

and strict time limits. Both sets of Regulations are administrative instruments rather than formal law and they focus on procedure.

UNHCR maintains a role in Israel, continuing its efforts to promote an Israeli refugee law and seeking a 'favourable asylum environment'.[36] It organizes capacity building and training, and assists the government and civil society in improving their treatment of and services for asylum seekers and refugees.[37] UNHCR also has permission to visit detained asylum seekers, many of whom are Eritreans.

The 2011 Regulations, as might be expected in a national system, are a blend of international standards and municipal idiosyncrasies. Some alignment with the EU's Procedures Directive[38] is evident, as are certain Member State policies. Registration and identification of asylum applicants involves biometric data being taken,[39] interpreters are provided for[40] and the presence of a lawyer is permitted (although he or she is forbidden from making any comments during the interview).[41] A two-stage process has been implemented, involving a basic interview, followed in certain cases by a comprehensive interview.[42] This has interesting parallels with the former process in the United Kingdom (UK). It is, however, a somewhat convoluted structure with a variety of players. For example, the individual in the Population, Immigration and Border Authority ('Infiltrators and Asylum Seekers Department' – Refugee Status Determination (RSD) Unit) conducting the basic and comprehensive interviews will not necessarily make the decision on the merits of the refugee claim.[43]

A 'dismissal out of hand' – that is, a summary refusal – can occur where, following the basic interview, 'the claim and facts on which the application is based, even if all of them were to be proven, do not constitute any of the elements set out in the refugee convention'.[44] In other words, this is an

---

[36] UNHCR, *Israel Fact Sheet: June 2010.*   [37] *Ibid.*

[38] Council Directive 2005/85/EC of 1 December 2005 on minimum standards on procedures in Member States for granting and withdrawing refugee status, 13 December 2005 (OJ 2005 No. L326/13) (Procedures Directive).

[39] Ministry of Interior, Population Immigration and Border Authority, *Procedure for Handling Political Asylum Seekers in Israel*, para. 2.

[40] *Ibid.*, paras. 3(b)(1) and 5(d).

[41] *Ibid.*, paras. 3(b)(2) and 5(d)(3) as per art. 16(3) Procedures Directive.

[42] *Ibid.*, paras. 3 and 5.

[43] Prior to the New Asylum Model being introduced in the UK, it was possible for the interviewer and decision maker to be two different people.

[44] Ministry of Interior, Population, Immigration and Border Authority, *Procedure for Handling Political Asylum Seekers in Israel*, para. 4(a).

BETWEEN EAST AND WEST: THE CASE OF ISRAEL   139

accelerated procedure. Though the interviewer/caseworker is required to refer the material to someone who has undergone RSD training for approval, it is clear that a decision with far-reaching implications can be taken by an individual with no refugee law training. This is deeply worrying and has been criticized by UNHCR.[45]

Applicants attending the comprehensive interview must complete a form no later than fourteen days before the interview; failure to do so will lead to refusal of the application.[46] An RSD-trained employee will decide whether to refer the application to the Advisory Committee (in effect the NSGB, as previously) for consideration.[47] There are two possible referrals to the Committee: for a summary procedure – if the claim is deemed not credible, groundless or not well founded and the case can be dismissed – or for full deliberation.[48] In the summary procedure, the ultimate decision is made by the Director of the Authority, taking account of the views of the Committee and of the RSD Unit. In the case of a full deliberation, the Committee's recommendation is then passed on to the Minister of the Interior for a final decision. A grant of refugee status entitles the bearer to a temporary residency licence (A/5) for one year only on a renewable basis, with the right to work and access to social security benefits.

Refused applicants have a number of routes to revisit decisions on their claims. For summary refusals, the applicant has no internal appeal but can petition the Court of Administrative Affairs.[49] However, it would appear that those rejected summarily are usually detained and removed from Israel within three days.[50] Indeed, although not clearly stated in the Regulations, the challenge to the court would seek to prevent deportation, which automatically arises on summary rejection. For other refusals

---

[45] UNHCR, 'Comments on Sections 2–4 of the Regulations Regarding the Processing of Asylum Seekers in Israel', 12 January 2011, cited in Yonatan Berman, 'The Israeli Refugee Status Determination Process: General Background' (Hotline for Migrant Workers, 20 September 2011), p. 4.

[46] In the UK, failure to complete the Statement of Evidence Form could result in outright refusal for 'non-compliance': see Dallal Stevens, *UK Asylum Law and Policy: Historical and Contemporary Perspectives* (London: Sweet & Maxwell, 2004), pp. 295–6.

[47] The Committee should comprise a retired judge or person qualified to serve as a district court judge, a representative of the Ministry of Justice, a representative of the Ministry of Foreign Affairs and a representative of the Ministry of the Interior's Population, Immigration and Border Authority.

[48] Ministry of Interior, Population, Immigration and Border Authority, *Procedure for Handling Political Asylum Seekers in Israel*, paras. 6 and 7.

[49] *Ibid.*, para. 4(a)(2).   [50] Berman, 'The Israeli Refugee Status Determination Process', 3.

(the minority of cases), the applicant can request reconsideration of the claim where there is a change of circumstances or new evidence.[51] A request for reconsideration suspends deportation.[52] The case goes back to the Infiltrators and Asylum Seekers Department but is handled by an RSD-qualified caseworker who did not consider the original claim. The caseworker's opinion is then provided to the Advisory Committee for decision. Somewhat bizarrely, however, '[t]he recommendation of the Committee regarding the request for reconsideration of a person whose application for asylum was denied by the Director of the Authority, will be referred to the Director of the Authority in order for him to decide on the matter'.[53] This recirculation of the revised claim to a number of the same decision makers is somewhat questionable in terms of transparency, independence and fairness.

There is also the possibility of petition to the Administrative Court against the decision of the Director of the Authority or of the Interior Minister, although this is not clearly specified in the Regulations other than for 'dismissals out of hand'. Administrative challenge requires legal representation and is costly. Yet, in a striking parallel with appeals and judicial review proceedings in countries such as the UK, there is a burgeoning caseload before the Administrative Court. The Ministry of the Interior has stated that in the first two months of 2011, there were some seven hundred challenges presented to the court.[54] In dismissing twenty asylum petitions in one week, the sitting judge claimed that the majority of asylum claims were 'baseless' and that appeals were filed in order to 'abuse the procedure and enjoy temporary immunity from expulsion'.[55] Thus, as elsewhere, the courts in Israel are beginning to feel the pressure of an increasing number of asylum applications.

A form of humanitarian protection can be said to exist in Israel, but it has been hard won. Once the government had resolved not to process Eritreans and Sudanese through RSD, arguably because they represent the overwhelming majority of asylum claimants and because of the high rate of refugee grants internationally, a decision had to be taken on the fate of the Africans. Under some pressure from UNHCR, it was agreed that they would not be returned to their countries of origin, nor to Egypt

---

[51] Ministry of Interior, Population, Immigration and Border Authority, *Procedure for Handling Political Asylum Seekers in Israel*, para. 9(a)(1).

[52] *Ibid.*, para. 9(f).   [53] *Ibid.*, para. 9(d).

[54] Ron Friedman, 'State says courts backing up stricter asylum policies', *Jerusalem Post*, 16 March 2011.

[55] *Ibid.*

because of the risk of *refoulement*, but would be permitted to remain in Israel. Eritreans and Sudanese are granted 'conditional release visas' under article 2(a)(5) Entry to Israel Law, which carry no entitlements, other than a right to remain in the territory, and are valid for one to three months on a renewable basis.[56] Interestingly, the government frequently refers to the Sudanese incomers as having been granted 'temporary protection', while refugee support groups dispute this, arguing that it in fact constitutes 'deferred deportation'. Though the Israeli government accepts that Sudanese and Eritreans should not be returned to their home countries, this blanket policy cannot be regarded as a form of complementary protection as understood in the EU. In fact, it has greater similarities with the approach to non-Palestinian refugees of its Arab neighbours – such as Jordan – which prefer to treat asylum seekers and refugees as 'guests', which often entails a form of territorial sanctuary but comes with few other rights.

The Israeli asylum process is thus a mixture of some positive elements – the entitlement to interpreters and legal advisers, and the right to reasons for refusal – and many negative elements – lack of an asylum law or incorporation of the Refugee Convention into national law; a complex administrative system that has been much criticized by non-governmental organizations (NGOs), and a power of summary dismissal with extreme consequences (deportation), to name a few. The refusal rate is very high.[57] Some similarity with EU Member State practice and with the EU Procedures Directive can be seen, but the correlation is relatively minor. Israel is behaving in the same way as many individual EU Member States: adopting a restrictive approach where so inclined. The RSD Unit is mirroring attitudes familiar in many countries and adopting a 'culture of disbelief'. For example, refugee advocates report that interviewers of asylum seekers assume an intimidating role as if interrogating a criminal suspect, and do not permit applicants to explain their cases in depth.[58] There is an apparent presumption of lack of credibility from the outset, and minor inconsistencies are relied upon to reject claims.[59] It is also suggested that country of origin information is misused and that the Ministry of the

---

[56] See below for discussion on employment rights.

[57] Hotline for Migrant Workers reports that of 3,400 applications lodged in 2009 and 5,390 in 2010, 4,178 were passed on to the Advisory Committee (NSGB) by the RSD Unit; not one applicant was determined by the RSD Unit to be a refugee (Berman, 'The Israeli Refugee Status Determination Process', 1).

[58] *Ibid.*, 4.   [59] *Ibid.*, 4–5.

Interior is selective about the information upon which it relies to reject asylum claims.[60] While this may be a familiar tale to those who have been examining asylum systems in European States, there is one major issue on which there is wide divergence between the EU and Israel: the approach adopted towards so-called 'enemy nationals', arguably the most contentious provision of the Regulations.

D   Political drivers

Israel's unique political situation adds an unusual dimension to the asylum/refugee issue. The State is established to provide a homeland for Jews, and in order to ensure the security of its citizens, a demographic majority is regarded as paramount.[61] The very construct of Israel, which encourages a right of return for Jews and a specific ethnic membership, necessitates some exclusion of the non-Jew and, consequently, the potential for stringent policies. This has been borne out in the asylum field. For example, Israel is very reluctant to consider asylum applications from citizens of countries it considers enemies of Israel – mainly neighbouring Arab States. In 1954, Israel enacted the Prevention of Infiltration (Offences and Jurisdiction) Law which stated that any person who is a citizen of, resident or visitor to, Egypt, Iraq, Lebanon, Saudi Arabia, Syria, Trans-Jordan (now Jordan) and Yemen, and who enters Israel knowingly and unlawfully, is defined as an 'infiltrator'. The sanction under the Law for Infiltration was up to five years in prison.[62] There is no exception for asylum. It was intended that the Law cease with the state of emergency, but, as the latter was never lifted, the Law is still in force. In a recent contentious amendment to the Prevention of Infiltration Law, passed by the Knesset in January 2012,[63] no distinction is made between asylum seekers, migrant workers and infiltrators: anyone failing to enter Israel via an official border will be deemed an 'infiltrator', and consequently subject to imprisonment. Furthermore, any person considered an infiltrator – asylum seeker, migrant, child – is

---

[60] *Ibid.*, 5.
[61] Euro-Mediterranean Human Rights Network, *Israel's Anti-Infiltration Bill: Another Aspect of Asylum Adhocracy* (June 2010), p. 7.
[62] An infiltrator is liable to imprisonment for a term of five years, or to a fine of I£5,000, or to both such penalties: Prevention of Infiltration (Offences and Jurisdiction) Law, 5714–1954, s. 2.
[63] Note that there was an attempt to introduce a similar bill in 2010 but it was withdrawn on account of significant objection and on request by the Ministry of Defence.

subject to mandatory detention and/or deportation, and can be held without charge for three years or more.[64] Indeed, the possibility of indefinite detention is very real.

When one considers that the previous period of detention was a maximum of sixty days under the Entry into Israel Law 1952, the change in policy is shocking.[65] But the clear aim is deterrence. As the Explanatory Notes to the new Law boldly claim: 'The expectation is that the detention period will stop the massive infiltration or at least minimize it.'[66] Despite the Explanatory Notes also stating that conditions in detention would not be deleterious to the health and dignity of detainees, and that they would not breach the Refugee Convention, the UNHCR representative in Israel, William Tall, demurred. In a letter to the Knesset Speaker, he strongly advocated that the Law should specifically exclude Refugee Convention refugees:

> Our serious concern with the current draft Legislation for the Prevention of Infiltration is that if applied to asylum-seekers in its current form, it could constitute a breach of Israel's rights and obligations as stipulated in the UN Convention for Refugees for which Israel was a founding signatory.[67]

The Knesset chose to ignore the advice.

The law does not simply endorse criminalization of the asylum seeker; it seeks also to target anyone who chooses to assist irregular entrants who are armed, or involved in drug or human trafficking. The sanction is five to fifteen years' imprisonment.[68]

Both the 2001 and 2011 procedural regulations take account of the 1954 Prevention of Infiltration Law and include a provision on 'Subjects of Enemy Hostile States'. The regulations grant the State the right 'not to absorb into Israel and not to grant permits to stay in Israel to subjects of enemy or hostile States – as determined from time to by the authorized

---

[64] Amnesty International, 'Israel: New Detention Law'.

[65] Shira Lawrence, 'Anti-Infiltration Bill Passes into Law', ARDC, 11 January 2012 www.ardc-israel.org/en/article/anti-infiltration-bill-passes-law (accessed 23 November 2012).

[66] Explanatory Notes to the Prevention of Infiltration Law 2012, as quoted in Elizabeth Tsurkov, 'Knesset basses bill on prolonged detention of refugees without trial', *972 Magazine*, 10 January 2012 http://972mag.com/knesset-passes-controversial-bill-on-prolonged-detention-of-asylum-seekers/32487/ (accessed 23 November 2012).

[67] See 'PM's Immigration Bill could violate refugee rights', *New Middle East News*, 19 March 2012; Lahav Harkov, 'Knesset passes Anti-Infiltration Bill', *Jerusalem Post*, 10 January 2012 www.jpost.com/DiplomacyAndPolitics/Article.aspx?id=252909 (accessed 23 November 2012).

[68] Lawrence, 'Anti-Infiltration Bill Passes into Law'.

authorities'.[69] While the 1954 law appears to have a definitive list of those Arab countries considered enemy States, in practice the list is longer due to the enormous discretion granted to the authorities to decide which States to include. It is assumed that Sudan and Iran are included, although attempts to obtain a definitive list by local NGOs have failed.[70] The obvious concern with the relevant provision (paragraph 10, as well as its former incarnation) is its inherent discrimination, which would appear to sanction the exclusion of refugees from 'enemy States'. Israel employed the provision to exclude Sudanese from the refugee status determination procedure and to subject them to indefinite detention, until their release was won by court action.[71] Many remain in Israel today in a precarious legal situation[72] and now face deportation. In the summer of 2011, Israel was one of the first countries to visit the newly independent South Sudan, and it was agreed that if South Sudanese chose to leave Israel on a voluntary basis by the end of March 2012, they would receive USD 1,300. From 1 April 2012, they would be deported by force.[73] Following a late petition to the Jerusalem Administrative Court by a range of NGOs, the court issued a temporary injunction barring removal until 15 April 2012 in view of the fact that conditions in the area were extremely severe and that sporadic fighting was still occurring in the country.[74] The Ministry of Foreign Affairs also recommended delaying the deportation while it reviewed the situation in Sudan, but subsequently changed its mind.[75] As a consequence, the

---

[69] Ministry of Interior, Population, Immigration and Border Authority, *Procedure for Handling Political Asylum Seekers in Israel*, para. 10.

[70] See, e.g., Hotline for Migrant Workers, 'New Regulations for the Treatment of Asylum Seekers in Israel: August 2010' (September 2010).

[71] *Ibid.*

[72] Except in the case of 452 Darfuris who received A5 (temporary residence) visas and 1,000 Eritreans who were granted B1 work visas: Refugees' Rights Forum (Hotline for Migrant Workers), 'Asylum Seekers and Refugees in Israel: August 2009 Update', 20 August 2009 www.acri.org.il/pdf/refugees0809en.pdf (accessed 23 November 2012).

[73] 'Israel begins deportation of South Sudanese refugees', *Real News*, http://therealnews.com/t2/index.php?option=com_content&task=view&id=31&Itemid=74&jumival=8042 (accessed 23 November 2012).

[74] Ben Hartman, 'Court delays deportation of South Sudanese', *Jerusalem Post*, 29 March 2012 www.jpost.com/DiplomacyAndPolitics/Article.aspx?id=264036 (accessed 23 November 2012).

[75] Jacob Blaustein Institute for the Advancement of Human Rights, 'Background: African Asylum Seekers and Migrants in Israel, June 13, 2012', www.jbi-humanrights.org/files/jbi-background_african-asylum-seekers-and-migrants-in-israel.pdf (accessed 23 November 2012).

court's judgment of 7 June 2012 was unsurprising. It determined that the South Sudanese in Israel did not have a right to temporary group protection and were therefore subject to deportation, so long as the right to lodge an individual asylum claim remained.[76]

As in the EU and elsewhere, then, in Israel securitization is a key impetus behind the development of asylum law and policy. Alongside changes to the Prevention of Infiltration Law, the government, with the agreement of the Knesset, has decided to invest millions (approximately USD 5.4 million) in the building of a fence/wall along 140- of the 250-kilometre border between Egypt and Israel – clearly with the aim of keeping out African migrants, whether asylum seekers or otherwise. This actual *cordon sanitaire* is reminiscent of 'Fortress Europe'. But, as with Europe, such policies rarely achieve their objective; the erection of the barrier will not necessarily deter everyone but it will certainly make the journey to Israel more hazardous. It is already evident that the journey across the desert can be a terrifying ordeal, with reports of violence, rape and starvation.[77] In alarming reports in September 2012, twenty Eritreans were refused entry at the Israeli–Egyptian border. Acting under orders, the Israeli army refused them food and only provided limited water in an apparent attempt to force their return to Egypt.[78] Clearly, such a policy raises serious concerns under international law. Israel is also constructing one of the largest detention centres in the world in the southern Negev desert, which will be able to house a minimum of 10,000 detainees. It is suggested that the running costs will amount to USD 3 million per annum.[79] For many who campaign against administrative detention, this is a shocking development.[80] The final initiative in the three-pronged attack is to fine employers that employ undocumented migrants – a time-honoured practice within EU Member States.

[76] *Ibid.*

[77] Paz, 'Ordered Disorder', 3; Anouk Lorié, 'Dangers await Africans seeking asylum in Israel', *Time Magazine*, 11 December 2009 www.time.com/time/world/article/0,8599, 1946861,00.html (accessed 23 November 2012).

[78] Harriet Sherwood, 'Eritrean refugees trapped by security fence at Israeli–Egyptian border', *Guardian*, 5 September 2012 www.guardian.co.uk/world/2012/sep/05/eritrean-refugees-at-israeli-egyptian-border (accessed 23 November 2012).

[79] Charlotte Silver, 'Tel Aviv no haven for asylum seekers', *Al Jazeera*, 23 February 2012 www.aljazeera.com/indepth/opinion/2012/02/2012215161243752551.html (accessed 23 November 2012).

[80] See, e.g., the Global Detention Project: www.globaldetentionproject.org (accessed 23 November 2012).

To deal with the influx of mainly African asylum seekers from the Sinai, Israel implemented a somewhat unusual policy of 'hot returns'. This has no exact equivalent in the EU, but it is not too dissimilar to the 'push back' arrangements that existed between Italy and Libya prior to the Libyan revolution in 2011. Simply put, 'hot returns' – or 'immediate coordinated returns' as they are more formally known – involve removing asylum seekers across the Sinai border to Egypt within 'a reasonable time' of crossing, without any opportunity to lodge an asylum claim.[81] This is, of course, a breach of article 33 Refugee Convention (the principle of *non-refoulement*) and of Israeli law, since the 1995 Supreme Court judgment in *El-Tai'i* v. *Minister of Interior* has declared the principle of *non-refoulement* to be binding.[82] According to Ben Dor and Kagan, '[t]he *El Tai'i* decision is of particular importance since it has recognized ... *non-refoulement* as a binding principle in ... Israeli law, based on international customary law, as well as on the sanctity of life enshrined in the Basic Law: Human Dignity and Liberty'.[83] Notwithstanding the strong legal endorsement of the principle of *non-refoulement*, a formal procedure for the examination, questioning and 'coordinated return' of individuals was introduced.[84] In August 2007, a group of forty-eight migrants were returned to Egypt a day after crossing into Israel. During their brief period in Israel, they were detained and were unable to lodge an asylum claim (despite Darfuris being among the group).[85] It is claimed that, in October 2007, Egypt returned at least five of the group to Sudan.[86]

A challenge to the 'hot returns' policy was instigated by a number of NGOs and it took four years before a decision was handed down by the High Court in July 2011.[87] The court conveniently relied upon

[81] Euro-Mediterranean Human Rights Network, *Israel's Anti-Infiltration Bill*, p. 7.
[82] 49(3) PD 843 [1994] (Isr.), cited in Avi Perry, 'Solving Israel's African Refugee Crisis' (2010) 51 *Virginia Journal of International Law* 157–84, at 162.
[83] Ben-Dor and Kagan, 'The Refugee from My Enemy Is My Enemy', 6.
[84] See for further discussion, Tally Kritzman-Amir and Thomas Spijkerboer, 'On the Morality and Legality of Borders: Border Policies and Asylum Seekers', pp. 27–32 http://works.bepress.com/tally_kritzman_amir/7 (accessed 23 November 2012).
[85] Jacob Blaustein Institute for the Advancement of Human Rights, 'African Asylum Seekers in Israel: Frequently Asked Questions', p. 2 www.ajc.org/atf/cf/%7B42d75369-d582-4380-8395-d25925b85eaf%7D/AFRICANASYLUMFAQS.PDF (accessed 23 November 2012).
[86] *Ibid.*
[87] *The Hotline for Migrant Workers* v. *Minister of Defence*, HCJ 7302/07, 7 July 2011 cited in Kritzman-Amir and Spijkerboer, 'On the Morality and Legality of Borders', 33–4; case available in Hebrew at http://elyon1.court.gov.il/files/07/020/073/n32/07073020.n32.htm (accessed 23 November 2012).

governmental assurances that the policy was no longer in force due to the resignation of the former President of Egypt, Mubarak, and the consequent political uncertainties, and thus dismissed the petition without consideration of the merits of the case.[88] However, the court did add that if the policy were to be reinstated, it should comply with the standards of international law and should guarantee the safety of any returnees as far as possible.[89] Despite the court accepting the government's argument that hot returns were now a non-issue, NGOs have reported that they continue to occur.[90]

E Case law and the judiciary: facilitating change?

Israeli jurisprudence on asylum and refugee issues is in the early stages of development, and the courts have tended, at times, to adopt a somewhat restrictive stance, with a reluctance to challenge the decisions of the Ministry of the Interior (see, for example, the case of *The Hotline for Migrant Workers* v. *Minister of Defence* discussed below).[91] However, there have been some notable recent victories, with indications that the judiciary is upholding principles of human rights protection where the government appears remiss.

The Hotline for Migrant Workers Association was involved in an important challenge to government policy – on this occasion in relation to detention. Until the arrival of Sudanese asylum seekers, the government had rarely felt the need to use the Prevention of Infiltrators Law to detain possible 'infiltrators', relying instead on the Entry into Israel Law of 1952. This changed in 2006. Frustrated with the decision of the Custody Review Court to release African detainees who had been held for longer than sixty days (a discretion provided by the Entry Law), the government began using the Prevention of Infiltrators Law to enable longer-term detention not subject to judicial oversight; detention orders are issued by the military under this Law.[92] The Hotline for Migrant

---

[88] *Ibid.,* 33.   [89] *Hotline for Migrant Workers* v. *Minister of Defence*, para. 12.

[90] Kritzman-Amir and Spijkerboer, 'On the Morality and Legality of Borders', 34.

[91] The University of Michigan Law School Refugee Case Law Site contains a number of judgments from the Israeli courts: http://refugeecaselaw.org/Home.aspx (accessed 23 November 2012).

[92] Refugees' Rights Forum Letter to Members of the Knesset: Infiltration, 4 June 2008 www.acri.org.il/en/2010/10/05/refugees-rights-forum-letter-to-mks-infiltration/ (accessed 23 November 2012); Refugees' Rights Forum, *Policy Paper: The Detention of Asylum Seekers and Refugees*, June 2008.

Workers Association and the Refugee Rights Program of Tel Aviv University filed petitions with the High Court in 2006,[93] and the Supreme Court held that judicial review needed to be undertaken for detained asylum seekers.[94] As a consequence, a judge from the Custody Review Court was appointed 'special advisor to the defence minister' with responsibility for examining the situation of each detainee and recommending release to the military authorities where appropriate.[95] The adviser recommended release of the Sudanese, since they neither presented a threat to the State, nor could be deported back to Sudan in view of the situation in the country at the time.[96] The government and military complied.

In the area of employment of asylum seekers, the intervention of the High Court was required, once more, to provide hope to the many Sudanese and Eritreans in possession of a conditional release visa which has no entitlement to work, healthcare or benefits. Such visas are stamped with the words: 'This temporary permit does not constitute a work permit'. Anyone found employing an individual in possession of such a visa was subject to fines. The High Court held in January 2011 that, until the 10,000-place detention centre is opened in the Negev desert, no sanction will be taken against employers who recruit asylum seekers with 2(A)(5) permits.[97] However, despite the ruling, there does appear to be some ongoing confusion, with employers nervous about recruiting holders of a permit that suggests they cannot work, and with evidence of some immigration officers threatening action against those employing asylum seekers.[98]

An important recent decision bears witness to a transnational approach to refugee law interpretation. In the case of *Hernandez* v. *Ministry of the Interior* (August 2011), the Israeli Central District Court (sitting as the Court for Administrative Affairs), overturned a decision of the Ministry of the Interior refusing refugee status.[99] The claimant, a Colombian national, entered Israel clandestinely via the Sinai crossing. (His mother, also a

---

[93] *4 Refugees* v. *Head of IDF Operations Division*, HCJ 3208, 3270, 3271, 3272/06.
[94] *Ibid.*
[95] Refugees' Rights Forum, *Policy Paper: The Detention of Asylum Seekers and Refugees.*
[96] *Ibid.*, p. 10.   [97] HCJ 6312/10, 19 January 2011.
[98] Orna Dickman, 'Employing of Asylum Seekers in Israel: Regulations and Problems' (Hotline for Migrant Workers, May 2011), p. 1.
[99] See abbreviated version of case details in English at http://refugeecaselaw.org/ CaseAdditionalInfo.aspx?caseid=1988 (accessed 23 November 2012). See also Yonatan Berman, 'Stop press: for the first time, Israeli court orders the government of Israel to grant asylum', *Fahamu Refugee Legal Aid Newsletter*, 31 October 2011.

Colombian national, had been living in Israel for some time on a temporary resident permit, as she is an 'essential witness' in an international
criminal case relating to forgery in Colombia.)[100] He claimed asylum on
the basis that he had been threatened, attacked and seriously injured on a
number of occasions between 2008 and 2009 by non-State actors. In
examining the merits of the claim, the court turned to the UNHCR
Handbook on Procedures and Criteria for Determining Refugee Status as
well as international case law. The court referred to the US case of *INS* v.
Cardoza-Fonseca[101] on the question of the appropriate standard of proof,
and to *Sanchez-Trujillo* v. *INS*[102] and *Shah & Islam*[103] in relation to
membership of a particular social group. It concluded that it was sufficient
for the applicant to present a reasonable case and that corroboration was
not a requirement; that the claimant was persecuted for reasons of his
membership of a particular social group (the family); and that persecution
by a non-State actor was possible if the State did not provide effective
protection. Though the decision has been appealed by the government to
the Supreme Court, Israeli refugee rights lawyers still regard it as a 'historic
moment'.[104]

These cases provide a few examples of the successes achieved before
the courts. The courts appear, on some issues, to be taking account of
international decisions, while in other areas it is the peculiar context of
Israel that influences case law. With the asylum jurisprudence of the
Court of Justice of the EU (CJEU) being relatively new, there is no
evidence, as yet, that Israeli judges are taking CJEU judgments into
account in their deliberations. This may, however, become clear in time.

F   The transformative effect of discourse

Israel has certainly adopted the familiar discourse of 'abuse of asylum'.
Indeed, the very name of the department of the Ministry of the Interior
that handles asylum applications is telling – the 'Infiltrators and Asylum
Seekers Department'. In fact, statistics for asylum seekers are often conflated
with infiltrators under the combined heading of 'infiltrators'.[105] The

---

[100] *Ibid.*   [101] 480 US 421 (1987).   [102] 801 F. 2d 1571 (9th Cir. 1986).

[103] *Islam* v. *Secretary of State for the Home Department; R* v. *Immigration Appeal Tribunal,
ex parte Shah* [1999] 2 AC 629.

[104] Berman, 'Stop press'.

[105] See, e.g., Gilad Natan, *National Programme to Meet the Problem of Infiltrators and
Asylum Seekers Entering Israel Across the Egyptian Border* (The Knesset, Research and
Information Center, 25 January 2011), p. 2.

unfortunate association between seeking asylum and threat is well known in
the EU, as is the assumption that incomers are rarely 'genuine' refugees.
Prime Minister Benjamin Netanyahu clearly considers the African incomers
to be economic migrants, but his objection to their arrival is not solely based
on the apparent bypassing of immigration law, but also on assumed cata-
strophic implications for the country: 'We must stop the mass entry of
illegal migrant workers', he said, 'because of the very serious threat to the
character and future to the State of Israel'.[106] For his part, Interior Minister
Eli Yishai has claimed (without justification) that African foreigners would
introduce diseases such as AIDS, hepatitis and tuberculosis into the host
Israeli population.[107] Such statements have been used to justify recent
exclusionary and restrictive initiatives, including the building of the barrier
along the Israeli–Egyptian border, and the construction of the Negev desert
detention centre. Familiar metaphors are also present. In presenting the
Prevention of Infiltration Bill to the Knesset in January, the Interior Affairs
Committee Chairman, Amnon Cohen, argued that the Bill was the best way
in which to address the 'plague' of people illegally entering Israel from the
south.[108] Prime Minister Netanyahu, by contrast, prefers water metaphors:
'We hear the outcry from Israel's cities. We will continue to care for
refugees, but they make up a minimal part of the human wave. Entire
populations are starting to move, and if we don't act to stop this, we will
be flooded.'[109] Similarly, the Interior Minister argued:

> The fence must be constructed immediately and by one contractor;
> military forces must be placed at the border fence as a human barrier;
> closed detention centers must be constructed near border crossings and
> efforts must be made to prevent infiltrators from getting work in Israel. It
> must be made clear that anyone employing an infiltrator is so doing
> against the law. The deluge must be stopped.[110]

[106] Tania Kepler, 'Israel Approves Detention Centre for Migrants, Refugees', *Alternative Information Center*, 30 November 2010 www.alternativenews.org/english/index.php/news/israeli-society/3049-israel-approves-detention-centre-for-migrants-refugees.html (accessed 23 November 2012).
[107] Ron Friedman, 'Health Ministry data refutes Yishai's Claims that African refugees bring in disease', *Jerusalem Post*, 5 April 2012 www.jpost.com/LandedPages/PrintArticle.aspx?id=159701 (accessed 23 November 2012).
[108] Harkov, 'Knesset passes Anti-Infiltration Bill'.
[109] Ethan Bronner, 'Israel acts to curb illegal immigration from Africa', *New York Times*, 11 December 2011 www.nytimes.com/2011/12/12/world/middleeast/israel-steps-up-efforts-to-stop-illegal-immigration-from-africa.html (accessed 23 November 2012).
[110] Kepler, 'Israel Approves Detention Centre'.

Yet, the refugee discourse is extremely powerful for historical reasons in Israel. Thus, it is evident that the arrival of refugees from an area of the world in which ethnic cleansing was emergent – Sudan – affected many Israelis deeply. Yonathan Paz has examined the role of what he terms 'ethnonational discourse' and 'the holocaust/genocide discourse',[111] and has determined that the 'holocaust discourse has an ongoing role in shaping policies and attitudes towards asylum seekers'. Interestingly, he argues that a more generous view was taken of Darfurian Sudanese because of the perception of a 'shared "intimacy" of the genocide experience between Israelis and Sudanese from Darfur'.[112] While NGOs appear to have used the Holocaust discourse to support advocacy and fundraising, with many Israelis proving sympathetic to the plight of the Sudanese,[113] there is a also a negative outcome: the ability to identify with one group of asylum applicants may result in a more restrictive stance being adopted towards others who do not generate quite the same sense of identification and moral responsibility in Israelis.[114]

A further familiar shift in attitude from the earlier generosity is evident among part of the Israeli population. The rise in numbers of Africans on the streets of Israel's main cities, and the increasingly hostile language of government ministers and elements in the media, have led to increasing antagonism towards the incomers. According to the Director of the African Refugee Development Centre (ARDC), there is growing hatred: 'people have been attacked on the streets; there is a reluctance to rent houses to African refugees';[115] and there have been demonstrations against the presence of foreigners (but also some in support). Yet, despite the invective, there have been few deportations and many are permitted to stay on 'humanitarian grounds'. As indicated above, this is likely to change soon in relation to South Sudan.

G The role of civil society

Civil society certainly plays an active and significant role in refugee and asylum law and policy development in Israel. Notable organizations are: ARDC, the Aid Organization for Refugees and Asylum Seekers in Israel (ASSAF), the Association for Civil Rights in Israel (ACRI), the Hotline for Migrant Workers and Physicians for Human Rights Israel (PHR-Israel). These bodies have succeeded in establishing an influential

---

[111] Paz, 'Ordered Disorder'.   [112] *Ibid.*, 13.   [113] *Ibid.*   [114] *Ibid.*, 14.
[115] Silver, 'Tel Aviv no haven for asylum seekers'.

network which not only provides much-needed support to asylum seekers and refugees in the country, but also acts as a conduit for information and guidance.[116] Through research and reports, they provide a counterbalance to the negative and restrictive voices in government and the media.[117] Perhaps the most important role of civil society has been to challenge government policy in the courts, as highlighted earlier. Working alone or in association with the Tel Aviv University Buchmann Faculty of law, Refugee Rights Clinic, NGOs have petitioned the courts on numerous occasions with considerable success. It is anticipated that, increasingly, the battleground on asylum will be within the courts, but civil society will continue to play a significant role in the politics of asylum-seeking in Israel.

H   Conclusion

Israel has had a close and generally fruitful relationship with the EU, with the EU constituting a significant trading partner. It was one of the first countries to enter into discussions with the then European Economic Community, and it established a diplomatic mission in Brussels very early on (in 1958).[118] Increasing cooperation at a diplomatic level, particularly in relation to finance,[119] has further cemented the relationship and, in many ways, Israel is expected to turn westward towards Europe when seeking to develop its laws. Legislative approximation is formally advocated in the EU/Israel Action Plan in the migration and asylum fields. However, while migration has long been on the agenda for the EU, until recently it was not considered a priority for Israel. Asylum, too, has been a peripheral concern, with Israel

---

[116] Examples of the work undertaken and publications can be found on their websites: for example, ASSAF www.assaf.org.il (accessed 26 November 2012); ARDC www.ardc-israel.org (accessed 26 November 2012); Hotline for Migrant Workers www.hotline.org.il (accessed 26 November 2012).

[117] See, e.g., Maya Paley, *Surviving in Limbo: Lived Experiences among Sudanese and Eritrean Asylum Seekers in Israel* (ASSAF, June 2011); Maya Paley, *Surviving in Limbo: Community Formation among Sudanese and Eritrean Asylum Seekers in Israel* (ASSAF, June 2011). Both reports are available at www.assaf.org.il/en/refugees/refugees-israel.

[118] Sharon Pardo and Joel Peters, *Uneasy Neighbours: Israel and the European Union* (Lanham, MD: Lexington Books, 2009), Introduction.

[119] For the first time, Israel is eligible for €14 million in EC financial cooperation over the next seven years: European Union External Action, *Israel* http://eeas.europa.eu/israel/index_en.htm (accessed 26 November 2012).

fulfilling any moral obligation towards refugees through the occasional provision of sanctuary. This remained the case until the dramatic events of 2005–06 when Israel was catapulted into the reality of migration in the twenty-first century, and the world of mixed migration flows, smuggling and desperate people.

These new challenges have tested the Israeli government. On account of an immigration and nationality policy that incorporates a right of return for the Jewish diaspora, and that favours *jus sanguinis* over *jus soli*,[120] there is nervousness within Israel about upsetting the demographic status quo. As a relatively small country, both in terms of territory and population,[121] and possessing a unique history and ethnicity, it has struggled to strike a balance between generosity and illiberalism. On the one hand, the influx of African migrants has tapped into a deep sense of (historical) obligation towards the suffering 'alien'; on the other hand, the African asylum seeker is rarely considered to be a true or 'genuine' refugee. This tension is borne out in policy. Recent legislative and administrative changes are tending towards a highly restrictive stance with the clear aim of deterring would-be migrants; yet, at the same time, though certain nationalities – Eritreans and Sudanese – are not permitted to apply for asylum, they are granted a form of temporary protection on a group basis.

A range of actors has been involved in formulating the new Israeli approaches to asylum, and their contributions to the debates have been striking. Under the framework of EU initiatives such as TAIEX and the ENP Action Plan, the EU has been able to present its asylum model to Israel within a broader context of managing global migration and ensuring the sanctity of European borders. Israel has certainly learned some lessons from its European partners, although these have generally been of the more stringent nature: the incorporation of an accelerated refusal procedure; the application of lack of credibility criteria to refuse many cases; a high asylum refusal rate; the widespread – and growing – use of detention as a form of deterrence; the adoption of push-back policies; and the creation of a literal 'fortress Israel' on the Egyptian border.

---

[120] It is possible to obtain Jewish citizenship through naturalization if the applicant has lived in Israel for three of the past five years and has a right to permanent residence in Israel. The grant is at the discretion of the Minister of the Interior.

[121] The 2012 statistic for the population of Israel is 7,836,000, with 5,901,000 being Jewish and 1,610,000 being Arab: Jewish Virtual Library, *Latest Population Statistics* (September 2012) www.jewishvirtuallibrary.org/jsource/Society_&_Culture/newpop.html (accessed 26 November 2012).

Minimum standards on the reception of asylum seekers have not been met in the majority of cases, with many having to fend for themselves – reliant upon food and clothing handouts, or eking out a living in an uncertain and sometimes exploitative employment environment. Nevertheless, judicial review of refusal decisions has not been withdrawn and, as a consequence, a nascent case law is developing in which international refugee and human rights law principles are emergent.

UNHCR, too, with its established role in Israel, has sought to advance the case for protection, and has encouraged Israel to fulfil its responsibilities towards refugees and developing a fair and effective RSD regime. Its influence seems, however, to be waning somewhat, despite a semi-formal articulation of the relationship between UNHCR and the State of Israel within the Procedural Regulations.[122] Successive governments have tended to negatively stereotype the majority of asylum seekers as economic migrants and have sought to minimize pull factors to Israel. This has been achieved by severely limiting asylum seekers' access to economic and social rights, and through the use of detention and deportation, both of which are set to rise. Indeed, within months of passing the Prevention of Infiltration Law in January 2012, further stringent amendments to Israeli law were proposed including: the criminalization of employment of asylum seekers; the prohibition of transfer of funds abroad by asylum seekers; increased powers for immigration officers; and the introduction of a non-suspensive appeal where entry has been refused.[123] It has now fallen to the NGO community and the courts to offer an alternative perspective to that of the government. The NGOs, in particular, are increasingly vocal and litigious and provide an effective liberal counterbalance to the discourse.

It is often said that Israel wishes to be considered part of the community of Western democracies. The appeal to fundamental human rights and democratic principles in the EU–Israeli documents is testament to such an objective. Israel is alone in its region in having assumed responsibility for refugee determination from UNHCR and established an asylum process. There are, however, two major problems. Israel's

---

[122] See above n. 35.
[123] Hotline for Migrant Workers, 'Legislation Targeting Asylum Seekers in 2012' (August 2012) http://hotline.org.il/english/pdf/HotlineReport080812LegislationEng.pdf (accessed 26 November 2012). A non-suspensive appeal permits an appeal from abroad rather than in-country following removal or deportation. Similar to UK law, there is an exception where torture or danger to life is claimed, but this can be overridden where such a claim is deemed unfounded, again mirroring UK provisions.

response to new challenges and uncertainties, particularly where it considers State interests to be under threat, tends towards the aggressive. It is consequently unafraid to adopt contentious and restrictive policies. Second, when the exemplar on asylum provided by the EU and its Member States is itself a mass of contradictions, it should come as no surprise if Israel, too, pursues a somewhat erratic path in its treatment of asylum seekers and refugees.

6

Is Switzerland an EU Member State? Asylum law harmonization through the backdoor

VINCENT CHETAIL AND CÉLINE BAULOZ

A   Introduction

Should the attitude of Switzerland towards the European Union (EU) be resumed in a couple of words, 'Je t'aime, moi non plus' would probably be the most pertinent expression.[1] The relationship of the Swiss Confederation with the EU has indeed always been one of ambivalence: in between isolationism and communitarianism, concurrence and acquaintance, dissension and cooperation, even sometimes at the verge of adhesion.[2]

Such ambiguity results from two main contradictory forces: a centripetal and a centrifugal one. On the one hand, both the EU and Switzerland share to a great extent common regional history, culture and values; for the Swiss Confederation is an enclave within the EU territory. On the other hand, Switzerland has always striven to preserve its peculiar identity, translating (through its foreign policies) into a traditional principle of neutrality.[3] Reconciling both forces has led the

---

[1] 'I Love You, Me Neither', 1969 song of the French singer, Serge Gainsbourg, with Jane Birkin.

[2] Despite the multiple attempts of the Swiss government, any adhesion to the EU has so far failed in the face of the direct democracy system in Switzerland. Indeed, as early as December 1992, the Swiss citizens rejected adhesion to the European Economic Area (EEA) with 50.3 per cent of negative votes. In 1997, the popular initiative 'Négociations d'adhésion à l'UE: que le peuple décide!' was also rejected by 74.1 per cent. A similar 2001 initiative was again refused by 76.8 per cent of the vote.

[3] On the neutrality of Switzerland, see, most notably, Stefan Aeschimann *et al.*, *Swiss Neutrality* (4th edn, Berne: Federal Department of Defence, Civil Protection and Sports, 2004); Laurent Goetschel, Magdalena Bernath and Daniel Schwarz, *Politique extérieure Suisse: Fondements et possibilités* (Lausanne: Payot, 2004), especially pp. 45–49; Georges-André Chevallaz, *The Challenge of Neutrality: Diplomacy and the Defense of Switzerland* (Lanham,

Swiss Confederation to develop a cherry-pick strategy through the adoption of sectoral agreements with the EU. The most recent of these are the 1999 Bilateral Agreements I and the 2004 Bilateral Agreements II.[4] While the Bilateral Agreements I encompass seven agreements mainly concerned with opening up the market,[5] cooperation with the EU has gone one step further with the Bilateral Agreements II. The nine Bilateral Agreements II not only cover economic matters but also

MD: Lexington Books, 2001); Luzius Wildhaber, 'Swiss Neutrality: Legal Base and Historical Background', in Bo Huldt and Atis Leijŋš (eds.), *Neutrals in Europe* (Stockholm: Swedish Institute of International Affairs, 1989), pp. 3–15; Paul André Ramseyer, 'Switzerland and Europe: Between the EC, the CSCE and Neutrality', *ibid.*, pp. 17–26.

[4] Preceding agreements also include the Agreement between the European Economic Community and the Swiss Confederation (OJ 1972 No. L300/189) (entered into force 1 January 1973) and the Agreement between the European Economic Community and the Swiss Confederation on direct insurance other than life assurance (OJ 1991 No. L205/3) (entered into force 1 January 1993). On the Bilateral Agreements I and II, see Alexandre Afonso and Martino Maggetti, 'Bilaterals II, Reaching the Limits of the Swiss Third Way?', in Clive H. Church (ed.), *Switzerland and the European Union: A Close, Contradictory and Misunderstood Relationship* (London: Routledge, 2007), pp. 215–33; Marius Vahl and Nina Grolimund, *Integration without Membership: Switzerland's Bilateral Agreements with the European Union* (Brussels: Centre for European Policy Studies, 2007); Sandra Lavenex, 'Switzerland: Between Intergovernmental Cooperation and Schengen Association', in Marina Caparini and Otwin Marenin (eds.), *Borders and Security Governance: Managing Borders in a Globalised World* (Münster: LIT Verlag, 2006), pp. 233–51; Christine Kaddous and Monique Jametti Greiner (eds.), *Accords bilatéraux II Suisse–UE et autres Accords récents* (Brussels: Bruylant, Paris: LGDJ, Basel: Helbing & Lichtenhahn, 2006); René Schwok and Nicolas Levrat, 'Switzerland's Relations with the EU after the Adoption of the Seven Bilateral Agreements' (2001) 6 *European Foreign Affairs Review* 335–54. On the relationship between Switzerland and the EU, see more generally among a prolific literature: Philippe Koch and Sandra Lavenex, 'The (Contentious) Human Face of Europeanization: Free Movement and Immigration', in Church, *Switzerland and the European Union*, pp. 148–65; René Schwok (ed.), *Switzerland–European Union: An Impossible Membership?* (Brussels: Peter Lang, 2009); René Schwok, 'Switzerland's Approximation of Its Legislation to the EU *Acquis*: Specificities, Lessons and Paradoxes' (2007) 9 *European Journal of Law Reform* 449–65; Alex Fischer, Sarah Nicolet and Pascal Sciarini, 'Europeanisation of a Non-EU Country: The Case of Swiss Immigration Policy' (2002) 25 *West European Politics* 143–70.

[5] The seven Bilateral Agreements I were negotiated following the rejection of EEA adhesion in 1992, and were signed on 21 June 1999 (all entered into force on 1 June 2002). They cover the free movement of persons, technical barriers to trade, public procurement markets, agriculture, research, civil aviation and overland transport. For more information on the Bilateral Agreements I, see Swiss Confederation, Federal Department of Foreign Affairs (FDFA)/Federal Department of Economic Affairs (FDEA), *Bilateral Agreements Switzerland–EU* (Berne: Integration Office FDFA/FDEA, 2009). See also the website of the Swiss Confederation dedicated to the Bilateral Agreements www.europa.admin.ch/themen/00500/index.html?lang=en (accessed 5 September 2012).

extend collaboration to politically sensitive areas, such as security and asylum.[6]

That asylum is now an issue of intergovernmental cooperation between the EU and Switzerland is all but logical. The Swiss Confederation faces the same challenges as any other EU Member State,[7] and is driven by an identical fear: (massive) asylum flows with real or perceived abuses of the asylum system. It therefore comes as no surprise that asylum practices of EU States and Switzerland have more or less mirrored each other in their developments. Contrary to some beliefs, the Swiss Confederation has not been such a generous *terre d'asile* in the middle of fortress Europe.[8] The 'asylum fatigue' felt in Europe in the late 1970s/early 1980s did not spare Switzerland.[9] As a result of this common stance, a battery of restrictive legislations has been adopted by the Swiss Confederation. This trend began in 1979 with the adoption of the first Swiss Act on asylum,[10] which was further revised in 1983 and 1986[11] and finally replaced in 1998 by the Asylum

---

[6] These nine agreements concern: Schengen/Dublin, taxation of savings, processed agricultural products, media, environment, statistics, fight against fraud, pensions, education and vocational training. See Swiss Confederation, *Bilateral Agreements Switzerland–EU*, pp. 4ff.

[7] Denise Efionayi *et al.*, *Switzerland Faces Common European Challenges* (Washington, DC: Migration Information Source, Migration Policy Institute, February 2005).

[8] This stereotype may be explained by the early post-Second World War asylum practice of the Confederation. It is true that, in the 1950s and 1960s, Switzerland had a particularly generous attitude towards Hungarian and Czechoslovakian refugees. However, its practice was soon questioned in the 1970s with the case of Chilean refugees. See Lorena Parini and Matteo Gianni, 'Enjeux et modifications de la politique d'asile en Suisse de 1956 à nos jours', in Hans Mahnig (ed.), *Histoire de la politique de migration, d'asile et d'intégration en Suisse depuis 1948* (Zurich: Seismo, 2005), pp. 189–252, at 196–209. It is further noteworthy that Switzerland is one of few countries to have enshrined the principle of *non-refoulement* within its Constitution: see art. 25(2) and (3) Federal Constitution of the Swiss Confederation of 18 April 1999, RS 101 (entered into force 1 January 2000; status as at 1 January 2011). Such reference is a novelty of the 1999 Constitution (see preceding Constitutions of 29 May 1874 and 12 September 1848). The Confederation has been a party to the 1951 Refugee Convention since 21 January 1955: Convention relating to the Status of Refugees, Geneva, 28 July 1951, in force 22 April 1954 (189 UNTS 137).

[9] On the history of asylum in Switzerland, see, most notably, Mahnig, *Histoire de la politique de migration*; Yvonne Riaño and Doris Wastl-Walter, 'Historical Shifts in Asylum Policies in Switzerland: Between Humanitarian Values and the Protection of National Identity' (2006) 27 *Refugee Watch* 1–18; Lorena Parini, *La politique d'asile en Suisse: Une perspective systémique* (Paris: L'Harmattan, 1997); Etienne Piguet, *L'immigration en Suisse* (Lausanne: Presses polytechniques et universitaires romands, 2004).

[10] Loi sur l'asile, FF 1977 III 105, 5 October 1979 (entered into force 1 January 1981).

[11] See Samuel Werenfels, *Der Begriff des Flüchtlings im schweizerischen Asylrecht* (Berne: Peter Lang, 1987), pp. 94–101; Parini and Gianni, 'Enjeux et modifications', 211–14.

Act (AsylA).[12] It is in this respect noteworthy that Switzerland was one of the pioneer countries to rely on the controversial concept of 'safe third country', already enshrined in its 1979 legislation.[13]

Within the EU, a similar pattern of restrictions has been erected in a comprehensive regime – the Common European Asylum System (CEAS).[14] This ambitious regional system has sought to harmonize the many facets of asylum law and policy: from determining the EU State responsible for examining asylum claims,[15] to creating a temporary protection status,[16] and laying down minimum standards relating to

---

[12] Asylum Act, RS 142.31, RO 1999, 2262, 26 June 1998 (entered into force 1 October 1999). A non-official English version of the Asylum Act is available on the Swiss Confederation's website: www.admin.ch/ch/e/rs/1/142.31.en.pdf (accessed 2 October 2012). This version of the Asylum Act is a consolidated one, as the Act has been amended multiple times. The most important revision was carried out in 2006, with all amendments in force since 1 January 2008: see Swiss Federal Office of Migrations (Office fédéral des migrations), 'Révision partielle de la loi sur l'asile' www.bfm.admin. ch/content/bfm/fr/home/dokumentation/rechtsgrundlagen/abgeschl_gesetzgebungspro jekte/teilrevision_asylgesetz.html (accessed 5 September 2012). Another partial revision is currently ongoing with the aim of accelerating the asylum procedure and systematically combating abuses of the asylum system: see Swiss Federal Office of Migrations (Office fédéral des migrations), 'Modifications de la loi sur l'asile et de la loi fédérale sur les étrangers' www.bfm.admin.ch/content/bfm/fr/home/dokumentation/rechtsgrundlagen/ laufende_gesetzgebungsprojekte/asyl-_und_auslaendergesetz.html (accessed 5 September 2012).

[13] See Mario Gattiker, 'Evolution et perspectives de la notion de pays tiers sûr dans la législation suisse sur l'asile', in Vincent Chetail and Vera Gowlland-Debbas (eds.), *Switzerland and the International Protection of Refugees* (The Hague, London, New York: Kluwer Law International, 2002), pp. 129–44, at 134.

[14] The CEAS was created following the Treaty of Amsterdam amending the Treaty on European Union, the Treaties establishing the European Communities and certain related acts (OJ 1997 No. C340/1) (entered into force 1 May 1999) and the Presidency Conclusions of the Tampere European Council (15–16 October 1999). With the Amsterdam Treaty, asylum was indeed brought within the competence of the European Community under Title IV (area of freedom, security and justice). Most notably, its art. 63(1) and (2) lays down a five-year programme to develop harmonized asylum standards.

[15] Council Regulation (EC) No. 343/2003 of 18 February 2003 establishing the criteria and mechanisms for determining the Member State responsible for examining an asylum application lodged in one of the Member States by a third-country national (OJ 2003 No. L50/1) (Dublin Regulation). The Regulation replaced the Dublin Convention determining the State responsible for examining applications for asylum lodged in one of the member states of the European Communities of 15 June 1990 (OJ 1997 No. C254/ 1) (entered into force 1 September 1997).

[16] Council Directive 2001/55/EC of 20 July 2001 on minimum standards for giving temporary protection in the event of a mass influx of displaced persons and on measures promoting a balance of efforts between Member States in receiving such persons and

eligibility for international protection,[17] asylum procedures,[18] the reception of asylum seekers[19] and returns of illegally staying third-country nationals.[20]

With such extensive reach, the CEAS has shed light on Swiss isolation in domains of inherently common concerns, such as the management of asylum flows and border control. This has prompted Switzerland to realize the need for a coordinated approach to asylum with the EU, while remaining loyal to its traditional ambivalent attitude towards it. As a result, the Swiss Confederation has opted for selective convergence through collaboration and association, but never attaining the level of CEAS integration. The 2004 Schengen/Dublin Association Agreements were eventually adopted with this aim, as part of the broader Swiss–EU Bilateral Agreements II.[21] But the Dublin Agreement has taken the form of the Trojan horse of the Swiss asylum normalization vis-à-vis the EU (see Part B below). With Pandora's box so opened, a dynamic of harmonization has been initiated. It is notably illustrated by the influence of the Qualification Directive on Swiss asylum jurisprudence (discussed in

bearing the consequences thereof (OJ 2001 No. L212/12) (Temporary Protection Directive).

[17] Council Directive 2004/83/EC of 29 April 2004 on minimum standards for the qualification and status of third-country nationals or stateless persons as refugees or as persons who otherwise need international protection and the content of the protection granted(OJ 2004 No. L304/12) (2004 Qualification Directive); recently replaced by the Recast Directive 2011/95/EU of the European Parliament and of the Council of 13 December 2011 on standards for the qualification of third-country nationals or stateless persons as beneficiaries of international protection, for a uniform status for refugees or for persons eligible for subsidiary protection, and for the content of the protection granted (OJ 2011 No. L337/9), to be transposed into Member States' national legislation by 21 December 2013 by virtue of art. 39(1) (Recast 2011 Qualification Directive).

[18] Council Directive 2005/85/EC of 1 December 2005 on minimum standards on procedures in Member States for granting and withdrawing refugee status (OJ 2005 No. L326/13) (Procedures Directive).

[19] Council Directive 2003/9/EC of 27 January 2003 laying down minimum standards for the reception of asylum seekers (OJ 2003 No. L31/18) (Reception Conditions Directive).

[20] Directive 2008/115/EC of the European Parliament and of the Council of 16 December 2008 on common standards and procedures in Member States for returning illegally staying third-country nationals (OJ 2008 No. L348/98) (Returns Directive).

[21] Agreement between the European Union, the European Community and the Swiss Confederation on the Swiss Confederation's association with the implementation, application and development of the Schengen acquis (OJ 2008 No. L53/52), signed 26 October 2004 (entered into force 1 March 2008) (Schengen Association Agreement); Agreement between the European Community and the Swiss Confederation concerning the criteria and mechanism for establishing the State responsible for examining a request for asylum lodged in a Member State or in Switzerland (OJ 2008 No. L53/5), signed 26 October 2004 (entered into force 1 March 2008) (Dublin Association Agreement).

Part C). Ultimately, such a process of convergence inevitably begs the question whether Switzerland is not itself becoming an EU Member State for the purposes of asylum.

B The Dublin Association Agreement: the Trojan horse of European harmonization in Switzerland

The Dublin Regulation was adopted by the European Council in 2003 with the aim, as its title indicates, of establishing 'the criteria and mechanisms for determining the Member State responsible for examining an asylum application lodged in one of the Member States by a third-country national'. Its main objective has been to suppress secondary movements of asylum seekers within the EU. It thus addresses the prime obsession of Member States to deter asylum shopping (the idea that asylum seekers may take advantage of the abolition of the EU's internal borders to move freely into States with the most favourable host conditions).[22] As analysed below, this obsession has constituted the main motivation behind the Swiss adhesion to the Dublin mechanism.

1 Rationale of the Dublin Association: the fear of becoming the asylum country of last resort

Under the logic of the Dublin system, asylum seekers have only one opportunity to lodge an asylum claim within EU territory. Only the 'responsible Member State' will be in charge of examining such an application, and this is usually the State which the asylum seeker first entered or in which he or she first lodged his or her claim.[23] In the event

[22] This objective is clearly restated in the Explanatory Memorandum to the Recast Proposal of the Dublin Regulation: 'to prevent abuse of asylum procedures in the form of multiple applications for asylum submitted by the same person in several Member States with the sole aim of extending his/her stay in the Member States'. See Commission of the European Communities, Proposal for a Regulation of the European Parliament and of the Council establishing the criteria and mechanisms for determining the Member State responsible for examining an application for international protection lodged in one of the Member States by a third-country national or a stateless person (recast) (COM(2008) 820 final), 3 December 2008, p. 3 (Dublin Recast Proposal).

[23] The Regulation sets out six criteria to identify the responsible Member State: family unity; the Member State having issued prior documentation (residence permits or visas); the State whose borders were irregularly crossed by the asylum seeker, or which allowed entry to its territory by waiving visa requirements; the State in whose international transit area of an airport the asylum seeker made his or her claim; and the State with which the first asylum claim was lodged (see arts. 6–13 Dublin Regulation). It nonetheless remains the case that the alternative

of the asylum seeker's secondary movement to another Member State, the latter will be entitled to ask the responsible Member State to take charge of him or her.[24]

As Switzerland was not originally a Dublin State, this single opportunity de facto translated into a 'double chance' scenario for asylum seekers. They benefited from two possibilities to apply for asylum in Europe: in the EU *and* in Switzerland.[25] This side effect of EU harmonization prompted the Swiss Confederation to make a first step towards the CEAS by associating itself with the Dublin system. The Schengen/Dublin Association Agreements were eventually adopted in October 2004 as two sides of the same coin: the Dublin Association Agreement aims to compensate for the free movement of persons promoted by the Schengen Agreement.[26] A twofold rationale can explain this first collaborative move on the part of Switzerland.

First and foremost, Switzerland feared becoming the country of last resort for asylum seekers rejected by EU Member States. Borrowing the government's words, there was a perceived risk that Switzerland would turn into a 'pays d'asile de réserve'.[27] From this angle, lessons learned from the previous 1990 Dublin Convention highlighted the high costs associated with Swiss exclusion from the Dublin regime.[28] The prospect

nature of these criteria usually implies that responsibility will fall to the State of first entry or first claim. See, in this sense, Vincent Chetail and Céline Bauloz, *The European Union and the Challenges of Forced Migration: From Economic Crisis to Protection Crisis?* (EU–US Immigration Systems 2011/07, Robert Schuman Centre for Advanced Studies, San Domenico di Fiesole: European University Institute, 2011), p. 12; Francesco Maiani and Vigdis Vevstad, 'Reflection Note on the Evaluation of the Dublin System and on the Dublin III Proposal' (European Parliament, Directorate-General of Internal Policies, Policy Department C, Citizens Rights and Constitutional Affairs, PE 410.690, March 2009), p. 2.

24 See Ch. V Dublin Regulation.

25 See Position of the Swiss Liberal-Radical Party of 28 January 1999, quoted in Parini and Gianni: 'les accords de Dublin et de Schengen, signés par les pays de l'UE, permettent avec efficacité d'éviter les abus en matière d'asile en Europe. Notre pays en est exclu et risque ainsi de devenir le dernier pays de recours pour les requérants d'asile en Europe ... Il n'est plus possible dans l'UE de présenter deux fois une requête d'asile. Le seul pays où cela reste possible est la Suisse' ('Enjeux et modifications', 241).

26 See arts. 15(4) and 14(2) respectively of the Schengen and Dublin Agreements which make implementation of each Agreement subordinate to the effective application of the other one.

27 Swiss Federal Council, *Message du Conseil fédéral du 13 mai 1998 relatif à l'arrêté fédéral sur les mesures d'urgence dans le domaine de l'asile et des étrangers*, FF 1998 2829, 13 May 1998.

28 For the Dublin Convention, see n. 15 above. As underlined by Hans Mahnig and Sandro Cattacin, 'une grande partie des décideurs politiques suisses voient dans l'harmonisation de la politique d'asile au sein de l'UE une menace pour la Confédération ... En effet, l'accroissement du nombre de demandes d'asile qui a eu lieu entre 1996 et 1997 ... est interprétée dans les médias comme l'effet de la Convention de Dublin' ('La

of Switzerland abolishing its internal border with its neighbours under the Schengen Association Agreement only exacerbated this anguish. Far from being buoyed by its humanitarian tradition, the pressure of potential secondary asylum flows from EU Member States prompted Switzerland to adopt the Dublin Agreement.

Second, Switzerland's association with the Dublin system came not only out of necessity, but also represented a strategic interest for the Confederation. Given the tendency of Dublin responsibility to be allotted to States where asylum seekers first entered or lodged their protection claims,[29] Member States located at the EU's external borders are typically found to be responsible. With its inner location in Europe, Switzerland's comparative advantage under the Dublin association is clear: it is rarely the State responsible for examining asylum claims. In other words, its geographical position effectively shields it from a high number of asylum applications under the Dublin mechanism.

Such 'positive' outcomes have not escaped the attention of the Swiss Confederation, and have even turned into a self-declared objective of Swiss asylum policy. In a 2009 communication, the Swiss Federal Office of Migration (Office fédéral des migrations) openly welcomed the fact that 'Switzerland has clearly sent more persons back to the other Dublin States than it has had to take charge of on the basis of this agreement'.[30] The data speaks for itself: in 2011, Switzerland asked other Dublin States to take charge of 9,347 applicants, out of which 7,014 were accepted by the States concerned.[31] In contrast, Switzerland received 1,611 of such requests, and accepted only 907 of them.[32]

In sum, the geographical location of Switzerland acts both as a push and pull factor for its association to the Dublin mechanism. This, in turn, constitutes the prime instance of EU influence over Swiss asylum law.

2   Behind the Dublin mechanism: a case of normative mimicry

While the Dublin Association Agreement evidences the centripetal force exercised by the EU on Switzerland, its consequences have extended

transformation de la constellation politique internationale', in Mahnig, *Histoire de la politique de migration*, pp. 405–15, at 414).

[29] See above n. 23.

[30] Swiss Federal Office of Migration, *Accord de Dublin: bilan positif pour la Suisse* (Département fédéral de Justice et Police, Communiqué, 7 April 2009) (authors' translation).

[31] Swiss Federal Office of Migration, *Statistique en matière d'asile 2011* (Département fédéral de Justice et Police, 6 January 2012), p. 4.

[32] *Ibid.*

beyond the mere identification of the responsible State for examining asylum requests. With the Dublin Agreement, Switzerland has not only agreed to implement the Dublin Regulation,[33] but also many other related-CEAS measures, including the 2000 Eurodac Regulation for comparing fingerprints,[34] the 1995 Directive on the protection of personal data[35] and all subsequent Dublin *acquis*.[36]

Conceived as a 'package agreement', these diverse measures ensure the effective functioning of the Dublin mechanism. For instance, the Eurodac system was established as a logistical support tool for the Dublin Regulation to identify asylum seekers and persons illegally present within the EU.[37] With this database, Member States are informed if an asylum seeker previously lodged an asylum claim within one of the other participating Dublin States.[38] The binding nature of this EU regulation for Switzerland, and the Dublin *acquis*, is thus the natural consequence of its association with the Dublin mechanism.

The notion of the Dublin *acquis*, however, is far from clear-cut in terms of its legal implications for Switzerland. The Dublin Association Agreement only gives a rather vague, and arguably restrictive, definition: 'The acts and measures taken by the European Community amending or building upon the provisions referred to in paragraph 1 [namely, the Dublin and Eurodac (Implementing) Regulations] and the decisions taken in accordance with the procedures set out in those provisions.'[39]

---

[33] This also includes the Dublin Implementing Regulation: Commission Regulation (EC) No. 1560/2003 of 2 September 2003 laying down detailed rules for the application of Council Regulation (EC) No. 343/2003 establishing the criteria and mechanisms for determining the Member State responsible for examining an asylum application lodged in one of the Member States by a third-country national (OJ 2003 No. L222/3).

[34] Council Regulation (EC) No. 2725/2000 of 11 December 2000 concerning the establishment of 'Eurodac' for the comparison of fingerprints for the effective application of the Dublin Convention (OJ 2000 No. L316/1). See art. 1 Dublin Association Agreement, which also requires Switzerland to implement Council Regulation (EC) No. 407/2002 of 28 February 2002 laying down certain rules to implement Regulation (EC) No 2725/2000 concerning the establishment of 'Eurodac' for the comparison of fingerprints for the effective application of the Dublin Convention (OJ 2002 No. L62/1).

[35] Dublin Association Agreement, preambular para. 3 and art. 1(4); Directive 95/46/EC of the European Parliament and of the Council of 24 October 1995 on the protection of individuals with regard to the processing of personal data and on the free movement of such data (OJ 1995 No. L281/31).

[36] Dublin Association Agreement, art. 1(3).   [37] Eurodac Regulation, Recital 2.

[38] On the Eurodac Regulation, see Pascal-Hervé Bogdanski, 'L'association de la Suisse au système de Dublin', in Kaddous and Jametti Greiner, *Accords bilatéraux II*, pp. 389–424, at 407–16.

[39] Dublin Association Agreement, art. 1(3). See also Swiss Federal Council, *Message relatif à l'approbation des accords bilatéraux entre la Suisse et l'Union européenne, y compris les*

Against such an elusive explanation, determining the precise scope of Switzerland's obligations under the Dublin *acquis* remains a key issue. Under the Schengen Association Agreement, a quasi-identical obligation to accept, implement and apply the Schengen *acquis* had already led to the adoption of the 2008 Returns Directive by the Swiss Confederation.[40] By analogy, then, should the other CEAS directives (such as the Qualification and Procedures Directives) be an integral part of the Dublin *acquis*? Two main arguments can be advanced in support of such unexpected extension of the Swiss obligations under the Dublin Association Agreement.

First, from an EU perspective, the Dublin Regulation is part and parcel of the broader CEAS. The overall coherence of the EU asylum system implies that its various components are treated as a whole. It is on this ultimate rationale that the Dublin system is built: returns to other Dublin States are conceivable due to the harmonized standards of protection in the EU. In other words, EU asylum harmonization is both a prerequisite[41] and a product[42] of the Dublin mechanism. From this stance, one could be tempted to consider that the Swiss Dublin Association also entails implementation of the EU directives. Stretching this reasoning even further, some experts have questioned whether removals to associate States (such as Switzerland) might not be precluded because of their disregard of EU standards.[43] This possibility is even more relevant in light of the Proposal on a Recast Dublin Regulation which recurrently refers to

actes législatifs relatifs à la transposition des accords ('accords bilatéraux II'), FF 2004 5593, 1 October 2004, p. 5696.

[40] Schengen Association Agreement, arts. 2(3) and 7. See also Swiss Federal Council, *Message sur l'approbation et la mise en œuvre de l'échange de notes entre la Suisse et la CE concernant la reprise de la directive CE sur le retour (directive 2008/115/CE) (développement de l'acquis de Schengen) et sur une modification de la loi fédérale sur les étrangers (contrôle automatisé aux frontières, conseillers en matière de documents, système d'information MIDES)*, FF 2009 8043, 18 November 2009, especially pp. 8048–9.

[41] See Commission of the European Communities, Commission Staff Working Document Accompanying the Proposal for a Regulation of the European Parliament and of the Council Establishing the Criteria and Mechanisms for Determining the Member State Responsible for Examining an Application for International Protection Lodged in One of the Member States by a Third-Country National or a Stateless Person (Recast), Impact Assessment, SEC(2008) 2962, 3 December 2008, p. 15: 'For the Dublin system to function adequately, all Member States have to provide harmonized and adequate standards of protection for asylum-seekers.'

[42] See Dublin Regulation, Recital 5 which itself acknowledges that the Dublin Convention already 'stimulated the process of harmonising asylum policies'.

[43] Francesco Maiani, 'Fitting EU Asylum Standards in the Dublin Equation: Recent Case Law, Legislative Reforms, and the Position of Dublin "Associates"' (2010) 2/10 *ASYL* 9–19, at 15: 'the failure by associate States to meet some (or all) of the EU asylum standards would eventually *hinder* the transfer of asylum seekers from CEAS States to associate States'. This

specific provisions of the various EU directives, such as the Qualification Directive.[44] Since this recast version will constitute part of the Dublin *acquis* once adopted at the EU level, these many *renvois* back to other directives should be taken into account one way or another by Switzerland.

Second, at the Swiss level, the attitude of the Confederation towards the CEAS appears to have evolved into a more receptive stance. Even though Switzerland considers itself as being not formally bound by the CEAS directives,[45] it demonstrates a growing willingness to participate in the EU harmonization process. Article 113 of its 1998 AsylA expressly provides that: 'The Confederation shall participate in the harmonization of European refugee policy at international level as well as in the resolution of refugee problems abroad.' Moreover, since 2002, the Swiss Federal Council has been

---

assertion was based on analysis of some national case law (mainly from Germany) which took the EU directives as the appropriate standards to assess the legality of Dublin transfers. These rulings nonetheless concerned returns to EU Member States and not associate States. Since then, the Court of Justice of the European Union (CJEU) has rendered a judgment relating, *inter alia*, to the relationship between the Dublin mechanism and EU asylum standards: see Joined Cases C-411/10 and C-493/10, *NS* v. *Secretary of State for the Home Department* and *ME, ASM, MT, KP and EH* v. *Refugee Applications Commissioner, Minister for Justice, Equality and Law Reform* (CJEU, Grand Chamber, 21 December 2011), at para. 70. One of the questions referred for preliminary ruling by the United Kingdom indeed asked 'whether the Member State which should transfer the asylum seeker to the Member State which Article 3(1) of Regulation No. 343/2003 indicates as responsible is obliged to assess the compliance, by that Member State, with the fundamental rights of the European Union, Directives 2003/9, 2004/83 and 2005/85 and with Regulation 343/2003' (para. 70). For the CJEU, 'any infringement of the individual provisions of the [CEAS] Directives' is not sufficient to preclude returns under the Dublin Regulation (paras. 82–5). It went on to conclude that: 'By contrast, if there are substantial grounds for believing that there are systemic flaws in the asylum procedure and reception conditions for asylum applicants in the Member State responsible, resulting in inhuman or degrading treatment, within the meaning of Article 4 of the [EU] Charter, of asylum seekers transferred to the territory of that Member State, the transfer would be incompatible with that provision' (para. 86); see also para. 94. In other words, a certain threshold has to be attained for a violation of an EU directive to preclude a Dublin return – namely, that of inhuman or degrading treatment. This ruling nonetheless leaves open the question of the appropriate standards to apply in the case of return to associate States, as it was only concerned with removals to EU Member States.

[44] As underlined by the Commission, 'the proposal aims to ensure consistency with developments in the EU asylum *acquis*, in particular with the Procedures Directive, with the Qualification Directive, and with the Council Directive 2003/9/EC on minimum standards for the reception of asylum seekers' (Dublin Recast Proposal, p. 4). The Recast Proposal even extends the Regulation's personal scope to subsidiary protection applicants, a protection status created by the Qualification Directive: see art. 1(b) Dublin Recast Proposal.

[45] See Swiss Federal Council, *Message relatif à l'approbation des accords bilatéraux entre la Suisse et l'Union européenne*, p. 5737; Swiss Federal Council, *Message concernant la modification de la loi sur l'asile*, FF 2010 4035, 26 May 2010, p. 4106.

officially requested to comment on the relationship between EU law and any domestic bills submitted to the Federal Assembly.[46] Thus, since that time, an EU-compatibility test of any amendments to AsylA has been systematically undertaken by the Federal Council.[47] A salient illustration is given by the Federal Council's 2010 statement on the ongoing revision of AsylA. It first declared that: 'The present modifications to AsylA essentially concern the Procedures Directive, the Reception Conditions Directive as well as the Qualification Directive.'[48] The Federal Council further displayed an even greater EU sensitivity when detailing its position on the recast Dublin proposal:

> Some provisions of the proposal of the new Dublin Regulation of 3 December 2008 refer to the above-mentioned four directives (as in its Article 2) [namely, the Temporary Protection, the Reception, the Qualification and the Asylum Procedures Directives]. Although the *renvois* back to these directives would not be legally binding for Switzerland, one has in principle to avoid differing unnecessarily from the minimum norms defined by the EU. Indeed, *the well-functioning of the Dublin system and the effectiveness of the containment of excessive migratory flows within the Dublin area suggest the adoption of similar norms in the field of asylum procedure.*[49]

---

[46] See Federal Act on the Federal Assembly, RS 171.10, 13 December 2002, unofficial English version available at www.admin.ch/ch/e/rs/171_10/index.html (accessed 5 September 2012). Article 141 provides:

    1. The Federal Council shall submit its bills to the Federal Assembly together with a dispatch.

    2. In the dispatch, the Federal Council shall provide justification for the bill and if necessary comment on the individual provisions. In addition, it shall explain the following points in particular, on condition that it is possible to provide a substantial amount of information thereon:

       a. the legal background, the consequences for constitutional rights, compatibility with superior law and the relationship with European law.

[47] See, e.g., Swiss Federal Council, *Message concernant la modification de la loi sur l'asile, de la loi fédérale sur l'assurance-maladie et de la loi fédérale sur l'assurance-vieillesse et survivants*, FF 2002 6359, 4 September 2002, especially pp. 6445–6, where the Council directly referred to the EU Asylum Procedures and Qualification Directives; Swiss Federal Council, *Message portant approbation et mise en œuvre de l'échange de notes entre la Suisse et l'Union européenne concernant la reprise du code frontières Schengen (développement de l'acquis Schengen) et relatif aux modifications du droit des étrangers et du droit d'asile en vue de la mise en œuvre totale de l'acquis de Schengen et Dublin déjà repris (compléments)*, FF 2007 7449, 24 October 2007, p. 34, referring to Swiss Federal Council, *Message relatif à l'approbation des accords bilatéraux entre la Suisse et l'Union européenne*, p. 5633.

[48] Swiss Federal Council, *Message concernant la modification de la loi sur l'asile*, p. 4106 (authors' translation).

[49] *Ibid.* (authors' translation; citations omitted; emphasis added).

As exemplified by this last statement, the similarity with EU law represents a key concern and arguably a driving force behind Swiss legislation. This process of legislative mimicry is triggered by the efficient implementation of the Dublin mechanism and the obsessive fear of massive asylum flows. It illustrates, in turn, the particularism of Switzerland: though not formally an EU Member State, Switzerland internalizes the substance of EU norms in its own domestic law in order to avoid discrepancies. This occurs through a bottom-up harmonization approach. This trend is further reinforced by the influence of the Qualification Directive on Swiss jurisprudence on the refugee definition.

C   Interpreting the refugee definition: a bottom-up harmonization

In parallel to these legislative developments, the Swiss courts have undertaken a similar exercise with respect to the refugee definition. Although the Qualification Directive is not formally binding on Switzerland, its domestic jurisprudence has been progressively engaged in a process of bottom-up harmonization of the core components of the refugee definition.[50]

1   Actors of persecution: the domino effect of the Qualification Directive

The notion of 'actors of persecution' is a clear illustration of the domino effect on Swiss asylum law generated by the Qualification Directive.[51]

---

[50] For the purpose of the present chapter, emphasis is placed on three elements of the refugee definition: actors of persecution, actors of protection and the concept of the internal flight alternative. Concerning the other definitional elements, it suffices to note that the notion of 'serious disadvantages' (*sérieux préjudices*) in AsylA mainly equates in substance to that of 'persecution' and covers the acts of persecution enumerated in the Qualification Directive (art. 9(2) Qualification Directive and its recast version). For further details, see Francesco Maiani, 'La définition de réfugié entre Genève, Bruxelles et Berne – différences, tensions, ressemblances', in United Nations High Commissioner for Refugees (UNHCR) and Schweizerische Flüchtlingshilfe (eds.), *Schweizer Asylrecht, EU-Standards und internationales Flüchtlingsrecht, eine Vergleichsstudie/Droit d'asile Suisse, normes de l'UE et droit international des réfugiés, une étude comparative* (Berne: Stämpfli Verlag, 2009), pp. 19–66, at 24–34.

[51] On the notion of actors of persecution, see generally James C. Hathaway, *The Law of Refugee Status* (Toronto, Vancouver: Butterworths, 1991), pp. 124–33; Walter Kälin, 'Non-State Agents of Persecution and the Inability of the State to Protect' (2001) 15 *Georgetown Immigration Law Journal* 415–31; Volker Türk, 'Non-State Agents of

Switzerland was indeed one of the last European countries to restrict the scope of 'actors of persecution' to State or State-like entities. This traditional understanding of actors of persecution relied on an 'accountability' logic[52] – namely, that any act of persecution had to be directly or indirectly attributable to the State or to de facto State entities in order to trigger the surrogate protection of an asylum country. Thus, the State of origin had to be the source of persecution through its own officials or, at the very minimum, encourage, condone or tolerate persecutory acts by private actors.[53] Alternatively, quasi-State entities 'exercising de facto control over an area uncontrolled by the government'[54] could be considered as legitimate sources of persecution.[55] This was, for instance, the position with respect to the Taliban in Afghanistan and the Kurdish parties in Northern Iraq.[56]

As a result of this State-centred approach, private persecution was not recognized as a ground for refugee eligibility, since neither the State nor

Persecution', in Chetail and Gowlland-Debbas, *Switzerland and the International Protection of Refugees*, pp. 95–109; Daniel Wilsher, 'Non-State Actors and the Definition of a Refugee in the United Kingdom: Protection, Accountability or Culpability?' (2003) 15 *International Journal of Refugee Law* 68–112.

[52] On the Swiss conception of actors of persecution before 2006, see Samuel Werenfels, *Der Begriff des Flüchtlings*, pp. 217–30; Walter Kälin, *Grundriss des Asylverfahrens* (Basel: Helbing & Lichtenhahn, 1990), pp. 61–71; Alberto Achermann and Christina Hausammann, *Handbuch des Asylrechts* (Berne: Paul Haupt, 1991), pp. 82–8; Astrid Epiney, Bernhard Waldmann, Andrea Egbuna-Joss and Magnus Oeschger, 'Die Anerkennung als Flüchtling im europäischen und schweizerischen Recht' (*Jusletter*, 26 May 2008) 1–43, at 30–1.

[53] See, e.g., Asylum Appeals Commission, *Jurisprudence et informations de la Commission suisse de recours en matière d'asile* (JICRA) 1995/25, para. 2(a)(b) which clearly links the accountability approach to the law of State responsibility for internationally wrongful acts (cf. International Law Commission, Articles on Responsibility of States for Internationally Wrongful Acts in *Report of the International Law Commission on the Work of Its Fifty-Third Session* (UN Doc A/56/10 (2001). For indirect State persecution, see, e.g., para. 5(b) and (c) JICRA 1993/9; para. 5(e) JICRA 1993/10; para. 5 JICRA 1995/1; para. 5 JICRA 1997/12; para. 4(c) and (d) JICRA 1998/17.

[54] JICRA 2000/15, p. 108. See the similar definition given by the Qualification Directive, art. 6(b).

[55] However, to qualify as quasi-State entities of persecution, their de facto control needs to attain a certain degree of effectiveness, durability and stability. See JICRA 1995/25: 'sont assimilables à des persécutions étatiques, les agissements d'un mouvement insurrectionnel, lorsque ledit mouvement s'est mû en autorité de fait et exerce, d'une manière effective, stable et durable, la puissance publique sur le territoire soumis au contrôle de sa propre administration' (para. 2(a)(b)). On these criteria, see also JICRA 1995/2; JICRA 1996/6; JICRA 1996/42; JICRA 1997/6; JICRA 1997/14; JICRA 2000/15; JICRA 2002/16; JICRA 2004/14; JICRA 2006/19.

[56] See JICRA 1997/4 for the Taliban and JICRA 2000/15 and 2006/19 for the Kurdistan Democratic Party (KDP) and the Patriotic Union of Kurdistan (PUK).

quasi-State entities could be accountable for persecutory acts in such cases. The prime victims of this restrictive stance were women fleeing private gender-based persecution (such as female genital mutilation),[57] despite the gender-mainstreaming approach to asylum advanced by the 1998 AsylA.[58] Even asylum seekers fleeing extreme situations of civil unrest were denied refugee status if the State could not be found accountable for private groups' persecution but only for failing to maintain its sovereign control.[59] Refugee claims based on persecution by Somalian warlords were thus precluded in Switzerland.[60]

However, the Swiss understanding of actors of persecution differed from that of the majority of European States. Most of them focused on the absence of effective protection in the State of origin, rather than on the source of persecution, be it of a State, quasi-State or non-State nature.[61] This 'protection approach' was ultimately endorsed in article 6 2004 Qualification Directive. Even the EU States traditionally the most recalcitrant to recognize non-State actors of persecution, such as France and Germany, eventually agreed to this harmonized approach.[62]

---

[57] JICRA 2004/14, paras. 6 and 7. See also JICRA 1996/16, 146, para. (c). See, in this sense, Organisation Suisse d'Aide aux Réfugiés (OSAR), *La Suisse finit elle aussi par accorder l'asile aux victimes de persécutions non-étatiques* (Communiqué de presse, Berne: OSAR, 15 June 2006).

[58] See art. 3(2) AsylA, which specifically states that '[m]otives for seeking asylum specific to women must be taken into account'.

[59] OSAR, *Manuel de la procédure d'asile et de renvoi* (Berne, Stuttgart, Vienna: Haupt, 2009), p. 176. For further criticisms of the accountability approach, see Christina von Gunten, 'Die Staatlichkeit der Verfolgung – eine Voraussetzung der Anerkennung als Flüchtling?' (2001) 1/01 *ASYL* 22–35.

[60] See, for instance, JICRA 1995/25, p. 242, para. 5(b).

[61] See UNHCR, *Asylum in the European Union: A Study of the Implementation of the Qualification Directive* (November 2007), pp. 41–2. At the European level, as early as 1996, a joint position of the Council timidly favoured recognition of such third parties as actors of persecution. See Joint Position of 4 March 1996 defined by the Council on the basis of Article K.3 of the Treaty on European Union on the harmonized application of the definition of the term 'refugee' in Article 1 of the Geneva Convention of 28 July 1951 relating to the status of refugees (OJ 1996 No. L63/2): 'Where the official authorities fail to act, such [private] persecution should give rise to individual examination of each application for refugee status, in accordance with national judicial practice, in the light in particular of whether or not the failure to act was deliberate' (para. 5.2). As Volker Türk explains, '[t]he primary motivation is the recognition of the international protection needs as compensation for the lack of effective national protection, including in situations where the state is willing but unable to provide such protection' ('Non-State Agents of Persecution', 99).

[62] On the changes generated by the Qualification Directive in France and Germany, see notably Vincent Chetail, 'The Implementation of the Qualification Directive in France: One Step

This acknowledgement of non-State actors of persecution at the EU level prompted the Swiss courts to revise their own position. In 2006, the Swiss Asylum Appeals Commission finally ruled out its accountability approach in favour of the protection one.[63] The importance and reach of this leading decision of 2006 call for three main remarks.

First, this jurisprudential shift was clearly presented by the Swiss Commission as a result of the Qualification Directive. It expressly mentioned article 6(c) of the Directive as a reference point.[64] Though not bound by the EU Directive, the Swiss tribunal considered it to be an authoritative frame of interpretation.[65]

Second, the Swiss Asylum Appeals Commission emphasized the relationship between the Dublin system and the EU harmonization process as a further ground for bringing its interpretation into line with the Qualification Directive.[66] It concluded that, in cases of doubt about the exact meaning of the refugee definition under article 3 AsylA, it should be interpreted 'in a way that makes possible the harmonization of the refugee definition to the greater extent in Europe'.[67] In other words, the Commission presented the CEAS internal coherence as an argument legitimating the harmonization of its national asylum law with (in this case) the Qualification Directive.

Third, this landmark judgment has paved the way for further changes within Swiss jurisprudence on the refugee definition. Not only has it consecrated article 6 Qualification Directive as a reference standard, but it has been repeatedly quoted in Swiss judgments on actors of

---

Forward and Two Steps Backwards', in Karin Zwaan (ed.), *The Qualification Directive: Central Themes, Problem Issues, and Implementation in Selected Member States* (Nijmegen: Wolf Legal Publishers, 2007), pp. 87–101; Roland Bank, 'Transposition of the Qualification Directive in Germany', *ibid.*, pp. 109–26.

[63] JICRA 2006/18, paras. 7 and 8.

[64] *Ibid.*, para. 8.1. The relevant article reads as follows: 'Actors of persecution or serious harm include: ... (c) non-State actors, if it can be demonstrated that the actors mentioned in (a) and (b) [i.e. the State and 'parties or organisations controlling the State or a substantial part of the territory of the State'], including international organisations, are unable or unwilling to provide protection against persecution or serious harm as defined in Article 7.' The same wording is retained in art. 6(c) recast 2011 Qualification Directive.

[65] For a similar account, see also Susanne Bolz and Kathrin Buchmann, 'Die Rechtsprechung der Schweizerischen Asylrekurskommission im Jahre 2006', in Alberto Achermann *et al.* (eds.), *Jahrbuch für Migrationsrecht/Annuaire du droit de la migration 2006/2007* (Berne: Stämpfli Verlag AG, 2007), pp. 183–214, at 185.

[66] JICRA 2006/18, para. 8.1.

[67] *Ibid.*: 'welche die grössere inhaltliche Angleichung des materiellen Flüchtlingsbegriffs innerhalb Europas ermöglicht' (authors' translation). See also para. 8.2.

persecution.[68] Further, by adopting the protection approach, it has also opened up new interpretative perspectives for Swiss judges and for further harmonization with EU asylum law. Indeed, in discarding the accountability reasoning, refugee eligibility assessment now focuses more squarely on the existence of effective protection against persecution in the country of origin and the possibility of an internal flight alternative.[69]

2   Effective protection: the ripple effect of the protection approach

When adopting the protection approach, the Swiss Asylum Appeals Commission laid down the legal requirements for protection to exist in the country of origin. These include: (a) the existence of operational and efficient infrastructures for protection; (b) the accessibility of such infrastructure for the concerned person; and (c) the reasonableness of access to and benefit of such protection.[70] Referred to as 'adequate protection', this definition does not fundamentally depart from the one of 'effective protection' prescribed by article 7(2) Qualification Directive.[71]

Harmonization with the Qualification Directive appears to be less straightforward with respect to the actors of protection, however. Article 7(1) Qualification Directive lists such actors as being the State and 'parties or organizations, including international organizations, controlling the State or a substantial part of the territory of the State'. While State and quasi-State entities have been acknowledged as actors of protection by the Swiss jurisprudence,[72] the position on international organizations (IOs) remains more ambiguous.

Prior to the existence of the 2004 Qualification Directive, Swiss case law had not had the occasion to clearly address the issue of IOs as actors of

---

[68] See, e.g., Federal Administrative Tribunal (Tribunal administratif fédéral; TAF): E-4412/2006, 25 April 2008, para. 8.2; E-4054/2006, 18 July 2007, para. 4.1; D-7035/2006, 1 February 2008, para. 4.2; E-3710/2006, 18 June 2008, para. 4.2; E-4110/2008, 18 December 2008, para. 6.4.2; D-313/2010, 2 March 2010, para. 6.2.1.

[69] JICRA 2006/18, para. 10.1.   [70] Ibid., paras. 10.3.1–10.3.3.

[71] See the similar wording of art. 7(2) Recast 2011 Qualification Directive, which even more stringently emphasizes the effective and non-temporary nature of such protection.

[72] Concerning quasi-State entities, see, e.g., JICRA 2000/2; JICRA 2000/15, paras. 10–12. Quasi-State entities do not, however, encompass clans or families, which are unable to provide adequate protection. See JICRA 2006/18, para. 10.2.1 and 10.2.3; TAF, D-4935/2007, 21 December 2011; TAF, D-4404/2006, 2 May 2008, paras. 7.2.6.2: 'Adäquater Schutz kann nur von einer stabilen und organisierten Autorität gewährt werden, die das betrefende Gebiet und dessen Bevölkkerung uneningeschränkt kontrolliert'. See further TAF, D-4404/2006, para. 7.2.6.3.

protection. Only a judgment in 2002 contemplated the protective character of IOs.[73] According to the Swiss Asylum Appeals Commission, two conditions needed to be fulfilled in such situations: first, IOs had to truly and completely replace the State authority; and, second, they had to be in a position to effectively guarantee protection.[74] This conclusion resulted from the Commission's consideration of the role played by the United Nations (UN) and its robust administrative mandates, such as in East Timor and Kosovo.[75] However, the weight of this case needs to be somehow nuanced for the present purpose of identifying actors of protection, since this judgment was indeed within the framework of article 1C(5) Refugee Convention concerning changes of circumstances in the country of origin as a ground for the cessation of refugee protection.

Following the adoption of the Qualification Directive, the issue of IOs as actors of protection does not seem to be completely resolved. The Swiss Commission addressed the question in a quite ambivalent manner in its 2006 leading decision. On the one hand, it closely followed the enumeration made under article 7 Qualification Directive when stating that protection 'can be assumed by the country of origin . . . by a quasi-State entity or, *possibly, by determined international organizations*'.[76] On the other hand, the Commission left the question to be further determined since it was not a concern in the case at hand.[77] The subsequent

---

[73] JICRA 2002/8, para. 8. An unofficial English version of the main findings of this leading decision is available at www.ark-cra.ch/emark/2002/english.htm (accessed 2 October 2012). See para. 3: 'Under certain circumstances, the protection provided by an UNO protecting power (Schutzmacht) can replace the necessary protection of the state of nationality and therefore result in the revocation of asylum as defined by art. 1 C ciph. 1 Geneva Convention.'

[74] *Ibid.*, para. 8(c)(ee).   [75] *Ibid.*, paras. 8(c)(cc) and (ee).

[76] JICRA 2006/18, abstract of the leading decision, para. 2 (authors' translation; emphasis added). See further para. 10.2.

[77] *Ibid.*, para. 10.2.2. The Commission invoked its previous 2002 ruling where it recognized IOs within the framework of art. 1C Refugee Convention. It nonetheless went on to conclude that it has never yet had the occasion to determine whether IOs could be considered as actors of protection for the purposes of refugee eligibility: 'Die Frage, ob und gegebenenfalls unter welchen Umständen neben Quasi-Staaten auch internationale Organisationen als Schutzgewährer im Sinne von Art. 1A Ziff. 2 FK anzuerkennen sind, ist von der ARK bisher nie beantwortet worden. Sie stellt sich auch im vorliegenden Beschwerdeverfahren nicht. Diese dogmatische Frage wird anhand eines geeigneten Verfahrens zu gegebener Zeit zu beantworten sein.'

See also para. 10.2.3: 'Die Frage, ob unter Umständen auch internationale Organisationen mit der gleichen Konsequenz schützen können, bleibt vorderhand offen.'

Swiss case law has since followed this ambiguous stance, mentioning IOs *en passant* within the list of actors of protection.[78]

At present, Swiss jurisprudence has not yet elaborated all the consequences of the new protection approach prompted by EU law. This is simply due to the fact that the question of IOs has so far never been a key issue to be determined by Swiss courts. While the Swiss interpretation will have to be clarified sooner or later, the rationale for a half-shade attitude might stem from a principled reticence to recognize all IOs as actors of protection. Indeed, in general, IOs rarely reach the necessary protection threshold.[79] As ruled in the 2002 judgment, only transitional administration operations as set up by the UN in Kosovo and East Timor would have the necessary means to ensure protection by virtue of their peace-enforcement mandate under Chapter VII of the UN Charter. Any other interpretation would risk precluding refugee eligibility because of the mere presence of a peacekeeping operation in a part of the country of origin through the concept of internal flight alternative, analysed below.[80]

3   The internal flight alternative: towards EU neutralization of Swiss particularism

The concept of the internal flight alternative (IFA), also referred to in the Qualification Directive as 'internal protection', acts as a ground of ineligibility when the applicant can be relocated to a part of the country of origin where he or she will be free from persecution.[81] Although not

---

[78]   TAF, D-356/2007, 2 April 2007, 4; TAF, D-4935/2007, 21 December 2011, para. 7.2.

[79]   Chetail and Bauloz, 'The European Union and the Challenges of Forced Migration', 16. This echoes the more fundamental question of the participation of IOs in human rights treaties, since only States and not IOs are parties to such treaties. See notably Bolz and Buchmann, 'Die Rechtsprechung der Schweizerischen Asylrekurskommission', 185.

[80]   Vincent Chetail, 'La réforme de l'asile: prélude à la banalisation européenne du droit des réfugiés' (2004) 131 *Journal de droit international* 817–65, at 849–50.

[81]   On the IFA notion, see generally James C. Hathaway and Michelle Foster, 'Internal Protection/Relocation/Flight Alternative as an Aspect of Refugee Status Determination', in Erika Feller, Volker Türk and Frances Nicholson (eds.), *Refugee Protection in International Refugee Law: UNHCR's Global Consultations on International Protection* (Cambridge: Cambridge University Press, 2003), pp. 357–417; Reinhard Marx, 'The Criteria of Applying the "Internal Flight Alternative" Test in National Refugee Status Determination Procedures' (2002) 14 *International Journal of Refugee Law* 179–218; Ninette Kelley, 'Internal Flight/Relocation/Protection Alternative: Is It Reasonable?' (2002) 14 *International Journal of Refugee Law* 4–44; Hugo Storey, 'The Internal Flight Alternative Test: The Jurisprudence Re-Examined' (1998) 10 *International Journal of Refugee Law* 499–532.

explicitly mentioned in the Refugee Convention,[82] its rationale stems from the surrogate nature of refugee protection: if an asylum seeker can be returned to a safe area within his or her country of origin, then he or she is not in need of international protection.

In Europe, this concept was rarely applied until the 1980s, and it eventually gained momentum in the 1990s.[83] In the early 1980s, Switzerland was one of the first countries to rely on it in its refugee determination decisions.[84] At the EU level, the notion was endorsed in the 2004 Qualification Directive. Article 8 Qualification Directive aims to harmonize the definition of 'internal protection' on the basis of a twofold requirement: (a) the absence of a well-founded fear of persecution in a part of the country of origin; and (b) the reasonableness for the applicant to relocate to that area.[85]

This second requirement was not traditionally part of the Swiss understanding of IFA.[86] Indeed, only the absence of persecution in the

---

[82] UNHCR, *Guidelines on International Protection: 'Internal Flight or Relocation Alternative' within the Context of Article 1A(2) of the 1951 Convention and/or 1967 Protocol relating to the Status of Refugees*, 23 July 2003 (UN Doc. HCR/GIP/03/04), para. 2.

[83] European Legal Network on Asylum (ELENA), *Research Paper on the Application of the Concept of Internal Protection Alternative* (London: ELENA, November 1998, updated as at 2000), p. 69. Attempts to define such a concept were first undertaken in the mid-1990s at the UNHCR and EU levels: UNHCR, *An Overview of Protection Issues in Western Europe: Legislative Trends and Positions Taken by UNHCR* (September 1995); *Joint Position of 4 March 1996 defined by the Council on the basis of Article K.3 of the Treaty on European Union* (OJ 1996 No. L63/2), s. 8. See also UNHCR Executive Committee, Conclusion No. 87(L) (8 October 1999), para. j; UNHCR, *Relocating Internally as a Reasonable Alternative to Seeking Asylum (the So-Called 'Internal Flight Alternative' or 'Relocation Principle')* (UNHCR Position Paper, February 1999).

[84] Maiani, 'La définition de réfugié', 57; Werenfels, *Der Begriff des Flüchtlings*, pp. 333-4. For further discussions on the Swiss understanding of IFA, see Kälin, *Grundriss des Asylverfahrens*, pp. 71-4; Werenfels, *Der Begriff des Flüchtlings*, pp. 333-41; Achermann and Hausammann, *Handbuch des Asylrechts*, pp. 89-90.

[85] These criteria were acknowledged by UNHCR as *broadly* corresponding to UNHCR criteria developed in its 2003 Guidelines on the internal flight alternative. See respectively, UNHCR, *UNHCR Annotated Comments on the EC Council Directive 2004/83/EC of 29 April 2004 on Minimum Standards for the Qualification and Status of Third Country Nationals or Stateless Persons as Refugees or as Persons Who Otherwise Need International Protection and the Content of the Protection Granted* (January 2005), p. 19; UNHCR, *Guidelines on International Protection* (2003), para. 7; but see UNHCR, *Asylum in the European Union*, p. 56. Further note that art. 8(1) of the Directive is not phrased in mandatory language but gives the possibility to Member States to rely on such a concept in their refugee status determinations.

[86] JICRA 1996/1, para. 5(d). See also Susanne Bolz, 'Wie EU-Kompatibel ist das Schweizer Asylrecht?' (2005) 1/05 *ASYL* 8-13, at 9-10.

concerned area of the country of origin (the first EU criterion) was examined.[87] On closer examination, however, this peculiar understanding is less significant than it might appear at first sight.

While it is not integrated within the refugee eligibility determination, the reasonableness of return is relevant at a subsequent stage, namely, when implementing removal orders against rejected asylum seekers. If the enforcement of such removals appears unreasonable, a person can benefit from temporary admission in accordance with article 83(4) Foreign Nationals Act (FNA).[88]

More fundamentally, a recent judgment delivered by the Swiss Federal Administrative Tribunal in December 2011 has opened the door to a neutralization of the traditional Swiss understanding of IFA. After long and sophisticated reasoning, the Tribunal concluded that:

> [T]he jurisprudence based on JICRA 1996/1 formerly relying on the accountability theory – under which the reasonableness of relocation ... in part of the country ... had to be exclusively examined under Article 83(4) FNA – can no longer be retained in light of the current practice of interpreting the Geneva Convention on the basis of the protection theory.[89]

Drawing on the Swiss Asylum Appeals Commission's leading 2006 judgment endorsing the protection approach, the Tribunal held that in order to show that effective protection exists in the country of origin, it is necessary to show that the person can reasonably access and benefit from the conditions identified in the 2006 decision.[90]

The relinquishment of Switzerland's traditional approach to persecution in 2006 has led to a harmonization dynamic within Swiss jurisprudence. The ripple effect of the EU's 'new' protection theory has indeed been felt beyond the mere recognition of non-State actors of persecution:

---

[87] JICRA 1996/1, para. 5(b) with assessment of such protection guarantee further detailed in para. 5(c). See also JICRA 1997/12, 30 January 1997, para. 6; OSAR, *Manuel de la procédure d'asile et de renvoi*, p. 190.

[88] RS 142.20, RO 2007 5437, 16 December 2005. See also AsylA: 'If the enforcement of the removal order is not admissible, unreasonable or impossible, the Federal Office shall regulate the conditions of stay in accordance with the statutory provisions of the FNA on temporary admission' (art. 44(2)).

[89] TAF, D-4935/2007, 21 December 2011, para. 8.7 (authors' translation).

[90] *Ibid.*, paras. 8.5–8.6. For the three conditions for assessing the existence of protection as defined by the Commission, see JICRA 2006/18, paras. 10.3.1–10.3.3. The 2011 judgment represents a significant change compared to previous decisions of the Federal Administrative Tribunal which insisted on the Swiss specificity of the IFA. See TAF, E-2553/2008, 16 August 2011, para. 6.5; TAF, E-7089/2009, 2 December 2009, para. 8.3.; TAF, D-4297/2006, 26 January 2009, para. 5.7; TAF, D-4404/2006, 2 May 2008, para. 7.3.

they have also extended to the Swiss interpretation of IFA and IOs as possible actors of protection. The minimum standards for eligibility as a refugee established by the Qualification Directive have had a mainstreaming influence on Swiss asylum jurisprudence. Thus, the Swiss interpretation of the refugee definition is being progressively reconsidered in light of the Qualification Directive.

D   Conclusion: Switzerland as the outsiders' insider within the EU

The EU has undeniably set the rules of the asylum game in Europe such that the Swiss 'free rider' position has become increasingly untenable. Switzerland's inner geographical location and its fear of secondary movements of asylum seekers prompted its first step towards the CEAS through the Dublin Association Agreement. What the Swiss Confederation perhaps did not contemplate is that this first step has set the pace for further EU integration. A cultural revolution has taken place within the Swiss judiciary with the adoption of the protection approach, ending its long restrictive conception of actors of persecution. Swiss courts are still in a process of drawing the systemic consequences of this jurisprudential shift, as demonstrated by their rulings on actors of protection and the IFA.

For the purposes of the present chapter, the following question appears more legitimate than ever: is Switzerland becoming a de facto EU Member State? The answer is perhaps as ambivalent as the Swiss attitude towards the EU. Switzerland continues to favour a double discourse – on the one hand, emphasizing that it is not an EU Member State, while on the other hand relying on an internalization process of the substance of EU norms. This policy translates into a bottom-up harmonization approach, notably carried out at the judicial level. Far from being ideal for its jurisprudential red tape,[91] this backdoor process of harmonization denotes an incremental convergence process with EU asylum law.

Ultimately, Switzerland has become the outsiders' insider within the EU by opening the door to further CEAS integration. The Dublin Association Agreement has set the first foundation stone, with subsequent legislative and jurisprudential developments still building the edifice. Far from the tower of Babel, the Swiss construction is slowly taking the form of a turret – one of fortress Europe.

---

[91] It is indeed notable that, in 2012, Swiss judges are still attempting to assess and implement the consequences of the 2006 ruling and the adoption of the protection approach.

7

The impact of European refugee law on the regional, subregional and national planes in Africa

MARINA SHARPE

A   Introduction

The governance of refugee affairs in Africa occurs on three separate planes: regional, subregional and national. This chapter surveys key historical and contemporary African regional, subregional and State refugee protection practices that originated in Europe and finds that they have been and continue to be employed at each level. The chapter begins with a brief overview of the European refugee law framework. It then describes aspects of what is arguably the most significant instance of African regional engagement with refugee protection: the Organization of African Unity's (OAU) adoption of the 1969 Convention Governing the Specific Aspects of Refugee Problems in Africa[1] (1969 Convention, or the Convention). This essentially began as an initiative to make the European 1951 Convention relating to the Status of Refugees[2] (1951 Convention) – originally limited to flight from events that occurred prior to 1 January 1951 and so largely irrelevant in Africa – applicable on the continent. The African Union (AU) succeeded the OAU in 2001, and the AU's approach to refugee protection continues to reflect elements of European refugee law. After surveying the regional plane, the chapter examines the Southern African Development Community's (SADC) now defunct initiative for the free movement of people within the subregion and the impact this could have had on refugee protection in light of European refugee law precedent. It also discusses SADC's current work to harmonize refugee protection in the bloc. Finally, recent national

[1] Organization of African Unity Convention Governing the Specific Aspects of Refugee Problems in Africa, Addis Ababa, 10 September 1969, in force 20 June 1974 (1001 UNTS 45).
[2] Convention relating to the Status of Refugees, Geneva, 28 July 1951, in force 22 April 1954 (189 UNTS 137).

approaches to refugee protection that mirror restrictive European practices are outlined.

This survey reveals that European practices are often clearly reflected in African regional, subregional and State approaches to refugee protection. However, the historical regional case is the only one in which the process of norm diffusion can be traced back to an explicit objective of emulating the European approach in Africa. By contrast, an explicit desire to implement European approaches in Africa is not evident in the modern context. Yet the appearance within the AU, SADC and national laws and policies of approaches to refugee protection pioneered by Europe certainly suggests that a process of norm diffusion is under way. That this process is not documented, makes it impossible to describe with precision, but it is evident that European approaches to refugee protection continue to hold sway in Africa.

B   The European asylum *acquis*

The 1992 Maastricht Treaty on the European Union[3] (EU) recognized immigration and asylum issues as coming under the EU's 'third pillar' on justice and home affairs. Subsequently, the 1997 Treaty of Amsterdam brought refugee protection within the purview of the EU's judicial European Court of Justice and its legislative Council of Ministers, mandating the latter to adopt, among other things

> measures on asylum, in accordance with the ... [1951] Convention ... and the [1967] Protocol ... within the following areas: (a) criteria and mechanisms for determining which Member State is responsible for considering an application for asylum ... (b) minimum standards on the reception of asylum seekers ... (c) minimum standards with respect to the qualification of nationals of third countries as refugees; (d) minimum standards on procedures in Member States for granting or withdrawing refugee status.[4]

This Directive ultimately gave rise to the European asylum *acquis*, which consists in large part of the 2003 Dublin Regulations,[5] the 2003

---

[3] Treaty on the European Union, Maastricht, 7 February 1992, in force 1 November 1993 (OJ C 191).

[4] Treaty of Amsterdam Amending the Treaty on the European Union, the Treaties Establishing the European Communities and Related Acts, Amsterdam, 2 October 1997, in force 1 May 1999 (OJ C 340), art. 63.

[5] Council Regulation (EC) No. 343/2003 of 18 February 2003 establishing the criteria and mechanisms for determining the Member State responsible for examining an asylum

Reception Conditions Directive,[6] the 2004 Qualification Directive (as amended in 2011)[7] and the 2005 Procedures Directive.[8] The Procedures Directive, the first supranational instrument to codify rules on the application of the restrictive 'safe third country', 'first country of asylum', 'safe country of origin' and 'manifestly unfounded' notions, forms a critical part of the legal framework underpinning Europe's increasingly exclusionary and globally influential approach to refugees,[9] as will be seen in the discussion of national law later in this chapter. As important as the European asylum *acquis* is, however, it is not the first European refugee law initiative to have effects around the world. The 1951 Convention was largely responsive to the events of the Second World War in Europe, and yet its influence ultimately extended across the globe, including to Africa, as is described below.

C   The regional level: the OAU's early emulation and contemporary AU practice[10]

The OAU was formed on 25 May 1963 to promote regional cooperation through policy harmonization among newly independent African States. It was eventually, however, judged ineffective. Zard explains that the

application lodged in one of the Member States by a third-country national (OJ 2003 No. L50/1); responsive to (a) in text above.

[6] Council Directive 2003/9/EC of 27 January 2003 laying down minimum standards for the reception of asylum seekers (OJ 2003 No. L31/18); responsive to (b) in text above.

[7] Directive 2011/95/EU of the European Parliament and of the Council of 13 December 2011 on standards for the qualification of third-country nationals or stateless persons as beneficiaries of international protection, for a uniform status for refugees or for persons eligible for subsidiary protection, and for the content of the protection granted (recast) (OJ 2011 No. L337/9) (Qualification Directive); responsive to (c) in text above.

[8] Council Directive 2005/85/EC of 1 December 2005 on minimum standards on procedures in Member States for granting and withdrawing refugee status (OJ 2005 No. L236/13) (Procedures Directive); responsive to (d) in text above. Also relevant are the Family Reunification Directive (2003/109/EC), the Third Country Nationals Directive (2003/109/EC) and the Return Directive (2008/115/EC). For a detailed description of the European asylum *acquis*, see Anja Klug, 'Harmonization of Asylum in the European Union: Emergence of an EU Refugee System?' (2004) 47 *German Yearbook of International Law* 594–628.

[9] See generally Satvinder Juss, 'The Decline and Decay of European Refugee Policy' (2005) 25 *Oxford Journal of Legal Studies* 749–92.

[10] This section draws on Marina Sharpe, 'Organization of African Unity and African Union Engagement with Refugee Protection: 1963–2011' (2013) 21 *African Journal of International and Comparative Law* 50–94, which goes into the drafting history of the 1969 Convention in far greater detail than is possible here.

OAU's 'strict adherence to the principle of non-intervention and its subordination to state interest, combined with chronic financial difficulties, often precluded . . . [it] from asserting any form of moral authority or leadership in tackling some of Africa's chronic problems'.[11] This was especially the case in the face of modern challenges facing the continent. Having focused on decolonization and liberation from minority rule and committed to the principle of non-interference,[12] the OAU was not equipped to deal with contemporary issues of economic growth and conflict. The first major move to revitalize the regional organization came in 1999 with the Sirte Declaration, which set out plans to establish what would become the AU.[13] This new body superseded the OAU with the entry into force of its Constitutive Act on 26 May 2001.[14]

1   The drafting of the 1969 Convention

Despite its overall ineffectiveness, the OAU was responsible for what is arguably Africa's most important regional achievement in the field of refugee protection: the adoption of the 1969 Convention. This instrument has – alongside the 1951 Convention – since 1974 governed the protection of refugees on the continent. The 1969 Convention is relatively short, containing a preamble and fifteen articles. Article I provides two refugee definitions. The first mirrors that found at article 1A(2) 1951 Convention, minus the 1 January 1951 date limit that most States later agreed, by way of a protocol[15] (1967 Protocol), not to apply. The second definition provides: 'the term refugee shall also apply to every person who, owing to external aggression, occupation, foreign domination or events seriously disturbing public order in either part or the whole of his country of origin or nationality, is compelled to leave his place of habitual residence in order to seek refuge in another place outside his

---

[11] Monette Zard, 'African Union', in Matthew Gibney and Randall Hansen (eds.), *Immigration and Asylum: From 1900 to the Present* (Santa Barbara: ABC-CLIO, 2005), pp. 6–7.

[12] Charter of the Organization of African Unity, Addis Ababa, 25 May 1963 (479 UNTS 39), art. III(2).

[13] Organization of African Unity (Assembly of Heads of State and Government), 'Sirte Declaration' (OAU Sirte, 9 September 1999), AHG/Draft/Decl. (IV) Rev. 1.

[14] Constitutive Act of the African Union, Lomé, 11 July 2000, in force 26 May 2001 (2158 UNTS 3).

[15] Protocol relating to the Status of Refugees, New York, 31 January 1967, in force 4 October 1967 (606 UNTS 267), art. 1(2).

country of origin or nationality'.[16] Article I also includes paragraphs on cessation[17] and exclusion.[18] Article II relates to asylum. The third article articulates refugees' duty to respect the laws and regulations of the host State and prohibits them from engaging in subversive activities against any OAU Member State. Article IV is on non-discrimination in the application of the Convention. The fifth article relates to voluntary repatriation. Article VI mandates contracting States to provide refugees with travel documents. Articles VII and VIII relate to State cooperation with the OAU and United Nations High Commissioner for Refugees (UNHCR), respectively. The final seven articles are technical provisions.[19]

Most accounts of the 1969 Convention attribute the OAU's initial interest in a regional refugee instrument to the failure of the Eurocentric, persecution-based 1951 Convention refugee definition to reflect African realities.[20] The historical record, however, reveals this to be largely false. When work on the 1969 Convention began in 1964, the OAU had two other concerns. First, the date line contained in the 1951 Convention refugee definition prevented the instrument from applying to new refugee situations that had arisen in Africa.[21] Accordingly, the first draft of the 1969 Convention, known as the 'Kampala Draft' because the OAU's first drafting committee[22] met in the Ugandan capital, 'employed the

---

[16] Art. I(2) 1969 Convention.   [17] Ibid., art. I(4).   [18] Ibid., art. I(5).

[19] It is notable that the 1969 Convention is silent on refugee rights. The elaborate rights framework found at arts. 3–34 1951 Convention finds no parallel in its African counterpart. This is because the 1969 Convention relates primarily to qualification for and disqualification from refugee status; rights are governed by the 1951 Convention, even in respect of individuals recognized only under art. I(2). See Marina Sharpe, 'The 1969 African Refugee Convention: Innovations, Misconceptions, and Omissions' (2012) 58 *McGill Law Journal* 95–147, section III.

[20] See, e.g., Ousmane Goundiam, 'African Refugee Convention' (1970) March/April, *Migration News* 3–12, at 8; Jennifer Turner, 'Liberian Refugees: A Test of the 1969 OAU Convention Governing the Specific Aspects of Refugee Problems in Africa' (1994) 8 *Georgetown Immigration Law Journal* 281–301, at 286; Jennifer Hyndman and Bo Victor Nylund, 'UNHCR and the Status of Prima Facie Refugees in Kenya' (1998) 10 *International Journal of Refugee Law* 21–45.

[21] George Okoth-Obbo, 'Thirty Years On: A Legal Review of the 1969 OAU Convention Governing the Specific Aspects of Refugee Problems in Africa' (2001) 20 *Refugee Survey Quarterly* 79–138, at 109–10. It should be noted that there was never any geographical limitation preventing the 1951 Convention from applying in Africa. Article 1B(1) 1951 Convention allows States to opt out of its geographical limitation to Europe upon signature, ratification or accession.

[22] This ad hoc commission consisted of representatives from Burundi, Cameroon, Congo-Léopoldville (as it then was), Ghana, Nigeria, Rwanda, Senegal, Sudan, Tanganyika (as it

form and much of the working of the 1951 Refugee Convention, although it eliminated the dateline contained therein'.[23] Subsequent drafts were also largely reflective of the 1951 Convention – though less liberal in some respects, as will be discussed below – and included just the refugee definition borrowed from the international refugee instrument, without the date line. That early drafts of the 1969 Convention included only the 1951 Convention refugee definition evidences that dissatisfaction with it was not a factor initially motivating the adoption of a regional instrument. Indeed, early in the drafting process Tanzania asserted that a regional convention was not even necessary, and instead proposed a simple protocol to extend the application of the 1951 Convention to Africa.[24] This approach was rejected because the newly formed Committee of Legal Experts[25] felt bound by the mandate conferred upon it by the OAU Council of Ministers.[26]

The OAU's second concern was with 'the security and peaceful relations among OAU member States, particularly in cases where the presence of refugees causes inter-State tension'.[27] This concern is evidenced by many provisions of the 1969 Convention, such as its third preambular paragraph, which recognizes that 'refugee problems are a source of friction among many Member States' and notes the aim of 'eliminating the source of such discord'. Thus the impetus to adopt an African refugee convention had nothing to do with the irrelevance of the 1951 Convention refugee definition to Africa. To the contrary, the OAU sought to make the 1951 Convention applicable in Africa by drafting a regional instrument largely reflective of it, with additional provisions

---

then was) and Uganda. In March 1965, in view of various shortcomings of the Kampala draft, drafting was handed from the ad hoc commission over to a Committee of Legal Experts, which consisted of legal experts from the same ten States represented on the ad hoc commission (Organization of African Unity (Council of Ministers), 'Resolution on the Problem of Refugees' (OAU Nairobi 26 February–9 March 1965) CM/Res. 52 (IV) para. 3).

[23] Philip Chartrand, 'The Organization of African Unity and African Refugees: A Progress Report' (1975) 137 *World Affairs* 265–85, at 270.

[24] Copy of incoming cable from HCR Léopoldville to HiComRef Geneva, received 12 July 1965, UNHCR archives, fonds 1/5/11/1.

[25] See above n. 22.

[26] The drafting committee's mandate emanates from Organization of African Unity (Council of Ministers), 'Resolution on the Problem of Refugees' (OAU Nairobi 26 February–9 March 1965) CM/Res. 52 (IV) para. 3.

[27] Jacob van Garderen and Julie Ebenstein, 'Regional Developments: Africa', in Andreas Zimmermann (ed.), *The 1951 Convention relating to the Status of Refugees and Its 1967 Protocol* (Oxford: Oxford University Press, 2011), p. 188.

that would address the Organization's concerns about inter-State tension.

About a year into the drafting process, after the 1964 Kampala draft and the subsequent July 1965 Léopoldville draft had come before the OAU's Council of Ministers, the OAU's stance on the form that the regional instrument should take started to shift. It then began to be recognized that the regional instrument should not duplicate its international counterpart, but rather should address refugee problems particular to Africa. At its October 1965 Assembly of Heads of State and Government in Accra, the OAU called on Member States to 'ratify the United Nations Convention relating to the Status of Refugees and ... apply meanwhile the provisions of the said Convention to refugees in Africa'.[28] According to Jackson, this request 'can be taken as the first clear indication that the African refugee convention should not cover the same ground as the 1951 Convention, the overriding character of which was implicitly recognised'.[29] Similarly, the then High Commissioner explained in his October 1965 Executive Committee statement that most delegations at the Accra meeting had agreed that instead of creating a convention 'covering all aspects of the problem of refugees in Africa', the OAU should 'recognise the universal principles of the 1951 Convention and supplement the latter with a view to regulating certain aspects of the refugee problems peculiar to the region in particular in so far as they concern relations between member states'.[30] UNHCR's April 1965 Bellagio Colloquium, the work of which ultimately led to the adoption of the 1967 Protocol,[31] likely played a role in this shift.

Despite the consensus that emerged from the 1965 Accra meeting, the third draft convention that followed it in 1966, known as the Addis Ababa draft, 'still tended to cover the same ground as the 1951 Convention, though its provisions were more liberal than those of the preceding drafts and it contained new articles felt to be essential for

---

[28] Organization of African Unity (Assembly of Heads of State and Government), 'Resolution on the Problem of Refugees in Africa' (OAU Accra 21–25 October 1965) AHG/Res. 26 (II), para. 6.

[29] Ivor Jackson, *The Refugee Concept in Group Situations* (Leiden: Martinus Nijhoff, 1999) p. 182.

[30] UNHCR, 'Statement by the High Commissioner to the 15th Session of the Executive Committee of the High Commissioner's Programme' (29 October 1965) A/AC.96/310, at 1.

[31] Louise Holborn, *Refugees: A Problem of Our Time: The Work of the United Nations High Commissioner for Refugees, 1951–1972* (Washington, DC: Scarecrow Press, 1974), pp. 185–6.

dealing with the refugee situations in Africa'.[32] Moreover, the Addis Ababa draft still included only one refugee definition, replicating that of the 1951 Convention. Possibly in response to the Addis Ababa draft's failure to reflect the OAU's new stance, at its Seventh Ordinary Session, the OAU's Council of Ministers handed the job of drafting the African refugee convention from the Committee of Legal Experts over to the OAU Secretariat.[33] Furthermore, the Council expressed in no uncertain terms the consensus that had emerged in Accra, noting its desire 'that the African instrument should govern the *specifically African aspects of the refugee problem* and that it should come to be the *effective regional complement* of the 1951 ... Convention'.[34] This approach was at this point clearly inspired by the 1967 Protocol's imminent adoption, which meant that the 1951 Convention would soon be fully applicable in Africa.[35] Holborn describes the OAU Council of Ministers' Seventh Ordinary Session as 'a turning point in the drafting of the OAU Convention; from then on drafts almost totally omitted any reference to matters already covered in the 1951 Convention and concentrated instead on matters particularly affecting refugees in Africa'.[36]

The OAU Secretariat presented its draft convention, now the fourth to come before the OAU's Council of Ministers, at the body's Ninth Ordinary Session, held in Kinshasa in September 1967. By this time, the 1967 Protocol had received three of the six accessions it needed to enter into force.[37] The impending complete applicability of the 1951 Convention in Africa did not, however, obviate the regional instrument. OAU Member States agreed in Kinshasa that in light of its now complementary character, the regional convention remained necessary in order to address refugee situations specific to Africa.[38] Furthermore, certain African States – notably Nigeria and Uganda – were critical of the 1967 Protocol because, while it removed the 1951 Convention's temporal limitation, it failed to address refugee protection concerns particular to Africa.[39] Yet while it was agreed that an African refugee convention

---

[32] Holborn, 'Refugees', 187.

[33] *Ibid.*; Organization of African Unity (Council of Ministers), 'Resolution on the Adoption of a Draft Convention on the Status of Refugees in Africa' (OAU Addis Ababa 31 October–4 November 1966) CM/Res. 88 (VII), para. 2.

[34] OAU, 'Resolution on the Adoption of a Draft Convention', preambular para. 6 (emphasis added).

[35] Okoth-Obbo, 'Thirty Years', 110.   [36] Holborn, 'Refugees', 187.   [37] *Ibid.*, 188.

[38] *Ibid.*

[39] Sara Davies, 'Redundant or Essential? How Politics Shaped the Outcome of the 1967 Protocol' (2007) 19 *International Journal of Refugee Law* 703–8, at 724–5.

remained necessary, the Council of Ministers did not accept the Secretariat's draft, and the OAU's Committee of Legal Experts was sent back to work on what would be the fifth, and final, draft of the regional refugee convention.

The Committee of Legal Experts met in Addis Ababa in June 1968. The OAU Secretariat provided the Committee with a draft convention to serve as a basis for their work.[40] This draft included the 1951 Convention refugee definition plus, for the first time, a second definition. It also included a conflict clause governing the regional instrument's relationship to the 1951 Convention, as well as provisions similar to or mirroring those in the final 1969 Convention. The Committee of Legal Experts maintained the Secretariat's draft with only minor revisions, including an amendment to the portion of the conflict clause that would have made the regional instrument supreme in specified instances.[41] At its Eleventh Ordinary Session, held in Algiers in September 1968, the OAU's Council of Ministers requested that 'Member States, who have not yet done so . . . communicate to the General Secretariat before 15 December 1968 their comments on the OAU draft Convention'.[42] In February 1969, once such comments had been received, the Committee of Legal Experts presented its final draft to the Council of Ministers. This time, the document won the Council's unanimous support, and was signed by forty-one African States on 10 September 1969.[43]

The OAU and UNHCR played critical roles in the process that ultimately led to the 1969 adoption of the African refugee convention, the former body by initiating the regional convention and, along with UNHCR, by guiding the process of drafting it. The initiative to address refugees at the regional level in Africa was spearheaded by the OAU's Council of Ministers, which in 1964 established an ad hoc commission to examine '(a) the refugee problem in Africa and make recommendations to the Council of Ministers on how it can be solved; [and] (b) ways and means of maintaining refugees in their country of asylum'.[44] It

---

[40] 'Report of the Administrative Secretary-General for the Meeting of the OAU Commission on Refugees Held in Addis Ababa from 17th to 23rd June 1968', UNHCR archives, fonds 1/5/11/1.

[41] No conflict clause ultimately made its way into the final draft of the 1969 Convention.

[42] Organization of African Unity (Council of Ministers), 'Resolution on the Problem of Refugees in Africa' (OAU Algiers 4–12 September 1968) CM/Res. 149 (XI), para. 1.

[43] Chartrand, 'Progress Report', 271.

[44] Organization of African Unity (Council of Ministers), 'Resolution on the Problem of Refugees in Africa' (OAU Lagos 24–29 February 1964) CM/Res. 19 (II); see above n. 22.

was this ad hoc Commission that recommended that the OAU draft a regional refugee instrument.[45] The Council of Ministers adopted the Commission's recommendation, directing it to draw up a draft convention.[46] However, owing to shortcomings of the Kampala draft, in 1965 drafting was handed from the ad hoc Commission over to the Committee of Legal Experts, which consisted of legal experts from the same ten States represented on the ad hoc Commission.[47] While responsibility for drafting the 1969 Convention rested with this Committee from 1965 onwards, its work and the work of the ad hoc Commission before it was at all times influenced by the OAU and UNHCR.

The OAU and UNHCR were concerned about the ad hoc Commission's and the Committee of Legal Experts' drafts, which as mentioned above generally replicated the 1951 Convention but were in many respects far less liberal. For example, in a letter of July 1965, then Deputy High Commissioner Prince Sadruddin Aga Kahn wrote

> [w]e are concerned at possibility of African Regional Convention which departs from universal 1951 Convention and provides substantially lesser standard of treatment for African refugees as for example on wage earning employment and expulsion ... Moreover believe present [Kampala] draft would seriously jeopardise protocol or other instrument to extend effects 1951 Convention to post dateline refugees.[48]

The Léopoldville draft was equally problematic. It 'failed to win OAU approval because, in the eyes of many OAU members, it on the one hand, overlapped with the 1951 Convention and, on the other, was still far less liberal than the 1951 Convention since it reduced its standards'.[49] Similarly, UNHCR's view of the Léopoldville draft was that it would 'dangerously impair the universal value of the principles of the 1951 Convention, and would hinder efforts currently being undertaken to extend the Convention's scope'.[50] Accordingly, the OAU and UNHCR worked together, largely behind the scenes, on reports and draft

---

[45] Holborn, 'Refugees', 185.

[46] Organization of African Unity (Council of Ministers), 'Resolution on the Commission on the Problem of Refugees in Africa' (OAU Cairo 13–17 July 1964) CM/Res. 36 (III), para. 6.

[47] Organization of African Unity (Council of Ministers), 'Resolution on the Problem of Refugees' (OAU Nairobi 26 February–9 March 1965) CM/Res. 52 (IV), para. 3; see above n. 22.

[48] Letter dated 14 July 1965, UNHCR archives, fonds 1/5/11/1.

[49] Chartrand, 'Progress Report', 270.   [50] Jackson, Group Situations, p. 181.

conventions to promote an African convention that would not undermine the 1951 instrument. For example, the OAU's Assistant Secretary
General prepared a report for the OAU's October 1965 Assembly of
Heads of State and Government in Accra, highlighting the concerns
shared by his organization and UNHCR. Furthermore, UNHCR provided a draft convention to serve as a basis of the Committee of Legal
Expert's work in Léopoldville[51] – which was largely ignored – and, as
mentioned above, the OAU Secretariat authored the penultimate draft of
the 1969 Convention.

That 1969 Convention's unique refugee definition and other provisions relating to refugee protection concerns specific to Africa appeared
only in the fifth and final draft of the instrument. This is evidence that,
until the time of the 1967 Protocol's adoption, work on the 1969
Convention was directed at making the 1951 Convention fully *applicable
in Africa*; only when the 1951 Convention became truly universal would
addressing refugee issues *particular to Africa* become a firm objective of
the project to draft a regional refugee instrument. Thus the first and
arguably the most significant regional refugee protection initiative in
Africa was initially an OAU project to make the fundamentally
European 1951 Convention apply on the continent; the OAU and
UNHCR played a critical role in facilitating this process, in particular
by ensuring that it would not undermine the 1951 Convention. This
regional historical example of norm diffusion represents a precedent:
elements of contemporary regional, subregional and national refugee
protection frameworks reproduce approaches, especially restrictive
ones, conceived in Europe.

2   The contemporary AU approach to refugee protection

At the regional level, contemporary European influence may be apparent in the way refugee protection has recently shifted from being a focal
issue on the AU's agenda to being one of several issues within a wider
humanitarian portfolio, including disaster response, internal displacement and the protection of civilians in armed conflict.[52] Elsewhere in

---

[51] Note Submitted by the United Nations High Commissioner for Refugees on Measures
Being Examined within the Framework of the Organization of African Unity for
Regulating Refugee Problems between Member States, June 1965, UNHCR archives,
fonds 1/5/11/1.

[52] See generally Sharpe, 'OAU and AU Engagement'.

this volume, Durieux speculates that the rise of temporary and subsidiary protection in Europe – the former through the 2001 Temporary Protection Directive[53] and the latter via the Qualification Directive[54] – may be undermining the specificity of refugee protection there.[55] With the AU now treating refugee protection as just one among several humanitarian issues confronting it, the same arguably dangerous phenomenon is apparent in Africa. The dilution of the AU's focus on refugees is most apparent in how the mandates of its once refugee-focused bodies are changing. For example, the AU's Coordinating Committee on Assistance and Protection to Refugees, Returnees and Internally Displaced Persons – which advises the political Permanent Representatives Committee's Sub-Committee on Refugees, Returnees and Internally Displaced Persons – will soon formally amend its mandate to cover humanitarian assistance generally, with a corresponding name change to the Coordinating Committee on Humanitarian Affairs.[56] Moreover, the director of the AU's most effective and therefore significant refugee protection body – the technical Division of Humanitarian Affairs, Refugees and Displaced Persons – is very keen to make the humanitarian element of his division's mandate its top priority.[57] It is not possible to attribute the AU's shift in focus from refugee protection in particular to humanitarian issues more generally to European influence, but it is certainly clear that the European trend described by Durieux has AU parallels. This highlights the importance of flagging dangerous trends before they take hold elsewhere; Europe's refugee protection missteps can at the very least put analysts and advocates on notice of detrimental approaches before they are adopted elsewhere in the world – such as in SADC. The section that follows discusses the subregional economic community's (REC) experimentation with two policies already in place in Europe: regional freedom of movement and a harmonized approach to refugee protection.

---

[53] Council Directive 2001/55/EC of 20 July 2001 on minimum standards for giving temporary protection in the event of a mass influx of displaced persons and on measures promoting a balance of efforts between Member States in receiving such persons and bearing the consequences thereof (OJ 2001 No. L212/12).

[54] Qualification Directive, chap. V.   [55] See Chapter 9 of this volume.

[56] Interview with Olabisi Dare, Director, AU Division of Humanitarian Affairs, Refugees and Displaced Persons, Addis Ababa, 16 January 2012.

[57] Ibid.

D   The subregional level: contemporary emulation in SADC

In the 1970s, States in Africa began to join forces to form subregional economic groupings that would transcend inherited colonial boundaries and further economic integration among Member States.[58] These RECs were to form the building blocks of an eventual African Economic Community (AEC), the plan for which was concretized in the 1994 Abuja Treaty.[59] This instrument sets out a process for the AEC's establishment by 2028. Today, the continent hosts fourteen RECs, including SADC. It was formed in 1992 as the successor organization to the Southern African Development Coordination Conference. SADC's mission is 'to promote sustainable and equitable economic growth and socio-economic development through efficient productive systems, deeper co-operation and integration, good governance, and durable peace and security, so that the region emerges as a competitive and effective player in international relations and the world economy'.[60] The institutional structure supportive of this mission includes the Summit of Heads of State and Government, the SADC Tribunal, the Council of Ministers, the Organ on Politics, Defence and Security Cooperation, sectoral ministerial committees, the Secretariat, the Standing Committee of Senior Officials and SADC National Committees. SADC has fifteen Member States: Angola, Botswana, Democratic Republic of Congo, Lesotho, Madagascar, Malawi, Mauritius, Mozambique, Namibia, the Seychelles, South Africa, Swaziland, Tanzania, Zambia and Zimbabwe.

The features of SADC of interest here are its initiative to promote visa-free movement within the subregion and its nascent project to harmonize refugee protection across all its Member States. The former initiative is not unique. Of Africa's fourteen RECs, SADC and five others[61] have protocols, articles or objectives in their founding treaties regarding visa-free movement.[62] What is, however, less common is SADC's goal of harmonizing

---

[58] John Oucho and Jonathan Crush, 'Contra Free Movement: South Africa and the SADC Migration Protocols' (2001) 48 *Africa Today* 139–57, at 139.
[59] Treaty Establishing the African Economic Community, Abuja, 3 June 1991, in force 12 May 1994 (30 ILM 1241).
[60] www.sadc.int/about-sadc (accessed 10 October 2012).
[61] The Common Market for East and Southern Africa, the East African Community, the Economic Community of Central African States, the Economic Community of West African States and the West African Economic and Monetary Union.
[62] Jonathan Martens, 'Moving Freely on the African Continent: The Experiences of ECOWAS and SADC with Free Movement Protocols', in Ryszard Cholewinski and

Member States' approaches to refugee protection.[63] Together, the proposed visa-free movement and harmonization activities make SADC an illuminating case study of how subregional approaches to refugee protection and related matters have mirrored European initiatives.

1   The free movement of people

A Belgian expert on Europe's Schengen Agreement and a Zimbabwean lawyer completed the first draft of the SADC Free Movement Protocol in 1995.[64] It proposed that free movement within SADC be effected in three phases. During phase one, visa-free entry for visits of up to six months would be implemented. In phase two, citizens of any one SADC Member State would have the right to enter and work in any other SADC country. Finally, during phase three all restrictions on permanent residence would be abolished in respect of citizens of SADC States, thereby affording them rights of establishment across the subregion. Regional power-house South Africa was, however, ultimately successful in blocking the Protocol's adoption. Fearful of the number of people from relatively less developed SADC States that would move to South Africa if given the chance, it redrafted the Protocol. The 1997 South African Draft Protocol on the Facilitation of Movement maintained the form of the 1995 SADC version but watered down its main objectives. SADC's response to South Africa's redraft was to amend its original Protocol. The resulting 1997 Protocol on the Facilitation of Movement of Persons in the Southern African Development Community (1997 SADC Protocol) was, like its 1997 South African counterpart, significantly less generous than the original 1995 Protocol. Oucho and Crush provide an overview of the main differences;[65] in this context it suffices to note that all references to rights were eliminated from the revised SADC document. Whereas the original SADC Protocol sought to 'confer, promote and protect the right to entry, residence and establishment', the revised version aimed only to 'facilitate entry, residence and establishment'. Ultimately, none of the proposed protocols has entered into force. The 1997 SADC Protocol has

---

Richard Perruchoud (eds.), *International Migration Law: Developing Paradigms and Key Challenges* (The Hague: TMC Asser Press, 2007), p. 349.

[63] Though East African Community Member States, for example, have also agreed to establish common mechanisms for the management of refugee affairs; see Treaty Establishing the East African Community, Arusha, 30 November 1999, in force 7 July 2000 (2144 UNTS 255), art. 124(4).

[64] Oucho and Crush, 'Contra Free Movement', 143.   [65] *Ibid.*, 152–3.

been signed by seven Member States; an unlikely ten ratifications are required before it can become law.

While some analysts have traced SADC's free movement initiatives to the European Schengen example,[66] such projects have considerable precedent within Africa. As mentioned above, SADC is only one of six RECs that have experimented with free movement, and some of these experiments pre-date the 1985 Schengen Agreement. The 1975 Treaty establishing the Economic Community of West African States, for example, identified the abolition of any obstacles to the free movement of people between its Member States as a goal of the union. Perhaps, then, it is not the birth of the SADC free movement initiative that should be traced back to European precedent, but rather its failure to enter into force. According to Klaaren and Rutinwa, '[t]he Protocol dealing with the cross-border migration of people within SADC . . . owed too much to European (Schengen) precedent and too little to the political and economic realities of the region',[67] in particular South Africa's resistance to free movement. Such failure may, from a refugee protection perspective at least, have been a good thing.

Although not a refugee protection issue as such, the free movement of people within SADC with corresponding rights of establishment would certainly have refugee protection implications, particularly in light of article 1E 1951 Convention. The drafters of the 1951 Convention included the article 1E exclusion clause to cover East Germans who fled to the Federal Republic of Germany, where the Constitution recognized them as possessing the rights and obligations attached to German nationality.[68] They were therefore seen as not in need of international protection. Article 1E accordingly states, '[t]his Convention shall not apply to a person who is recognized by the competent authorities of the country in which he has taken residence as having the rights and obligations which are attached to the possession of the nationality of that country'. The provision has been incorporated in Europe at article 12(1)(b) Qualification Directive. UNHCR literature on article 1E explains, '[t]his exclusion clause may only apply if the applicant has taken up regular or permanent residence in a country, and if the status

---

[66] *Ibid.*, 140.

[67] Jonathan Klaaren and Bonaventure Rutinwa, *Towards the Harmonization of Immigration and Refugee Law in SADC* (Johannesburg: Institute for Democracy in South Africa, 2000), p. 1.

[68] UNHCR, 'Note on the Interpretation of Article 1E of the 1951 Convention relating to the Status of Refugees' (Geneva: UNHCR, 2009), para. 3.

given to him or her by that country means that he or she effectively enjoys the rights and obligations of its own nationals'.[69] UNHCR further notes that it is 'of crucial importance that the status provides protection against *refoulement* as well as the right to return, re-enter, and remain in the country where the person concerned has taken residence'.[70]

Despite this guidance and the highly particular origins of article 1E, there is a danger that the clause will be relied upon by States seeking to limit their protection obligations, in this case to refugees from other States within a common free movement area. Indeed, there are hints of this in Europe's Protocol on Asylum for Nationals of Member States of the European Union,[71] also known as the Aznar Protocol for the Spanish prime minister who was its champion. Under the Aznar Protocol, EU Member States may declare any refugee claim from the national of another EU Member State to be inadmissible; the Qualification Directive correspondingly applies only to third-country (i.e., non-EU) nationals and stateless persons. It was never explicitly intended that the Aznar Protocol should operationalize the 1951 Convention's article 1E. In other words, that EU nationals have rights of establishment, and hence most of 'the rights and obligations which are attached to the possession of . . . nationality', in all other EU Member States was not the Aznar Protocol's primary rationale. Rather, the instrument is mainly premised upon the assumption that the level to which fundamental freedoms are protected within the EU renders all EU Member States 'safe countries of origin' for asylum purposes.[72] However, establishment rights are acknowledged in the Aznar Protocol. Its seventh preambular paragraph bears in mind that the 'Constitution establishes an area without internal frontiers and grants every citizen of the Union the right to

---

[69] UNHCR, 'Self-Study Module on Refugee Status Determination' (Geneva: UNHCR, 2005), p. 73.

[70] *Ibid.*

[71] Protocol on Asylum for Nationals of Member States, 16 December 2004 (OJ C 310/362), to the Treaty of Amsterdam amending the Treaty on European Union, the Treaties Establishing the European Communities and Related Acts, 2 October 2007 (OJ 1997 No. C340/1) (Aznar Protocol).

[72] The Aznar Protocol's sole article provides, '[g]iven the level of protection of fundamental rights and freedoms by the Member States of the European Union, Member States shall be regarded as constituting safe countries of origin in respect of each other for all legal and practical purposes in relation to asylum matters'. The recent case of *MSS* v. *Belgium and Greece* (App. No. 30696/09 (Grand Chamber, 21 January 2011)) has highlighted that human rights are not in fact uniformly protected across Europe, and in so doing has underlined just how problematic the Aznar Protocol is.

move and reside freely within the territory of the Member States'. Thus it is difficult to completely divorce the Aznar Protocol from the fact that EU nationals benefit from rights of establishment across the region; such rights could well have had a role in obviating refugee protection within the EU.

The Aznar Protocol is problematic in several respects. For our purposes, it suffices to note that while an EU national who experiences persecution at home may indeed relocate to any other EU Member State and enjoy rights of establishment there, the most important refugee right – *non-refoulement* – does not form part of the establishment rights bundle. A State's duty of readmission – and by implication the prohibition of expulsion – is at international law limited to its own nationals.[73] Rights of establishment may therefore complement,[74] but are no substitute for, refugee protection. It is in this regard that the failure of the 1997 SADC Protocol to enter into force may have been an unwitting boon for refugee protection in Southern Africa. With the 1997 SADC Protocol firmly shelved, there is no danger that freedom of movement will undermine refugee status in the subregion as internal refugee protection has been excised from the EU.

Yet SADC was perhaps mindful of the refugee protection implications of subregional freedom of movement in drafting its 1997 Protocol. In what may have been a nod to the specificity of refugee protection not seen in the EU, States parties reaffirmed 'their commitment to their obligations under international agreements to which they are parties, and which relate to refugees'.[75] However, Member States went on to agree that the 'management of refugees in the Region shall be regulated by a specific Memorandum of Understanding … between State Parties',[76] thereby – as in Europe – indicating a possible link between subregional free movement on the one hand and the creation of a regionally specific refugee protection regime on the other. Only recently has such a subregional refugee regime begun to take shape.

---

[73] International Covenant on Civil and Political Rights, New York, 16 December 1966, in force 23 March 1976 (999 UNTS 171), art. 12(4).

[74] How rights of establishment may complement refugee protection can be seen in Uganda. Section 9 of that country's Refugees Regulations provide that '[a] person who applies and is granted refugee status in Uganda and is a national of the East Africa Community shall enjoy all the rights and privileges bestowed on the "Community nationals" and as set out in the Treaty and Protocols for the establishment of the East Africa Community'.

[75] Draft Protocol on the Facilitation of Movement of Persons, Gaborone, 18 August 2005, art. 28(1).

[76] *Ibid.*, art. 28(2).

2   Towards the harmonization of refugee protection in SADC

As mentioned above, SADC's institutional structure includes sectoral ministerial committees, one of which has a subcommittee of refugee commissioners. Below this sits a sub-subcommittee chaired by South Africa and charged with spearheading the drive to harmonize asylum within the subregion pursuant to a SADC decision from mid-2012.[77] The regional or subregional harmonization of refugee laws and policies does not undermine refugee protection as such. Rather, protection is undercut when standards converge around problematic practices, as has been the case in Europe. European refugee law doctrines such as 'safe third country', 'safe country of origin', 'first country of asylum' and 'manifestly unfounded' – all of which are codified in the Procedures Directive and are discussed below – have prevented many needy individuals from finding safe haven in Europe.[78] The SADC initiative to harmonize the subregion's approach to refugee protection is so new that the content of its harmonized approach has yet to be articulated. It is hoped that it will not follow the European example. State practice, however, does not auger well in this regard. Countries in Africa have recently adopted restrictive practices pioneered in Europe, as detailed below.

E   The national level: modern indicators of influence

The approach of African States to refugees has shifted considerably in recent years. This shift has been described in detail by Rutinwa,[79] among

---

[77] Interview with Kaajal Ramjathan-Keogh, Head, Refugee and Migrant Rights Programme, Lawyers for Human Rights (South Africa), Cape Town, 13 September 2012. Also mentioned by Lindile Kgasi (Director, Asylum Seeker Management, Department of Home Affairs, Republic of South Africa) in her opening remarks at UNHCR's Expert Roundtable on International Protection for Persons Fleeing Armed Conflict and Other Situations of Violence, Cape Town, South Africa, 13–14 September 2012.

[78] See Elspeth Guild, 'The Europeanisation of Europe's Asylum Policy' (2006) 18 *International Journal of Refugee Law* 630–51. Other more general aspects of European integration have also threatened refugee protection there; see, e.g., James Hathaway, 'Harmonizing for Whom? The Devaluation of Refugee Protection in the Era of European Economic Integration' (1993) 26 *Cornell International Law Journal* 719–35.

[79] Bonaventure Rutinwa, 'The End of Asylum? The Changing Nature of Refugee Policies in Africa' (2002) 21 *Refugee Survey Quarterly* 12–41.

others,[80] who has grouped African State practice regarding refugees into
two distinct periods:

> [t]he first is the period between [the] early 1960s and 1990, and the
> second is the period thereafter. In the first period, African countries,
> both individually and collectively, exhibited a very generous attitude
> toward refugees. Through the 1969 ... Convention ... African states
> implemented what became known as an 'open door policy'. African
> countries readily admitted all those in search of security and safety, and
> refugees were hardly ever rejected at the frontier or returned ... Even
> though refugees were normally required to remain in camps, the stand-
> ards of treatment of refugees were adequate and refugees enjoyed security
> rights, basic dignity rights as well as self-sufficiency rights. There was also
> a strong commitment to durable solutions.[81]

By contrast, since the 1980s, Rutinwa explains that 'there has been a
marked shift in refugee policies in Africa, which became particularly
pronounced in the 1990s. While the refugee problem has on the whole
increased, African States have become less committed to asylum'.[82] He
cites a number of reasons for this shift, among them the restrictive
policies employed in the West, which 'set bad examples for the rest of
the world'[83] and have 'emboldened African states to take steps within
their means to achieve the same ends'.[84] For example, when Tanzania
closed its borders with Burundi and Rwanda to forestall the influx of
further refugees from the Rwandan genocide, the Minister of Foreign
Affairs said it was 'a double standard to expect weaker countries to live
up to their humanitarian obligations when major powers did not do so
when their national rights and interests were at stake'.[85] European and
American practices have been of particular influence in this regard.[86] In
particular, restrictive approaches to refugee protection codified in
Europe have, in recent years, emerged in African laws and as features
of African State practice.

Of Africa's fifty-four States, it would seem that twenty-seven have
domestic refugee legislation.[87] Nine[88] of these acts have been passed since

---

[80] See, for example, James Milner, *Refugees, the State and the Politics of Asylum in Africa*
(London: Palgrave Macmillan, 2009), ch. 2.
[81] Rutinwa, 'End of Asylum', 12.   [82] *Ibid.*   [83] Rutinwa, 'The End of Asylum', 13.
[84] *Ibid.*   [85] Rutinwa, 'End of Asylum', 33.   [86] *Ibid.*
[87] It is impossible to state this figure with any certainty, as African State legislation is not
consistently available outside of each State's legislative collection.
[88] Tanzania (1998), Guinea (2000), Rwanda (2001), Democratic Republic of Congo (2002),
Ethiopia (2004), Mauritania (2004), Cameroon (2005), Uganda (2006) and Kenya (2007).

the Amsterdam Treaty laid the foundation of the European asylum *acquis* in 1997 and three[89] coincided with or postdated the Procedures Directive's 2005 codification of the 'safe third country', 'first country of asylum', 'safe country of origin' and 'manifestly unfounded' notions. While the list of restrictive asylum practices employed in Europe runs much longer than these four – it would include, for example, the notion of an internal flight alternative and attempts at interdiction through visa regimes, carrier sanctions, readmission agreements and extraterritorial processing – locating the full range of restrictive European practices within the twenty-seven laws and innumerable policies of African States would be a prohibitively arduous exercise and would not necessarily yield evidence of norm diffusion from Europe to Africa. A more sensible exercise, and the one undertaken here, is to look for those restrictive practices that were codified in the Procedures Directive in the three African refugee acts that coincided with or postdated it – those of Cameroon, Kenya and Uganda – as well as in the post-2005 practice of African States more generally.[90] This is followed by a broader discussion of similarities between European and African State practice.

The safe third-country doctrine, which appears in article 27 Procedures Directive, allows States to reject asylum applications from individuals who have transited through countries where protection might have been found.[91] Further along the continuum considering ties to countries other than that determining refugee status lies the related notion of first country of asylum. This doctrine, codified at article 26 Procedures Directive, provides for the rejection of asylum applications from individuals whose refugee status has already been recognized in a third State or who are otherwise protected by a third State.[92] Both concepts negate a refugee's agency to choose his or her country of asylum and fail to take account of individual circumstances. Cameroon's 2005 refugee law explicitly recognizes the first country of asylum concept,[93] as

---

[89] Cameroon (2005), Uganda (2006) and Kenya (2007).

[90] The research in this regard was greatly facilitated by reference to Soo-Ryun Kwon's unpublished research report 'The influence of the European Union's Common European Asylum System on the domestic legislation of African States', which was written in 2009 during her James E. Tolan Fellowship at the International Refugee Rights Initiative in Kampala, Uganda and is on file with this author.

[91] See generally Rosemary Byrne and Andrew Shacknove, 'The Safe Country Notion in European Asylum Law' (1996) 9 *Harvard Human Rights Journal* 185–228.

[92] See generally Morten Kjaerum, 'The Concept of Country of First Asylum' (1992) 4 *International Journal of Refugee Law* 514–30.

[93] Cameroon Law No. 2005/006, art. 7(5).

do the 2008 Regulations to operationalize Uganda's 2006 Refugees Act.[94] The concept is also a feature of the practice of many African countries. Morocco, for example, in 2005 returned hundreds of asylum seekers to the Algerian desert, alleging that they had already found protection in Algeria.[95] Senegal's National Eligibility Commission does not recognize 'secondary movers' as refugees, even if the individual left his or her 'first country of asylum' for security reasons.[96] South Africa recently used the safe third-country concept to reject refugee applicants from Fiji and Nepal,[97] despite the practice having been rejected by a South African court in 2002.[98]

The notion of safe country of origin, found at article 29 Procedures Directive, precludes the substantive consideration of asylum applications made by nationals of countries deemed 'safe'. It underpins the Aznar Protocol, discussed above, under which all EU Member States are deemed to be safe countries of origin. This doctrine, and in particular the Aznar Protocol's legislation of EU Member States as 'safe', has not been adopted to any significant degree in Africa. By contrast, States in Africa have exhibited a tendency to recognize the status of refugees from the same subregion while rejecting applications from further afield; the practice of SADC States provides an example.[99] The concept of a manifestly unfounded asylum application, by contrast, has found expression in Africa. The concept was first articulated in Europe in the 1992 Resolution on Manifestly Unfounded Applications for Asylum,[100] and was subsequently codified at article 28 Procedures Directive. Pursuant to this provision, asylum applications may be deemed manifestly unfounded if the applicant falsified information relating to his or her

---

[94] Section 14.

[95] Kwon, 'European Union's Common European Asylum system', p. 26.

[96] Lisa Laurel Weinberg, *Senegal Legal Aid Assessment* (Dakar: WARIPNET, 2008) (on file with the author).

[97] Tal Schreier, 'An Evaluation of South Africa's Application of the OAU Refugee Definition' (2008) 25 *Refuge* 53–63, at 55.

[98] *Katambayi and Lawyers for Human Rights* v. *Minister of Home Affairs et al.*, No. 02/ 5312, South African High Court, Witwatersrand Local Division, 24 March 2002; see also Anais Tuepker, 'On the Threshold of Africa: OAU and UN Definition in South African Asylum Practice' (2002) 15 *Journal of Refugee Studies* 409–23, at 413. One wonders if the court would have reached the same decision post-2005, once safe third country had been codified in, and hence perhaps legitimated by, Europe.

[99] James Hathaway, *The Rights of Refugees under International Law* (Cambridge: Cambridge University Press, 2005), p. 241.

[100] Council of the European Union, Council Resolution of 30 November 1992 on manifestly unfounded applications for asylum.

identification or nationality, seems to have destroyed or disposed of his or her travel document, applied for asylum immediately prior to deportation and could have applied earlier, presents no legal grounds for protection, is from a safe country of origin or has submitted a new application that raises no new facts. This concept finds expression in section 20(6) of Uganda's Refugees Act and is a feature of South African practice.[101]

The appearance of restrictive approaches to refugee protection in the law and practice of African States after Europe codified such approaches is at least suggestive of a process of Europe to Africa norm diffusion. Yet the practices described herein – as well as other restrictive asylum practices – were employed in Europe well before the Procedures Directive codified them in 2005; therefore a broader examination of the similarities between European and African State practice is warranted, yielding a laundry list of examples. Just as Europe has sought to make its external frontier impenetrable to migrants,[102] so too have African States attempted to prevent refugees from penetrating their borders. For example, hundreds of refugees fleeing conflict in Sierra Leone were summarily returned by Guinea.[103] Namibia imposed a dusk-to-dawn curfew, enforced by gun-wielding soldiers, along its border with Angola, effectively keeping out refugees in flight from the Angolan civil war.[104] As mentioned above, Tanzania closed its borders to refugees from the Rwandan genocide.[105] Similarly, in 2007 Kenya closed its border with Somalia.[106] European States have imposed carrier sanctions on airlines to make their territories inaccessible to refugees, and African countries have done the same. Uganda provides an example.[107]

F   Conclusion

European approaches to refugees have animated African engagement with refugee protection since the beginning of the post-colonial era.

---

[101] Roni Amit, 'No Refuge: Flawed Status Determination and the Failures of South Africa's Refugee System to Provide Protection' (2011) 23 *International Journal of Refugee Law* 458–88, at 475–6.

[102] See Violeta Moreno-Lax, 'Seeking Asylum in the Mediterranean: Against a Fragmentary Reading of EU Member States' Obligations Accruing at Sea' (2011) 23 *International Journal of Refugee Law* 174–220, 180–5.

[103] Hathaway, *Rights of Refugees*, p. 280.   [104] *Ibid.*

[105] Rutinwa, 'End of Asylum', 33.

[106] BBC, 'Kenyans close door to Somalia' (3 January 2007) http://news.bbc.co.uk/2/hi/africa/6227083.stm (accessed 7 October 2012).

[107] Uganda Refugees Act 2006, s. 27.

Africa's first major refugee protection project began as an effort to make the 1951 Convention applicable on the continent, with the first four drafts of the 1969 Convention copying in many respects the 1951 instrument. Only once the 1967 Protocol was well on its way to adoption did refugee protection challenges particular to Africa move up the OAU agenda. The other instances of emulation discussed above are perhaps less explicit, but a broad trend in which European practices subsequently appear as features of African law and policy is almost certainly apparent at the regional, subregional and national levels. At the regional level, the AU's specific focus on refugees is giving way to the prioritization of more general humanitarian issues, much like temporary and subsidiary protection have assumed increased prominence in Europe. At the subregional level, the SADC case study demonstrates the rise of and challenges to freedom of movement within RECs on the continent, and provides an example of efforts towards the subregional harmonization of refugee protection; the Aznar Protocol is a cautionary tale in this regard. The failure of the 1997 SADC Protocol may have prevented free movement from threatening refugee protection in Southern Africa, as has been the case in Europe. It is hoped that SADC's current harmonization efforts also diverge from the European example, where harmonization has meant the codification of many restrictive approaches to refugee protection. At the national level, such approaches have emerged in State laws as well as in practice. It is nearly impossible to pinpoint the origins of legislative rules and State practice. Yet when the rules and practices of one region subsequently emerge as features of the law and practice of another, it is at the very least plausible and possibly even likely that norm diffusion is under way; it seems that such a process is occurring between Europe and Africa.

8

Stealth emulation: the United States and European protection norms

MARYELLEN FULLERTON

A   Introduction

The ambitious project to build a Common European Asylum System (CEAS) has been under way for more than a decade, making this an opportune moment to explore the diffusion of European legal norms in non-European settings. Studying the process of diffusion, a 'vast and complex range of phenomena' in circumstances when the 'motives, agents, recipients [and] impact' are opaque,[1] is always challenging, and there are unique factors that intensify the challenges of identifying and evaluating EU norm diffusion in the United States. US legal training and the resulting legal system are chauvinistic and solipsistic. The dualist tradition in US law results in great attention to domestic implementation of international norms, with little focus on the underlying international norms themselves. Furthermore, while sociological institutionalists predict that weak States on the periphery of the world system are likely to emulate the policies developed by the European Union, what should be expected of an advanced State that is an economic competitor and cultural rival?

To an extent that may be difficult for outsiders to perceive, the United States views itself as *the* centre of the current world order. The United States imagines that it exports human rights norms to the rest of the world, not vice versa. The United States sees itself, not Europe, as a nation of immigrants and a haven for the persecuted. Moreover, 'European' has

Thanks to William Hine-Ramsberger and Margaret Garrett for their research assistance and to Brooklyn Law School for research support.
[1] William Twining, 'Social Science and Diffusion of Law' (2005) 32 *Journal of Law and Society* 203–40, at 240, 228.

become an epithet in the current political and culture wars in the United States. Charges that the Obama Administration desires to transform the United States into a European (read: socialist, elitist, secular) nation have been staple insults during the past few years.[2] These potent circumstances do not favour emulation of EU asylum norms, and they inhibit acknowledgement of emulation when it occurs.

This chapter argues, nonetheless, that we are witnessing partial emulation of EU asylum norms in the United States. The 2004 Qualification Directive (QD),[3] setting forth the eligibility criteria for those entitled to protection, is the focal point for this examination. There is evidence that two QD norms – the definition of a 'particular social group' and the right to subsidiary protection – have shaped recent US discourse concerning asylum and refugee protection. US attention to these norms came into focus several years after the QD was adopted, and the timing suggests that norm diffusion is under way. Although direct evidence of emulation is sparse, close examination of contemporary US administrative and judicial decisions reveals substantial resonance with EU asylum law.

B   Setting the stage: the context for emulation in the United States

The contemporary political, cultural and legal context in the United States includes both factors that facilitate adoption of European norms and factors that inhibit emulation. As a former colony of a European power, the United States has close ties to Europe, including a 'special relationship' with the United Kingdom.[4] The US legal system consciously adopted the English common law structure, and US law studies

---

[2] See, e.g., John Harwood, 'A blurring of the lines in the populist vs. capitalist debate', *New York Times*, 12 January 2012, p. A19 ('"President Obama wants to . . . turn America into a European-type welfare state . . . This president takes his inspiration from the capitals of Europe; we look to the cities and small towns of America", said Republican primary candidate Mitt Romney.'); Matt DeLong, 'Joe Miller: Obama moving America "toward socialism"', *Washington Post*, 2 September 2010 http://voices.washingtonpost.com/44/2010/09/joe-miller-obama-moving-americ.html (accessed 11 October 2012).

[3] Directive 2011/95/EU of the European Parliament and of the Council of 13 December 2011 on standards for the qualification of third-country nationals or stateless persons as beneficiaries of international protection, for a uniform status for refugees or for persons eligible for subsidiary protection, and for the content of the protection granted (recast) (OJ 2011 No. L. 337/9) (QD).

[4] Winston Churchill, 'The Sinews of Peace' (Speech delivered at Westminster College, Fulton, Missouri, 5 March 1946) www.winstonchurchill.org/learn/speeches/speeches-of-winston-churchill/120-the-sinews-of-peace (accessed 11 October 2012).

are steeped in reverence for the Anglo-American adversarial system. Thus, the discussion and analysis of CEAS provisions in judicial decisions rendered by UK courts form an important channel for introducing European norms to the United States. These historical ties and cultural 'fit' can be seen as factors that facilitate emulation, though they are offset, to some extent, by a powerful chauvinism that objects to the explicit emulation of norms that originate elsewhere. The worship of American exceptionalism and the rejection of the relevance of international and foreign law are examples of these counter forces.

1 American exceptionalism

Alexis de Tocqueville used the term 'American exceptionalism' in 1831 to suggest that the origins, political and religious institutions, national credo and historical evolution of the United States made it qualitatively different from other nations.[5] In recent years there has been a powerful reflex to describe every American perspective as exceptional and there is an ever-growing cottage industry of academics who study and comment on American exceptionalism.[6] Current political conservatives cite 'American exceptionalism' to refer to, among other notions, political differences between the United States and Europe.[7]

Progressive legal scholars generally oppose the American exceptionalism rhetoric and note that it does not accurately describe the US legal system.[8] For example, although the United States did fail to ratify the 1951 Convention, the United States ultimately became a party to the 1967 Protocol and has created a legal framework that provides substantial protection to refugees. That the American exceptionalism rhetoric has power cannot be doubted, but it does not convey the complex reality of US asylum policy. Nonetheless, it ensures that a search for US emulation of CEAS provisions will require subtlety.

---

[5] Alexis de Tocqueville, *Democracy in America*, 2 vols. (ed. Phillips Bradley, trans. Henry Reeve) (New York: Knopf, 1948), vol. II, pp. 36–7 (1835).

[6] See Sabrina Safrin, 'The Unexceptionalism of US Exceptionalism' (2008) 41 *Vanderbilt Journal of Transnational Law* 1307–54, at 1309 (referring to more than 1,000 English-language law review articles that have discussed 'American exceptionalism' in the past two decades).

[7] See, e.g., Robert Kagan, *Of Paradise and Power: America vs. Europe in the New World Order* (New York: Knopf, 2003).

[8] See, e.g., Harold Koh, 'On American Exceptionalism' (2003) 55 *Stanford Law Review* 1479–1527, at 1482–3.

2   The debate about foreign law

The raging debate concerning the relevance of foreign law to US legal decisions complicates investigations of EU norm diffusion. Closely entwined with the notion of American exceptionalism, the foreign law controversy flared into public consciousness in recent years, in part due to several high-profile Supreme Court opinions that referred to European perspectives on contemporary legal issues. In 2003, in *Lawrence* v. *Texas*,[9] the Supreme Court reviewed a statute criminalizing sexual intercourse between individuals of the same sex. In his appraisal of prior jurisprudence, Justice Kennedy, writing for the Court, paid particular attention to the *Dudgeon* v. *United Kingdom* judgment rendered by the European Court of Human Rights.[10]

A year later, in *Roper* v. *Simmons*,[11] the Supreme Court ruled that sentencing an offender to death for crimes committed when he was younger than 18 years old was unconstitutional because it violated the prohibition against 'cruel and unusual punishments'.[12] Justice Kennedy, writing for the majority, noted that the EU and other entities had submitted *amici curiae* briefs, and the Court drew support from the evidence of State practice elsewhere.

Justice Kennedy's discussions of foreign law provoked chauvinistic reactions from other Supreme Court Justices, politicians, journalists and academics. The US House of Representatives entertained a resolution declaring that 'judicial interpretations regarding the meaning of the Constitution . . . should not be based in whole or in part on judgments, laws, or pronouncements of foreign institutions'.[13] Multiple State legislatures considered similar proposals.[14] Indeed, voters in Oklahoma amended the State constitution to instruct judges that they 'shall not look to the legal precepts of other nations or cultures'.[15] Some called Justice Kennedy's use of foreign law an impeachable offence.[16]

---

[9]   539 US 558 (2003).

[10]   *Dudgeon* v. *United Kingdom* (European Court of Human Rights, App. No. 7525/76, 22 October 1981), 45 ECtHR (1981).

[11]   543 US 551 (2004).

[12]   US Constitution, Amendment VIII ('Excessive bail shall not be required, nor excessive fines imposed, nor cruel and unusual punishments inflicted').

[13]   HR Res. 97, 109th Congress (2005).

[14]   See Donna Leinwand, 'States enter debate on sharia law: are bans like Oklahoma's necessary, constitutional, anti-Islamic?', *USA Today*, 9 December 2010, p. A3.

[15]   *Awad* v. *Ziriax*, 754 F. Supp. 2d 1298 (WD Okla. 2010) (temporarily enjoining amendment adopted by large majority in State ballot initiative).

[16]   Jason DeParle, 'In battle to pick next justice, right says avoid a Kennedy', *New York Times*, 27 June 2005, p. A1.

To be sure, there are many judges, scholars and commentators who support the use of foreign law in US judicial decisions. Justice Breyer, a member of the US Supreme Court, has publicly debated with Justice Scalia on this issue, arguing that courts should consider foreign laws and judicial rulings. Scholars such as Slaughter view courts as an emerging global community, with judges working as 'fellow professionals in an endeavor that transcends national borders'.[17] But, as events in Oklahoma have demonstrated, a significant portion of the voting public condemns the use of 'foreign' law in American courts. This antipathy to 'foreign' law also casts a shadow over the US legal system for dealing with 'foreigners', the refugee and immigration framework of the United States.

3   The dualist emphasis on domestic law

In addition to the notion of American exceptionalism and the debate over reliance on foreign law, the US legal system has a long tradition of dualism, requiring international law to be translated into domestic legislation before judges can apply it and individuals can rely on it.[18] The emphasis on domestic legislation to implement international norms has the result of focusing on the text and structure of the US statutes, with little discussion of the underlying norms themselves.

This is compounded by a large and robust system of domestic adjudicators and published judicial opinions; there is an ever-expanding body of domestic law to analyse and apply, overshadowing norms from other legal sources. To provide a quantitative context, there were more than 365,000 new cases filed with federal trial courts in 2011, along with more than 55,000 new appeals;[19] roughly 1,000 federal trial judges and 200 appellate judges were available to adjudicate these lawsuits.[20] The US common law system results in thousands of opinions per year,

---

[17] Anne-Marie Slaughter, 'A Global Community of Courts' (2003) 44 *Harvard International Law Journal* 191–219, at 193.

[18] Although there are mixed monist and dualist elements in the US legal framework, US law strongly favours domestic legislation to implement international obligations.

[19] US Courts, Judicial Business of the US Courts, '2011 Report' www.uscourts.gov/Statistics/JudicialBusiness.aspx (accessed 11 October 2012) (reporting that in 2011 289,252 new civil cases were filed, along with 78,440 criminal cases and 55,126 new appeals).

[20] US Courts, 'Judicial Facts and Figures 2010' www.uscourts.gov/Statistics/JudicialFactsAndFigures/JudicialFactsAndFigures2010.aspx (accessed 11 October 2012) (reporting that there were 158 active judges and 95 senior judges on the courts of appeals and 590 active judges and 356 senior judges in the federal trial courts in 2010).

which future litigants need to read and analyse. The magnitude of the research effort exacerbates the parochialism of the corpus of case law.

C   The US asylum system and European refugee law

1   Direct emulation in the past

The US participated in the Conference of Plenipotentiaries that drafted the 1951 Convention, but never ratified the benchmark international refugee law treaty. Ultimately, though, the US did adopt both the substance and the basic procedural approach of European refugee law and practice. Turning first to the substantive dimension, in the years following the Second World War and the 1951 Convention, the United States enacted legislation and created programs to relocate hundreds of thousands of displaced persons and refugees.[21] The US did not attribute its actions to international legal obligations, however, and indeed departed from international norms in significant areas. For example, US legislation included a cramped definition of refugees: those fleeing persecution in a communist or communist-dominated country or the Middle East.[22] When the United States ratified the 1967 Protocol to the Refugee Convention, it finally assented to the refugee definition and the obligations specified in the 1951 Convention. Nonetheless, the US did not adopt implementing legislation until 1980,[23] when it deleted the regional and ideological limitations from the statute. Thus, three decades later, the US explicitly emulated the international refugee law norms born in Europe in 1951.

A somewhat speedier emulation occurred in the context of asylum procedures. Neither the 1951 Convention nor the US Refugee Act of 1980 established procedures for determining refugee status. As a result, asylum applications in the US were folded in with migration control litigation concerning non-citizens who wanted to remain in the United States. Immigration judges held adversarial hearings and resolved

---

[21] E.g., Displaced Persons Act of 1948, Pub. L. No. 80–774, ch. 647, 62 Stat. 1009 (1948) (resettled approximately 400,000 to the United States); Refugee Relief Act of 1953, Pub. L. No. 83–203, 67 Stat. 400 (1953) (resettling more than 200,000 from 1953 to 1956).

[22] INA Amendments of 1965, Pub.L. No. 89–236, §3, 79 Stat. 911, 913, amending § 203 (a)(7) INA.

[23] Refugee Act of 1980, Pub. L. No. 96–212, 94 Stat. 102, codified at 8 USC §§ 1101(a)(42), 1157–1159 (1980).

disputed factual and legal issues.[24] After years of criticism that this format was inadequate for evaluating claims of persecution, a major reform of asylum adjudication occurred in 1990, with the creation of an Asylum Division within the Immigration and Naturalization Service (INS).[25] This reform followed a major study of European asylum systems,[26] and a key component of the new system was the adoption of a European-style non-adversarial interview with the asylum seeker.[27] The emulation of a European approach to asylum adjudication was clear, but partial; the adversarial system remains ensconced in all later stages of the US asylum procedure.

2   Pathways of emulation in the present

(a)   Training in international norms

Despite the general ignorance of and antipathy to foreign law in much of the US legal system, recent years have witnessed significant efforts to highlight the importance of international and comparative law. Prominent law schools have revamped their curricula to require all students to enrol in at least one international law course. Many law schools have added academic journals focusing on international or comparative research. More specifically in the asylum process, regulations require that asylum officers receive 'special training in international human rights law, nonadversarial interview techniques, and other relevant national and international refugee laws and principles'.[28] They have a documentation centre with information on human rights conditions and access to information concerning persecution, torture, and other circumstances relevant to asylum determinations.[29] Currently, asylum officers must attend two six-week residential training programmes when they start work, receiving training in international

---

[24] See David A. Martin, T. Alexander Aleinikoff, Hiroshi Motomura and Maryellen Fullerton, *Forced Migration: Law and Policy* (St Paul, MN: Thomson/West Publishing, 2007) (discussing the evolution of Immigration Court from an enforcement arm to an adjudicative body, at pp. 81–3).

[25] Asylum and Withholding of Deportation Procedures, Final Rule, 55 Federal Register 30674 (1990), codified at 8 CFR § 208. See Gregg Beyer, 'Reforming Affirmative Asylum Processing in the United States: Challenges and Opportunities' (1994) 9 *American University International Law Review* 43–78.

[26] David A. Martin, 'Reforming Asylum Adjudication', *Report to the Administrative Conference of the United States*, May 1989, at 36–60.

[27] See 8 CFR § 208.9(b).   [28] *Ibid.*, § 208.1(b).   [29] *Ibid.*

refugee law, worldwide refugee protection needs and US asylum law.[30] The regulations instruct asylum officers that they may rely on a wide range of materials to assess the application for protection, including information provided by international organizations, private voluntary agencies, news organizations and other credible sources.[31]

The Asylum Division, which was created in 1990, now numbers roughly three hundred asylum officers in eight asylum offices within the United States.[32] In addition to the initial training, each office sets aside four hours per week for training.[33] On occasion, weekly training sessions have addressed recent CEAS developments and legal decisions in other regions of the world.[34] Senior staff have occasionally attended in-depth programmes, such as the Summer School in Forced Migration at Oxford University in the United Kingdom.[35] As a result, there is an increasing awareness that the CEAS and other legal standards advanced outside the United States may be relevant to US asylum policy.

(b)   Legal education

Asylum officers have substantially increased in numbers in the past five years,[36] and many of the asylum officers who have been hired in the last decade are recent graduates of US law schools.[37] Their exposure to European asylum law, as well as to basic international refugee law, is wider than in prior generations. In addition to the greater attention to international law required by many US law schools today, there has

---

[30] US Citizenship and Immigration Services, 'Asylum Division Training Programs' www.uscis.gov/portal/site/uscis/menuitem.5af9bb95919f35e66f614176543f6d1a/?vgnextoid=38292f81eb478110VgnVCM1000004718190aRCRD&vgnextchannel=4db791de70c98110VgnVCM1000004718190aRCRD (accessed 11 October 2012).

[31] 8 CFR § 208.12(a).

[32] The offices are located in Arlington, Chicago, Houston, Miami, Newark, New York City, Los Angeles and San Francisco. US Citizenship and Immigration Services, 'USCIS Service and Office Locator' https://egov.uscis.gov/crisgwi/go?action=offices.type&OfficeLocator.office_type=LO (accessed 11 October 2012).

[33] See above n. 30.

[34] For example, the author presented a training session on 19 May 2010 for the New York Asylum Office concerning subsidiary protection and CJEU jurisprudence including Case C-465/07, *Elgafaji* v. *Staatssecretaris van Justitie* (Court of Justice of the European Union, Grand Chamber, 17 February 2009), ECR [2009] 1–921.

[35] See above n. 30.

[36] E.g., the number of Asylum Officers in New York has almost doubled since 2008. Letter, 23 March 2012, Ashley Caudill-Mirillo, Deputy Director, New York Asylum Office.

[37] Letter, 27 March 2012, Caudill-Mirillo.

been an explosion in the numbers of law school courses focusing on refugees and migration.[38] The major academic texts used by US law teachers all acknowledge and address, to some extent, the significant developments in the European asylum system. Although these casebooks target an audience attentive to US law, each of them includes explicit references to CEAS norms. The titles – *Refugee Law and Policy: A Comparative and International Approach*;[39] *Forced Migration: Law and Policy*;[40] *Immigration and Refugee Law and Policy*[41] – open a window to a wider world of refugee protection.

In addition, many law professors who teach migration and refugee law courses in US law schools have studied or been involved in refugee protection issues in Europe and elsewhere.[42] They are aware of European and other refugee norms, and they believe it is important for US law students to understand them. Further, more law school clinical education during the past decade has adopted an international human rights dimension.[43] This includes supervising law students in preparing reports and cases for regional human rights bodies, and focusing US law students to recognize the importance of law developed outside the United States. US law graduates during the first decade of the twenty-first century are more likely to have been exposed to comparative perspectives and to be aware of refugee law developments outside the United States, facilitating the diffusion of CEAS norms during the next decades.

---

[38] This is reflected in the growth in the number of faculty members attending the biannual Immigration Law Teachers workshop: 50 attended in 2002, 55 in 2004, 75 in 2006, 105 in 2008, 130 in 2010, Hiroshi Motomura, Memorandum on 2012 Immigration Workshop, 14 March 2012.

[39] Karen Musalo, Jennifer Moore and Richard Boswell, *Refugee Law and Policy: A Comparative and International Approach* (4th edn, Durham, NC: Carolina Academic Press, 2011).

[40] Martin *et al.*, *Forced Migration*.

[41] Stephen Legomsky and Cristina Rodriguez, *Immigration and Refugee Law and Policy* (5th edn, New York: Foundation Press, 2009).

[42] E.g., based on the author's personal knowledge and confirmed by law faculty websites, Aleinikoff, Deputy High Commissioner, UNHCR, 2010 to present; Legomsky, Portugal, 2010; Nessel, Spain, 2007–08; Pistone, Malta, 2006; Caplow, Ireland, 2006; Medina, Greece, 2003; Fullerton, Spain, 2001–02, Hungary, 1994–5, Belgium,1986–7; Jastram, UNHCR, 1991–2001; Moore, Tanzania, 2002–03, UNHCR; 1990–5.

[43] There are more than 100 legal education clinics that focus on migration; of these, at least 30 have a specific emphasis on refugee and international human rights law. Anju Gupta, 'Immigration Clinics List' (July 2012) https://dl.dropbox.com/u/61625492/immigration clinicslist.xlsx (accessed 15 October 2012).

(c)   Transnational networks

Several members of the Board of Immigration Appeals, the administrative appellate tribunal that reviews asylum claims litigated in the
Immigration Courts, have joined the International Association of
International Refugee Law Judges, which feature discussions of refugee
law developments in Europe and around the world.[44] In addition, there
are multiple other transnational legal networks concerned with migration and human rights issues. To give one example, Migration Policy
Institute (MPI), a non-partisan non-profit think-tank studying the
movement of people worldwide, issues analytical reports about
European asylum and immigration developments, as well as studies,
reports, and proposals concerning the United States and other nations.[45]
MPI includes a Transatlantic Council on Migration to develop policy
proposals for Europe as well as the Americas, and MPI has partnered
with the European University Institute to form a US–EU Immigration
Systems Project to generate approaches for improving the treatment of
refugees and other migrants in the US and in Europe.[46]

There also are extensive transnational academic networks, with many
US refugee law scholars active in multiple undertakings with European
colleagues. To name just a few salient examples, the author has been an
active participant in the European-based Refugee Law Reader for close to
a decade, and has published widely on the development of European
protection norms.[47] The Director of the Center for Gender and Refugee
Studies at the University of California Hastings College of Law has been
involved in multiple transnational projects,[48] and has returned repeatedly to Spain to speak on gender and asylum.[49] The Director of the
International Human Rights Program at Boston College of Law, has
researched asylum in Germany, and has been a visiting professor on
law faculties in France and the United Kingdom.[50]

---

[44] Letter, 7 May 2012, Immigration Judge Paul Schmidt, former BIA Chairman, 1995–2001.
[45] Migration Policy Institute, 'About MPI' www.migrationpolicy.org/about/index.php
      (accessed 11 October 2012).
[46] Migration Policy Institute, 'European Migration' www.migrationpolicy.org/Europe/
      (accessed 11 October 2012).
[47] Professor Maryellen Fullerton, Brooklyn Law School http://www.brooklaw.edu/faculty/direc
      tory/facultymember/biography.aspx?id=maryellen.fullerton (accessed 11 October 2012).
[48] Professor Karen Musalo, University of California Hastings College of Law http://uchast
      ings.edu/faculty-administration/faculty/musalo/index.html (accessed 11 October 2012).
[49] Ibid.
[50] Professor Daniel Kanstroom, Boston College of Law www.bc.edu/schools/law/fac-staff/
      deans-faculty/kanstroomd.html (accessed 11 October 2012).

Other prominent refugee advocates and scholars who have undertaken major research concerning asylum law and policy in Europe are working or have worked in the US government recently. To illustrate, the new Chief Counsel to the US Citizenship and Immigration Service spent 2010 in the EU as a Research Professor at the Catholic University of Portugal.[51] The Deputy General Counsel of the Department of Homeland Security from 2009 to 2011 has done extensive research on European asylum adjudication,[52] as has Aleinikoff, now on leave from academia to serve as the UN Deputy High Commissioner for Refugees.[53]

Through their various policy analyses and legal positions these institutions and individuals have served as conduits of ideas and practices adopted in Europe, and they disseminate knowledge of CEAS norms. The transnational networks, together with the changes in contemporary US legal education, the enhanced asylum officer training, and the historical and cultural ties between Europe and the US, all facilitate European norm diffusion.

D   Partial emulation of CEAS norms

As sketched above, the US context includes powerful factors that both facilitate and hinder the diffusion of European norms. In this setting, it is notable that recent US case law replicates two of the hallmark changes embodied in the Qualification Directive.

1   Membership of a particular social group

(a)   Early US jurisprudence

The 1951 Convention defines refugees to include individuals who have a well-founded fear of persecution on account of their membership in a particular social group. Considered one of the most elusive terms of the Convention, 'particular social group' has engendered much commentary and jurisprudence; the reciprocal nature of the norm diffusion process[54]

---

[51] Professor Stephen H. Legomsky, University of Washington School of Law http://law. wustl.edu/news/pages.aspx?id=8966 (accessed 11 October 2012); http://law.wustl.edu/ Faculty_profiles/documents/legomsky/cvcurrentupd.pdf (accessed 11 October 2012).

[52] Professor David A. Martin, University of Virginia School of Law www.law.virginia.edu/ lawweb/faculty.nsf/FHPbI/1187875 (accessed 11 October 2012).

[53] Professor T. Alexander Aleinikoff, Georgetown University Law Center www.law.george town.edu/news/releases/December.2.2009TAA.html (accessed 11 October 2012).

[54] Twining, 'Social Science and Diffusion of Law', 215–16.

and the impact of transnational judicial dialogue[55] can be seen as differ-ent legal systems have wrestled with the meaning of this term. The BIA's landmark *Matter of Acosta* decision in 1985 defined a particular social group as one whose members share a common characteristic that they 'either cannot change or should not be required to change because it is fundamental to their individual identities or consciences'.[56] The *Acosta* 'immutability or fundamental to identity' approach took hold in the United States, leading to the recognition of particular social groups encompassing former members of the Salvadoran national police,[57] Cuban homosexuals,[58] Somali clans[59] and women in Togo who opposed female genital mutilation.[60]

Acosta was cited approvingly by many tribunals in Europe, as well as courts in other parts of the world.[61] To give just one prominent example, in 1999 the highest court in the UK relied on the *Acosta* analytical framework in deciding *Islam* v. *Secretary of State for the Home Department*,[62] which held that women who had suffered domestic violence in Pakistan satisfied the refugee definition. The *Acosta* frame-work did not resolve all concerns, however, and decision makers on both sides of the Atlantic continued to grapple with persecution claims founded on membership in particular social groups. It was, therefore, not surprising that the Qualification Directive addressed this aspect of the refugee definition.

(b) The CEAS norm

Although the QD's inclusion of provisions regarding a particular social group was not surprising, the content was unexpected. With little com-mentary or discussion, the QD set forth a new definition of the particular social group term:

---

[55] See Hélène Lambert, 'Transnational Judicial Dialogue, Harmonization and the CEAS', 58 *International and Comparative Law Quarterly* 519–43 (2009).

[56] I & N Dec. 211, at 233 (BIA 1985).

[57] *Matter of Fuentes*, 19 I & N Dec. 658 (BIA 1988).

[58] *Matter of Toboso-Alfonso*, 20 I & N Dec. 819 (BIA 1990); *Hernandez-Montiel* v. *INS*, 225 F.3d 1084 (9th Cir. 2000).

[59] *Matter of H*, 21 I & N Dec. 337 (BIA 1996).

[60] *Matter of Kasinga*, 12 I & N Dec. 357 (BIA 1996).

[61] E.g., *Re GJ*, Refugee Appeal No. 1312/93, New Zealand: Refugee Status Appeals Authority, 30 August 1995 [1995] 1 NLR 387.

[62] *Islam* v. *Secretary of State for the Home Department*; *R* v. *Immigration Appeal Tribunal, ex parte Shah* [1999] 2 AC 629.

[A] group shall be considered to form a particular social group where in particular:

Members of that group share an innate characteristic, or a common background that cannot be changed, or share a characteristic or belief that is so fundamental to identity or conscience that a person should not be forced to renounce it, *and*

that group has a distinct identity in the relevant country, because it is perceived as being different by the surrounding society.[63]

This definition adopts the *Acosta* factors – immutable *or* fundamental – but it superimposes an additional requirement concerning the social perception of a group's distinct identity. The addition of the social perception element places a heavier burden on asylum applicants, thus narrowing the scope of persecuted individuals eligible for refugee status. The negative impact has been clearly visible in the post-QD decisions issued by German courts, and to a lesser extent in Austria and Belgium.[64] It appears that other EU States may not have put the restrictive norm into practice, exercising their prerogative to adopt more generous standards than the minimum required by the QD.[65]

(c)   New challenges in the United States

Shortly after the enactment of the QD, the notion of society's perception of the 'social visibility' of a group began appearing prominently in BIA opinions. The BIA faced a series of asylum claims that involved members of transnational criminal gangs, such as Mara Salvatrucha (MS-13). The flourishing of MS-13 and similar gangs, which had originated in Los Angeles, California and spread to other cities in Latin America, Canada

---

[63] Art. 10(d) (emphasis added). The early Commission draft did not include the social perception text; it was added after UNHCR commented on the proposed text, see UNHCR, *Observations on the European Commission's proposal for a Council Directive on minimum standards for the qualification and status of third country nationals and stateless persons as refugees or as persons who otherwise need international protection* (November 2001); UNHCR, *Some Additional Observations and Recommendations on the European Commission 'Proposal for a Council Directive on minimum standards for the qualification and status of third country nationals and stateless persons as refugees or as persons who otherwise need international protection'* (July 2002). The original QD set forth this definition in 2004 and the recast 2011 version maintains the same provision regarding a particular social group.

[64] Michelle Foster, 'The "Ground with the Least Clarity": A Comparative Study of Jurisprudential Developments relating to the Ground of "Membership of a Particular Social Group"' (UNHCR, Legal and Protection Policy Research Series, August 2012).

[65] *Ibid.*; European Council on Refugees and Exiles, 'The Impact of the EU Qualification Directive on International Protection' (October 2008) www.ecre.org/component/content/article/150.html (accessed 11 October 2012).

and the United States, presented new challenges to the US asylum framework.[66] Gang members frequently possess undisputed ties to their gang
and powerful evidence of life-threatening violence. Furthermore, large
groups of their non-violent neighbours are at risk: those who refuse to
join gangs, actively oppose gangs, rebuff sexual liaisons with gang members, defect from gangs or are family members of individuals who resist
gangs.[67] Some decision makers feared that the *Acosta* refugee definition
would extend asylum to gang members and other individuals unworthy of
asylum, as well as to large numbers of individuals who live in neighbour-
hoods frequented by gangs and criminal organizations.[68] Such fears made
this an opportune moment for emulation of a new, more restrictive
definition of 'particular social group'.

Coincident with the drafting and enactment of the QD, US judicial
opinions bore witness to an increasing number of gang-related claims. In
2007 a federal court denied protection to a long-time resident of the
United States who faced removal to El Salvador, despite his argument
that his *indelible* gang tattoos marked him as a member of a particular
social group who would be targeted for persecution by the Salvadoran
police and by rival gangs.[69] A similar result occurred when a tattooed
former gang member argued that his membership in a particular social
group would make him a target for extra-judicial killing by Honduran
security forces and paramilitary groups.[70] Despite the well-founded fears
of persecution and the immutability of their past gang membership, their
past criminal activities may have excluded both of these asylum seekers
from refugee status, or made them ineligible for *non-refoulement*
protection.

But exclusion based on criminal acts does not apply to non-gang
members who are menaced by gangs, such as extortion targets, street
gang recruits, and informants, and this is where the QD norm began to
play a role. In 2008 the BIA announced a momentous change in US law

[66] See generally Steven Dudley, *Transnational Crime in Mexico and Central America: Its
Evolution and Role in International Migration* (Washington, DC: Migration Policy
Institute, 2012).
[67] Harvard International Human Rights Clinic, 'No Place to Hide: Gang, State and Clandestine
Violence in El Salvador' (February 2007) www.law.harvard.edu/programs/hrp/documents/
FinalElSalvadorReport(3-6-07).pdf (accessed 11 October 2012) (discussion of groups vulnerable to persecution, from p. 76); Thomas Boerman, 'Youth Gangs in El Salvador:
Unpacking the State Department 2007 Issue Paper', *Immigration Daily*, 2010 www.ilw.
com/articles/2010,1117-boerman.shtm (accessed 11 October 2012).
[68] E.g., *Arteaga* v. *Mukasey*, 511 F. 3d 940, at 945–6 (9th Cir. 2007).   [69] *Ibid.*
[70] *Castellano-Chacon* v. *INS*, 341 F. 3d 533 (6th Cir. 2003).

in its denial of asylum to a young man who had *resisted recruitment* by a gang. In *Matter of SEG*,[71] the BIA directed immigration judges and asylum officers to apply two additional requirements – social visibility and particularity – to all claims premised on membership in a particular social group. Prior to this, the BIA had sometimes considered the relevance of social perceptions;[72] henceforth the BIA applied a more stringent definition that, as in the EU approach, narrows the scope of individuals eligible for refugee status. Subsequent BIA decisions have applied both criteria, leading to the rejection of many asylum claims.

Some of the federal courts that have reviewed the BIA's 'social visibility' requirement have approved, while others have not. For example, the First Circuit concluded that Brazilian individuals who provided information to US officials concerning smuggling were not eligible for asylum because their purported group of 'noncriminal government informants' lacked social visibility.[73] In contrast, the Seventh Circuit harshly criticized the BIA's application of the 'social visibility' factor in protection claims filed by former members of MS-13,[74] and in asylum applications filed by defecting members of a secret sect in Kenya.[75] The Third Circuit reversed the denial of protection to a Honduran threatened with violence for refusing to join MS-13, commenting that the 'social visibility' criterion would have precluded asylum in many of the BIA's prior landmark opinions, such as those granting protection to homosexuals, former police officers and women who opposed female genital mutilation.[76] The court instructed the BIA to explain its reinterpretation of the law. To date, the BIA has not responded, and the debate over the social visibility requirement rages on.

(d)   Emulation or coincidence?

Several years after the CEAS added a 'social perception' element, arguments about 'social visibility' resounded loudly in US legal discourse. The timing is suggestive that EU norm diffusion is under way, but direct

---

[71] 24 I & N Dec. 579, at 584, 586 (BIA 2008).

[72] E.g., *Matter of RA*, 22 I & N Dec. 906 at 919 (BIA 1999) ('While *not determinative*, the prominence of importance of a characteristic within a society is another factor bearing on whether we will recognize that factor as part of a "particular social group" under our refugee provisions ... The factors we look to in this case, beyond *Acosta's* immutableness test, are *not prerequisites*') (emphasis added).

[73] *Scatambulli* v. *Holder*, 558 F. 3d 53, at 59–60 (1st Cir. 2009).

[74] *Ramos* v. *Holder*, 589 F. 3d 426, at 430 (7th Cir. 2009).

[75] *Gatimi* v. *Holder*, 578 F. 3d 611, at 615–16 (7th Cir. 2009).

[76] *Valdiviezo-Galdamez* v. *Attorney General*, 663 F. 3d 582, at 600–3 (3rd Cir. 2011).

evidence is hard to come by. Legislative history is unavailing, as the norm emerged in the US via case law. The *Matter of SEG* opinion did not refer to CEAS or to any European developments, nor did the subsequent federal judicial decisions. A search of all BIA opinions referring to 'social visibility' turns up no mention of European or other foreign sources of law.[77] Nor has a search of the literature uncovered articles or advocacy policy papers acknowledging the QD's addition of 'social perception' as a prerequisite for defining particular social groups.

Moreover, it must be acknowledged that the QD was not the only source that mentioned a 'social perception' norm. Aleinikoff argued in 2001 that a 'social perception' element should be added to the *Acosta* analysis in order to broaden protection.[78] Starting in 2002, UNHCR Guidelines identified 'social perception' as an element in defining particular social group for refugee law purposes.[79] Both of these efforts, however, envisioned 'social perception' as an expansion, not a contraction, of *Acosta*. Accordingly, they do not support the BIA's adoption of the 'social visibility' limitation in *Matter of SEG*.

The BIA's lack of reference to European norms is unsurprising due to the rarity with which US tribunals refer to foreign law. Indeed, to US scholars, the ease with which judges in Australia (as can be observed in Chapter 2) and other countries refer to legal developments abroad is startling.

Therefore, at this juncture, several matters can be emphasized. The QD was the first instance of a restrictive use of the 'social perception' concept; this QD norm fits the new challenges faced in the US, a classic setting that drives decision makers to emulate approaches pioneered elsewhere; the BIA's restrictive 'social visibility' approach emerged a few short years after the QD went into effect; and no other explanation has been proffered for the parallel development. Thus, we can say emulation appears to be taking place by stealth.

---

[77] A search was done on the terms 'social visibility', 'social perception', 'European', 'EU', and 'foreign law'. William Hine-Ramsberger, research report to author, 14 May 2012.

[78] T. Alexander Aleinikoff, 'Protected Characteristics and Social Perceptions: An Analysis of the Meaning of "Membership in a Particular Social Group"', in Erika Feller, Volker Türk and Frances Nicholson (eds.), *Refugee Protection in International Law: UNHCR's Global Consultations on International Protection* (Cambridge: Cambridge University Press, 2003), pp. 294–301. Aleinikoff also prepared a background paper on this topic as a basis for discussion at the San Remo Expert Roundtable organized by UNHCR and the International Institute of Humanitarian Law, San Remo, Italy, 6–8 September 2001.

[79] UNHCR, *Guidelines on International Protection: 'Membership of a Particular Social Group' within the Context of Article 1A(2) of the 1951 Convention and/or 1967 Protocol relating to the Status of Refugees*, 7 May 2002 (UN Doc. HCR/GIP/02/02).

2 Subsidiary protection

Another example that the process of emulating CEAS norms is under way concerns the QD's expansion of international protection to individuals who suffer refugee-like harm but do not satisfy the legal 'refugee' definition. As long ago as 1976, the Council of Europe Parliamentary Assembly recommended common policies for asylum seekers in refugee-like situations.[80] The late 1990s featured discussions and drafts of what a common policy should entail, but a wide variety of national laws continued to exist.[81] Finally, in 2004, the QD brought uniformity to the fore and mandated renewable residence permits and employment authorization for those who face a real risk of suffering 'serious harm', defined as death penalty, execution, torture, inhuman or degrading treatment or a serious threat to a civilian on account of indiscriminate violence in armed conflict.[82]

The scope of the last clause, indiscriminate violence in armed conflict, engendered controversy and led to the first judgment of the Court of Justice of the European Union (CJEU) interpreting the QD.[83] As analysed in greater detail in Chapter 1, the CJEU's *Elgafaji* opinion adopted an expansive view of 'serious harm' and rejected the argument that article 15c QD requires applicants to provide evidence of a high degree of individualized threat. Further, the CJEU concluded that the QD's definition of serious harm provided protection to a broader scope of individuals than those already protected by other QD provisions or by the European Convention on Human Rights.[84] The *Elgafaji* judgment sparked legal commentary and political discussions in Europe and in the United States.[85] It cast a spotlight on the need for new avenues for

---

[80] Council of Europe, Parliamentary Assembly, Recommendation 773 (1976) on the situation of de facto refugees.

[81] See, e.g., Daphné Bouteillet-Paquet, 'Subsidiary Protection: Progress or Set-Back of Asylum Law in Europe? A Critical Analysis of the Legislation of the Member States of the European Union', in Daphné Bouteillet-Paquet (ed.), *Subsidiary Protection of Refugees in the European Union: Complementing the Geneva Convention?* (Brussels: Bruylant, 2002) p. 226, n. 37.

[82] Art. 15.

[83] Case C-465/07, *Elgafaji* v. *Staatssecretaris van Justitie* (Court of Justice of the European Union, Grand Chamber, 17 February 2009), ECR [2009] 1–921.

[84] Convention for the Protection of Human Rights and Fundamental Freedoms, Rome, 4 November 1950, in force 3 September 1053, ETS No. 5.

[85] See, e.g., Maryellen Fullerton, 'A Tale of Two Decades: War Refugees and Asylum Policy in the European Union' (2011) 10 *Washington University Global Studies Law Review* 87–132; UNHCR, *Safe At Last? Law and Practice in Selected EU Member States with Respect to Asylum-seekers Fleeing Indiscriminate Violence* (July 2011).

protection of people fleeing armed violence and intense generalized harm. Two years after the *Elgafaji* judgment, the European Court of Human Rights expressly stated that article 3 European Human Rights Convention also could, in exceptional cases, protect against *refoulement* to situations of generalized violence.[86]

(a)   US responses to the protection gap

US legislation has been slow to address the protection needs of forced migrants who do not qualify for refugee status. There have been numerous ad hoc and discretionary responses to crises, such as special immigrant visas for Iraqis who worked on behalf of US forces,[87] and there is statutory authorization for Temporary Protected Status (TPS) in situations of mass displacement.[88] While it extends protection beyond those who face persecution, the availability of TPS is severely limited; it applies only when US officials exercise their discretion to designate a country's nationals for TPS protection and it protects only those nationals already in the US. It falls far short of subsidiary protection in the EU: had they travelled to the US rather than to the Netherlands, the Elgafajis could not have accessed TPS protection.

Therefore, it was noteworthy when the BIA issued an opinion that strongly resonates with the European subsidiary protection norm. In February 2012, almost three years to the day after the CJEU interpreted the QD's scope of 'serious harm', the BIA interpreted a US regulation authorizing protection for those who fear 'serious harm'.[89] As the CJEU did in *Elgafji* and similar to the perspective articulated by the European Court of Human Rights in *Sufi and Elmi* v. *United Kingdom*,[90] the BIA took an expansive approach in its interpretation of this term. The case arose under regulations promulgated in 2001 that authorize humanitarian asylum for those who establish 'a reasonable possibility that [they] may suffer other serious harm' if returned to their homeland.[91] The regulation does not define 'serious harm' and this avenue of

[86] *Sufi and Elmi* v. *United Kingdom* (European Court of Human Rights, App. Nos. 8319/07 and 11449/07, 28 June 2011).
[87] Special Immigrant Visa Program, National Defense Authorization Act for Fiscal Year 2006, Pub. Law No. 109–163, §1059; National Defense Authorization Act for Fiscal Year 2008, Pub. Law No. 110–181, §1244.
[88] Immigration and Nationality Act, §244, Pub. L. No. 101–649, 104 Stat. 5030, §244, codified at 8 USC §1254(a) (2006).
[89] *Matter of LS*, 25 I & N Dec. 705 (BIA 2012).   [90] *Sufi and Elmi* v. *United Kingdom*.
[91] Asylum Procedures, 65 Federal Register 76121, at 76133 (final rule Dec. 6, 2000) (effective 5 January 2001); see also 8 CFR §208.13(b)(1)(iii)(B).

protection has remained underutilized.[92] In *Matter of LS*, the BIA high-lighted for the first time this term and uncoupled it from persecution and refugee status: '[T]he focus should be on current conditions and the potential for new physical or psychological harm that the applicant might suffer ... [N]o nexus between the 'other serious harm' and [a protected] asylum ground ... need be shown'.[93]

The asylum claim that brought into focus protection from 'serious harm' began in communist Albania in the 1970s and 1980s.[94] The Hoxha regime arrested Leonard Sholla, his wife, and his 2-year-old child and sent them all to a labour camp. Things improved vastly in the 1990s, but late in the decade the Shollas again faced police interrogations, armed attacks and bombings of their property. They ultimately fled Albania and sought asylum in the United States, where they were deemed credible, but unable to prove a well-founded fear of future persecution. On appeal, Sholla expressly requested humanitarian asylum. The BIA chastised the Immigration Court for failing to consider fully the circumstances that can constitute 'serious harm'.

> The 'other serious harm' provision ... differs in nature from [past] persecution ... [T]he inquiry is forward-looking. When considering the possibility of 'other serious harm', the focus should be on current conditions and the potential for new physical or psychological harm that the applicant might suffer. While 'other serious harm' must equal the severity of persecution, it may be wholly unrelated to the past harm. Moreover ... the asylum applicant need only establish a 'reasonable possibility' of such 'other serious harm' ... We also emphasize that *no nexus* between the 'other serious harm' and an asylum ground protected under the Act need be shown.
>
> [A]djudicators considering 'other serious harm' should be cognizant of conditions in the applicant's country of return and should pay partic-ular attention to major problems that large segments of the population face or conditions that might not significantly harm others but that could severely affect the applicant. Such conditions may include, but are not limited to, those involving civil strife, extreme economic deprivation beyond economic disadvantage, or situations where the claimant could experience severe mental or emotional harm or physical injury.[95]

The BIA's approach echoes that of the QD; conditions that face large swaths of the population are relevant; civil strife in the country of origin

---

[92] Prior to *Matter of LS*, discussion of this regulation focused generally on the severity of past persecution, the alternative ground for humanitarian asylum.

[93] *Matter of LS*, p. 714.   [94] *Sholla v. Gonzalez*, 492 F.3d 946 (8th Cir. 2007).

[95] *Matter of LS*, p. 714 (emphasis in original).

is expressly mentioned. Moreover, the BIA listed examples of a wide variety of injuries that might constitute 'serious harm', including life-threatening situations for AIDS patients unable to obtain the necessary medications if returned home,[96] suffering likely to be faced by Somali women returned to an unstable area without protection of their clan[97] and anguish of mothers who had experienced genital mutilation and now saw their daughters at risk of the same fate.[98] Calling for a case-by-case analysis based on the totality of the circumstances in each application,[99] *Matter of LS* expands the possibilities of protection in the United States.

Although *Matter of LS* contains echoes of the QD's subsidiary protection norm, humanitarian asylum in the US remains substantially more limited than subsidiary protection in the EU. Its delineation of 'serious harm' is far less detailed than the QD, and the humanitarian asylum regulation is only triggered if an applicant can point to evidence of persecution in the past. Nonetheless, in its response to a grave humanitarian need, the *Matter of LS* opinion resonates with the CEAS norm.

(b)   The case for norm diffusion

Although the claims for protection presented by Sholla and by the Elgafajis arose out of different historical circumstances and under different legal instruments, both judgments recognized that States must offer protection to individuals who face the risk of suffering severe non-persecution harm. Both judgments acknowledge that 'serious harm' may be linked to widespread conditions in the applicant's home country; both judgments recognize that civil strife and lethal violence may constitute 'serious harm'. The judgments confirm that both the EU and the US asylum systems include a subsidiary (or complementary) protection norm.

May we conclude that the *Matter of LS* is evidence of partial emulation of the CEAS subsidiary protection norm? The BIA did not credit EU law in its discussion of 'other serious harm'. Further, not one of the 150

---

[96] *Ibid.*, p. 715 (referring to *Boer-Sedano v. Gonzales*, 418 F. 3d 1082 (9th Cir. 2005)).

[97] *Ibid.* (referring to *Mohammed v. Gonzales*, 400 F. 3d 785 (9th Cir. 2005)).

[98] *Ibid.* (referring to *Kone v. Holder*, 596 F. 3d 1141 (2nd Cir. 2010)).

[99] *Ibid.* The BIA also referred to other instances that might constitute serious harm: the unavailability of necessary medical care, in certain extreme circumstances, see *Pllumi* v. *Attorney General of US*, 642 F. 3d 155 (3rd Cir. 2011), the unavailability of psychiatric medications needed for daily functioning, see *Kholyavskiy v. Mukasey*, 540 F. 3d 555 (7th Cir. 2008); economic extortion and private expropriation, see *Belishta v. Ashcroft*, 378 F. 3d 1078 (9th Cir. 2004).

judicial decisions analysing the humanitarian asylum regulation referred to EU or other sources of law,[100] although this is unsurprising when a review of all BIA opinions concerned with asylum identifies only one, involving the Convention Against Torture, with any mention of European law.[101] Similarly, the adoption of the underlying humanitarian asylum regulation did not refer to European developments.

Nonetheless, despite the lack of attribution or other direct proof, norm diffusion may be at work. The QD requirement that Member States provide subsidiary protection has sparked commentary in US academic and policy circles, and has been looked on favourably by US advocates.[102] Asylum officer training sessions have been devoted to the *Elgafji* opinion, and US law school courses have highlighted the CEAS subsidiary protection norm. Further, the CJEU's *Elgafaji* judgment was a pathbreaking interpretation of this norm, and US decision makers, raised in a common law system, are likely to find judicial opinions a more accessible source of EU law than the text of EU directives.

Most important, the US asylum system has confronted new challenges in recent years that the QD's extension of protection to those who suffer 'other serious harm' can address. There has been a horrifying upsurge in lethal violence in Mexico, and claims by Mexican applicants seeking protection in the United States have increased substantially.[103] News stories of exploding homicide rates, mass graves, beheadings, assassinations of journalists and other gruesome crimes have filled the US media.[104] The US State Department has posted a travel advisory warning

---

[100] A search was done of the terms 'humanitarian asylum', 'European', 'EU', 'foreign law' and '8 CFR §208.13(b)(1)(iii)'. William Hine-Ramsberger, research report to author, 18 March 2012.

[101] *Matter of JE*, 23 I & N Dec. 291, at 297–8 (BIA 2002) (discussion of jurisprudence of European Court of Human Rights regarding the definition of torture).

[102] See, e.g., Fullerton, 'War Refugees'.

[103] US Department of Justice, Executive Office of Immigration Review, 'Asylum Statistics by Nationality' (FY 2007-FY 2011) www.justice.gov/eoir/efoia/foiafreq.htm (accessed 11 October 2012) (reporting that roughly 3,000 Mexican nationals applied for asylum each year in 2007, 2008 and 2009, with applications rising to 4,510 in 2010 and to 6,133 in 2011; on average, 75 were granted asylum each year).

[104] E.g., Randal Archibold, 'Drug cartel violence spills over from Mexico, alarming US', *New York Times*, 23 March 2009, p. A1; Clint McDonald, 'Danger on the US–Mexico border', *Washington Post*, 31 March 2011 www.washingtonpost.com/opinions/danger-on-the-us-mexico-border/2011/03/30/AFQp4KCC_story.html (accessed 13 October 2012); Randal Archibold, 'Mexico's drug war bloodies areas thought safe', *New York Times*, 19 January 2012, p. A1; Ashely Fantz, 'The Mexico drug war: bodies for billions', CNN.com,

US citizens of dangers they may face in Mexico.[105] The violence is deadly, publicly visible, and affects innocent bystanders close to the United States. But much of it does not fall within the refugee law paradigm. This gap in the standard US asylum framework can be minimized by partial emulation of the QD subsidiary protection norm.

We confront another example of stealth emulation in the BIA's generous expansion of humanitarian asylum to those suffering not persecution, but 'serious harm'. The social and political circumstances conform to the constructivist account of the process of norm diffusion.[106] A transnational conversation had begun concerning the need to protect individuals likely to face serious harm if forced to return home. The US faced pressure to bridge the protection gap; the QD's 'serious harm' norm was internalized in the US protection framework, appearing in a localized version in the US humanitarian asylum mechanism. Here we can see the 'jurisprudential glow' of the CJEU at work beyond the EU.

E   Conclusion

Theorists in International Relations and in sociological institutionalism suggest that norm emulation is more likely to occur in weaker, peripheral States than in the hegemon. Compounding the expectation that there might be less emulation of European norms, the US scene presents additional negative factors: a reflexive American exceptionalism mindset, compounded by contemporary public antipathy to reliance on foreign law. Other hurdles include the US dualist tradition and the extensive multitiered US asylum system that generates thousands of published asylum opinions every year. These combined factors have impeded emulation of European refugee norms in the US.

20 January 2012 www.cnn.com/2012/01/15/world/mexico-drug-war-essay/index.html? iref=allsearch (accessed 11 October 2012); Karla Zabludovsky, 'Photographers found dead in Mexico', *New York Times*, 4 May 2012, p. A12; Karla Zabludovsky, 'Police find 49 bodies by a highway in Mexico', *New York Times*, 14 May 2012, p. A4; Karla Zabludovsky, 'Mexico: bodies found on bridge', *New York Times*, 15 September 2012, p. A8. See generally Steven Dudley, *Transnational Crime in Mexico and Central America: Its Evolution and Role in International Migration* (Washington, DC: Migration Policy Institute, 2012).

[105] US Department of State, 'Travel Warning' (8 February 2012) http://travel.state.gov/travel/cis_pa_tw/tw/tw_5665.html (accessed 11 October 2012).

[106] See, e.g., Amitav Acharya, 'How Ideas Spread: Whose Norms Matter? Norm Localization and Institutional Change in Asian Regionalism' (2004) 58 *International Organization* 239–75.

Nonetheless, despite these obstacles and the absence of public acknowledgement of EU law in US asylum decisions, the process of norm diffusion is under way. This chapter posits a rational account for the emulation of European norms. The chief emulation drivers are the new challenges to the US protection regime that have been posed by the widespread and seemingly unstoppable violence in Mexico and by transnational activity involving Central American–US criminal gangs. The uncertainties generated by these high profile instances of violence and criminal activities have pushed the BIA to search for new solutions. The chapter further argues that though evidence is elusive there are at least two examples of partial emulation of EU norms, one that restricts international protection and one that expands it. After the QD formulated a more constrained definition of 'membership of a particular social group', the BIA adopted a similar limiting definition in a precedent opinion expressly intended to provide clarification of US asylum standards. After the CJEU propounded a broad reading of article 15c QD, the BIA instructed US decision makers to take an expansive view of humanitarian asylum based on 'serious harm'.

This chapter also contends the strong Anglo-American heritage of the US legal system and the special relationship with the UK provide a certain degree of 'fit' for the adoption of a norm developed in the EU. In addition, the multiple vibrant transnational legal networks concerned with migration and related human rights issues contain many who are aware of European norms, have studied asylum and forced migration in Europe, and have generated interest in and knowledge of European developments.

The lack of explicit discussion of European norms in the US legislative and regulatory processes and in administrative and judicial opinions necessitates tentative conclusions about the extent of the norm diffusion process. The parallel appearance of these norms in EU and US asylum law, with the US adoption taking place several years after the completion of stage one of the CEAS, suggests that the years of ferment accompanying the Tampere Programme have contributed to the diffusion of EU protection norms across the Atlantic. At this moment the suggestion is faint, but it would be unlikely at this early stage to see an avowed emulation of European norms in the US legal system. It is important not to ignore evidence of emulation, even though it is only partial and has been occurring by stealth.

To European scholars and jurists, the CEAS has been under development for a long time. To outsiders in the US, it is a very recent undertaking and one taken seriously only in 2009 when the CJEU issued its first interpretations of the CEAS. It is a dynamic process and in future years more US lawyers, judges and activists will be aware of European refugee law. More US law graduates conversant with European norms will have advanced in the profession to positions that wield influence in developing the law. There will be more European judgments casting a 'jurisprudential glow', a development likely to have a strong impact on common law systems.

Thus, the early evidence from the US predicts that the future will witness wide diffusion of CEAS norms beyond Europe. European asylum norms have already wielded influence in the solipsistic US legal system. Over a longer term, it can be expected that the ripple effects of the CEAS will continue to wash US shores and will ultimately reach many States around the globe.

9

The vanishing refugee: how EU asylum law blurs the specificity of refugee protection

JEAN-FRANÇOIS DURIEUX

A Introduction

The United Nations (UN) refugee regime, which was ushered in by the adoption of the 1951 Refugee Convention and the establishment of the UN High Commissioner for Refugees (UNHCR), was crafted in large part by European States and was designed to deal with a European refugee problem.[1] In the decades that followed, the principles, norms and institutions created radiated beyond the original European ambit, so that nowadays one can reasonably speak of a universal protection regime. Today, as a substantial number of European States, bound together in a powerful Union, equip themselves with a common asylum system, a similar process of diffusion is a distinct possibility. Some have argued that the European Union (EU) is actually bound to export its own devices, at times aggressively, in order to preserve the internal system.[2]

Thank you to Marie Schirrmeister for research assistance.

[1] Out of nineteen original signatories to the 1951 Refugee Convention (Convention relating to the Status of Refugees, Geneva, 28 July 1951, in force 22 April 1954, 189 UNTS 137), fourteen were European States. The Convention allowed Contracting Parties to make a declaration according to which only events occurring prior to 1951, in Europe, would give rise to refugee status. While the time limitation was lifted by the 1967 Protocol relating to the Status of Refugees (Protocol relating to the Status of Refugees, New York, adopted 31 January 1967, in force 4 October 1967, 606 UNTS 267), a few States have maintained the geographical limitation. For a history of the refugee regime before and after the Second World War, see Guy S. Goodwin-Gill and Jane McAdam, *The Refugee in International Law* (3rd edn, Oxford: Oxford University Press, 2007), pp. 421–36; James C. Hathaway, 'The Evolution of Refugee Status in International Law: 1920–1950' (1984) 33 *International and Comparative Law Quarterly* 348–80.

[2] Philippe C. Schmitter points to the incentive of forging common positions and policies to increase the collective bargaining power of the European Community vis-à-vis the outside world, as well as involuntary motives, such as the demands of the extra-Community environment reacting to successful developments within the regional integration project ('Three

Be that as it may, the 'export value' of the Common European Asylum System (CEAS) is likely to be as great, if not greater, than that of individual Member States' laws and policies precisely because it presents itself *as a system*: that is, a comprehensive and coherent whole. In other words, it is tempting to regard the CEAS as a mini-regime[3] of international protection, based upon the 1951 Refugee Convention.[4] However, it also addresses some of the human rights and international cooperation issues that the Convention alone does not satisfactorily resolve.

To be effective, an international refugee regime must, at a minimum, formalize the participating States' agreement on inclusion and exclusion: that is, on who needs and deserves, and who either does not need or does not deserve, protection; and it must include a mix of substantive standards and procedures that make it possible to: (a) promptly and conclusively identify those individuals who are in need of protection; (b) provide them with an adequate status; and (c) ensure fairness in the distribution of responsibilities and costs among participating States. On its face, the CEAS contains all of these elements to some extent, as well as additional ones: notably, the system reaches out to persons who are not Convention refugees but nonetheless require a form of international protection.[5] This is a remarkable achievement which in all likelihood increases – in the eyes of non-EU States – the attractiveness of the CEAS, consequently enhancing its global impact.

A warning therefore seems necessary. While it is possible to represent the CEAS as a regional asylum system,[6] nested within the global refugee regime, such a representation is misleading because it misses a most significant fact: at no point in time did the Member States of the EU

Neo-Functional Hypotheses about International Integration' (1969) 23 *International Organization* 161–6).

[3] Emek M. Uçarer, 'Guarding the Borders of the European Union: Paths, Portals, and Prerogatives', in Sandra Lavenex and Emek M. Uçarer (eds.), *Migration and the Externalities of European Integration* (Lanham, MD: Lexington Books, 2003), pp. 16–17.

[4] The 1999 European Council in Tampere, Finland, 'agreed to work towards establishing a Common European Asylum System, based on the full and inclusive application of the Geneva Convention' (Presidency Conclusions of the Tampere European Council (15–16 October 1999), Presidency Conclusion 13).

[5] See Treaty on the Functioning of the European Union (Consolidated Version) (OJ 2010 No. C83/47) (TFEU), art. 78, for the most current description of CEAS elements.

[6] Including an increasingly significant 'external' dimension, which corroborates Schmitter's externalization hypothesis ('Three Neo-Functional Hypotheses', 165). On this, see Lavenex and Uçarer, *Migration*; Philippe De Bruycker, Marie-Claire Foblets and Marleen Maes (eds.), *External Dimensions of European Migration and Asylum Law and Policy* (Brussels: Bruylant, 2011).

deliberately or consciously set out to craft a piece of regional or supra-national refugee law. Indeed, the CEAS can only fully be understood in relation to the broader European integration project in which it is embedded, and which imposes upon it a very particular logic.

Of course, regional integration is not an exclusively European phe-nomenon.[7] Nonetheless, the 'EU project' represents a uniquely ambi-tious and advanced form of integration. It is ambitious with regard to the policy areas it encompasses, which stretch far beyond the trade and economic goals that characterize most regional integration schemes; and it is advanced in its modes of functioning, including the voluntary transfer to supranational decision-making institutions and enforcement powers traditionally vested in individual States.

As Niemann has rightly observed, such a complex endeavour is necessarily dialectical, subject to both dynamics and countervailing forces.[8] This is all the more so once non-material values, such as free-dom, security and justice, enter the field of 'communitarization'.[9] Indeed, as he has noted:

> Treaty revision in the context of visa, asylum and immigration policy is a particularly interesting and significant research question: on the one hand, this domain has become one of the most dynamic and fastest moving sectors of the European integration project. On the other hand, it is very close to the heart of national sovereignty. The revision of decision rules and the institutional set-up in this 'high politics' area is a substantial constitutional question.[10]

From a historical perspective, it is essential to bear in mind that asylum dawned upon the EU project as an afterthought, not as a primary motivation. Consequently, it bears the legacy of earlier integration

---

[7] See Walter Mattli, *The Logic of Regional Integration: Europe and Beyond* (Cambridge: Cambridge University Press, 1999); ch. 1 and the tables therein provide a comprehensive overview of European and non-European regional integration schemes.

[8] Arne Niemann, 'Explaining Visa, Asylum and Immigration Policy Treaty Revision: Insights from a Revised Neofunctionalist Framework' (Constitutionalism Web-Papers ConWEB No.1/ 2006) www.qub.ac.uk/schools/SchoolofPoliticsInternationalStudiesandPhilosophy/File Store/ConWEBFiles/Filetoupload,38372,en.pdf (accessed 3 October 2012).

[9] TFEU, art. 3(2): 'The Union shall offer its citizens an area of freedom, security and justice without internal frontiers, in which the free movement of persons is ensured in conjunction with appropriate measures with respect to external border controls, asylum, immigration and the prevention and combating of crime.' Title V (arts. 67–89) of the companion TFEU is devoted to EU action in this area, encompassing policies on border checks, immigration and asylum; judicial cooperation in civil and criminal matters; and police cooperation.

[10] Niemann, 'Explaining Visa, Asylum and Immigration Policy Treaty Revision', p. 2 (citations omitted).

efforts, but also – and above all – the powerful logic which drives the EU project forward.

The 'story of integration in the field of immigration and asylum can be told in many different ways'.[11] With due deference to the comprehensive analyses of Noll[12] and Guild,[13] among others, this chapter sheds an admittedly selective light on this story. First, with regard to European law, it is chiefly concerned with those premises of the EU project that have imposed their own peculiar logic upon the design and development of the CEAS. By stressing these idiosyncrasies, it is hoped that the chapter's focus on the *logic* underpinning the CEAS can stimulate reflection on the degree to which EU asylum law can be replicated in other jurisdictions and contexts.

Second, with regard to the international refugee regime, this chapter is concerned with the spirit, at least as much as the letter, of the law. It postulates that a regime of international cooperation, geared towards the protection of a particular category of people (refugees), can only thrive if it is grounded in a *positive* inclination to protect refugees, reflecting a *positive* image of the refugee as a person of concern. While it may represent an ideal rather than a reality, this positive spirit is the guarantor of the specificity of an international regime based on the Refugee Convention. In the analysis that follows, therefore, the figure of the refugee occupies a central place.

In short, this chapter argues that the EU concept of asylum induces the phenomenon of a 'vanishing refugee', whereby the central character of the 1951 Convention regime, namely the refugee, is blurred, marginalized or ignored. It also argues that although this result may not be intended, neither is it accidental, since its logical premises are inherent in the EU project. Two such premises are explored in the following sections: mutual trust among participating States; and free internal movement (a space without internal borders). The chapter then turns to the fairly unique human rights foundation of the CEAS which, while not truly coextensive with EU integration, has come to affirm itself as an inescapable factor of its development.

---

[11] Gregor Noll, *Negotiating Asylum: The EU Acquis, Extraterritorial Protection and the Common Market of Deflection* (The Hague: Martinus Nijhoff, 2000), p. 117.

[12] Noll, *Negotiating Asylum*; Gregor Noll and Jens Vedsted-Hansen, 'Non-Communitarians: Refugee and Asylum Policies', in P. Alston (ed.), *The EU and Human Rights* (Oxford: Oxford University Press, 1999).

[13] Elspeth Guild, *The Legal Elements of European Identity: EU Citizenship and Migration Law* (The Hague: Kluwer Law International, 2004); Elspeth Guild, 'The Europeanisation of Europe's Asylum Policy' (2006) 18 *International Journal of Refugee Law* 630–51.

B   Mutual trust

Mutual trust is key to the constitution of the EU as an area governed (in an increasing number of policy domains) by supranational law and institutions. Granted, the whole of international law is predicated on the sovereign equality of States and on mutual respect for sovereignty. Likewise, the conclusion of any inter-State agreement supposes a measure of trust – at a minimum, some confidence that each party has both the capacity and the will to implement the agreement in good faith. Nonetheless, mutual trust acquires a special meaning and plays a special role within an integration project such as that of the EU. Here, Member States share more than simply a desire to cooperate, which would be present in any bilateral or multilateral agreement. Rather, their resolve to cooperate in giving effect to the goals of the EU is grounded in a bedrock of shared values, common destiny and other determinants of a 'European identity'. Inherent in the EU project is a notion that Member States are, in Orwellian fashion, 'more equal than others'. It seems fairly easy to dismiss this equality as a fiction considering the wide disparities that continue to exist between the legal systems, let alone the practices and attitudes, of the EU Member States, even within the relatively narrow policy area of migration and asylum.[14] It is important to bear in mind, however, that, as a foundation of mutual trust, equality between Member States is in part axiomatic – a given – and in part programmatic – something to be built, not least through solidarity and mutual support. Thus, while there exists a presumption of common legal references and comparable, if not identical, standards of performance, there is now also a process of validation, namely an admission test. EU membership criteria require:

> that the candidate country has achieved stability of institutions guaranteeing democracy, the rule of law, human rights and respect for and protection of minorities, the existence of a functioning market economy

---

[14] On the lack of effective harmonization despite the CEAS, see Eiko Thielemann and Nadine El-Enany, 'Common Laws, Diverse Outcomes: Can EU Asylum Initiatives Lead to More Effective Refugee Protection?' (Paper prepared for the European Union Studies Association's 12th Biennial International Conference, Boston, 3–5 March 2011) www. euce.org/eusa/2011/papers/1a_thielemann.pdf (accessed 3 October 2012); European Council on Refugees and Exiles (ECRE), *Broken Promises – Forgotten Principles: An ECRE Evaluation of the Development of EU Minimum Standards for Refugee Protection, Tampere 1999–Brussels 2004* (2004) www.ecre.org/component/downloads/downloads/ 63.html (accessed 3 October 2012); UNHCR, *Asylum in the European Union: A Study of the Implementation of the Qualification Directive* (November 2007), www.unhcr.org/ refworld/docid/473050632.html (accessed 3 October 2012).

as well as the capacity to cope with competitive pressure and market forces within the Union.[15]

Among other things, these conditions guarantee that EU legislation, once transposed into the domestic order, will be implemented effectively. They are 'building blocks' for the mutual trust inherent in EU membership.

1   The EU definition of 'refugee'

There is, however, one issue around which mutual trust seems to be firmly axiomatic: EU Member States seem confident that none of them will produce refugees. In other words, all Member States regard themselves as safe enough to ensure that the premise for a need for protection – namely, a well-founded fear of persecution for one of the reasons outlined in the 1951 Convention – is not, and cannot be, realized within the EU. This was the basic message of the so-called Aznar Protocol, annexed to the Amsterdam Treaty,[16] whose declared objective was to ensure that no citizen of a Member State would have access to an asylum procedure anywhere within the territory of the EU. This position, spearheaded by Spain,[17] understandably raised alarm within UNHCR. Summarizing its concerns, Landgren argued that the Aznar Protocol violated the letter and the spirit of the Refugee Convention in several ways, including through discrimination on the basis of nationality.[18] According to UNHCR, an automatic bar to refugee status determination would amount to introducing *a posteriori* a geographical limitation to

---

[15] Presidency Conclusions of the Copenhagen European Council (21–22 June 1993), Presidency Conclusion 7 http://ec.europa.eu/bulgaria/documents/abc/72921_en.pdf (accessed 3 October 2012).

[16] Protocol on asylum for nationals of Member States of the European Union, annexed to the Treaty establishing the European Community (OJ 1997 No. C340/103).

[17] This move, led by Spanish Prime Minister, José Maria Aznar, was a political response to the protection extended by some European countries, notably Belgium and France, to members of the Basque nationalist organization Euzkadi ta Askatasuna (ETA). These countries had also refused to extradite ETA members to Spain, the consequences of which are reflected in the 1996 European Convention on Extradition (Convention drawn up on the basis of Article K.3 of the Treaty on European Union, relating to extradition between the Member States of the European Union (OJ 1996 No. C313/12).

[18] Karin Landgren, 'Deflecting International Protection by Treaty: Bilateral and Multilateral Accords on Extradition, Readmission and the Inadmissibility of Asylum Requests' (UNHCR, *New Issues in Refugee Research*, Working Paper No. 10, June 1999), p. 13.

the application of the Convention refugee definition, which is precluded by article 42.[19]

By way of compromise, the Council adopted a Declaration (alongside the Protocol) which added:

> The Protocol on asylum for nationals of Member States of the European Union does not prejudice the right of each Member State to take the organisational measures it deems necessary to fulfil its obligations under the Geneva Convention of 28 July 1951 relating to the status of refugees.[20]

This may knock the wind out of the Aznar Protocol's sails, so to speak. Nevertheless, the Declaration confirms that the personal scope of the EU asylum system is, through its exclusion of EU nationals, narrower than that of the universal regime, and that it is not the business of the EU (but rather of any Member State that may be so inclined) to fill the *ratione personae* gap between the two regimes through its own 'organisational measures'. Thus, deference to the Refugee Convention goes hand in hand with an admission that EU law per se falls short of a full and inclusive application of the international instrument.

Although the Aznar Protocol is only representative of a singular moment of European (if not merely Spanish) history, and not all Member States were as eager as Spain to push it through,[21] the *ratione personae* gap it introduced between EU law and international refugee law has not been closed. If anything, it has solidified. Article 2(d) (formerly 2(c)) EU Qualification Directive delimits the 'refugee' definition under that instrument to third-country nationals, and article 2(f) (formerly 2(e)) does the same with regard to the category of persons eligible for subsidiary protection.[22]

---

[19] *Ibid.*, p. 17. Pursuant to art. 42 Refugee Convention, any reservations must be entered at the time of signature, accession or ratification, and no reservations are allowed with respect to arts. 1, 3, 4, 16(1), 33 and 36–46.

[20] Declaration (No. 48) relating to the Protocol on asylum for nationals of Member States of the European Union (OJ 1997 No. C340/141).

[21] Belgium made it known that it would continue to 'carry out an individual examination of any asylum request made by a national of another Member State': Declaration by Belgium on the Protocol on asylum for nationals of Member States of the European Union (OJ 1997 No. C340/144). See also Landgren, 'Deflecting International Protection by Treaty', pp. 12–13.

[22] The Council Directive 2004/83/EC of 29 April 2004 on minimum standards for the qualification and status of third-country nationals or stateless persons as refugees or as persons who otherwise need international protection and the content of the protection granted (OJ 2004 No. L304/12) (Qualification Directive) was agreed in April 2004 and came into effect in October of that same year. A recast version was adopted in December 2011: Directive 2011/

The CEAS provides a dual justification for excluding EU nationals from international protection. The first, which can be traced directly to the premise of mutual trust, refers to an expectation, possibly a non-rebuttable presumption,[23] that Member States respect, protect and fulfil the fundamental rights of their nationals, with the effect that EU citizens have no reason to seek asylum. The second justification is inspired by another basic principle of the EU scheme: free movement. Since this is discussed in detail in the next section, it is addressed only briefly here.

The preamble to the Aznar Protocol refers to the EU's central objective of establishing an area without internal frontiers and granting 'every citizen of the Union the right to move and reside freely within the territory of the Member States'. What this reference suggests is that even in the highly unlikely case of an EU national needing to escape from persecution, there would be no need in the EU destination country for a mechanism called asylum, since the right of free establishment would achieve the same protection objective. This seemingly reasonable proposition may have a seriously damaging impact, however, particularly if it were to be emulated in other parts of the world where regional groupings favour and facilitate free movement and establishment within the region of participating countries' citizens, but lack comparable human rights guarantees.[24]

Where sufficient human rights guarantees do exist, assimilating asylum with freedom of establishment is less objectionable. Nonetheless, by focusing on an available non-refugee-specific remedy, this assimilation downplays the specific causes of the refugee's flight. Taken to the extreme, such a posture would make the entire refugee regime redundant. Even at a limited

---

95/EU of the European Parliament and of the Council of 13 December 2011 on standards for the qualification of third-country nationals or stateless persons as beneficiaries of international protection, for a uniform status for refugees or for persons eligible for subsidiary protection, and for the content of the protection granted (recast), 20 December 2011 (OJ 2011 No. L337/9) (Recast 2011 Qualification Directive). Arguably, EU citizens may still seek protection directly under the Refugee Convention, which is not affected by the EU directives. This is, however, a rather theoretical remedy: in practice, no Member State has established procedures for determining refugee status outside the 'regular' asylum procedures, and the latter are geared towards assessing claims pursuant to domestic law that incorporates binding EU instruments. Only Belgium, consistent with the reservation mentioned in above n. 21, omitted the 'third country national' phrase when it transposed the Qualification Directive into the national legal order.

[23] See Part D at p. 244 below.

[24] This is the case, for example, in the Economic Community of West African States (ECOWAS). See other examples in Landgren, 'Deflecting International Protection by Treaty', pp. 12–13.

regional level, it contributes to blurring the image of the refugee by obviating the need to consider those essential features that, ultimately, justify the existence of a specific regime.

2   The distribution of protection responsibilities

Mutual trust finds an arguably more straightforward, but certainly no less worrying, application in another element of the CEAS, namely the allocation of Member State responsibility for processing a claim to international protection. The development of a 'clear and workable' system for determining which State is responsible for the examination of an asylum application lodged within the EU was listed in the Tampere Conclusions as a short-term objective, higher in the order of EU priorities than any other element of the CEAS.[25] This sense of urgency can be traced to article 63 Treaty establishing the European Community (as amended by the Amsterdam Treaty), under which 'criteria and mechanisms' to enable such a determination appear as the very first of the 'measures of asylum' to be adopted within five years. In this area of the CEAS more than in any other, however, it would be unwise to ignore the enduring legacy of prior extra-Community arrangements – from the early cooperation of a limited number of Member States under the Schengen Agreement and its Implementation Convention, through to the 1990 Dublin Convention and the 2003 Dublin Regulation in the CEAS (known as 'Dublin II').[26] While this has been a long and tense journey, the fundamentals have not changed significantly.

The basic tenet of the Dublin system is fairly straightforward: each application for asylum made anywhere in the 'Dublin area'[27] shall be examined by one – and only one – Member State. The operation of such a system obviously requires a considerable measure of trust among participating States, at two levels. First, the 'one shot only' principle necessarily implies a mutual recognition of asylum decisions. In this regard, however,

---

[25] Presidency Conclusions of the Tampere European Council (15–16 October 1999), Presidency Conclusion 14.

[26] For a history of EU harmonization in this area, see Guild, 'Europeanisation of Europe's Asylum Policy'; Noll, *Negotiating Asylum*; Agnès Hurwitz, *The Collective Responsibility of States to Protect Refugees* (Oxford: Oxford University Press, 2009) and references therein; Violeta Moreno-Lax, 'Dismantling the Dublin System: *MSS* v. *Belgium and Greece*' (2012) 14 *European Journal of Migration and Law* 1–31.

[27] This area actually extends beyond the EU since Norway, Iceland and Switzerland are also part of the system.

the system suffers from a strange asymmetry, discussed in the next section. Second, in allocating processing responsibilities among States, Dublin relies on objective criteria which are 'performance neutral' – that is, the criteria refer neither to the will, nor to the capacity, of any State to offer the protection required by EU law or international law. This is because such will and capacity are presumed to exist – a massive show of mutual trust indeed.[28]

In its critical appraisal of the Dublin system, the Court of Justice of the European Union (CJEU) acknowledged that the CEAS 'was conceived in a context making it possible to assume that all the participating States . . . observe fundamental rights, including the rights based on the Geneva Convention and the 1967 Protocol, and on the ECHR, and that the Member States can have confidence in each other in that regard'.[29] The court proceeded to explain why this presumption cannot be absolute and to describe the threshold that must be met before this presumption can be validated (discussed in Part D below). This is not, however, the focus of the argument here. States should not be allowed blindly to trust each other's compliance with refugee protection norms. At the same time, some measure of trust is implicit in any legal regime – for example, within the 'community of obligations' which binds all Contracting Parties to the Refugee Convention. But for the fact that it overstates equality of performance, an inter-State agreement à la Dublin is not incompatible at all with the principles of the international refugee regime. Even though the Refugee Convention does not set out criteria for responsibility sharing, its efficacy is predicated on such a principle, and, critically, the responsibilities to be shared include the early identification of a need for international protection.[30] In Conclusion No. 15 (XXX) of 1979, the Executive Committee of UNHCR confirmed that the phenomenon of refugees without an asylum country undermines the

---

[28] Note that another presumption is implicit in the Dublin allocation system, namely that its criteria – including, for example, family unity or the existence of a visa – reflect, if not the preference of the asylum seeker, at least his or her legitimate expectations as regards the country of his or her asylum.

[29] Joined Cases C-411/10 and C-493/10, para. 78.

[30] On the issue of timing, see Jean-François Durieux, 'Opinion: Protection Where? – Or When? First Asylum, Deflection Policies and the Significance of Time' (2009) 21 *International Journal of Refugee Law* 75–80. For a comprehensive discussion of responsibility allocation for the protection of refugees, see Hurwitz, *Collective Responsibility*; Savitri Taylor, 'Protection Elsewhere/Nowhere' (2006) 18 *International Journal of Refugee Law* 283–312; Michelle Foster, 'Protection Elsewhere: The Legal Implications of Requiring Refugees to Seek Protection in Another State' (2007) 28 *Michigan Journal of International Law* 223–86.

credibility of the international regime. It recommended that efforts 'be made to resolve the problem of identifying the country responsible for examining an asylum request by the adoption of common criteria' that should make it possible to identify that country 'in a positive manner' and 'to avoid possible disagreement between States'.[31] This is, evidently, what the Dublin system has attempted to achieve in Europe.

There is, however, one substantial – even substantive – difference between what the Executive Committee called for, and the approach chosen by the EU. The former took, as one should, the interest of the refugee herself as a primary consideration; it called for any return agreements to be applied 'with due regard to [the] special situation' of asylum seekers; and it recalled that the concept of asylum relates to the refugee's 'right to reside' and 'possibility of taking up residence in a country other than one where [she] may have reasons to fear persecution'.[32]

In contrast, the Dublin system erects a conceptual wall between the asylum process and the refugee. It allocates responsibility for a process, rather than for a person. The territorial distribution formula concerns asylum applications and the locus of their *processing*, rather than asylum seekers or refugees and the locus of their *protection*.

3 Summary

Does the lens of mutual trust give any relief to the refugee character within the EU landscape? Have we come any closer to understanding who the intended beneficiary of 'European asylum' may be?[33] At this stage, we only know who this beneficiary – the refugee – *cannot* be: she is

---

[31] UNHCR Executive Committee, Conclusion No. 15 (XXX) (16 October 1979), paras. (h)(i), (ii).

[32] *Ibid.*, paras. (h)(vi), (m). The criteria 'should take into account the duration and nature of any sojourn of the asylum-seeker in other countries' (para. (h)(ii)). 'The intentions of the asylum-seeker as regards the country in which he wishes to request asylum should as far as possible be taken into account' (para. (h)(iii)).

[33] The phrase 'European asylum' appeared for the first time in the TFEU, art. 78(2):

> For the purposes of paragraph 1, the European Parliament and the Council, acting in accordance with the ordinary legislative procedure, shall adopt measures for a common European asylum system comprising:
> (a) a uniform status of asylum for nationals of third countries, valid throughout the Union;
> (b) a uniform status of subsidiary protection for nationals of third countries who, without obtaining European asylum, are in need of international protection.

not an EU national. The reasons for this negative definition have been analysed above, and it can be concluded that these demonstrate a profound misunderstanding of what refugee law stands for, if not a blatant disregard for it.

As for the Dublin system of allocation – a pivotal element of the CEAS – this chapter suggests that the asylum seeker, not the refugee, is the principal focus of attention of EU asylum law. Furthermore, the 'person' of the asylum seeker disappears behind her application, which needs to be processed. Other components of the CEAS confirm this focus, notably the Directives on asylum procedures and on reception conditions, which aim at harmonizing Member States' practices to a degree sufficient for making the Dublin system 'workable'.[34] The combined effect of these instruments is to emphasize the *processing* of an asylum application as a duty owed by Member States to each other, which is to obfuscate the process – and, above all, the rationale – of asylum-seeking as a personal démarche. A conceptual wall separates the asylum process from the protection seeker. Even the Temporary Protection Directive contributes to spiriting the refugee away from the EU discourse on asylum, albeit that the circumstance of mass influx may provide *some* justification for this approach.[35]

C A space without internal borders

In order to comprehend fully the roots of this phenomenon, it is necessary to refer to another EU premise: the EU as a common space without internal borders. Its influence on EU asylum law and policy has been amply documented, in particular by Guild from whose work this section takes much of its inspiration. This section argues that mutual trust

---

[34] Council Directive 2005/85/EC of 1 December 2005 on minimum standards on procedures in Member States for granting and withdrawing refugee status (OJ 2005 No. L326/13) (Procedures Directive); Council Directive 2003/9/EC of 27 January 2003 laying down minimum standards for the reception of asylum seekers (OJ 2003 No. L31/18) (Reception Conditions Directive).

[35] Council Directive 2001/55/EC of 20 July 2001 on minimum standards for giving temporary protection in the event of a mass influx of displaced persons and on measures promoting a balance of efforts between Member States in receiving such persons and bearing the consequences thereof (OJ 2001 No. L212/12). For a discussion of this aspect of the CEAS, see Jean-François Durieux and Agnès Hurwitz, 'How Many Is Too Many? African and European Legal Responses to Mass Influxes of Refugees' (2004) 47 *German Yearbook of International Law* 105–59.

within the EU is reflected not only in mistrust towards the asylum seeker, but also in further alienation of the refugee.

Since the Single European Act of 1986, the EU's primary objective has been to create an internal market characterized by the abolition between Member States of obstacles to the free movement of goods, persons, services and capital.[36] Controls at inter-State borders obviously constitute a significant obstacle to the free movement of persons (which is, of course, the focus here). Through a gradual and often painstaking process, such controls have been removed almost entirely within the territory of the EU. This is no small achievement. It would be wrong, however, to interpret this as a manifestation of a laissez-faire approach, as though Member States considered that the free movement of persons across previously guarded borders was devoid of any security risk. This is definitely not the case: the urge to control remains, but it is exercised differently, and 'elsewhere'. The first (non-EU) experimentation with 'unchecked borders', the Schengen Agreement, made it clear that such a move had to be accompanied by 'complementary measures to safeguard internal security and prevent illegal immigration'.[37] Likewise, but with greater precision, the Amsterdam Treaty mandates the adoption of 'flanking measures' that are directly related to the free movement of persons in the areas of 'external border controls, asylum and immigration'[38] – language which lives on in the definition of an 'area of freedom, security and justice' in the Treaty on European Union.[39]

Put simply, the topic of 'asylum' had no *raison d'être* within the EU integration project until it imposed itself as a concern – perhaps even an

---

[36] Single European Act (OJ 1987 No. L169/1), signed 17 February 1986 in Luxembourg and 28 February 1986 in The Hague (entered into force 1 July 1987). Article 13 reads:

> The EEC Treaty shall be supplemented by the following provisions:
> The Community shall adopt measures with the aim of progressively establishing the internal market over a period expiring on 31 December 1992 ... The internal market shall comprise an area without internal frontiers in which the free movement of goods, persons, services and capital is ensured in accordance with the provisions of this Treaty.

[37] Agreement between the Governments of the States of the Benelux Economic Union, the Federal Republic of Germany and the French Republic on the gradual abolition of controls at their common borders, 14 June 1985 (OJ 2000 No. L239/13), art. 17.

[38] Treaty establishing the European Community (Consolidated Version) (OJ 2002 No. C325/33), art. 61 (previously art. 73).

[39] TEU, art. 3(2): 'The Union shall offer its citizens an area of freedom, security and justice without internal frontiers, in which the free movement of persons is ensured in conjunction with appropriate measures with respect to external border controls, asylum, immigration and the prevention and combating of crime.'

annoyance – confronting the EU's ambition to establish an internal market.[40] Without controls at the intra-EU State borders, it became imperative to: (a) strengthen controls at the external border of the EU; (b) regulate the intra-EU movement of third-country nationals at the EU level, including that of long-term lawful residents (but also asylum seekers); and (c) harmonize the reception, qualification and treatment of migrants – including those evading external border controls – in order to minimize forum-shopping among Member States. The perverse effect of this functional spillover has been described by Carlier:

> Non seulement la politique migratoire commune est la conséquence de la libre circulation interne, mais elle est aussi une condition pour la pleine réalisation de cette dernière. Ce lien consubstantiel explique, plus qu'il ne le devrait, le développement d'une politique commune d'asile au sein de l'Union européenne. Plus qu'il ne le devrait, car cette perspective induit une approche guidée par la gestion et la limitation des migrations plus que par la sauvegarde des droits fondamentaux, quand bien même les textes de droits de l'homme, dont la Convention de Genève, sont abondamment cités dans les textes adoptés.[41]

This perspective conditions every aspect of EU asylum law and policy and conflicts on a number of fronts with the protection logic of the Refugee Convention. The following paragraphs outline some ways in which the logic of control pushes the refugee to the margins not only of EU territory, but also of EU concerns and, in the final analysis, of the EU's self-image.

---

[40] This dominant neo-functionalist explanation has been questioned by Guiraudon and Bigo, among others. Both argue, on different grounds, that the compensatory measures rationale cannot provide a sufficient explanation for the restrictiveness of the policies and practices adopted. According to Guiraudon, the acceleration of vertical integration in migration and asylum resulted from a tactical choice by Member States' law and order officials, whose primary concern was to circumvent domestic constraints on migration control. According to Bigo, any internal market rationale is agnostic as to the restrictiveness or otherwise of external barriers, but simply requires the application of common rules. For example, for internal free trade in goods, there must be a common external tariff and commercial policy, but not of any particular degree of restrictiveness. In contrast, in relation to the movement of persons, there are no common immigration rules but rather a restrictive entry control system. See Virginie Guiraudon, 'European Integration and Migration Policy: Vertical Policy-Making as Venue Shopping' (2000) 38 *Journal of Common Market Studies* 251–71; Didier Bigo, 'Border Regimes, Police Cooperation and Security in an Enlarged European Union', in Jan Zielonka (ed.), *Europe Unbound: Enlarging and Reshaping the Boundaries of the European Union* (London and New York: Routledge, 2002).

[41] Jean-Yves Carlier, *Droit d'asile et des réfugiés: de la protection aux droits* (Leiden and Boston: Martinus Nijhoff, 2008), pp. 52–3.

1   The logic of external border control

The abolition of checks at intra-EU borders is compensated by three levels of control around, or beyond, the external frontier.

At the first level, a special responsibility to control immigration (in other words, to block entry into the EU) is vested in the States that flank the external borders of the EU. The Dublin Regulation makes it possible for a Member State to transfer an asylum seeker – and the responsibility for processing her application – to the Member State which the asylum seeker first entered, or to another Member State if the asylum seeker has family members lawfully staying there. This latter point represents a significant protection advance over the predecessor Dublin Convention, which had been much criticized for being insensitive to the well-being of the individuals concerned, let alone to their wishes.[42] However, all other criteria for transfer remain 'strongly grounded in the so-called "authorisation principle", according to which the State responsible for examining the application is the one responsible for [the asylum seeker's] presence in the common territory, be it through legal author-isation or unnoticed entry or stay'.[43] In practice, the vast majority of Dublin transfers are based on the rather artificial 'objective link' of unauthorized entry or stay, and transfers are mainly to one of the States 'guarding' the external border of the EU on its southern or eastern front. Here we can plainly see the legacy of the pre-Dublin Regulation agreements. According to Guild, the determination of refugee status by the Member State through whose territory the individual first entered the EU has always 'fitted into an internal market logic which was operating strongly with the full support of the Member States'.[44] Her analysis of the 1990 Schengen Implementation and Dublin Conventions largely rings true to this day:

> [R]esponsibility for determining asylum applications and responsibility for the body that goes with the application is treated . . . as a burden and a punishment for the Member State which permitted the individual to arrive in the Union.[45]

At the second level, responsibility is shifted to countries on the other side of the external border. The Dublin Regulation, like its predecessor, suggests that wherever possible, 'the asylum seeker should be allocated

---

[42] See Hurwitz, *Collective Responsibility*, pp. 89–125.
[43] Moreno-Lax, 'Dismantling the Dublin System', 4.
[44] Guild, 'Europeanisation of Europe's Asylum Policy', 635.   [45] *Ibid.*, 637.

to a country outside the Union'.[46] Article 3(3) specifies that any Member State shall retain the right, pursuant to its national law, to send an asylum applicant to a third State 'in compliance with the provisions of the Geneva Convention'. In other words, the Dublin system is not closed, and if it allegedly 'resolves "orbit" situations within the European Union, Member States may still contribute to such situations in the rest of the world'.[47]

Within the CEAS, the Dublin Regulation must be read in conjunction with the Procedures Directive which codifies a dubious and long-standing practice in Europe, namely the 'safe third country' mechanism.[48] Technically, and from the narrow viewpoint of a Member State, the proclaimed 'safety' of a third country functions as a rule of inadmissibility within – and indeed at the very outset of – an asylum procedure.[49] From the vantage point of the international refugee regime, however, it is wholly inappropriate for the EU to deal with (the possibility of) transferring an asylum seeker to a third State as though this were merely a technical or procedural matter. A system of responsibility allocation *à la* Dublin, open to the outside world through a 'safe third country' window, is an extremely poor model of international cooperation. It is bad enough that it operates inside the EU on the basis of one set of criteria, and on the basis of different criteria in its 'third country' dimension. But it is even worse that the latter criteria have not been agreed, or even negotiated, with the third countries potentially affected, the determination of safety being entirely unilateral. The EU should be honest enough to situate this discussion where it belongs, namely in a fair dialogue with third countries, in particular those that share with EU Member States a commitment to protect refugees as defined by, and according to the standards of, the 1951 Convention.

At the third level, it can be seen that over time, the 'safe third country' mechanism has lost much of its exclusionary power. Non-EU Member States have become braver in resisting transfers of asylum seekers, or have resisted EU efforts to make them 'safe' (through their enhanced protection capacity, for example), or are simply considered to be

---

[46] Noll, *Negotiating Asylum*, p. 193.   [47] Hurwitz, *Collective Responsibility*, p. 93.

[48] Procedures Directive, art. 27. See Cathryn Costello, 'The Asylum Procedures Directive and the Proliferation of Safe Third Countries Practices: Deterrence, Deflection and the Dismantling of International Protection?' (2005) 7 *European Journal of Migration and Law* 35–69.

[49] For a comprehensive analysis, see Hurwitz, *Collective Responsibility* and references therein.

unworthy of such efforts. At the same time, the Dublin system of 'internal' control is marred by a host of technical and political problems, and the axiomatic trust upon which it was built is being slowly but surely eroded (a point that is examined briefly in the next section). When those levels of control become untrustworthy, the logic of 'protection elsewhere' suggests the creation of filters (controlled by the EU) further afield, effectively pushing the external borders ever closer to the countries of origin of uninvited migrants. In other words, it 'takes us to the next step on the road to extraterritorial processing of asylum applications'.[50] Other chapters in this volume document the very special appeal which EU visions of extraterritorial processing exert on industrialized States in other parts of the world.[51]

2   The logic of internal control

Although this is not the preferred option of Member States, some third-country nationals do enter EU territory uninvited and seek asylum there. Many – although these days not the majority – succeed in their asylum applications and are formally recognized as refugees. How these categories of persons of concern to the international community – asylum seekers and refugees – fit within or fall outside the free movement equation is arguably the litmus test of EU law's compatibility with the universal refugee regime. The previous section showed how the movement of asylum seekers is restricted and governed by an allocation system based on 'objective' criteria that leave precious little room for what UNHCR's Executive Committee wisely called their 'special situation'.[52] But what about recognized refugees?

A strange asymmetry affects the mutual recognition of asylum decisions within the EU: 'if one Member State considers the asylum application of an individual and rejects it, that rejection is valid for all the Member States (notwithstanding that the recognition of refugee status remained and remains nationally limited)'.[53]

---

[50] Guild, 'Europeanisation of Europe's Asylum Policy', 636. See also Madeline Garlick, 'The EU Discussions on Extraterritorial Processing: Solution or Conundrum?' (2006) 18 *International Journal of Refugee Law* 601–29; Lavenex and Uçarer, *Migration and the Externalities*, p. 19 on the 'expansive notion of the external border' of the EU.

[51] See also McAdam, Chapter 2 and Macklin, Chapter 4 of this volume.

[52] UNHCR Executive Committee, Conclusion No. 15, para. (h)(vi).

[53] Guild, 'Europeanisation of Europe's Asylum Policy', 636.

Once recognized in one Member State, the refugee is supposed to stay
there. Her refugee status is respected by all other Member States, but it is
devoid of EU-wide effect since it does not entail a right to free movement
or establishment beyond that first country.[54] This disconnect is deeply
revealing of the way that EU law and policy has kept the refugee away,
not only from the asylum equation, but more fundamentally from the
integration project itself. When the EU was conceived as a space without
internal borders, refugees lawfully residing there were simply not
regarded as being among those 'persons' whose free movement should
be ensured by the EU treaties. Guild's denunciation of this 'original sin'
(a sin of omission, at the very least) deserves to be quoted in full:

> [T]he failure to integrate refugees into the project has led directly to the
> current hostility of the EU towards refugee protection ... By leaving this
> part of the population out of the free movement equation, the EU became
> hostage to its own failure towards refugees as these became the people on
> the basis of whom the creation of substantial coercive flanking measures
> to compensate for the loss of control at the intra-Member-State borders
> was based.[55]

It is sadly telling that, after affirming the principle of free movement of
persons in the Single European Act, it took the EU a full twenty-five years to
afford refugees the right to move and establish themselves freely within the
EU (after satisfying the condition of five years' lawful residence in a Member
State). It is doubly remarkable that this benefit should be granted on a
par with other long-staying third-country nationals, rather than as something incidental to their status as refugees.[56] Far from being a component of
the EU *demos*, refugees have been treated as third-class residents ever since
the inception of the integration project, less worthy of inclusion than other
third-country nationals legally residing in the EU.

One may debate whether or to what extent such exclusion is a necessary
condition, and/or an inevitable by-product, of regional integration. After all,

---

[54] Note, however, that it remains an ambition of the CEAS in its ongoing second phase to
establish a refugee status that is valid throughout the EU.
[55] Guild, 'Europeanisation of Europe's Asylum Policy', 634.
[56] On 11 May 2011, the European Parliament and the Council of the EU adopted an
extension of the EU rules on long-term residents by amending Directive 2003/109/EC,
whereby refugees and beneficiaries of subsidiary protection will be able to acquire long-
term resident status on a similar basis as other third-country nationals legally living in
the EU for more than five years: Directive 2011/51/EU of the European Parliament and
of the Council of 11 May 2011 amending Council Directive 2011/51/EU to extend its
scope to beneficiaries of international protection (OJ 2011 No. 132/1).

an integrationist environment such as that of the EU project contains the germs of exclusion, since, in the words of Mouffe, 'the very process of constituting the "people"' necessarily implies 'a moment of closure'. She adds that '[t]his cannot be avoided, even in a liberal democratic model; it can only be negotiated differently. But this can only be done if this closure and the paradox that it implies are acknowledged'.[57]

One cannot help but think that as far as refugees in the EU are concerned, the closure in question could have been negotiated differently, and that the paradox it implies is still to be openly acknowledged.

3 Summary

Can we distinguish the refugee in the EU landscape? This section does not seem to have produced a positive answer to this question. If anything, the 'free movement' lens has had the effect of further blurring the image of the refugee. Be that out of hostility or neglect, the migration narrative of EU integration posits the asylum seeker as an alien and an intruder, and asylum as a guarded narrow gate that is designed to be more forbidding than inviting. As for the refugee, who is after all the person of concern to the universal refugee regime, she is simply 'not there' – absent from the original *demos* of the EU, and admitted with suspicion (and restrictions) once recognized.

Although there is not space in this chapter to dwell on this point, it is worth noting that the refugee is also absent from the catalogue of those legal migrants whom the EU needs and welcomes. Despite the efforts of UNHCR, it has not been possible so far to obtain a mandatory commitment to an EU-wide programme of refugee resettlement (namely, admission through selection from third countries), and the annual resettlement quotas set by individual Member States, where they exist, remain alarmingly low.[58] Stressing the need to reshape the CEAS as an integral part of a holistic

---

[57] Chantal Mouffe, 'Carl Schmitt and the Paradox of Liberal Democracy', in David Dyzenhaus (ed.), *Law as Politics: Carl Schmitt's Critique of Liberalism* (Durham, NC: Duke University Press, 1998), p. 164. On the same topic, see Noll and Vedsted-Hansen, 'Non-Communitarians', p. 361.

[58] On 29 March 2012, the EU adopted a joint resettlement programme, participation in which is voluntary. The joint programme will provide EU Member States with additional funding for the reception and integration of resettled refugees in local communities, in particular in those countries that are considering developing resettlement programmes. Twelve Member States currently run resettlement programmes, together contributing to less than 8 per cent of the annual resettlement places on offer around the world.

approach to migration, Chetail and Bauloz observe that a 'major systemic flaw in the current system ... stems from the EU's one-sided attitude towards migration which has created an inextricable bias both as regards its relationship with third countries and its disproportionate focus on irregular migration'.[59] The EU would certainly have adopted a radically different and more positive approach to refugees and asylum seekers had it been conceived of as a region of immigration, and asylum as a mechanism for admission rather than border control. Such an admission perspective is noticeable, for example, in the deliberations leading to the adoption of the 1980 Refugee Act in the United States,[60] which stressed that an asylum application had to be treated as a proactive *démarche*, rather than as a defence to deportation.[61]

D   Enter human rights

If the logic of control trumps the humanitarian imperative that under-pins the international legal regime for refugees, could the latter reassert its authority through recourse to another set of principles rooted in human rights law? This is the hypothesis examined in this section. In the process, a new, rather insidious threat to the specificity of the international regime will come to light.

While human rights per se were not part of the EU's original scheme, the fact that all Member States are also members of the Council of Europe, and hence bound by the provisions of the European Convention on Human Rights (ECHR),[62] is relevant to the understanding and development of EU law, including the CEAS. The construction of EU law is grounded in a specific European human rights terrain, and EU law will inevitably be influenced by the ECHR, even though the two legal orders are separate. According to article 6 Treaty on European Union: 'Fundamental rights, as guaranteed by the European Convention

---

[59] Vincent Chetail and Céline Bauloz, *The European Union and the Challenges of Forced Migration: From Economic Crisis to Protection Crisis?* (EU–US Immigration Systems 2011/07, Robert Schuman Centre for Advanced Studies, San Domenico di Fiesole: European University Institute 2011), p. 32.

[60] See Edward M. Kennedy, 'Refugee Act of 1980' (1981) 15 *International Migration Review* 141–56.

[61] Deborah Anker and Michael Posner, 'The Forty Year Crisis: A Legislative History of the Refugee Act of 1980' (1981) 19 *San Diego Law Review* 9–90, at 46 (n. 177) (testimony of A. Whitney Ellsworth and Hurst Hannum, Amnesty International).

[62] Convention for the Protection of Human Rights and Fundamental Freedoms, Rome, 4 November 1950, in force 3 September 1953 (213 UNTS 221).

for the Protection of Human Rights and Fundamental Freedoms and as they result from the constitutional traditions common to Member States, shall constitute general principles of the Union's law.'[63]

Since the European Council of Tampere in 1999, this common legal heritage has been affirmed as an important foundation of the CEAS, alongside the 1951 Refugee Convention and its 1967 Protocol.[64] For the purposes of this chapter, it is sufficient to highlight its influence on two aspects of EU asylum law, namely: the presumption underpinning mutual trust, discussed in Part B above; and the harmonization of criteria for subsidiary protection, which was a significant achievement of the 2004 Qualification Directive.

1   The limits of trust

Membership in the ECHR-based regime serves to legitimize, but also to circumscribe, mutual trust and its application to components of the CEAS, in particular the exclusion of EU nationals from the ambit of EU asylum law and the Dublin system of responsibility allocation.

With respect to the first of these, the exclusion of EU nationals from EU asylum law is based on the assumption that 'the level of protection of fundamental rights and freedoms [provided] by the Member States' makes refugee protection unnecessary – indeed, unthinkable – for their nationals.[65] According to the Protocol on Asylum for Nationals of Member States of the EU, an asylum claim by an EU national may be heard if a Member State derogates from its obligations under the ECHR. Fortunately, such exceptional circumstances have not arisen since the Protocol was adopted. Noll and Landgren's argument that the Protocol directly conflicts with the ECHR because it discriminates against EU nationals in the exercise of a fundamental right remains to be tested in a court.[66]

---

[63] TEU, art. 6(3).

[64] *Ibid.*, art. 78(1): 'The Union shall develop a common policy on asylum, subsidiary protection and temporary protection with a view to offering appropriate status to any third-country national requiring international protection and ensuring compliance with the principle of *non-refoulement*. This policy must be in accordance with the Geneva Convention of 28 July 1951 and the Protocol of 31 January 1967 relating to the status of refugees, and *other relevant treaties*' (emphasis added). See also the rulings of the CJEU discussed in Lambert, Chapter 1 of this volume.

[65] Preamble to Aznar Protocol.

[66] Noll, *Negotiating Asylum*, pp. 536–57; Landgren, 'Deflecting International Protection by Treaty', pp. 17–18.

With respect to the Dublin system of responsibility allocation, Member States' commitment to ECHR standards is relied upon to justify the regime, both in its mutual recognition dimension and in its pro-claimed harmlessness to asylum seekers. However, this human rights underpinning is increasingly assuming the role of a protective fence against an abusive reliance on inter-State trust. The assumption of safety underlying the Dublin system has been found to lead to breaches of both the ECHR[67] and the EU Charter of Fundamental Rights.[68] Though the line between rights-based trust and rights-based suspicion is not yet entirely clear, these judgments usefully signal that '[n]either the uneven distribution of migration burdens, nor a minimalistic reading of the Dublin Regulation absolves Member States of their human rights responsibilities'.[69]

This is an important clarification which could have been articulated much earlier had it not been for the obstinate belief of a few Member States – and not those on the EU's external border – in the deterrent effect of an otherwise rather dysfunctional system. The *MSS* and *NS* decisions of the European Court of Human Rights and the CJEU, respectively, are particularly significant in their affirmation of both the overriding character of the principle of *non-refoulement*, and Member States' duty to pay attention to the specific vulnerabilities of asylum seekers. Whether these human rights duties exhaust States' obligations under the Refugee Convention is another matter altogether, of which the judges in the cases above were not seized, but which forms the texture of the following discussion.

2   Human rights-based protection

Up until now, this chapter has made scant reference to the Qualification Directive, even though it is, undoubtedly, the CEAS instrument that relates most closely to the Refugee Convention. Not only does this Directive contain, like the Convention itself, criteria to define refugees and minimum standards for their treatment, but it also explicitly acknowledges the Convention as the instrument of reference. It does

---

[67] *MSS* v. *Belgium and Greece* (European Court of Human Rights, Grand Chamber, App. No. 30696/09, 21 January 2011).

[68] Joined Cases C-411/10 and C-493/10, *NS* v. *Secretary of State for the Home Department and ME, ASM, MT, KP and EH* v. *Refugee Applications Commissioner, Minister for Justice, Equality and Law Reform* (CJEU, Grand Chamber, 21 December 2011).

[69] Moreno-Lax, 'Dismantling the Dublin System', 28–9.

not seek to replace the Convention, but rather interprets it for the sake of a harmonized application within the EU.[70] Furthermore, the Qualification Directive affirms the primacy of Convention refugee status over other forms of 'international protection', which it also describes and regulates. Through this instrument, the refugee seems to have re-entered the CEAS with great pomp to occupy central stage. There is, however, more than one twist in this plot.

EU asylum law is genuinely innovative and exemplary in that, without expanding the definition of a refugee, its concepts of 'asylum' (the 'A' in CEAS) and 'international protection' (in the Qualification Directive) cover more than Convention refugees. The reference to persons other than refugees being in need of international protection (and benefiting from 'measures on asylum') is the first of its kind in any legal instrument binding more than one State. It is testimony to the impressive penetration of human rights law, in particular the ECHR, into the European asylum discourse. Its legal manifestation within the CEAS is a novel 'subsidiary protection status' which consolidates and (where necessary) clarifies the previous practice of Member States – albeit, for the time being, at a minimum standard level. It also codifies the jurisprudence of the European Court of Human Rights on article 3 ECHR – possibly in an attempt to freeze it. Subsidiary protection under article 15(b) of the Directive is directly inspired by article 3 ECHR, and it is clear from the legislative history that it must be read in the light of the relevant Strasbourg case law.[71] The CJEU in *Elgafaji* described article 15(b) as corresponding 'in essence, to Article 3 of the ECHR'.[72]

It is worth recalling, however, that the ECHR does not actually deal with asylum, if that concept is construed to mean the sum total of protection afforded by a State to refugees on its territory or under its jurisdiction. The so-called asylum provisions of the ECHR, like those of other human rights treaties,[73] were not drafted with the plight of refugees

---

[70] Hugo Storey, 'EU Refugee Qualification Directive: A Brave New World?' (2008) 20 *International Journal of Refugee Law* 1–49, at 16.

[71] See, e.g., Nuala Mole, *Asylum and the European Convention on Human Rights* (4th edn, Strasbourg: Council of Europe Publishing, 2007); Goodwin-Gill and McAdam, *Refugee in International Law*, pp. 310–30.

[72] Case C-465/07, *Elgafaji* v. *Staatssecretaris van Justitie* (CJEU, Grand Chamber, 17 February 2009), para. 28.

[73] See especially the United Nations Convention against Torture and Other Cruel, Inhuman or Degrading Treatment, New York, 10 December 1984, in force 26 June 1987 (1465 UNTS 85), and the International Covenant on Civil and Political Rights, New York, adopted 16 December 1966, in force 23 March 1976 (999 UNTS 171). See also Kees Wouters,

in mind. Rather, it is through a human rights 'supplementation' of the *non-refoulement* principle expressed in article 33(1) Refugee Convention that the ECHR has contributed to the development of 'asylum law'.[74] This is no small contribution, obviously, given that the principle of *non-refoulement* is routinely and aptly presented as the cornerstone of the international refugee protection regime. In the art of legal construction, however, it may be dangerous to mistake a cornerstone for a foundation – a point discussed further below.

In several of its 'asylum' decisions, starting with *Soering* in 1989,[75] the European Court of Human Rights has taken notice of other international instruments of potential application to *non-refoulement* cases, including the Refugee Convention. In keeping with its specific mandate, it has ruled that the application of the ECHR is not excluded by the existence of these other treaties. Impeccable as this finding may be, it prompts an important question: *how supplementary* is the protection afforded by article 3 ECHR, over and above that afforded to refugees by the Refugee Convention? With the adoption of the Qualification Directive, this question has landed in the domain of EU law. There is real potential for the Directive – and, most importantly, its implementation by Member States – to answer it in a way that is both logical and respectful of refugee status. However, one should not underestimate the attendant risk that subsidiary protection may aggravate the phenomenon of the 'vanishing refugee'. The following subsections examine the opportunity and the risk entailed by the importation of ECHR-based protection into the CEAS.

(a)   Subsidiary protection: the opportunity

As noted above, the Qualification Directive uses the term 'subsidiary protection'. In so far as it can be traced to the protection offered by article 3 ECHR, however, subsidiary protection under EU law is both *complementary* and *subsidiary* to Convention refugee status. Indeed, there can be no doubt that article 3, as interpreted by the European Court of Human Rights, can protect from *refoulement* individuals who are not Convention refugees. In this sense it offers a true *complement* to refugee

---

International Legal Standards for the Protection from Refoulement (Antwerp: Intersentia, 2009).

[74] For a comprehensive discussion, see Jane McAdam, *Complementary Protection in International Refugee Law* (Oxford: Oxford University Press, 2007).

[75] *Soering* v. *United Kingdom* (1989) 11 EHRR 439.

protection.[76] In view of its absolute character,[77] article 3 also provides a 'safety net' for individuals who fall within one of the exclusion clauses in article 1 Refugee Convention, as well as for those to whom the exception in article 33(2) applies. This may be seen as genuinely *subsidiary* protection. Neither modality seems to threaten the integrity or specificity of the Refugee Convention regime. Furthermore, the Directive provides one important mechanism to make the Convention's primacy work in practice: the definitional criterion, according to which a 'person eligible for subsidiary protection' is a person who 'does not qualify as a refugee,'[78] in effect requires a sequencing of assessments, namely that eligibility is assessed against the refugee criteria before any grounds for subsidiary protection are considered.[79] Finally, by eliminating most of the pre-existing disparities between the content of refugee status and subsidiary protection status, the recast 2011 version of the Qualification Directive removes an important incentive for States to grant the latter in lieu of the former.[80] Prior to this welcome amendment, Member States may have been more easily tempted to skip a full assessment of the claim against the Refugee Convention criteria. It can be argued, therefore, that the definitions and procedures stipulated by the CEAS, if properly applied, not only help but in fact compel decision makers to interrogate the specificity of refugee protection more so than in the past.

(b) Subsidiary protection: the risk

Old legal habits die hard, however.[81] And, regrettably, the history of human rights-based protection in Europe, prior to its formal incorporation in the

---

[76] One may think of cases in which 'inhuman or degrading treatment' does not meet the severity threshold of 'persecution', and/or in which a nexus cannot be established between the feared treatment and the ethnic, political, religious or other affiliation of the claimant.

[77] Unlike the Refugee Convention, which excludes certain persons from protection (see art. 1F), art. 3 ECHR is absolute, and the European Court of Human Rights has consistently affirmed that it cannot be balanced against the public interest or any other matter, irrespective of the applicant's criminal or personal conduct. See, e.g., *Chahal v. United Kingdom* (1996) 23 EHRR 413; *Saadi v. United Kingdom* (2007) 44 EHRR 50.

[78] Qualification Directive, art. 2(f).

[79] See also Procedures Directive: '"application" or "application for asylum" means an application made by a third country national or stateless person which can be understood as a request for international protection from a Member State under the Geneva Convention. Any application for international protection is presumed to be an application for asylum, unless the person concerned explicitly requests another kind of protection that can be applied for separately' (art. 2(b)).

[80] Recast 2011 Qualification Directive, Ch. VII.

[81] Storey, 'EU Refugee Qualification Directive', 45.

CEAS, does not bear out the neat delineation of concepts which the language of the Directive suggests. Instead, it reveals a worrying trend of using the *non-refoulement* potential of article 3 ECHR not as subsidiary or complementary to, but rather as a substitute for, refugee status. For over two decades, so-called 'asylum' cases have been litigated in the European Court of Human Rights, and adjudicated on ECHR grounds by domestic courts in proceedings that often amount to de facto appeals against denials of Convention refugee claims. They are de facto, indeed, since judicial decisions of this type are made without reference, let alone deference, to Convention refugee criteria. On the occasion of a colloquium hosted by the Council of Europe in 2000, UNHCR's Director of International Protection voiced serious concerns in this respect:

> As an individual remedy, the European Court's interpretation of Article 3, together with its useful procedure for injunctive interim relief, will ensure that a 'safety net' exists for those cases that slip, for whatever reason, through a national asylum system ... However, from UNHCR's perspective, the frequency of recourse to Strasbourg may also have a downside. Although Article 3 can be helpful in individual cases, it has to be of concern where resort to it is symptomatic of a more deep-rooted but unaddressed problem in national asylum systems in the region. It would be worrying if states were tempted to use Article 3 more frequently so as to avoid their broader obligations to genuine refugees under the Refugee Convention.[82]

Helpful as it may be in the individual case, recourse to ECHR protection is an incomplete, and at any rate inappropriate, remedy against the deficiencies of refugee status determination. Unless these deficiencies are tackled within the parameters of the Refugee Convention, rather than in its margins, the risk identified by Gilbert cannot be ruled out:

> [B]ecause the Member States of the European Union can always rely on the ECHR as the ultimate safety net, their attempts at watering down the level of obligation under the universal 1951 Convention will be applied outside the Council of Europe in states that do not have that same safety net.[83]

---

[82] Erika Feller, 'Opening Statement', in Council of Europe, *Second Colloquy on the European Convention on Human Rights and the Protection of Refugees, Asylum-Seekers and Displaced Persons: Proceedings* (Strasbourg: Council of Europe, 2000).

[83] Geoff Gilbert, 'Is Europe Living Up to Its Obligations to Refugees?' (2004) 15 *European Journal of International Law* 963–87, at 987. See also Richard Plender and Nuala Mole, 'Beyond the Geneva Convention: Constructing a *De Facto* Right of Asylum from International Human Rights Instruments', in Frances Nicholson and Patrick Twomey (eds.), *Refugee Rights and Realities: Evolving International Concepts and Regimes* (Cambridge: Cambridge University Press, 1999); Brian Gorlick, 'Human Rights and

It is true that the *non-refoulement* provisions of the ECHR – and now also subsidiary protection under the CEAS – may offer a safety net to refugees by preventing their forcible return to persecution. They do not, however, remedy the basic flaw of an erroneous determination of refugee status unless – and here comes the dangerous slippage – non-return is regarded as the only protection that matters in refugee status. The danger that such an approach would represent for the refugee concept is self-evident: robust protection against forcible return, such as that provided by the European human rights regime, would make refugee status redundant.

In a rather ironic twist, the human rights background of EU legislation on subsidiary protection makes it easy, conceptually, to reduce the benefits of the Refugee Convention to *non-refoulement*. The prohibitions on inhuman or degrading treatment and discrimination may suffice to guarantee to all lawful residents, including refugees, all the other rights and benefits which the Refugee Convention stipulates for recognized refugees. When McAdam argues that persons eligible for complementary or subsidiary protection should, upon recognition, benefit from the same treatment as Convention refugees, she is definitely right. It is a different matter altogether, however, to argue, as she does, that the Convention dictates standards of treatment, not only for refugees, but indeed for all persons legally protected against *refoulement*, regardless of the source of such protection.[84] Such an argument obscures the specificity of refugee protection which does not lie in a particular set of rights, but in a *specific rationale* for the granting of such rights.

Two points should be highlighted about this rationale. First, what distinguishes refugee protection from any other form of protection is the discriminatory element which is inherent in the Refugee Convention's concept of persecution.[85] The reference to 'race, religion, nationality,

---

Refugees: Enhancing Protection through International Human Rights Law' (UNHCR, *New Issues in Refugee Research*, Working Paper No. 30, October 2000).

[84] McAdam, *Complementary Protection*, pp. 210–11.

[85] Although refugee law and international criminal law obviously pursue different objectives, it is not irrelevant that the crime of persecution, as defined by the Statutes of the International Tribunals for the Former Yugoslavia and for Rwanda, encompasses an act which denies fundamental human rights coupled with a discriminatory intent. '[T]he distinctive feature of a persecution as a crime against humanity lies in ... the intent of the perpetrator to discriminate on one of the [stipulated] grounds': see Guido Acquaviva, 'Forced Displacement and International Crimes' (UNHCR, Legal and Protection Policy Research Series, PPLA/2011/05, June 2011), p. 16. The Rome Statute of the International Criminal Court, 17 July 1998, in force 1 July 2002 (2187 UNTS 90), art. 7(1)(h) provides that '[p]ersecution against any identifiable group or collectivity on

membership of a particular social group, or political opinion' is not there in order to place an additional burden of proof on the asylum seeker, but rather in order to clarify what characteristics justify the status of refugees as 'privileged aliens' in our midst. As noted by Goodwin-Gill and McAdam, such 'characteristics of individuals and groups which are considered worthy of special protection . . . have figured in the development of the fundamental principle of non-discrimination in general international law, and have contributed to the formulation of other fundamental human rights'.[86] That *non-refoulement* obligations also arise in other contexts, and for the protection of equally worthy interests, should not make us lose sight of this specificity of refugee protection.

Second, if at any point in history a refugee definition is vested with a universal vocation – which is clearly the case for article 1A Refugee Convention – this definition necessarily represents the international consensus over a *positive* and collective commitment to protect specific categories of persons, and to resolve the problems caused by their exodus and exile. This positive inclination, which, significantly, extends to solutions as well as protection, sets refugees (however defined at a particular moment) apart from those other persons who also, subsidiarily, need protection against forcible return to personal or collective danger. In short, the refugee definition is not intended to describe those aliens whom we cannot deport – that is, negatively – but rather 'positively' to describe those aliens whom we want to protect.

McAdam's assertion that 'since the scope of *non-refoulement* has been broadened by subsequent human rights instruments, this necessarily widens the Convention's application'[87] would be valid only if one would regard the Refugee Convention as based on the *non-refoulement* principle alone. This would actually amount to mistaking the cornerstone (that is, the piece that holds the edifice together) with the foundation (which supports the edifice). The founding rationale of the Convention is a positive duty to protect refugees on safe territories, albeit that the sharing of responsibilities in this regard is itself not adequately regulated. The beneficiary class of the Refugee Convention

---

political, racial, national, ethnic, cultural, religious, gender as defined in paragraph 3, or other grounds that are universally recognized as impermissible under international law, in connection with any act referred to in this paragraph or any crime within the jurisdiction of the Court' is a 'crime against humanity'. It defines 'persecution' as 'the international and severe deprivation of fundamental rights contrary to international law by reason of the identity of the group or collectivity' (art. 7(2)(g)).

[86] Goodwin-Gill and McAdam, *Refugee in International Law*, pp. 92–3.

[87] McAdam, *Complementary Protection*, p. 209.

'is not ... defined by the duty of *non-refoulement*'.[88] Of course, the protection they are owed *includes* protection against forcible return to danger, which is what article 33 provides. This is why article 33 Refugee Convention – which prohibits the *refoulement* of refugees – appears where it does, and not as the first or second provision of the treaty.

Matters of treaty interpretation aside, this conceptual/teleological distinction between refugee status and a status based on *non-refoulement* must be preserved for another reason: it matters for the survival of the international refugee regime. For how does one build a regime of international cooperation upon a negative obligation? The basic commitment at the heart of the international regime – namely, that for each refugee there will be a State willing and able to offer asylum – is both hugely ambitious and worryingly diffuse, but it is what it is. Despite its limitations, it is an acceptable proposition and a proper positive basis for international cooperation and solidarity. It is impossible to express this obligation in the negative without losing these critical dimensions of the regime. Even if it could be 'universalized', '*non-refoulement* law' would not justify, much less sustain, a regime of international cooperation.

(c) Summary

There is no questioning the potential of human rights law to supplement the protection offered by the Refugee Convention. People who are not Convention refugees must also be protected against return to conditions that threaten their lives, physical integrity, liberty or dignity. Once identified and allowed to remain, they must be treated as lawful residents with all the rights, benefits and duties which this condition implies. On the other hand, the subsidiarity of subsidiary protection should not be put into question. Subsidiary protection is not a remedy against erroneous decisions on refugee status, nor is it an appropriate substitute for refugee protection where the latter is warranted. It is not easy to articulate a legal, political or ethical justification for a 'refugee privilege', and to do so is clearly beyond the remit of this chapter.[89] However, such an

---

[88] James C. Hathaway, 'Leveraging Asylum' (2010) 45 *Texas International Law Journal* 503–36, at 530.

[89] McAdam asserts that it is both historically inaccurate and legally flawed to 'invoke the Convention refugee definition as intrinsically and exclusively legitimate in giving rise to a privileged alien status' (*Complementary Protection*, p. 198). One may agree that there is nothing forever exclusive about it. Although unlikely, EU States might at some point

articulation is essential to the universal regime, and the question of refugee specificity must be answered *somehow*. It would be sad, and possibly devastating, should EU law inadvertently contribute to concealing this essential question behind the screen of an otherwise positive human rights approach.

Despite the guarantees surrounding the 'primacy' of Convention refugee status, which we have outlined above, there is a residual risk that the specificity of refugee protection may be lost on Member States as they implement the Qualification Directive. Indeed, to prioritize the refugee definition in the assessment of international protection claims under the Directive may not come naturally to EU Member States' officials and judges, who face two types of obstacles. First, there is a matter of legal construction. Article 15(b), which defines serious harm as 'torture or inhuman or degrading treatment or punishment of an applicant in the country of origin', could be interpreted as all-encompassing, namely as realizing a synthesis of grounds imported from both the Refugee Convention and the ECHR. Indeed, most forms of persecution can be subsumed under the notion of 'inhuman or degrading treatment or punishment', with the added advantage that the latter notion does not require the type of nexus (with a reason or ground for ill-treatment) as found in the refugee definition. As a result, the asylum officer or judge may be tempted to simply forego the niceties of the Refugee Convention definition, resulting in a negative decision on refugee status and the grant of subsidiary protection instead.

The second obstacle is not to be found in either the letter or the architecture of the Qualification Directive. Rather, it is hidden in its human rights subtext, which predates the emergence of the CEAS. To date, EU Member States have tended to attach greater importance to their *non-refoulement* obligations stemming from the ECHR than to a 'full and inclusive application' of the 1951 Refugee Convention. One explanation for this may be that the ECHR expresses values that are central to European identity, and that the European Court of Human Rights articulates the legal lingua franca of European nations more clearly than any instrument of universal scope. However true this may be, a more straightforward explanation can be found in the asymmetrical enforcement mechanisms of the two treaties. Whereas European States are genuinely wary of being found in

adopt a broader, or a different, refugee definition. On the other hand, this author contends that the Convention definition, as it stands today, intrinsically represents a deliberate intention to grant specific categories of aliens a privileged status, including over other people who cannot be deported.

breach of their ECHR obligations by the binding decision of a supranational court, they know that no such outcome is likely to result from an erroneous interpretation or restrictive application of the Refugee Convention. It seems natural that States should fight legal battles more energetically wherever the stakes are higher. Is this about to change? While no progress has been made towards an authoritative judicial interpretation of the Refugee Convention, it is significant that the CJEU has started issuing preliminary rulings on the interpretation of Qualification Directive provisions (as noted in Chapter 1 of this book). In doing so, the court can hardly avoid referring to concepts and phrases directly imported from the Refugee Convention, or taking notice of such things as UNHCR's views on its interpretation. It remains to be seen whether, and in what terms, the CJEU will dare to cross the systemic lines and admit that its reading of the Qualification Directive – including, should the question arise, the rationale for the primacy of refugee status – is not just a matter of EU law, but indeed a matter of international refugee law to be interpreted with the interests of the Contracting States to the Refugee Convention in mind.

In the final analysis, what is required is a tripartite conversation between EU asylum law, as authoritatively interpreted by the CJEU, and its two international law sources of 'international protection', namely the Refugee Convention, on the one hand, and the ECHR, on the other. It seems, for example, that only the European Court of Human Rights has sufficient strength to confront the risk of *non-refoulement*-based protection becoming a substitute for refugee status. Who, if not the Strasbourg Court itself, can expose the absurdity of trying to address what are essentially refugee definition matters in the ECHR forum? It is problematic that, in applying article 3 ECHR in expulsion cases, the court does not consider itself authorized to scrutinize whether the State concerned has properly applied the 1951 Convention refugee definition to the applicant. As a result, even a ruling by the European Court of Human Rights that demolishes the State's arguments against the original refugee claim will not entail a 'righting of the wrong' – that is, a grant of refugee status.[90] Such inconclusiveness can only add to the conceptual confusion and raise yet another smoke screen behind which the refugee is allowed – if not encouraged – to quietly vanish.

---

[90] Nonetheless, when observing that the risk assessment conducted by the State authorities was deficient, the court may on occasion refer to the asylum procedure, implicitly recognizing a principle of convergence between an assessment of refugee status and an assessment of a risk of violation of art. 3 ECHR: see, e.g., *MSS* v. *Belgium and Greece*, paras. 358–9.

E   Conclusion

It would be dishonest to deny that the EU harmonization process has enhanced refugee protection in Europe in several important respects.[91] It has also been increasingly possible to discuss asylum in the EU as a relatively autonomous subject area, rather than just a sideshow of migration control.[92] This positive development is largely attributable to the activism of the EU institutions, namely the Commission, the Parliament and now – in a nascent but promising form – the CJEU. One may wonder whether Member States would have dealt with their 'asylum problems' in an even more defensive way had it not been for the pressure of vertical integration.

At the same time, the very premises of the EU integration project constrain the laudable human rights impetus which the Tampere Council gave to the CEAS and risk taking the CEAS construction away from the universal regime of refugee protection. This chapter has shown how the premise of mutual trust, applied within an internal market logic, distorts the figure of the refugee as a person of concern to the international community. Of gravest concern, perhaps, is the alienation of refugees from the *demos* of the EU, which ignores the fact that refugees have much to say about the values that the EU claims as an essential part of its identity. Where those values are allowed to influence the development of EU asylum law through human rights-based protection, we find that the remedy may well be a double-edged sword. Unless the Qualification Directive is applied with great care, namely with attention to the specificity of refugee protection, the *non-refoulement* obligations corresponding to non-derogable rights under the ECHR risk displacing the positive inclination to protect, which is the *raison d'être* of the international refugee regime. In sum, essential questions of identity, inclusion and solidarity, which lie at the heart of the universal regime, are being obscured, rather than clarified, by the construction of the CEAS.

---

[91] See Lambert, Chapter 1 of this volume.

[92] Cf. Guiraudon, who argued that since the primary concern of Member States' law and order officials was to circumvent domestic constraints on migration control, they would resist the 'liberal' influence of supranational institutions. The risk of amalgamation still lingers, however. See, e.g., Council of the European Union, *Roadmap to Ensure Coherent EU Response to Continued Migration Pressures*, 7262/12 MIGR 25, 8 March 2012, and the related note from the Belgian, French, German, Dutch, Austrian, Swedish and UK delegations in Council of the European Union, *Common Responses to Current Challenges by Member States Most Affected by Secondary Mixed Migration Flows*, 7431/12 JAI 156 ASIM 26, 9 March 2012.

There is, however, a mildly reassuring side to this conclusion. Since the analytical lenses applied here trace the seeds of normative conflict to a 'genetic material' that is EU specific, they may also serve to pre-empt an unreasoned, mechanical replication of problematic EU standards and practices in other parts of the world. As the EU exports its own devices, other countries would be well advised not to take elements of the CEAS at face value, but to interpret and gauge them within their unique context.

10

Conclusion: Europe's normative power
in refugee law

HÉLÈNE LAMBERT

In its core, this volume is about the emulation of European legal norms of refugee protection in other parts of the world. The main purpose of the volume is threefold: to gather evidence that emulation is happening (if it is); to explore the extent of such emulation and identify the processes through which it is happening; and to examine the implications of these findings in terms of trends. Thus, the chapters investigate existing patterns of emulation and discuss, where appropriate, how these might continue in the future.

A review of the case studies reveals that all but one of these cases (the United States) provides clear evidence of emulation at some point in time. The EU protection regime, which has been most influenced by the *non-refoulement* jurisprudence of the European Court of Human Rights, is 'naturally' evolving transnationally and is spreading internationally. The role of 'formal' processes also cannot be ignored (e.g., bilateral agreements and treaties), and these are illustrated by the case studies of Israel and Switzerland. However, what this volume reveals is another picture of 'natural' diffusion and emulation into the legal systems of non-EU countries through more 'informal' transnational processes. Crucially also, this volume accounts for a complex set of rules, practices and ideas, that lies behind European refugee law. Notably, the EU (and all of its twenty-seven Member States) has a normative 'safety mechanism' in place that is unique to Europe (namely, the ECHR with the European Court of Human Rights, and the CJEU). As a result, EU norms are constantly evolving, and many of them are becoming more liberal under the influence of this double-judicial check. Not all States outside Europe may be aware of these constant adjustments being made to restrictive norms.[1]

---

[1] I thank Jane McAdam for this point.

The case study of Australia reveals a complex picture of partial emulation of European concepts in the Australian legislative framework and in some judicial decisions. This is particularly so in relation to 'complementary protection', where EU law and practice on 'subsidiary protection' seems to have had an enormous influence on its codification in Australia. European influence can also be discerned with respect to the 'safe third country' concept. Interestingly, other proposed practices considered 'bad' in the EU, such as those relating to 'transit processing centres', also failed in Australia. McAdam's discussion of these centres offers a striking illustration of the 'global' phenomenon of refugee law-making. Indeed, there is clear evidence that Australia's Pacific Solution, created in 2001, was in fact a source of inspiration for the UK's proposal to create offshore processing centres in Europe, and the Pacific Solution was itself reminiscent of the United States' offshore processing of Cuban and Haitian asylum seekers in Guantánamo Bay in the 1990s. Further similarities and emulation between Europe and Australia is explored in relation to a (failed) 'transfer arrangement' with Malaysia and the collection, storage and use of biometric data belonging to 'unauthorized' non-citizens entering or leaving Australia. In both these contexts (processing centres and transfer arrangements), explicit evidence that Europe (particularly the CEAS) was considered a model for Australian legislative change was found.

Crucially, these examples show that local conditions (such as the absence of a Bill of Rights in Australia or anything akin to a regional human rights treaty like the ECHR) have played a crucial role; thus emulation is only partial, and it is driven by new challenges for Australia, such as having to cope with an increased number of mixed flows of refugees. Emulation of European norms is facilitated by a range of actors and processes. Some are to be expected: decisions by domestic courts and tribunals, and policies adopted by the Department of Immigration necessarily contribute to such emulation. Other input is perhaps less obvious: submissions by NGOs, UNHCR and academics before Parliament in Committee hearings during the development of legislation and policy, and discussions between the Australian Immigration Minister and his/her overseas counterparts, can have significant influence on the direction of Australian practice. Parliamentary debates further show the desire to legitimize any such emulation as part of a growing international consensus (i.e., international best practice). The greatest risk with Australia emulating some of Europe's restrictive practices is that without an ECHR-like safety net, these practices (e.g., on detention) could be interpreted more restrictively in the Australian context and those affected may have no effective remedy available.

The chapter on Colombia, Ecuador, Panama and Venezuela discusses the recent adoption by these four States of accelerated status determination procedures for dealing with 'manifestly unfounded' and 'clearly abusive' asylum claims, as a form of admissibility screening. It traces the origins of these procedures through a recommendation of the Council of Europe that was subsequently adopted in UNHCR's EXCOM conclusions and disseminated by UNHCR, before it was finally developed in EU legislation. Emulation of these procedures has only been partial, and the standards provided in Europe have been adapted to local conditions. The main drivers for this emulation seem to be new asylum challenges in the region fuelled by an increased number of Colombian refugees believed to pose a 'national security' threat to the other three countries, as well as the dramatic increase in irregular migration from Africa and Asia. Two key facilitators are identified in this European influence: first, the compatibility or 'fit' between Latin American and Spanish legal systems (and language) which has made Spain, an EU Member State since 1986, a direct source of inspiration; and, second, UNHCR as an external but strong mediating actor in the region. There is a risk, however, noted by Cantor, that (restrictive) European asylum policies may serve to channel migratory flows to other parts of the world. If other regions emulate the same kind of restrictive asylum practices as Europe then it cannot be excluded that irregular migration routes might simply reorient themselves back towards Europe.

The possibility of this happening is illustrated by the case study on Canada. For many years, Canada has imposed visa requirements on the Czech Republic (and Hungary, to a lesser extent) as a means of deterring large numbers of Roma seeking asylum in Canada. However, in 2012, Canada introduced a new safe country of origin (SCO) provision in its revised refugee law, which acts as a visa substitute. This was done to facilitate the conclusion of the Canada–EU Comprehensive Economic Trade Agreement. The new provision on SCO is directly traceable to the 'white lists' of safe countries introduced by several European countries in the 1990s, including the UK, as well as, crucially, the Aznar Protocol. Emulation is partial in this case due to variation in the jurisprudential context. Established intergovernmental networks and the 'fit' in shared common law traditions between Canada and the UK (where the concept has been judicially scrutinized) are identified as key facilitators in the SCO norm transmission between Canada and the EU Member States. Macklin argues that the motivation for Canada's appeasement of the

European SCO concept as an alternative to a visa requirement was 'the power and influence of the EU'.[2] In other words, Canada chose to copy the EU as a powerful and successful international actor, in dealing with the challenge posed by the Roma. Since the EU has set the standards (all EU Member States regard themselves as safe), it can hardly complain if Canada adopts the same ones. This case study provides a clear illustration of the EU operating as a normative power in this area of law. Further discussion of the Aznar Protocol, and its implications for the EU and beyond, is provided by Durieux in Chapter 9.

Israel, too, has learned lessons from the EU in developing more restrictive approaches to refugee protection. It has an accelerated refusal procedure, applies credibility criteria to reject cases, has a high asylum refusal rate, increasingly uses detention as a form of deterrence, has push-back policies, and has sought to create a 'fortress Israel' on the Egyptian border. Law and jurisprudence on asylum and refugee protection are in the early stages of development in Israel, which provides an opportunity to look at what is being done elsewhere and 'fish for ideas'.[3] Israel's long-standing relationship with the EC/EU (trading, financial and diplomatic) means that it may be expected to turn towards Europe when seeking to develop its laws. Legislative approximation is formally advocated in the EU/Israel Action Plan in the migration and asylum fields. Under the framework of EU initiatives, the EU has been able to present its asylum model to Israel, within a broader context of managing global migration and ensuring the sanctity of European borders. UNHCR, too, has played a formal role in the diffusion of ideas from Europe to Israel. However, local conditions or 'culture' are powerful, particularly the right of return for the Jewish diaspora, a small territory and population, and the 'Holocaust discourse'. Hence, Israel has learned some lessons from the EU, but these have generally been of the restrictive kind.

Even more so than Israel, the Swiss case study provides a strident example of formal diffusion of EU norms through the (bilateral) Dublin Association Agreement. This diffusion is having such influential effect on both legislation and courts' decisions that Chetail and Bauloz question whether Switzerland isn't becoming a de facto EU Member State for the purposes of asylum. The Swiss Confederation faces identical challenges to the other EU Member States and is influenced by a deep fear of massive asylum flows with real or perceived abuses of the asylum system. Geographically an enclave within EU territory, it is not

---

[2] Macklin, Chapter 4, pp. 103 and 128.   [3] Lambert, Chapter 1, p. 7.

surprising that asylum practice of EU States and Switzerland have mirrored each other in their developments. An issue of contention concerns the notion of the Dublin *acquis*, which Switzerland is expected to implement and apply following ratification of the Dublin Association Agreement. However, the extent of these legal obligations for Switzerland remains unsettled. The influence of the EU Qualification Directive on the Swiss courts' interpretation of the refugee definition is equally profound. When Switzerland adopted the more liberal EU 'protection approach' to actors of persecution, this had a ripple effect on new interpretations of the concepts of 'effective protection by actors of protection' as well as 'internal flight alternative', both to be found in the Qualification Directive. As observed by Chetail and Bauloz, the definition of a refugee in the Refugee Convention in Switzerland no longer is interpreted without reference to EU law.

The chapter on Africa provides a striking example of historical emulation of the 1951 Refugee Convention to make it applicable in Africa. The evidence is clear and 'can be traced back to an explicit objective of emulating the European approach in Africa'[4] facilitated by the OAU and UNHCR. The 1969 OAU Convention indeed combines provisions of the 1951 Refugee Convention (e.g., the refugee definition which the OAU found to be very relevant) with specific provisions particular to Africa (relating to the dateline and the refugee problem as a source of tension between States, as well as a broader refugee definition). Since then, elements of contemporary regional, subregional and national refugee protection frameworks have been found to reflect European approaches, especially restrictive ones (such as 'safe third country', 'safe country of origin' and 'manifestly unfounded' asylum applications), but explicit evidence of this process is hard to find. Nonetheless, a broad trend of European (restrictive) practices appearing in African law and policy is clearly identifiable.

The United States is the only case study where *explicit* evidence of emulation (past or present) appears to be missing, not because EU asylum law is new (as some people might suggest), but because of local requirements that cause the United States to resist the influence of foreign law and practice. This case study is therefore particularly interesting in testing the prediction put forward by sociological institutionalists that weaker States are more likely to emulate the policies developed by the EU than advanced States. Political circumstances (the United States views itself as '*the* centre'[5] of the world order) do not favour US

---

[4] Sharpe, Chapter 7, p. 179.   [5] Fullerton, Chapter 8, p. 201.

emulation of European asylum law. This chapter nevertheless argues that partial emulation occasionally happens by stealth, and that this is facilitated by strong historical ties with Europe, and a cultural 'fit' with the UK. When such emulation occurs, acknowledgement is generally absent. The focal point of Fullerton's chapter is the EU Qualification Directive, particularly the definition of a 'particular social group' and the notion of 'subsidiary protection'. Although there is no explicit evidence of CEAS law having been emulated in the United States, the timing and presence of strong transnational legal networks support the view that a process of diffusion is under way between US administrative and judicial decisions, and EU asylum law. The main drivers seem to be new challenges to the United States protection regime, and uncertainty posed by the widespread and extreme violence in Mexico and activities of transnational criminal gangs. In addition, this case study offers a powerful illustration of the reciprocal nature of the norm diffusion process when discussing the requirement of 'particular social group' in the refugee definition.

The evidence provided in Chapters 2–8 of this volume can be taken to support the conclusion that European norms of refugee protection are being emulated around the world. Some of these norms are clearly restrictive to start with (e.g., 'accelerated procedures', 'safe third country', 'safe first country', 'safe country of origin'); others are of a more liberal tradition (e.g., the protection approach to actors of persecution, 'subsidiary protection'). While their character (i.e., restrictive or liberal) appears to remain unchanged following emulation, the meaning of these norms can be the subject of transformation in the country of emulation.[6] For instance, in Latin America, (European) accelerated procedures are used as a means of screening admissibility for refugee status. In the United States, 'serious harm', which is derived from the 2004 Qualification Directive, is interpreted to include risk caused by civil strife or extreme economic deprivation and is entirely forward-looking, in contrast to 'persecution' which can be based entirely on past harm. Thus, emulation can never be absolute. It can only be partial because the norms being emulated are deeply dependent on local conditions and requirements; they are 'localized' in the process of selective adoption by States.[7] This volume also confirms diffusion as an

---

[6] Teubner, for instance, refutes the idea of legal transplant as misleading. Gunther Teubner, 'Legal Irritants: Good Faith in British Law or How Unifying Law Ends up in New Divergences' (1998) 61 *Modern Law Review* 11–32, at 12.

[7] Amitav Acharya, 'How Ideas Spread: Whose Norms Matter? Norm Localization and Institutional Change in Asian Regionalism' (2004) 58 *International Organization*

iterative process, which may be formal (e.g., Switzerland), informal (e.g., Australia, Canada or Latin America) or mixed (e.g., Israel). Transnational networks can facilitate one-way transfer or reciprocal influence, or even re-export legal norms.[8]

To come back to the distinction between drivers and facilitators introduced in Chapter 1, all case studies find 'new challenges and uncertainty' as the main driver for emulation of European refugee law; in addition, in the cases of Israel and Switzerland, the normative motivation of emulation (through association and bilateral agreements) can also be said to be at work. A degree of fit between the EU norm and local requirements, politics, laws and culture is also present in all the case studies. The role of transnational policy, legal or advocacy networks, such as UNHCR or the IARLJ, in transmitting the foreign norms is found to be important, if not key, but the role of advocacy groups, academics, judges and other decision makers is also found to be at least as important.

While drivers and facilitators are useful in helping us understand the traffic in norms between different legal systems (i.e., why a particular State would look elsewhere for ideas or norms and how these ideas or norms would 'travel' and be emulated), their role is limited when it comes to explaining why the EU is such a source of inspiration. The idea that the EU may be setting world standards in normative terms is not new and has been explored in the writing of numerous scholars.[9] Here, we argue that the EU's normative power is clearly at work in the emulation of European refugee law. The long-standing commitments of the EU to peace, liberty, democracy, the rule of law, human rights, and its aspirations to social solidarity, antidiscrimination, sustainable development and good governance provide the EU with a broad normative basis.[10] In European refugee law more specifically, this normative basis is anchored in the 1951 Refugee Convention, the ECHR (and now also the Charter of Fundamental Rights of the EU) and other human rights treaties. It is strengthened with a set of supranational institutions competent to legislate on refugee law and interpret provisions of refugee law. With this basis, the EU is able 'to define what passes for "normal"[11] in refugee law and international protection.

239–75. See also William Twining, 'Diffusion of Law: A Global Perspective' (2004) 49 *Journal of Legal Pluralism* 1–45, at 26.

[8] Twining, 'Diffusion of Law', table I, 17.

[9] For a review of this literature, see Ian Manners, 'Normative Power Europe: A Contradiction in Terms?' (2002) 40 *Journal of Common Market Studies* 235–58.

[10] *Ibid.*, at 242–4.

[11] Manners argues that '[T]he ability to define what passes for "normal" in world politics is, ultimately, the greatest power of all' (*ibid.*, at 253).

Thus emulation of European refugee law involves more than a process of diffusion of an ideology or of a solution to a problem; it defines Europe's international identity in international protection.

There are problems associated with this exercise in 'normality', discussed by Durieux in Chapter 9. These include the logic underpinning the CEAS (i.e., mutual trust and freedom of movement between the Member States) and the vanishing, at least in Europe, of the 1951 Convention 'refugee'. Another risk in emulation is that, as mentioned above, whereas the EU has a normative 'safety mechanism' in place, namely the ECHR, many other countries do not. No matter how restrictive the law might be in Europe, its application in practice is subject to a double-judicial check that is unique to Europe: one by the CJEU, and the other by the European Court of Human Rights. Furthermore, EU norms are constantly evolving, and many of them are becoming more liberal under the influence of this double-check. This is true of EU asylum legislation, which continues to be revised, and both courts (the CJEU and the European Court of Human Rights) play a key role in the enhancement of the standards set in the legislation. Thus, where some of the EU legislative measures may appear to be restrictive in their wording or in their aims and objectives, the CJEU and European Court of Human Rights force their application in practice to be much more liberal than might be thought possible at first sight. The danger of non-EU countries emulating some of Europe's restrictive rules, practices and ideas without the more liberal 'interpretation package' that comes with it in a European context, is clearly illustrated by the findings in some of the case studies in this volume, such as Australia and Latin America.

The picture that emerges from this volume is of a natural diffusion of European norms around the world, mostly of a restrictive character, by a range of actors and for a number of motives. However, emulation of European norms of refugee protection is unlikely to produce convergence in international protection and uniformity of concepts.[12] Rather, it may lead instead to new differences for two reasons. First, these norms become 'localized' in the process of selective adoption by States, and in this process their original meaning transforms to meet the State's own requirements. Second, within Europe, these norms continue to evolve, under the influence of both the CJEU and the European Court of Human Rights and therefore at the moment of adoption by a non-EU State they may 'freeze in time' and then be out of step with European interpretations.[13]

---

[12] See Teubner, 'Legal Irritants'.   [13] I thank Jane McAdam for this point.

The refugee law regime, and human rights more generally, are historically 'European constructs' in origin (e.g., the Refugee Convention and the ECHR). This original 'European' regime has evolved transnationally and spread internationally through regional instruments, State practice and UNHCR doctrine. This book argues that the same pattern is in fact repeating itself. Thus refugee law is constitutive of Europe's identity, and likewise becomes so of the States that emulate Europe. In this real sense, European refugee law is global.

BIBLIOGRAPHY

Domestic constitutional and legislative instruments

Asylum and Withholding of Deportation Procedures, Final Rule, 55 Federal Register 30674 (1990), codified at 8 CFR § 208. 55

Asylum Act, RS 142.31, RO 1999, 2262, 26 June 1998 (entered into force 1 October 1999)

Asylum Procedures, 65 Federal Register 76121, at 76133 (final rule 6 December 2000) (effective 5 January 2001)

Balanced Refugee Reform Act, SC 2012, c. 8

Bill C-31, Protecting Canada's Immigration System Act, 1st Sess., 41st Parl., 2012 (assented to 28 June 2012), SC 2012, c. 17

Border Protection (Validation and Enforcement Powers) Act 2001 (Cth)

Code of Federal Regulations (US), Title 8 (8 CFR)

Decree 2817/84 (Colombia), 20 November 1984

Decree 4503/09 (Colombia), 19 November 2009

Decree 36831-G (Costa Rica), 28 September 2011

Decree 3293/87 (Ecuador), 30 September 1987

Decree 3301/92 (Ecuador), 6 May 1992

Decree 1635/09 (Ecuador), 25 March 2009

Decree 79/05 (El Salvador), 7 September 2005

Decree 23/98 (Panama), 10 February 1998

Decree 2491/03 (Venezuela), 28 July 2003

Displaced Persons Act of 1948, Pub. L. No. 80–774, ch. 647, 62 Stat. 1009 (1948)

Federal Act on Foreign Nationals, RS 142.20, RO 2007 5437, 16 December 2005

Federal Act on the Federal Assembly, RS 171.10, 13 December 2002

Federal Constitution of the Swiss Confederation of 18 April 1999, RS 101 (entered into force 1 January 2000)

HR Res. 97, 109th Congress (2005)

Immigration Act 2009 (NZ)

Immigration and Nationality Act (INA) Amendments of 1965 (US), Pub. L. No. 89–236, §3, 79 Stat. 911, 913, amending § 203(a)(7) of the INA

Immigration and Refugee Protection Act, SC 2001, c. 27

Law 5/1984 (Spain), 26 March 1984, as amended by Law 9/1994 (Spain), 19 May 1994

Law 12/2009 (Spain), 30 October 2009

Law No. 2011–672 of 16 June 2011 on Immigration, Integration and Nationality (France), JO No. 0139 of 17 June 2011

Law No. 2005/006 (Cameroon)

Law on Refugees and Complementary Protection (Mexico), 27 January 2011

Loi sur l'asile, FF 1977 III 105, 5 October 1979 (entered into force 1 January 1981)

Migration Act 1958 (Cth)

Migration Amendment Act 1992 (Cth)

Migration Amendment (Complementary Protection) Bill 2011 (Cth), Explanatory Memorandum

Migration Amendment (Excision from Migration Zone) Act 2001 (Cth)

Migration Amendment (Excision from Migration Zone) (Consequential Provisions) Act 2001 (Cth)

Migration Amendment Regulations 2004 (No. 4) (Cth)

Migration Legislation Amendment Bill (No. 2) 1995 (Cth)

Migration Legislation Amendment Bill (No. 4) 1994 (Cth), Explanatory Memorandum, Supplementary Explanatory Memorandum and Revised Explanatory Memorandum

Migration Legislation Amendment (Identification and Authentication) Bill 2003 (Cth), Explanatory Memorandum

Ministerial Accord 003 (Ecuador), 11 January 2011 (unpublished, on file with David J. Cantor)

Order Respecting the Interim Federal Health Program, 2012, in force 30 June 2012, SI 2012-26, Canada Gazette Vol. 146(9) 2012, repealing Order in Council PC 157-11/848 of June 20, 1957, as amended by Order Amending the Order Respecting the Interim Federal Health Program, 2012, in force 18 July 2012, SI 2012-49, Canada Gazette Vol. 146(15) 2012

Organic Law on Refugees and Asylees (Venezuela), 3 October 2001

Passports Law (Israel), 5712–1952

Political Constitution of Ecuador, 2008

Prevention of Infiltration (Offences and Jurisdiction) Law (Israel), 5714–1954

Proposed Regulations Amending the Immigration and Refugee Protection Regulations, SC 2012, c. 17 http://www.gazette.gc.ca/rp-pr/p1/2012/2012-08-04/html/reg1-eng.html

Refugee Act of 1980, Pub. L. No. 96–212, 94 Stat 102, codified at 8 USC §§ 1101(a)(42), 1157–1159 (1980)

Refugee Relief Act of 1953, Pub. L. No. 83–203, 67 Stat. 400 (1953)

Refugees Act 2006 (Uganda)

Special Immigrant Visa Program, National Defense Authorization Act for Fiscal Year 2006, Pub.

Law No. 109–163, §1059; National Defense Authorization Act for Fiscal Year 2008, Pub. Law No. 110–181, §1244

Temporary Protected Status, Immigration and Nationality Act, §244, Pub.
L. No. 101–649, 104 Stat. 5030, §244, codified at 8 USC §1254(a)(2006)
US Constitution

Documents of government departments

Bolkus, Nick, 'Refugee Decisions for 17 Boat People' (Media Release, 29 August 1994).
Canada Border Services Agency (Intelligence, GTA Region – Analytical Unit), 'Project SARA: International and Domestic Activities Final Report', 31 January 2012 https://www.documentcloud.org/documents/470868-cbsa-project-sara.html
Citizenship and Immigration Canada, 'Backgrounder: Designated Countries of Origin' http://www.cic.gc.ca/english/department/media/backgrounders/2012/2012-06-29a.asp
Citizenship and Immigration Canada, 'Backgrounder: Summary of Changes to Canada's Refugee System in Protecting Canada's Immigration System Act' http://www.cic.gc.ca/english/department/media/backgrounders/2012/2012-02-16f.asp
Citizenship and Immigration Canada, 'Backgrounder: The Visa Requirement for the Czech Republic' (13 July 2009) http://www.cic.gc.ca/english/department/media/backgrounders/2009/2009-07-13a.asp
Citizenship and Immigration Canada, 'Canada: Total Entries of Refugee Claimants by Top Source Countries' http://www.cic.gc.ca/english/resources/statistics/facts2010/temporary/25.asp
Citizenship and Immigration Canada, 'Interim Federal Health Program: Summary of Benefits' http://www.cic.gc.ca/english/refugees/outside/summary-ifhp.asp
Citizenship and Immigration Canada, 'News Release: Making Canada's Asylum System Faster and Fairer' (14 December 2012) http://www.cic.gc.ca/english/department/media/releases/2012/2012-12-14.asp?utm_source=media-centre-email&utm_medium=email-eng&utm_campaign=generic
Department of Citizenship and Immigration, Order Establishing Quantitative Thresholds for the Designation of Countries of Origin; Order Designated Countries of Origin, Canada Gazette, Part I, Vol. 146, No. 15 December 2012, 3378–3380 http://www.gazette.gc.ca/rp-pr/p1/2012/2012-12-15/html/index-eng.html
Department of Finance and Administration, *Parliamentarians' Travel paid by the Department of Finance and Administration: January to June 2002* (December 2002).
Department of Immigration and Citizenship, Submission No. 31 to Legal and Constitutional Affairs References Committee, *Inquiry into Australia's Arrangement with Malaysia in relation to Asylum Seekers* (September 2011).

Department of Immigration, Multicultural and Indigenous Affairs, 'Complementary Protection and Australian Practice', in UNHCR Regional Office for Australia, New Zealand, Papua New Guinea and the South Pacific, *Discussion Paper: Complementary Protection* (No. 2, 2005).

Department of Immigration and Multicultural and Indigenous Affairs, *Interpreting the Refugees Convention: An Australian Contribution* (Cth of Australia, 2002).

Department of Parliamentary Services (Cth), *Bills Digest: Border Protection (Validation and Enforcement Powers) Bill 2001*, No. 62 of 2001–02, 20 September 2001.

Department of Parliamentary Services (Cth), *Bills Digest: Migration Amendment (Complementary Protection) Bill 2009*, No. 70 of 2009–10, 24 November 2009.

Department of Parliamentary Services (Cth), *Bills Digest: Migration Amendment (Complementary Protection) Bill 2011*, No. 79 of 2010–11, 11 March 2011.

Department of Parliamentary Services (Cth), *Bills Digest: Migration Laws Amendment Bill (No. 4) 1994*, No. 151 of 1994, 23 September 1994.

Dirección General de Refugiados, *Política del Ecuador en materia de refugio* (Ministerio de Relaciones Exteriores, Comercio e Integracíon, Quito, 2008).

Foreign Affairs and International Trade Canada, 'EU Ambassadors Show Support for Canada–EU Economic and Trade Agreement' (Media Release, 2 October 2012) http://www.international.gc.ca/media_commerce/release_photo_distribu tion/2012/10/02b.aspx?lang=eng&view=d

House of Lords European Union Committee, *Handling EU Asylum Claims: New Approaches Examined* (HL Paper 74, 11th Report of Session 2003–04).

House of Lords Select Committee on the EU, *Defining Refugee Status and Those in Need of International Protection* (HL Paper 156, 28th Report of Session 2001–02).

Immigration and Refugee Board, Refugee Protection Division, 'Claims Referred and Finalized: Hungary' (on file with Audrey Macklin).

Immigration and Refugee Board, 'Women Refugee Claimants Fearing Gender-Related Persecution: Guidelines Issued by the Chairperson Pursuant to Section 65(3) of the Immigration Act' (effective 13 November 1996) http://www.irb-cisr.gc.ca/eng/brdcom/references/pol/guidir/pages/women.aspx

Joint Standing Committee on Migration, *Immigration Detention in Australia: Community-Based Alternatives to Detention* (Cth of Australia, 2009).

Joint Standing Committee on Migration, *Immigration Detention in Australia: Facilities, Services and Transparency* (Cth of Australia, 2009).

Legal and Constitutional Legislation Committee, *Provisions of the Migration Legislation Amendment (Identification and Authentication) Bill 2003* (Cth of Australia, 2003)

Minister for Immigration and Ethnic Affairs, *Guidelines for Stay in Australia on Humanitarian Grounds* (24 May 1994) http://parlinfo.aph.gov.au/parlInfo/

download/media/pressrel/IMAA6/upload_binary/imaa63.pdf;fileType=appli
cation/pdf

Minister for Immigration, Multicultural and Indigenous Affairs, 'UK Asylum
Proposals Worth Consideration' (Media Release, MPS 21/2003, 3 April 2003).

Ministry of Interior, Population, Immigration and Border Authority (Israel),
Procedure for Handling Political Asylum Seekers in Israel, entered into
force 2 January 2011 http://piba.gov.il/Regulations/Procedure%20for%
20Handling%20Political%20Asylum%20Seekers%20in%20Israel-en.pdf

National Refugee Commission (Venezuela), Internal Regulations, 28 January 2010.

Prime Minister and Minister for Immigration and Citizenship, 'Australia and
Malaysia Sign Transfer Deal' (Media Release, 25 July 2011) http://www.pm.
gov.au/press-office/australia-and-malaysia-sign-transfer-deal

Prime Minister and Minister for Immigration and Citizenship, 'Transcript of
Joint Press Conference' (12 September 2011) http://www.pm.gov.au/
press-office/transcript-joint-press-conference-canberra-15

Ruddock, Philip, 'Address to UNHCR Executive Committee Meeting' (Speech delivered at UNHCR Executive Committee Meeting, Geneva, 30 September 2002)
http://parlinfo.aph.gov.au/parlInfo/download/media/pressrel/ZHJ76/upload_
binary/zhj764.pdf;fileType=application/pdf

Ruddock, Philip, Minister for Immigration and Multicultural and Indigenous
Affairs, 'Managed Migration: Who Does the Managing?' (Presentation to
Senior Government Officials and Academics, Australia House, London, 16
August 2002).

Senate Legal and Constitutional Affairs References Committee, *A Sanctuary
under Review: An Examination of Australia's Refugee and Humanitarian
Determination Processes* (Cth of Australia, 2000).

Senate Legal and Constitutional Affairs References Committee, *Australia's
Arrangement with Malaysia in relation to Asylum Seekers* (Cth of
Australia, October 2011).

Senate Legal and Constitutional Legislation Committee, *Migration Legislation
Amendment (Judicial Review) Bill 1998* (Cth of Australia, 1999).

Senate Legal and Constitutional Legislation Committee, *Provisions of the
Migration Amendment (Judicial Review) Bill 2004* (Cth of Australia, 2004).

Senate Standing Committee on Legal and Constitutional Affairs, *Migration
Legislation Amendment Bill (No. 4) 1994: Report by the Senate Standing
Committee on Legal and Constitutional Affairs* (October 1994).

'Speaking Notes for The Honourable Jason Kenney, PC, MP Minister of Citizenship,
Immigration and Multiculturalism at a News Conference to Announce Royal
Assent of the Protecting Canada's Immigration System Act' (29 June 2012)
http://www.cic.gc.ca/english/department/media/speeches/2012/2012-06-29.asp

Standing Committee on Citizenship and Immigration, 41st Parl., 1st Sess.,
CIMM-37, 2 May 2012.

Standing Committee on Citizenship and Immigration, 41st Parl., 1st Sess., CIMM-40, 7 May 2012.

Submissions of the Solicitor-General in *Plaintiff M70 and Plaintiff M106/2011* v. *Minister for Immigration and Citizenship* [2011] HCATrans. 224 (23 August 2011).

Swiss Confederation, Federal Department of Foreign Affairs (FDFA)/Federal Department of Economic Affairs (FDEA), *Bilateral Agreements Switzerland–EU* (Berne: Integration Office FDFA/FDEA, 2009).

Swiss Federal Council, *Message concernant la modification de la loi sur l'asile*, FF 2010 4035, 26 May 2010.

Swiss Federal Council, *Message du Conseil fédéral du 13 mai 1998 relatif à l'arrêté fédéral sur les mesures d'urgence dans le domaine de l'asile et des étrangers*, FF 1998 2829, 13 May 1998.

Swiss Federal Council, *Message portant approbation et mise en œuvre de l'échange de notes entre la Suisse et l'Union européenne concernant la reprise du code frontières Schengen (développement de l'acquis Schengen) et relatif aux modifications du droit des étrangers et du droit d'asile en vue de la mise en œuvre totale de l'acquis de Schengen et Dublin déjà repris (compléments)*, FF 2007 7449, 24 October 2007.

Swiss Federal Council, *Message relatif à l'approbation des accords bilatéraux entre la Suisse et l'Union européenne, y compris les actes législatifs relatifs à la transposition des accords ('accords bilatéraux II')*, FF 2004 5593, 1 October 2004.

Swiss Federal Council, *Message sur l'approbation et la mise en œuvre de l'échange de notes entre la Suisse et la CE concernant la reprise de la directive CE sur le retour (directive 2008/115/CE) (développement de l'acquis de Schengen) et sur une modification de la loi fédérale sur les étrangers (contrôle automatisé aux frontières, conseillers en matière de documents, système d'information MIDES)*, FF 2009 8043, 18 November 2009.

Swiss Federal Office of Migrations, *Accord de Dublin: bilan positif pour la Suisse* (Département fédéral de Justice et Police, Communiqué, 7 April 2009).

Swiss Federal Office of Migrations, *Statistique en matière d'asile 2011* (Département fédéral de Justice et Police, 6 January 2012).

UK Government, 'New Vision for Refugees' (Summary), 7 March 2003, p. 4 http://www.proasyl.de/texte/mappe/2003/76/3.pdf

US Citizenship and Immigration Services, 'Asylum Division Training Programs' http://www.uscis.gov/portal/site/uscis/menuitem.5af9bb95919f35e66f6141765 43f6d1a/?vgnextoid=38292f81eb478110VgnVCM1000004718190aRCRD&vg nextchannel=4db791de70c98110VgnVCM1000004718190aRCRD

US Citizenship and Immigration Services, 'USCIS Service and Office Locator' https://egov.uscis.gov/crisgwi/go?action=offices.type&OfficeLocator. office_type=LO

US Courts, Judicial Business of the US Courts, '2011 Report' http://www.uscourts.
gov/Statistics/JudicialBusiness.aspx
US Courts, 'Judicial Facts and Figures 2010' http://www.uscourts.gov/Statistics/
JudicialFactsAndFigures/JudicialFactsAndFigures2010.aspx
US Department of Justice, Executive Office of Immigration Review, 'Asylum
Statistics by Nationality (FY 2007-FY 2011)' http://www.justice.gov/eoir/
efoia/foiafreq.htm

Regional and international instruments and documents of the United Nations, European Union and other intergovernmental organizations

Agreement between the European Community and the Swiss Confederation concerning the criteria and mechanism for establishing the State responsible for
examining a request for asylum lodged in a Member State or in Switzerland, OJ
2008 No. L53/5, signed 26 October 2004 (entered into force 1 March 2008).
Agreement between the European Economic Community and the Swiss Confederation,
OJ 1972 No. L300/189 (entered into force 1 January 1973).
Agreement between the European Economic Community and the Swiss Confederation
on direct insurance other than life assurance, OJ 1991 No. L205/3 (entered into
force 1 January 1993).
Agreement between the European Union, the European Community and the Swiss
Confederation on the Swiss Confederation's association with the implementa-
tion, application and development of the Schengen *acquis*, OJ 2008 No. L53/52,
signed 26 October 2004 (entered into force 1 March 2008).
Agreement between the Government of Canada and the Government of the
United States of America for Cooperation in the Examination of Refugee
Status Claims from Nationals of Third Countries, 29 December 2004.
Agreement between the Governments of the States of the Benelux Economic Union,
the Federal Republic of Germany and the French Republic on the gradual
abolition of controls at their common borders, OJ 2000 No. L239/13, 14 June
1985.
Amsterdam Treaty, OJ 1997 No. C340.
Arrangement between the Government of Australia and the Government of
Malaysia on Transfer and Resettlement (25 July 2011).
Barcelona Declaration adopted at the Euro-Mediterranean Conference (27–28
November 1995).
Cartagena Declaration on Refugees, adopted by the Colloquium on the International
Protection of Refugees in Central America, Mexico, and Panama, 22 November
1984, in 'Annual Report of the Inter-American Commission on Human Rights'
(1984–5) OAS Doc. OEA/Ser.L/V/II.66/doc.10, rev. 1, 190–3.
Charter of Fundamental Rights of the European Union, OJ 2000 No. C364/1.
Charter of the Organization of African Unity, Addis Ababa, 25 May 1963, 479
UNTS 39.

Commission of the European Communities, Commission staff working document accompanying the proposal for a Regulation of the European Parliament and of the Council establishing the criteria and mechanisms for determining the Member State responsible for examining an application for international protection lodged in one of the Member States by a third-country national or a stateless person (recast), Impact Assessment, SEC(2008) 2962, 3 December 2008.

Commission of the European Communities, Impact Assessment: Annexes to the Commission staff working document accompanying the proposal of the European Parliament and of the Council on minimum standards on procedures in Member States for granting and withdrawing international protection, SEC(2009) 1376 (Part II) (21 October 2009).

Commission of the European Communities, Implementation of the European Neighbourhood Policy in 2008: Progress Report Israel, SEC(2009) 516/2, 23 April 2009.

Commission of the European Communities, Proposal for a Regulation of the European Parliament and of the Council establishing the criteria and mechanisms for determining the Member State responsible for examining an application for international protection lodged in one of the Member States by a third-country national or a stateless person (recast), COM(2008) 820 final, 3 December 2008.

Commission Regulation (EC) No 1560/2003 of 2 September 2003 laying down detailed rules for the application of Council Regulation (EC) No 343/2003 establishing the criteria and mechanisms for determining the Member State responsible for examining an asylum application lodged in one of the Member States by a third-country national, OJ 2003 No. L222/3.

Communication from the Commission to the Council and the European Parliament of 10 May 2005 – The Hague Programme: ten priorities for the next five years. The Partnership for European renewal in the field of Freedom, Security and Justice, COM(2005) 184 final, OJ 2005 No. C236.

Conclusiones de la Reunión del Grupo Regional de Consulta sobre Migración de la Conferencia Regional sobre Migración (Querétaro, Mexico, 16–18 November 2010).

Constitutive Act of the African Union, Lomé, 11 July 2000, in force 26 May 2001, 2158 UNTS 3.

Convention determining the State responsible for examining applications for asylum lodged in one of the Member States of the European Communities, OJ 1997 No. C254/1.

Convention drawn up on the basis of Article K.3 of the Treaty on European Union, relating to extradition between the Member States of the European Union, OJ 1996 No. C313/12.

Convention for the Protection of Human Rights and Fundamental Freedoms, Rome, 4 November 1950, in force 3 September 1953, 213 UNTS 221.

Convention implementing the Schengen Agreement of 14 June 1985 between the Governments of the States of the Benelux Economic Union, the Federal Republic of Germany and the French Republic on the gradual abolition of checks at their common borders, OJ 2000 No. L239/19.

Convention on Territorial Asylum, Caracas, 28 March 1954, in force 29 December 1954, *OAS Treaty Series* No. 18.

Convention relating to the Status of Refugees, Geneva, 28 July 1951, in force 22 April 1954, 189 UNTS 137.

Council Directive 2001/55/EC of 20 July 2001 on minimum standards for giving temporary protection in the event of a mass influx of displaced persons and on measures promoting a balance of efforts between Member States in receiving such persons and bearing the consequences thereof, OJ 2001 No. L212/12.

Council Directive 2003/9/EC of 27 January 2003 laying down minimum standards for the reception of asylum seekers, OJ 2003 No. L31/18.

Council Directive 2004/83/EC of 29 April 2004 on minimum standards for the qualification and status of third-country nationals or stateless persons as refugees or as persons who otherwise need international protection and the content of the protection granted, OJ 2004 No. L304/12.

Council Directive 2005/85/EC of 1 December 2005 on minimum standards on procedures in Member States for granting and withdrawing refugee status, OJ 2005 No. L326/13.

Council of Europe, Parliamentary Assembly, *Assessment of Transit and Processing Centres as a Response to Mixed Flows of Migrants and Asylum Seekers*, Doc. 11304 (Committee on Migration, Refugees and Population, 15 June 2007).

Council of Europe, Parliamentary Assembly, Recommendation 773 (1976) on the situation of de facto refugees.

Council of Europe, Recommendation No. R (81) 16 of the Committee of Ministers to Member States on the harmonization of national procedures relating to asylum, 5 November 1981.

Council of the European Union, *Common Responses to Current Challenges by Member States Most Affected by Secondary Mixed Migration Flows*, 7431/12 JAI 156 ASIM 26, 9 March 2012.

Council of the European Union, Council Resolution of 30 November 1992 on manifestly unfounded applications for asylum.

Council of the European Union, Council Resolution of 20 June 1995 on minimum guarantees for asylum procedures, OJ 1996 No. C274/13.

Council of the European Union, *Roadmap to Ensure Coherent EU Response to Continued Migration Pressures*, 7262/12 MIGR 25, 8 March 2012.

Council Regulation (EC) No. 343/2003 of 18 February 2003 establishing the criteria and mechanisms for determining the Member State responsible for examining an asylum application lodged in one of the Member States by a third-country national, OJ 2003 No. L50/1.

Council Regulation (EC) No. 407/2002 of 28 February 2002 laying down certain rules to implement Regulation (EC) No 2725/2000 concerning the establishment of 'Eurodac' for the comparison of fingerprints for the effective application of the Dublin Convention, OJ 2002 No. L62/1.

Council Regulation (EC) No. 2000/2725/EC of 11 December 2000 concerning the establishment of 'Eurodac' for the comparison of fingerprints for the effective application of the Dublin Convention, OJ 2000 No. L316/1.

Declaration by Belgium on the Protocol on asylum for nationals of Member States of the European Union, OJ 1997 No. C340/144.

Declaración de Brasilia sobre la protección de personas refugiadas y Apátridas en el continente americano (Brazil, 11 November 2010).

Declaración de San José sobre refugiados y personas desplazadas (San José, 5–7 December 1994).

Declaration (No. 48) relating to the Protocol on asylum for nationals of Member States of the European Union, OJ 1997 No. C340/141.

Directive 95/46/EC of the European Parliament and of the Council of 24 October 1995 on the protection of individuals with regard to the processing of personal data and on the free movement of such data, OJ 1995 No. L281/31.

Directive 2003/9/EC of the European Council of 27 January 2003 laying down minimum standards for the reception of asylum seekers, OJ 2003 No. L31/18.

Directive 2004/38/EC of the European Parliament and of the Council of 29 April 2004 on the right of citizens of the Union and their family members to move and reside freely within the territory of the Member States, OJ 2004 No. L158/77.

Directive 2005/85/EC of the European Council of 1 December 2005 on minimum standards on procedures in Member States for granting and withdrawing refugee status, OJ 2005 No. L236/13.

Directive 2008/115/EC of the European Parliament and of the Council of 16 December 2008 on common standards and procedures in Member States for returning illegally staying third-country nationals, OJ 2008 No. L348/98.

Directive 2011/51/EU of the European Parliament and of the Council of 11 May 2011 amending Council Directive 2003/109/EC to extend its scope to beneficiaries of international protection, OJ 2011 No. L132/1.

Directive 2011/95/EU of the European Parliament and of the Council of 13 December 2011 on standards for the qualification of third-country nationals or stateless persons as beneficiaries of international protection, for a uniform status for refugees or for persons eligible for subsidiary protection, and for the content of the protection granted (recast), OJ 2011 No. L337/9.

Draft Protocol on the Facilitation of Movement of Persons (South African Development Committee), Gaborone, 18 August 2005.

EU/Israel Action Plan: http://ec.europa.eu/world/enp/pdf/action_plans/israel_enp_ap_final_en.pdf

Euro-Mediterranean Agreement establishing an association between the European Communities and their Member States, of the one part, and the State of Israel, of the other part, OJ 2000 No. L147/3.

European Commission, Amended Proposal for a Directive of the European Parliament and of the Council on common procedures for granting and withdrawing international protection status (recast), COM(2011) 319 final, 1 June 2011.

European Commission, Communication from the European Commission to the Council and the European Parliament: Towards more accessible, equitable and managed asylum systems, COM(2003) 315 final, 3 June 2003.

European Commission, 'European Neighbourhood Policy' (30 October 2010) http://ec.europa.eu/world/enp/policy_en.htm

European Commission, Implementation of the European Neighbourhood Policy in 2009: Progress Report Israel, SEC(2010) 520, 12 May 2010.

European Council, Joint Position of 4 March 1996 defined by the Council on the basis of Article K.3 of the Treaty on European Union on the harmonized application of the definition of the term 'refugee' in Article 1 of the Geneva Convention of 28 July 1951 relating to the status of refugees, OJ 1996 No. L63/2.

European Council, The Stockholm Programme – An Open and Secure Europe Serving and Protecting Citizens, OJ 2010 No. C115/1.

International Covenant on Civil and Political Rights, New York, adopted 16 December 1966, in force 23 March 1976, 999 UNTS 171.

International Law Commission, Articles on Responsibility of States for Internationally Wrongful Acts in *Report of the International Law Commission on the Work of Its Fifty-Third Session*, UN Doc A/56/10 (2001).

Lisbon Treaty, OJ 2007 No. C306.

Montevideo Treaty on Political Asylum and Refuge, adopted 4 August 1939.

Organization of African Unity (Assembly of Heads of State and Government), 'Resolution on the Problem of Refugees in Africa' (OAU Accra 21–25 October 1965) AHG/Res. 26 (II).

Organization of African Unity (Assembly of Heads of State and Government), 'Sirte Declaration' (OAU Sirte 9 September 1999) AHG/Draft/Decl. (IV) Rev. 1.

Organization of African Unity Convention Governing the Specific Aspects of Refugee Problems in Africa, Addis Ababa, 10 September 1969, in force 20 June 1974, 1001 UNTS 45.

Organization of African Unity (Council of Ministers), 'Resolution on the Adoption of a Draft Convention on the Status of Refugees in Africa' (OAU Addis Ababa 31 October–4 November 1966) CM/Res. 88 (VII).

Organization of African Unity (Council of Ministers), 'Resolution on the Commission on the Problem of Refugees in Africa' (OAU Cairo 13–17 July 1964) CM/Res. 36 (III).

Organization of African Unity (Council of Ministers), 'Resolution on the Problem of Refugees' (OAU Nairobi 26 February–9 March 1965) CM/Res. 52 (IV).

Organization of African Unity (Council of Ministers), 'Resolution on the Problem of Refugees in Africa' (OAU Algiers 4–12 September 1968) CM/Res. 149 (XI).

Organization of African Unity (Council of Ministers), 'Resolution on the Problem of Refugees in Africa' (OAU Lagos 24–29 February 1964) CM/Res. 19 (II).

Organization of American States, *Informe anual de la Comisión Interamericana de Derechos Humanos 1981–1982* (San José: OAS, 1982) OEA/Ser.L/V/II.57, Doc. 6, Rev.1.

Organization of American States, Comisión Especial de Asuntos Migratorios, *Memoria: Migración extracontinental en la Américas* (6 April 2010).

Protocol on Asylum for Nationals of Member States of the European Union, OJ 2004 No. C310/362.

Protocol relating to the Status of Refugees, New York, adopted 31 January 1967, in force 4 October 1967, 606 UNTS 267.

Presidency Conclusions of the Copenhagen European Council (21–22 June 1993).

Presidency Conclusions of the Tampere European Council (15–16 October 1999).

Protocol on asylum for Nationals of Member States of the European Union, annexed to the Treaty establishing the European Community, OJ 1997 No. C340/103 (Aznar Protocol).

Rome Statute of the International Criminal Court, 17 July 1998, in force 1 July 2002, 2187 UNTS 90.

Single European Act, OJ 1987 No. L169/1, signed 17 February 1986 in Luxembourg and 28 February 1986 in The Hague (entered into force 1 July 1987).

Treaty Establishing the African Economic Community, Abuja, 3 June 1991, in force 12 May 1994, 30 ILM 1241.

Treaty Establishing the East African Community, Arusha, 30 November 1999, in force 7 July 2000, 2144 UNTS 255.

Treaty Establishing the European Community (Consolidated Version), OJ 2002 No. C325/33.

Treaty of Amsterdam amending the Treaty on European Union, the Treaties establishing the European Communities and certain related acts, OJ 1997 No. C340/1 (entered into force 1 May 1999).

Treaty on the European Union, Maastricht, 7 February 1992, in force 1 November 1993, OJ 1992 No. C191.

Treaty on the European Union (Consolidated Version), OJ 2010 No. C83/13

Treaty on the Functioning of the European Union, as amended by the Treaty of Lisbon, entered into force 1 December 2009, OJ 2010 No. C83/47.

UN Convention against Torture and Other Cruel, Inhuman or Degrading Treatment, New York, 10 December 1984, in force 26 June 1987, 1465 UNTS 85.

UNHCR, *2005 UNHCR Statistical Yearbook: Israel*.

UNHCR, *2010 Global Trends* (June 2011).

UNHCR, 'A Year of Crises: UNHCR Global Trends 2011', 18 June 2012 http://www.unhcr.org/4fd6f87f9.html

UNHCR, 'Africans and Asians Attracted to Latin America as a Migration Route', 10 November 2010 http://www.unhcr.org/refworld/docid/4cdba5f82.html

UNHCR, *An Overview of Protection Issues in Western Europe: Legislative Trends and Positions Taken by UNHCR* (September 1995).

UNHCR, *Asylum in the European Union: A Study of the Implementation of the Qualification Directive* (November 2007) http://www.unhcr.org/refworld/docid/473050632.html

UNHCR, 'Comments on Sections 2–4 of the Regulations Regarding the Processing of Asylum Seekers in Israel', 12 January 2011.

UNHCR, *Documentos y conclusiones de Reuniones Regionales* http://www.acnur.org/paginas/index.php?id_pag=3170

UNHCR, *Follow-up on Earlier Conclusions of the Sub-Committee on the Determination of Refugee Status, inter alia, with Reference to the Role of UNHCR in National Refugee Status Determination Procedure*, 3 September 1982, UN Doc. EC/SCP/22/Rev.1.

UNHCR, *Follow-up on Earlier Conclusions of the Sub-Committee on the Determination of Refugee Status with Regard to the Problem of Manifestly Unfounded or Abusive Applications*, UN Doc. EC/SCP/29, 26 August 1983.

UNHCR, *Guidelines on International Protection: 'Internal Flight or Relocation Alternative' within the Context of Article 1A(2) of the 1951 Convention and/or 1967 Protocol relating to the Status of Refugees*, UN Doc. HCR/GIP/03/04, 23 July 2003.

UNHCR, *Guidelines on International Protection: 'Membership of a Particular Social Group' within the Context of Article 1A(2) of the 1951 Convention and/or 1967 Protocol relating to the Status of Refugees*, UN Doc. HCR/GIP/02/02, 7 May 2002.

UNHCR, *Memoria del Vigésimo Aniversario de la Declaración de Cartagena sobre los Refugiados 1984–2004* (San José: Editorama, 2005).

UNHCR, *Note on International Protection*, UN Doc. A/AC.96/799, 25 July 1992.

UNHCR, *Note on the Interpretation of Article 1E of the 1951 Convention relating to the Status of Refugees* (March 2009).

UNHCR, *Observations on the European Commission's proposal for a Council Directive on minimum standards for the qualification and status of third-country nationals and stateless persons as refugees or as persons who otherwise need international protection* (November 2001).

UNHCR, *Proposed Measures to Extend the Personal Scope of the Convention relating to the Status of Refugees of 28 July 1951*, UN Doc. A/AC.96/346, 12 October 1966.

UNHCR, 'Q&A: Growing Caseload of Asylum Seekers for UNHCR Officers in Israel', 13 July 2007 http://www.unhcr.org/469797404.html

UNHCR, *Refugees and Others of Concern to UNHCR: 1998 Statistical Overview* (July 2000).

UNHCR, *Relocating Internally as a Reasonable Alternative to Seeking Asylum (the So-Called 'Internal Flight Alternative' or 'Relocation Principle')* (UNHCR Position Paper, February 1999).

UNHCR, Submission No. 20 to the Senate Standing Committee on Legal and Constitutional Affairs, *Inquiry into the Migration Amendment (Complementary Protection) Bill 2009* (30 September 2009).

UNHCR, 'Regional Cooperative Approach to Address Refugees, Asylum-Seekers and Irregular Movement' (Manila, 22–23 November 2010) http://www.baliprocess.net/files/Regional%20Cooperation%20Approach%20Discussion%20document%20-%20final.pdf

UNHCR, *Safe at Last? Law and Practice in Selected EU Member States with respect to Asylum-seekers Fleeing Indiscriminate Violence* (July 2011).

UNHCR, *Self-Study Module on Refugee Status Determination* (2005).

UNHCR, *Some Additional Observations and Recommendations on the European Commission 'Proposal for a Council Directive on minimum standards for the qualification and status of third country nationals and stateless persons as refugees or as persons who otherwise need international protection'* (July 2002).

UNHCR, *Statement by the High Commissioner to the 15th Session of the Executive Committee of the High Commissioner's Programme*, UN Doc. A/AC.96/310, 29 October 1965.

UNHCR, *Summary Report: Regional Conference on Refugee Protection and International Migration in the Americas – Protection Considerations in the Context of Mixed Migration* (San José, Costa Rica, 19–20 November 2009).

UNHCR, *Annotated Comments on the EC Council Directive 2004/83/EC of 29 April 2004 on Minimum Standards for the Qualification and Status of Third Country Nationals or Stateless Persons as Refugees or as Persons Who Otherwise Need International Protection and the Content of the Protection Granted* (January 2005).

UNHCR, 'UNHCR's Recommendations to Belgium for its EU Presidency, July–December 2010' (June 2010).

UNHCR, 'UNHCR's Recommendations to Poland for its EU Presidency, July–December 2011' www.unhcr.org/4df8d00f9.html

UNHCR archives, Copy of incoming cable from HCR Léopoldville to HiComRef Geneva, received 12 July 1965, fonds 1/5/11/1.

UNHCR archives, Letter dated 14 July 1965, fonds 1/5/11/1.

UNHCR archives, Note Submitted by the United Nations High Commissioner for Refugees on Measures Being Examined within the Framework of the Organization of African Unity for Regulating Refugee Problems Between Member States, June 1965, fonds 1/5/11/1.

UNHCR archives, 'Report of the Administrative Secretary-General for the Meeting of the OAU Commission on Refugees Held in Addis Ababa from 17th to 23rd June 1968', fonds 1/5/11/1.

UNHCR Executive Committee, Conclusion No. 8 (XXVIII) (12 October 1977).

UNHCR Executive Committee, Conclusion No. 15 (XXX) (16 October 1979).

UNHCR Executive Committee, Conclusion No. 28 (XXXIII) (20 October 1982).

UNHCR Executive Committee, Conclusion No. 30 (XXXIV) (20 October 1983).

UNHCR Executive Committee, Conclusion No. 46 (XXVIII) (12 October 1987).

UNHCR Executive Committee, Conclusion No. 65 (XLII) (11 October 1991).

UNHCR Executive Committee, Conclusion No. 79 (XLVII) (11 October 1996).

UNHCR Executive Committee, Conclusion No. 85 (XLIX) (9 October 1998).

UNHCR Executive Committee, Conclusion No. 87(L) (8 October 1999).

UNHCR's oral submission in *NS* v. *Secretary of State for the Home Department* and *ME and Others* v. *Refugee Applications Commissioner and Minister for Justice, Equality and Law Reform*, Joined Cases C-411/10 and C-493/10, 28 July 2011.

UNHCR's written observations in *NS* v. *Secretary of State for the Home Department* and *ME and Others* v. *Refugee Applications Commissioner and Minister for Justice, Equality and Law Reform*, Joined Cases C-411/10 and C-493/10, 1 February 2011.

UN Human Rights Council, *Report of the Working Group on Arbitrary Detention: Mission to Malaysia*, UN Doc. A/HRC/16/47/Add., 28 February 2011.

UN Human Rights Council, *Report of the Special Rapporteur on Contemporary Forms of Racism, Racial Discrimination, Xenophobia and Related Intolerance, Githu Muigai*, A/HRC/11/36 19, May 2009.

Case law

4 Refugees v. *Head of IDF Operations Division*, HCJ 3208, 3270, 3271, 3272/06

A v. *Secretary of State for the Home Department* [2004] UKHL 56

AC (Syria) [2011] NZIPT 800035

Adan v. *Secretary of State for the Home Department* [1999] 1 AC 293

Al-Kateb v. *Godwin* [2004] HCA 37 (6 August 2004), (2004) 219 CLR 562

Al-Rahal v. *Minister for Immigration and Multicultural Affairs* [2001] FCA 1141

Amuur v. *France* (1992) 22 EHRR 533

Applicant A v. *Minister for Immigration and Ethnic Affairs* (1997) 190 CLR 225

Applicant M38/2002 v. *Minister for Immigration and Multicultural and Indigenous Affairs* [2003] FCA 458 (15 May 2003)

Applicants M160/2003 v. *Minister for Immigration and Multicultural and Indigenous Affairs* [2005] FCA 195 (8 March 2005)

Applicant S100 of 2004 v. *Minister for Immigration and Multicultural and Indigenous Affairs* [2004] FCA 1364 (26 October 2004)

Arteaga v. *Mukasey*, 511 F 3d 940 (9th Cir. 2007)

Asylum Case (Colombia v. *Peru)* (1950) ICJ Rep 266

Awad v. *Ziriax*, 754 F. Supp. 2d 1298 (WD Okla. 2010)

BB v. *France* (European Commission of Human Rights, App. No. 30930/96, 9 March 1998)

Belishta v. *Ashcroft*, 378 F3d 1078 (9th Cir. 2004)

BG (Fiji) [2012] NZIPT 800091

Boer-Sedano v. *Gonzales*, 418 F 3d 1082 (9th Cir. 2005)

Canadian Council for Refugees v. *Canada* (2007), 2007 FC 1262, reversed (2008), 2008 FCA 229, leave to appeal refused, 5 February 2009, 395 NR 387n

Case C-465/07, *Elgafaji* v. *Staatssecretaris van Justitie* (Court of Justice of the European Union, Grand Chamber, 17 February 2009), ECR [2009] 1–921

Case C-133/06, *Parliament* v. *Council* [2008] ECR I-3189; [2008] 2 CMLR 54

Case No. 0106-2005-RA, Constitutional Tribunal of Ecuador, 11 May 2006

Castellano-Chacon v. *INS*, 341 F 3d 533 (6th Cir. 2003)

Chahal v. *United Kingdom* (1996) 23 EHRR 413

D-356/2007, Swiss Federal Administrative Tribunal, 2 April 2007

D-7035/2006, Swiss Federal Administrative Tribunal, 1 February 2008

D-4404/2006, Swiss Federal Administrative Tribunal, 2 May 2008

D-4297/2006, Swiss Federal Administrative Tribunal, 26 January 2009

D-313/2010, Swiss Federal Administrative Tribunal, 2 March 2010

D-4935/2007, Swiss Federal Administrative Tribunal, 21 December 2011

Dudgeon v. *United Kingdom* (European Court of Human Rights, App. No. 7525/76, 22 October 1981), 45 ECtHR (1981)

E-4054/2006, Swiss Federal Administrative Tribunal, 18 July 2007

E-4412/2006, Swiss Federal Administrative Tribunal, 25 April 2008

E-3710/2006, Swiss Federal Administrative Tribunal, 18 June 2008

E-4110/2008, Swiss Federal Administrative Tribunal, 18 December 2008

E-7089/2009, Swiss Federal Administrative Tribunal, 2 December 2009

E-2553/2008, Swiss Federal Administrative Tribunal, 16 August 2011

El-Tai'i v. *Minister of Interior* 49(3) PD 843 [1994]

Frydlender v. *France* (2001) 31 EHRR 52

Gatimi v. *Holder*, 578 F3d 611 (7th Cir. 2009)

Geza v. *Canada (Minister of Citizenship and Immigration)* [2005] 3 FCR 3; 2004 FC 1039 (Federal Court)

Geza v. *Canada (Minister of Citizenship and Immigration)* [2006] 4 FCR 377; 2006 FCA 124

GJ, Re, Refugee Appeal No. 1312/93, New Zealand: Refugee Status Appeals Authority, 30 August 1995 [1995] 1 NLR 387

Golder v. *United Kingdom* (1975) 1 EHRR 524

HCJ 6312/10, 19 January 2011

Hercegi v. *Canada (Minister of Citizenship and Immigration)* [2012] 2012 FC 250 (Federal Court)

Hernandez v. *Ministry of the Interior*, 14 August 2011, case details in English available
   at: http://refugeecaselaw.org/CaseAdditionalInfo.aspx?caseid=1988
Hernandez-Montiel v. *INS*, 225 F.3d 1084 (9th Cir. 2000)
Hirsi and Others v. *Italy* (European Court of Human Rights, Grand Chamber,
   App. No. 27765/09, 23 February 2012)
Hornsby v. *Greece* (1997) 24 EHRR 250
Hotline for Migrant Workers v. *Minister of Defence*, HCJ 7302/07, 7 July 2011
Huber v. *Switzerland*, European Court of Human Rights, 23 October 1990, Ser. A,
   No. 188
Husan v. *Secretary of State for the Home Department* [2005] EWHC 189 (Admin.)
INS v. *Cardoza-Fonseca*, 480 US 421 (1987)
Islam v. *Secretary of State for the Home Department*; *R* v. *Immigration Appeal
   Tribunal, ex parte Shah* [1999] 2 AC 629
JICRA 1993/9, Swiss Asylum Appeals Commission
JICRA 1993/10, Swiss Asylum Appeals Commission
JICRA 1995/1, Swiss Asylum Appeals Commission
JICRA 1995/2, Swiss Asylum Appeals Commission
JICRA 1995/25, Swiss Asylum Appeals Commission
JICRA 1996/6, Swiss Asylum Appeals Commission
JICRA 1996/16, Swiss Asylum Appeals Commission
JICRA 1996/42, Swiss Asylum Appeals Commission
JICRA 1997/4, Swiss Asylum Appeals Commission
JICRA 1997/6, Swiss Asylum Appeals Commission
JICRA 1997/12, Swiss Asylum Appeals Commission
JICRA 1997/14, Swiss Asylum Appeals Commission
JICRA 1998/17, Swiss Asylum Appeals Commission
JICRA 2000/15, Swiss Asylum Appeals Commission
JICRA 2002/2, Swiss Asylum Appeals Commission
JICRA 2002/8, Swiss Asylum Appeals Commission
JICRA 2002/16, Swiss Asylum Appeals Commission
JICRA 2004/14, Swiss Asylum Appeals Commission
JICRA 2006/18, Swiss Asylum Appeals Commission
JICRA 2006/19, Swiss Asylum Appeals Commission
Joined Cases C-57/09 and C-101/09, *Bundesrepublik Deutschland* v. *B and D*, ECR
   [2010] I-000
Joined Cases C-175, 176, 178, 179/08, *Salahadin Abdulla and Others* v. *Germany*,
   ECR [2009] I-1493
Joined Cases C-411/10 and C-493/10, *NS* v. *Secretary of State for the Home
   Department* and *ME, ASM, MT, KP and EH* v. *Refugee Applications
   Commissioner, Minister for Justice, Equality and Law Reform* (Court of
   Justice of the European Union, Grand Chamber, 21 December 2011)
Katambayi and Lawyers for Human Rights v. *Minister of Home Affairs et al.*, No. 02/
   5312, South African High Court, Witwatersrand Local Division, 24 March 2002

Katinszki v. *Canada* (Minister of Citizenship and Immigration) [2012] 2012 FC
      1326
Kholyavskiy v. *Mukasey*, 540 F 3d 555 (7th Cir. 2008)
Kokkinakis v. *Greece* (1993) 17 EHRR 397
Kone v. *Holder*, 596 F 3d 1141 (2nd Cir. 2010)
Lawrence v. *Texas*, 539 US 558 (2003)
Lorenzo v. *Minister for Immigration and Multicultural and Indigenous Affairs and
      Commonwealth of Australia* [2004] FCA 435
Matter of Acosta, I & N Dec. 211 at 233 (BIA 1985)
Matter of Fuentes, 19 I & N Dec. 658 (BIA 1988)
Matter of H, 21 I & N Dec. 337 (BIA 1996)
Matter of JE, 23 I & N Dec. 291 at 297–8 (BIA 2002)
Matter of Kasinga, 12 I & N Dec. 357 (BIA 1996)
Matter of LS, 25 I & N Dec. 705 (BIA 2012)
Matter of RA, 22 I & N Dec. 906 at 919 (BIA 1999)
Matter of SEG, 24 I & N Dec. 579, at 584, 586 (BIA 2008)
Matter of Toboso-Alfonso, 20 I & N Dec. 819 (BIA 1990)
Minister for Immigration and Ethnic Affairs and Refugee Review Tribunal v. *Singh*
      [1997] FCA 354 (7 May 1997)
Minister for Immigration and Multicultural Affairs, Re; ex parte Epeabaka (2001)
      206 CLR 128
Minister for Immigration and Multicultural Affairs v. *Gnanapiragasam* (1998)
      88 FCR 1
Minister for Immigration and Multicultural Affairs v. *Haji Ibrahim* (2000)
      204 CLR 1
Minister for Immigration and Multicultural Affairs v. *Kabail* [1999] FCA 344
Minister for Immigration and Multicultural Affairs v. *Respondents S152/2003*
      (2004) 222 CLR 1
Minister for Immigration and Multicultural Affairs v. *Thiyagarajah* (1997)
      80 FCR 543
Minister for Immigration and Multicultural and Indigenous Affairs v. *Al Masri*
      [2003] FCAFC 70 (15 April 2003)
Minister for Immigration and Multicultural and Indigenous Affairs v. *QAAH of
      2004* (2006) 231 CLR 1
Mohammed v. *Gonzales*, 400 F3d 785 (9th Cir. 2005)
MSS v. *Belgium and Greece* (European Court of Human Rights, Grand Chamber,
      App. No. 30696/09, 21 January 2011)
MZ RAJ v. *Minister for Immigration and Multicultural and Indigenous Affairs*
      [2004] FCA 1261 (29 September 2004)
NABD of 2002 v. *Minister for Immigration and Multicultural and Indigenous
      Affairs* (2005) 216 ALR 1

NAEN v. *Minister for Immigration and Multicultural and Indigenous Affairs* [2003] FCA 216

NAGV and NAGW of 2002 v. *Minister for Immigration and Multicultural and Indigenous Affairs* [2005] HCA 6 (2 March 2005) (2005) 222 CLR 161

NAIS v. *Minister for Immigration and Multicultural and Indigenous Affairs* (2005) 228 CLR 470

Osman v. *United Kingdom* (1998) 29 EHRR 245

Ovcharuk v. *Minister for Immigration and Multicultural Affairs* [1998] FCA 1314 (16 October 1998)

Patto v. *Minister for Immigration and Multicultural Affairs* [2000] FCA 1554

Plaintiff M61/2010E v. *Commonwealth of Australia* [2010] HCA 41 (11 November 2010) (2010) 243 CLR 319

Plaintiff M70/2011 and Plaintiff M106/2011 v. *Minister for Immigration and Citizenship* [2011] HCA 32 (31 August 2011) (2011) 280 ALR 18

Pllumi v. *Attorney General of US*, 642 F 3d 155 (3rd Cir. 2011)

R v. *Secretary of State for the Home Department, ex parte Abdi* [1996] 1 WLR 298

R v. *Secretary of State for the Home Department* v. *Javed* [2001] EWCA Civ. 789 (Court of Appeal, Civ. Div.)

Ram v. *Minister for Immigration and Ethnic Affairs* (1995) 57 FCR 565

Ramos v. *Holder*, 589 F 3d 426 at 430 (7th Cir. 2009)

Refugee Appeal No. 76044 (11 September 2008)

Rezmuves v. *Canada (Minister of Citizenship and Immigration)* [2012] 2012 FC 334

Roper v. *Simmons*, 543 US 551 (2004)

Ruddock v. *Vadarlis* [2001] FCA 1329 (18 September 2001)

Saadi v. *United Kingdom* (2007) 44 EHRR 50

Sanchez-Trujillo v. *INS*, 801 F 2d 1571 (9th Cir. 1986)

SBZD v. *Minister for Immigration and Citizenship* [2008] FCA 1236 (14 August 2008)

Scatambulli v. *Holder*, 558 F 3d 53 (1st Cir. 2009)

Secretary of State for the Home Department v. *K* [2006] UKHL 46

Sentencia T-704/03, Reza Pirhadi v. *Ministerio de Relaciones Exteriores y el Departamento Administrativo de Seguridad DAS*, Constitutional Court of Colombia, 14 August 2003

Sholla v. *Gonzalez*, 492 F.3d 946 (8th Cir. 2007)

SHKB v. *Minister for Immigration and Multicultural and Indigenous Affairs* [2005] FCAFC 11 (18 February 2005)

Silva Pontes v. *Portugal* (1994) 18 EHRR 156

Singh v. *Minister for Immigration and Multicultural Affairs* [1998] FCA 619 (9 June 1998)

Soering v. *United Kingdom* (1989) 11 EHRR 439

Sufi and Elmi v. *United Kingdom* (European Court of Human Rights, App. Nos. 8319/07 and 11449/07, 28 June 2011)

SZBBP v. *Minister for Immigration and Multicultural and Indigenous Affairs* [2005] FCAFC 167 (19 August 2005)

Valdiviezo-Galdamez v. *Attorney General*, 663 F 3d 582 (3rd Cir. 2011)

VRAW v. *Minister for Immigration and Multicultural and Indigenous Affairs* [2004] FCA 1133 (3 September 2004)

Ward v. *Canada (Minister of Employment and Immigration* (1993), 20 Imm. LR (2d) 85; 103 DLR (4th) 1

Secondary sources

'3 paquistaníes detenidos en Quito aceptan vínculos con terrorismo', *El Comercio*, 14 September 2011.

'A Regional Refugee Protection Framework: A Joint Statement by Australian Non-Government Organisations' (1 August 2010) http://www.refugeecouncil.org.au/docs/releases/2010/100801_Regional_Protection_Framework.pdf

Acharya, Amitav, 'How Ideas Spread: Whose Norms Matter? Norm Localization and Institutional Change in Asian Regionalism' (2004) 58 *International Organization* 239–75.

Achermann, Alberto and Hausammann, Christian, *Handbuch des Asylrechts* (Berne: Paul Haupt, 1991).

Acquaviva, Guido, 'Forced Displacement and International Crimes' (UNHCR, Legal and Protection Policy Research Series, PPLA/2011/05, June 2011).

Aeschimann, Stefan *et al.*, *Swiss Neutrality* (4th edn, Berne: Federal Department of Defence, Civil Protection and Sports, 2004).

Afeef, Karin Fathimath, 'The Politics of Extraterritorial Processing: Offshore Asylum Policies in Europe and the Pacific', RSC Working Paper No. 36 (October 2006).

Afonso, Alexandre and Maggetti, Martino, 'Bilaterals II, Reaching the Limits of the Swiss Third Way?', in Clive H. Church (ed.), *Switzerland and the European Union: A Close, Contradictory and Misunderstood Relationship* (London: Routledge, 2007), pp. 215–33.

Aleinikoff, T. Alexander, 'Protected Characteristics and Social Perceptions: An Analysis of the Meaning of "Membership in a Particular Social Group"', in Erika Feller, Volker Türk and Frances Nicholson (eds.), *Refugee Protection in International Law: UNHCR's Global Consultations on International Protection* (Cambridge: Cambridge University Press, 2003), pp. 263–311.

Amit, Roni, 'No Refuge: Flawed Status Determination and the Failures of South Africa's Refugee System to Provide Protection' (2011) 23 *International Journal of Refugee Law* 458–88.

Amnesty International, 'Abused and Abandoned: Refugees Denied Rights in Malaysia' (June 2010) http://www.amnesty.org/en/library/asset/ASA28/010/2010/en/2791c659-7e4d-4922-87e0-940faf54b92c/asa280102010en.pdf

'Israel: New Detention Law Violates Rights of Asylum Seekers', 11 January 2012 http://www.amnesty.org/en/news/new-israeli-detention-law-violates-asylum-seekers-rights-2012-01-10

'Malaysia: Human Rights at Risk in Mass Deportation of Undocumented Migrants' (December 2004) http://www.amnesty.org/en/library/asset/ASA28/008/2004/en/a4e9ce8d-d57c-11dd-bb24-1fb85fe8fa05/asa280082004en.html

'Mind the Legal Gap: Roma and the right to housing in Romania', AI Index: EUR 39/004/2011, 23 June 2011.

'UK/EU/UNHCR: Unlawful and Unworkable: Amnesty International's Views on Proposals for Extraterritorial Processing of Asylum Claims', AI Index: IOR 61/004/2003, 17 June 2003.

Anker, Deborah and Posner, Michael, 'The Forty Year Crisis: A Legislative History of the Refugee Act of 1980' (1981) 19 *San Diego Law Review* 9–90.

Archibold, Randal, 'Mexican drug cartel violence spills over from Mexico, alarming US', *New York Times*, 23 March 2009, p. A1.

'Mexico's drug war bloodies areas thought safe', *New York Times*, 19 January 2012, p. A1.

Armstrong, David, Farrell, Theo and Lambert, Hélène, *International Law and International Relations* (2nd edn, Cambridge: Cambridge University Press, 2012).

Australian Refugee Law Academics, Submission No. 25 to Senate Legal and Constitutional Affairs References Committee, *Inquiry into Australia's Agreement with Malaysia in relation to Asylum Seekers* (15 September 2011).

Azuara, Araceli, 'Panorama general de la migración extracontinental en las Américas', in OAS Comisión Especial de Asuntos Migratorios, *Memoria: Migración extracontinental en las Américas* (6 April 2010), pp. 3–11.

Badie, Bertrand, *The Imported State: The Westernization of Political Order* (Stanford: Stanford University Press, 2000).

Baldaccini, Anneliese, Guild, Elspeth and Toner, Helen (eds.), *Whose Freedom, Security and Justice? EU Immigration and Asylum Law and Policy* (Oxford: Hart, 2007).

Bank, Roland, 'Transposition of the Qualification Directive in Germany', in Karin Zwaan (ed.), *The Qualification Directive: Central Themes, Problem Issues, and Implementation in Selected Member States* (Nijmegen: Wolf Legal Publishers, 2007), pp. 109–26.

Barkin, Samuel and Cronin, Bruce, 'The State and the Nation: Changing Norms and the Rules of Sovereignty in International Relations' (1994) 48 *International Organization* 107–30.

Barnes, Steve, 'The Real Cost of Cutting Refugee Health Benefits', Wellesley Institute, 23 May 2012 http://www.wellesleyinstitute.com/publication/the-real-cost-of-cutting-refugee-health-benefits/

Barnett, Laura, 'Global Governance and the Evolution of the International Refugee Regime' (2002) 14 *International Journal of Refugee Law* 238–62.

Battjes, Hemme, *European Asylum Law and International Law* (Leiden and Boston: Martinus Nijhoff, 2006).

Bell, John 'The Argumentative Status of Foreign Legal Arguments' (2012) 8 *Utrecht Law Review* 8–19.

Ben-Dor, Anat and Adut, Rami, *Israel: A Safe Haven? Problems in the Treatment Offered by the State of Israel to Refugees and Asylum Seekers* (Report and Position Paper, Tel Aviv University, Buchmann Faculty of Law, Public Interest Law Resource Centre, and Physicians for Human Rights, September 2003).

Ben-Dor, Anat and Kagan, Michael, 'The Refugee from My Enemy is My Enemy: The Detention and Exclusion of Sudanese Refugees in Israel' (Minerva Center for Human Rights, Working Paper, 19 November 2006).

Berman, Yonatan, 'Stop press: for the first time, Israeli court orders the government of Israel to grant asylum', *Fahamu Refugee Legal Aid Newsletter*, 31 October 2011.

'The Israeli Refugee Status Determination Process: General Background' (Hotline for Migrant Workers, 20 September 2011).

Betts, Alexander (ed.), *Global Migration Governance* (Oxford: Oxford University Press, 2011).

'The International Relations of the "New" Extraterritorial Approaches to Refugee Protection: Explaining the Policy Initiatives of the UK Government and UNHCR' (2004) 22 *Refuge* 58–70.

Beyer, Gregg, 'Reforming Affirmative Asylum Processing in the United States: Challenges and Opportunities', (1994) 9 *American University International Law Review* 43–78.

Bigo, Didier, 'Border Regimes, Police Cooperation and Security in an Enlarged European Union', in Jan Zielonka (ed.), *Europe Unbound: Enlarging and Reshaping the Boundaries of the European Union* (London and New York: Routledge, 2002), pp. 213–39.

Boccardi, Ingrid, *Europe and Refugees: Towards an EU Asylum Policy* (The Hague, London, New York: Kluwer Law International, 2002).

Boerman, Thomas, 'Youth Gangs in El Salvador: Unpacking the State Department 2007 Issue Paper', *Immigration Daily*, 2010 http://www.ilw.com/articles/2010,1117-boerman.shtm

Bogdanski, Pascal-Hervé, 'L'association de la Suisse au système de Dublin', in Christine Kaddous and Monique Jametti Greiner (eds.), *Accords bilatéraux II Suisse–UE et autres Accords récents* (Brussels: Bruylant, Paris: LGDJ, Basel: Helbing & Lichtenhahn, 2006), pp. 389–424.

Bolz, Susanne, 'Wie EU-Kompatibel ist das Schweizer Asylrecht?' (2005) 1/05 *ASYL* 8–13.

Bolz, Susanne and Buchmann, Kathrin, 'Die Rechtsprechung der Schweizerischen Asylrekurskommission im Jahre 2006', in Alberto Achermann *et al.* (eds.), *Jahrbuch für Migrationsrecht/Annuaire du droit de la migration* (Berne: Stämpfli Verlag AG, 2006/2007), pp. 183–214.

Bouteillet-Paquet, Daphné, 'Subsidiary Protection: Progress or Set-Back of Asylum Law in Europe? A Critical Analysis of the Legislation of the Member States of the European Union', in Daphné Bouteillet-Paquet (ed.), *Subsidiary Protection of Refugees in the European Union: Complementing the Geneva Convention?* (Brussels: Bruylant, 2002), pp. 211–64.

Bronner, Ethan, 'Israel acts to curb illegal immigration from Africa', *New York Times*, 11 December 2011 http://www.nytimes.com/2011/12/12/world/middleeast/israel-steps-up-efforts-to-stop-illegal-immigration-from-africa.html

Brownlie, Ian, *Principles of Public International Law* (5th edn, Oxford: Oxford University Press, 1998).

Burley, Anne-Marie and Mattli, Walter, 'Europe before the Court: A Political Theory of Legal Integration' (1993) 47 *International Organization* 41–76.

Byrne, Rosemary, Noll, Gregor and Vedsted-Hansen, Jens, 'Understanding Refugee Law in an Enlarged European Union' (2004) 15 *European Journal of International Law* 355–79.

Byrne, Rosemary and Shacknove, Andrew, 'The Safe Country Notion in European Asylum Law' (1996) 9 *Harvard Human Rights Journal* 185–228.

Campbell, Will, 'Federal government considers detaining Roma refugee claimants, report suggests', *Globe and Mail*, 18 August 2012 http://www.theglobeandmail.com/news/politics/federal-government-considers-detaining-roma-refugee-claimants-report-suggests/article4487855/

Cantor, David J., 'Restitution, Compensation, Satisfaction: Transnational Reparations and Colombia's Victims' Law' (UNHCR, *New Issues in Refugee Research*, Research Paper No. 215, August 2011).

Carlier, Jean-Yves, *Droit d'asile et des réfugiés: de la protection aux droits* (Leiden and Boston: Martinus Nijhoff, 2008).

Carlson, Kathryn Blaze, 'Record number of Hungarian asylum-seekers landing on Canada's doorstep', *National Post*, 4 November 2011 http://news.nationalpost.com/2011/11/04/record-number-of-hungarian-asylum-seekers-landing-on-canadas-doorstep/

Carrera, Sergio, Guild, Elspeth and Merlino, Massimo, 'The Canada–Czech Republic Visa Dispute Two Years On: Implications for the EU's Migration and Asylum Policies' (Centre for European Policy Studies Paper on Liberty and Security in Europe, October 2011).

Caudill-Mirillo, Ashley, Deputy Director, New York Asylum Office, 23 March 2012 (on file with Maryellen Fullerton).

New York Asylum Office, 27 March 2012 (on file with Maryellen Fullerton).

Chartrand, Philip, 'The Organization of African Unity and African Refugees: A Progress Report' (1975) 137 *World Affairs* 265–85.

Checkel, Jeffrey, 'Norms, Institutions, and National Identity in Contemporary Europe' (1999) 50 *International Studies Quarterly* 83–111.

Chetail, Vincent, 'La réforme de l'asile: prélude à la banalisation européenne du droit des réfugiés' (2004) 131 *Journal de droit international* 817–65.

'The Implementation of the Qualification Directive in France: One Step Forward and Two Steps Backwards', in Karin Zwaan (ed.), *The Qualification Directive: Central Themes, Problem Issues, and Implementation in Selected Member States* (Nijmegen: Wolf Legal Publishers, 2007), pp. 87–101.

Chetail, Vincent and Bauloz, Céline, *The European Union and the Challenges of Forced Migration: From Economic Crisis to Protection Crisis?* (EU–US Immigration Systems 2011/07, Robert Schuman Centre for Advanced Studies, San Domenico di Fiesole: European University Institute, 2011).

Chevallaz, Georges-André, *The Challenge of Neutrality: Diplomacy and the Defence of Switzerland* (Lanham, MD: Lexington Books, 2001).

Chimni, B. S. 'Reforming the International Refugee Regime: A Dialogic Model' (2001) 14 *Journal of Refugee Studies* 151–68.

Churchill, Winston, 'The Sinews of Peace' (Speech delivered at Westminster College, Fulton, Missouri, 5 March 1946) http://www.winstonchurchill.org/learn/ speeches/speeches-of-winston-churchill/120-the-sinews-of-peace

Clark, Campbell, 'Visa feud clouds Harper's free-trade dream with Europe', *Globe and Mail*, 26 April 2012 www.theglobeandmail.com/news/politics/. . ./article4102974/

Clarke, Anne-Marie, *Diplomacy of Conscience: Amnesty International and Changing Human Rights Norms* (Princeton: Princeton University Press, 2002).

Cortell, Andrew and Davis, James, 'Understanding the Domestic Impact of International Norms: A Research Agenda' (2000) 2 *International Studies Review* 65–90.

Costello, Cathryn, 'The Asylum Procedures Directive and the Proliferation of Safe Country Practices: Deterrence, Deflection and the Dismantling of International Protection?' (2005) 7 *European Journal of Migration and Law* 35–69.

Cotterrell, Roger, *Law, Culture and Society* (Aldershot: Ashgate, 2006).

Cuéllar, Roberto *et al.*, 'Refugee and Related Developments in Latin America: Challenges Ahead' (1991) 3 *International Journal of Refugee Law* 482–98.

Dastyari, Azadeh, 'Refugees on Guantánamo Bay: A Blue Print for Australia's "Pacific Solution"?' (2007) 79 *Australian Quarterly* 4–8.

Dauvergne, Catherine, *Making People Illegal* (Cambridge: Cambridge University Press, 2008).

Davies, Sara, 'Redundant or Essential? How Politics Shaped the Outcome of the 1967 Protocol' (2007) 19 *International Journal of Refugee Law* 703–28.

De Bruycker, Philippe, Foblets, Marie-Claire and Maes, Marleen (eds.), *External Dimensions of European Migration and Asylum Law and Policy* (Brussels: Bruylant, 2011).

De Tocqueville, Alexis, *Democracy in America*, vol. II (ed. Phillips Bradley, trans. Henry Reeve) (New York: Knopf, 1948) (1835).

DeLong, Matt, 'Joe Miller: Obama moving America "toward socialism"', *Washington Post*, 2 September 2010 http://voices.washingtonpost.com/44/ 2010/09/joe-miller-obama-moving-americ.html

Den Heijer, Maarten, 'Europe Beyond Its Borders: Refugee and Human Rights Protection in Extraterritorial Immigration Control', in Bernard Ryan and Valsamis Mitsilegas (eds.), *Extraterritorial Immigration Control: Legal Challenges* (Leiden and Boston: Martinus Nijhoff, 2010), pp. 169–98.

DeParle, Jason, 'In battle to pick next justice, right says avoid a Kennedy', *New York Times*, 27 June 2005, p. A1.

Dickman, Orna, 'Employing of Asylum Seekers in Israel: Regulations and Problems' (Hotline for Migrant Workers, May 2011).

DiMaggio, Paul and Powell, Walter, 'The Iron Cage Revisited: Institutional Isomorphism and Collective Rationality', in Walter Powell and Paul DiMaggio (eds.), *The New Institutionalism in Organizational Analysis* (Chicago: Chicago University Press, 1991), pp. 41–62.

Dudley, Steven, *Transnational Crime in Mexico and Central America: Its Evolution and Role in International Migration* (Washington, DC: Migration Policy Institute, 2012).

Durbach, Andrea, Renshaw, Catherine and Byrnes, Andrew, '"A Tongue but No Teeth?": The Emergence of a Regional Human Rights Mechanism in the Asia Pacific Region' (2009) 31 *Sydney Law Review* 211–38.

Durieux, Jean-François, 'The Many Faces of "Prima Facie": Group-Based Evidence in Refugee Status Determination' (2008) 25 *Refuge* 151–63.

'Opinion: Protection Where? – Or When? First Asylum, Deflection Policies and the Significance of Time' (2009) 21 *International Journal of Refugee Law* 75–80.

Durieux, Jean-François and Hurwitz, Agnès, 'How Many Is Too Many? African and European Legal Responses to Mass Influxes of Refugees' (2004) 47 *German Yearbook of International Law* 105–59.

Eggenschwiler, Alejandro, 'The Canada–Czech Republic Visa Affair: A Test for Visa Reciprocity and Fundamental Rights in the European Union' (Centre for European Policy Studies Paper on Liberty and Security in Europe, November 2010).

Efionayi, Denise *et al.*, *Switzerland Faces Common European Challenges* (Migration Information Source, Washington, DC: Migration Policy Institute, February 2005).

Efraim, Omri, 'Who are the Sinai infiltrators?', *Ynetnews.com*, 12 December 2011 www.ynetnews.com/articles/0,7340,L-4160678,00.html

Einarsen, Terje, 'Drafting History of the 1951 Convention and the 1967 Protocol', in Andreas Zimmermann (ed.), *The 1951 Convention relating to the Status of Refugees and Its 1967 Protocol: A Commentary* (Oxford: Oxford University Press, 2011), pp. 37–74.

El-Enany, Nadine, 'Who Is the New European Refugee?' (2008) 33 *European Law Review* 313–35.

Epiney, Astrid, Waldman, Bernhard, Egbuna-Joss, Andrea, and Oeschger, Magnus, 'Die Anerkennung als Flüchtling im europäischen und schweizerischen Recht' (*Jusletter*, 26 May 2008) 1–43.

Esponda Fernández, Jaime, 'La tradición latinoamericana de asilo y la protección internacional de los refugiados', in Leonardo Franco (ed.), *El asilo y la protección internacional de los refugiados en América Latina* (San José: Editorama, 2004), pp. 79–125.

Euro-Mediterranean Human Rights Network, *Israel's Anti-Infiltration Bill: Another Aspect of Asylum Adhocracy* (June 2010).

European Council on Refugees and Exiles, *Broken Promises – Forgotten Principles: An ECRE Evaluation of the Development of EU Minimum Standards for Refugee Protection, Tampere 1999–Brussels 2004* (2004) http://www.ecre.org/component/downloads/downloads/63.html

'Comments from the European Council on Refugees and Exiles on the Amended Commission Proposal to Recast the Asylum Procedures Directive' (COM (2011) 319 final) (1 September 2011) http://www.ecre.org/component/content/article/57-policy-papers/248-ecrecommentsrecastapd2011.html

'Comments from the European Council on Refugees and Exiles on the European Commission Proposal to Recast the Asylum Procedures Directive' (May 2010). http://www.ecre.org/topics/areas-of-work/protection-in-europe/162.html

'The Impact of the EU Qualification Directive on International Protection' (October 2008) http://www.ecre.org/component/content/article/150.html

Memorandum on the Occasion of the Belgian Presidency of the EU (July–December 2010).

European Legal Network on Asylum (ELENA), *Research Paper on the Application of the Concept of Internal Protection Alternative* (London: ELENA, November 1998, updated as of 2000).

European Roma Rights Centre, 'Roma under Attack: Violence against Roma Surges in Central and Eastern Europe' (27 September 2012) http://www.errc.org/article/roma-under-attack-violence-against-roma-surges-in-central-and-eastern-europe/4059

Facultad Latinoamericana de Ciencias Sociales (Costa Rica), *Diagnóstico sobre la situación actual, tendencias y necesidades de protección y asistencia de las personas migrantes y refugiadas extracontinentales en México y América Central* (2011).

Fantz, Ashley, 'The Mexico drug war: bodies for billions', *CNN.com*, 20 January 2012 http://www.cnn.com/2012/01/15/world/mexico-drug-war-essay/index.html?iref=allsearch

'Federal government mulls detaining Roma refugee claimants', *CBCNews*, 18 August 2012 http://www.cbc.ca/news/canada/story/2012/08/18/canada-roma-detain.html

Feller, Erika, 'Opening Statement', in Council of Europe, *Second Colloquy on the European Convention on Human Rights and the Protection of Refugees, Asylum-Seekers and Displaced Persons: Proceedings* (Strasbourg: Council of Europe, 2000).

Finnemore, Martha, *National Interests in International Society* (Ithaca, NY: Cornell University Press, 1996).

'Norms, Culture and World Politics: Insights from Sociology's Institutionalism' (1996) 52 *International Organization* 325–47.

Finnemore, Martha and Sikkink, Kathryn, 'International Norm Dynamics and Political Change' (1998) 52 *International Organization* 887–917.

Fischel de Andrade, José H., 'Regional Policy Approaches and Harmonization: A Latin American Perspective' (1998) 10 *International Journal of Refugee Law* 389–409.

Fischer, Alex, Nicolet, Sarah and Sciarini, Pascal, 'Europeanisation of a Non-EU Country: The Case of Swiss Immigration Policy' (2002) 25(4) *West European Politics* 143–70.

Foster, Michelle, 'Protection Elsewhere: The Legal Implications of Requiring Refugees to Seek Protection in Another State' (2007) 28 *Michigan Journal of International Law* 223–86.

'The "Ground with the Least Clarity": A Comparative Study of Jurisprudential Developments relating to the Ground of "Membership of a Particular Social Group"' (UNHCR, Legal and Protection Policy Research Series, August 2012).

Foster, Michelle and Pobjoy, Jason, Submission No. 9 to Senate Standing Committee on Legal and Constitutional Affairs, *Inquiry into the Migration Amendment (Complementary Protection) Bill 2009* (28 September 2009).

Francis, Angus, 'Bringing Protection Home: Healing the Schism between International Obligations and National Safeguards Created by Extraterritorial Processing' (2008) 20 *International Journal of Refugee Law* 273–313.

Franco, Leonardo (ed.), *El asilo y la protección internacional de los refugiados en América Latina* (San José: Editorama, 2004).

'El derecho internacional de los refugiados y su aplicación en América Latina', in *Anuario Jurídico Interamericano 1982* (Organización de Estados Americanos: Washington, DC, 1983).

Franco, Leonardo and Santistevan de Noriega, Jorge, 'La contribución del proceso de Cartagena al desarrollo del derecho internacional de refugiados en América Latina', in UNHCR, *Memoria del Vigésimo Aniversario de la Declaración de Cartagena sobre los Refugiados 1984–2004* (San José: Editorama, 2005), pp. 81–138.

Friedman, Ron, 'Health Ministry data refutes Yishai's claims that African refugees bring in disease', *Jerusalem Post*, 5 April 2012 http://www.jpost.com/LandedPages/PrintArticle.aspx?id=159701

'State says courts backing up stricter asylum policies', *Jerusalem Post*, 16 March 2011.

Fullerton, Maryellen, 'Inadmissible in Iberia: The Fate of Asylum Seekers in Spain and Portugal' (2005) 17 *International Journal of Refugee Law* 659–87.

'A Tale of Two Decades: War Refugees and Asylum Policy in the European Union' (2011) 10 *Washington University Global Studies Law Review* 87–132.

Garlick, Madeline, 'The EU Discussions on Extraterritorial Processing: Solution or Conundrum?' (2006) 18 *International Journal of Refugee Law* 601–29.

Gattiker, Mario, 'Evolution et perspectives de la notion de pays tiers sûr dans la législation suisse sur l'asile', in Vincent Chetail and Vera Gowlland-Debbas (eds.), *Switzerland and the International Protection of Refugees* (The Hague, London, New York: Kluwer Law International, 2002), pp. 129–44.

Geddes, Andrew, *Immigration and European Integration: Beyond Fortress Europe?* (2nd edn, Manchester: Manchester University Press, 2008).

Gil-Bazo, Maria-Teresa, 'Accelerated Procedures in European Union Law', in Ashley Terlouw (ed.), *Binnen 48 uur. Zorgvuldige behandeling van asielver-zoeken?* (Nijmegen: Wolf Legal Publishers, 2003), pp. 265–76.

'The Charter of Fundamental Rights of the European Union and the Right to be Granted Asylum in the Union's Law' (2008) 27 *Refugee Survey Quarterly* 33–52.

'The Role of Spain as a Gateway to the Schengen Area: Changes in Asylum Law and their Implications for Human Rights' (1998) 10 *International Journal of Refugee Law* 214–29.

Gilbert, Geoff, 'Is Europe Living up to Its Obligations to Refugees?' (2004) 15 *European Journal of International Law* 963–87.

'Gillard Reaches Asylum Agreement with Malaysia', *Q&A*, 7 May 2011 http://www.abc.net.au/news/stories/2011/05/07/3210503.htm?site=qanda

Goetschel, Laurent, Bernath, Magdalena and Schwarz, Daniel, *Politique extérieure Suisse: Fondements et possibilités* (Lausanne: Payot, 2004).

Goldman, Emily and Eliason, Leslie (eds.), *The Diffusion of Military Technology and Ideas* (Stanford: Stanford University Press, 2003).

Goodwin-Gill, Guy S. and Lambert, Hélène (eds.), *The Limits of Transnational Law: Refugee Law, Policy Harmonization and Judicial Dialogue in the European Union* (Cambridge: Cambridge University Press, 2010).

Goodwin-Gill, Guy S. and McAdam, Jane, *The Refugee in International Law* (3rd edn, Oxford: Oxford University Press, 2007).

Gorlick, Brian, 'Human Rights and Refugees: Enhancing Protection through International Human Rights Law' (UNHCR, *New Issues in Refugee Research*, Working Paper No. 30, October 2000).

Gottwald, Martin, 'Protecting Colombian Refugees in the Andean Region: The Fight against Invisibility' (2004) 16 *International Journal of Refugee Law* 517–46.

Goundiam, Ousmane, 'African Refugee Convention' (1970) March/April, *Migration News* 3–12.

Grahl-Madsen, Atle, 'The European Tradition of Asylum and the Development of Refugee Law' (1966) 3 *Journal of Peace Research* 278–89.

Guild, Elspeth, *The Legal Elements of European Identity: EU Citizenship and Migration Law* (The Hague: Kluwer Law International, 2004).

'The Europeanisation of Europe's Asylum Policy' (2006) 18 *International Journal of Refugee Law* 630–51.

Security and Migration in the 21st Century (Cambridge: Polity, 2009).

'Seeking Asylum: Storm Clouds between International Commitments and EU Legislative Measures' (2004) 29 *European Law Review* 198–218.

Guild, Elspeth and Harlow, Carol (eds.), *Implementing Amsterdam: Immigration and Asylum Rights in EC Law* (Oxford: Hart, 2001).

Guiraudon, Virginie, 'European Integration and Migration Policy: Vertical Policy-Making as Venue Shopping' (2000) 38 *Journal of Common Market Studies* 251–71.

Gupta, Anjum, Immigration Clinics List, July 2012 https://dl.dropbox.com/u/61625492/immigrationclinicslist.xlsx

Haas, Peter 'Epistemic Communities and International Policy Coordination' (1992) 41 *International Organization* 1–35.

Hammarberg, Thomas, Council of Europe, 'European Migration Policies Discriminate against Roma' (22 February 2010) http://www.coe.int/t/commissioner/Viewpoints/100222_en.asp

Harkov, Lahav, 'Knesset passes Anti-Infiltration Bill', *Jerusalem Post*, 10 January 2012 http://www.jpost.com/DiplomacyAndPolitics/Article.aspx?id=252909

Hartman, Ben, 'Court delays deportation of South Sudanese', *Jerusalem Post*, 29 March 2012 http://www.jpost.com/DiplomacyAndPolitics/Article.aspx?id=264036

Harvard International Human Rights Clinic, 'No Place to Hide: Gang, State and Clandestine Violence in El Salvador' (February 2007) http://www.law.harvard.edu/programs/hrp/documents/FinalElSalvadorReport(3-6-07).pdf

Harwood, John, 'A blurring of the lines in the populist vs. capitalist debate', *New York Times*, 12 January 2012, p. A19.

Hathaway, James, 'The Evolution of Refugee Status in International Law: 1920–1950' (1984) 33 *International and Comparative Law Quarterly* 348–80.

'Harmonizing for Whom? The Devaluation of Refugee Protection in the Era of European Economic Integration' (1993) 26 *Cornell International Law Journal* 719–35.

The Law of Refugee Status (Toronto: Butterworths, 1991).

'Leveraging Asylum' (2009–10) 45 *Texas International Law Journal* 503–36.

The Rights of Refugees Under International Law (Cambridge: Cambridge University Press, 2005).

Hathaway, James and Foster, Michelle, 'Internal Protection/Relocation/Flight Alternative as an Aspect of Refugee Status Determination', in Erika Feller, Volker Türk and Frances Nicholson (eds.), *Refugee Protection in International Refugee Law: UNHCR's Global Consultations on International Protection* (Cambridge: Cambridge University Press, 2003), pp. 357–417.

Higgins, Rosalyn, *Problems and Process: International Law and How We Use It* (Oxford: Clarendon Press, 1995).

Holborn, Louise, *Refugees: A Problem of our Time – The Work of the United Nations High Commissioner for Refugees, 1951–1972* (Washington, DC: Scarecrow Press, 1974).

Hotline for Migrant Workers, 'Legislation Targeting Asylum Seekers in 2012' (August 2012) http://hotline.org.il/english/pdf/HotlineReport080812LegislationEng.pdf
  'New Regulations for the Treatment of Asylum Seekers in Israel: August 2010' (September 2010).
Human Rights Research and Education Centre, University of Ottawa, 'By the Numbers: Refugee Statistics' http://www.cdp-hrc.uottawa.ca/projects/refugee-forum/projects/Statistics.php
  'IRB Refugee Status Determinations (1989–2011 Calendar Years)' http://www.cdp-hrc.uottawa.ca/projects/refugee-forum/projects/documents/REFUGEESTATS COMPREHENSIVE1999–2011.pdf
Human Rights Watch, 'Everyday Intolerance: Racist and Xenophobic Violence in Italy' (New York: Human Rights Watch, 2011).
  'France: One Year On, New Abuses against Roma' (29 September 2011) http://www.hrw.org/news/2011/09/29/france-one-year-new-abuses-against-roma
  'France's Compliance with the European Free Movement Directive and the Removal of Ethnic Roma EU Citizens: A Briefing Paper Submitted to the European Commission in July 2011' (28 September 2011) http://www.hrw.org/news/2011/09/28/france-s-compliance-european-free-movement-directive-and-removal-ethnic-roma-eu-citi
  'World Report 2011: Malaysia' (January 2011) http://www.hrw.org/world-report-2011/malaysia
Hurwitz, Agnès, *The Collective Responsibility of States to Protect Refugees* (Oxford: Oxford University Press, 2009).
Hyndman, Jennifer and Nylund, Bo Victor, 'UNHCR and the Status of Prima Facie Refugees in Kenya' (1998) 10 *International Journal of Refugee Law* 21–48.
Imaz, Cecilia, 'El asilo diplomático en la política exterior de México' (1993) 40–41 *Revista Mexicana de Política Exterior* 53–71.
International Organization for Migration, *Informe preliminar a la XI Conferencia Sudamericana sobre Migraciones: Migrantes extracontinentales en Sudamérica* (August 2011).
Interview with Foreign Minister Alexander Downer, 'Foreign minister discusses withdrawal of migration bill and response from Indonesia', *Lateline* (ABC television, 14 August 2006).
Interview with Kaajal Ramjathan-Keogh, Head, Refugee and Migrant Rights Programme, Lawyers for Human Rights (South Africa), Cape Town, 13 September 2012.
Interview with Olabisi Dare, Director, AU Division of Humanitarian Affairs, Refugees and Displaced Persons, Addis Ababa, 16 January 2012.
Interview with Senator Helen Coonan, *Breakfast*, ABC Radio (2 October 2001).
'Israel begins deportation of South Sudanese refugees', *Real News*, http://therealnews.com/t2/index.php?option=com_content&task=view&id=31&Itemid=74&jumival=8042

Jackson, Ivor, *The Refugee Concept in Group Situations* (Leiden: Martinus Nijhoff, 1999).

Jacob Blaustein Institute for the Advancement of Human Rights, 'African Asylum Seekers in Israel: Frequently Asked Questions', p. 2 http://www.ajc.org/atf/cf/% 7B42d75369-d582-4380-8395-d25925b85eaf%7D/AFRICANASYLUMFAQS. PDF

'Background: African Asylum Seekers and Migrants in Israel, June 13, 2012' http://www.jbi-humanrights.org/files/jbi-background_african-asylum-see kers-and-migrants-in-israel.pdf

John-Hopkins, Michael, 'The Emperor's New Safe Country Concepts: A UK Perspective on Sacrificing Fairness on the Altar of Efficiency' (2009) 21 *International Journal of Refugee Law* 218–55.

Jubilut, Liliana Lyra and Carneiro, Wellington Pereira, 'Resettlement in Solidarity: A New Regional Approach towards a More Humane Durable Solution' (2011) 30 *Refugee Survey Quarterly* 63–86.

Juss, Satvinder, 'The Decline and Decay of European Refugee Policy' (2005) 25 *Oxford Journal of Legal Studies* 749–92.

Kaddous, Christine and Jametti Greiner, Monique (eds.), *Accords bilatéraux II Suisse–UE et autres Accords récents* (Brussels: Bruylant, Paris: LGDJ, Basel: Helbing & Lichtenhahn, 2006).

Kagan, Michael and Ben-Dor, Anat, *Nowhere to Run: Gay Palestinian Asylum Seekers in Israel* (Tel Aviv University, Buchmann Faculty of Law, Public Interest Law Program, April 2008).

Kagan, Robert, *Of Paradise and Power: America vs. Europe in the New World Order* (New York: Knopf, 2003).

Kälin, Walter, *Grundriss des Asylverfahrens* (Basel: Helbing & Lichtenhahn, 1990). 'Non-State Agents of Persecution and the Inability of the State to Protect', (2001) 15 *Georgetown Immigration Law Journal* 415–31.

Kelley, Ninette, 'Internal Flight/Relocation/Protection Alternative: Is it Reasonable?' (2002) 14 *International Journal of Refugee Law* 4–44.

Kennedy, Edward M., 'Refugee Act of 1980' (1981) 15 *International Migration Review* 141–56.

'Kenney defends visa rules for Czech nationals', *CTV News*, 15 July 2009 http:// www.ctv.ca/CTVNews/TopStories/20090714/visas_immigration_09071

Kepler, Tania, 'Israel Approves Detention Centre for Migrants, Refugees', *Alternative Information Center*, 30 November 2010 http://www.alternativenews.org/eng lish/index.php/news/israeli-society/3049-israel-approves-detention-centre-for-migrants-refugees.html

Kjaergaard, Eva, 'Opinion: The Concept of "Safe Third Country" in Contemporary European Refugee Law' (1994) 6 *International Journal of Refugee Law* 649–55.

Kjaerum, Morten, 'The Concept of Country of First Asylum' (1992) 4 *International Journal of Refugee Law* 514–30.

Klaaren, Jonathan and Rutinwa, Bonaventure, *Towards the Harmonization of Immigration and Refugee Law in SADC* (Johannesburg: The Institute for Democracy in South Africa, 2000).

Klotz, Anne, *Norms in International Relations* (Ithaca, NY: Cornell University Press, 1995).

Klug, Anja, 'Harmonization of Asylum in the European Union: Emergence of an EU Refugee System?' (2004) 47 *German Yearbook of International Law* 594–628.

Koch, Philippe and Lavenex, Sandra, 'The (Contentious) Human Face of Europeanization: Free Movement and Immigration', in Clive H. Church (ed.), *Switzerland and the European Union: A Close, Contradictory and Misunderstood Relationship* (London: Routledge, 2007), pp. 148–65.

Koh, Harold, 'On American Exceptionalism' (2003) 55 *Stanford Law Review* 1479–1527.

Kritzman-Amir, Tally and Spijkerboer, Thomas, 'On the Morality and Legality of Borders: Border Policies and Asylum Seekers' http://works.bepress.com/tally_kritzman_amir/7

Kwon, Soo-Ryun, 'The influence of the European Union's Common European Asylum System on the domestic legislation of African States', unpublished research report written during 2009 James E. Tolan Fellowship at the International Refugee Rights Initiative in Kampala, Uganda (on file with Marina Sharpe).

Lambert, Hélène, 'The Next Frontier: Expanding Protection in Europe for Victims of Armed Conflict and Indiscriminate Violence' (2013) 25 *International Journal of Refugee Law* (forthcoming).

'Transnational Judicial Dialogue, Harmonization and the Common European Asylum System' (2009) 58 *International and Comparative Law Quarterly* 519–43.

Lambert, Hélène and Goodwin-Gill, Guy S., (eds.), *The Limits of Transnational Law: Refugee Law, Policy Harmonization and Judicial Dialogue in the European Union* (Cambridge: Cambridge University Press, 2010).

Landgren, Karin, 'Deflecting International Protection by Treaty: Bilateral and Multilateral Accords on Extradition, Readmission and the Inadmissibility of Asylum Requests' (UNHCR, New Issues in Refugee Research, Working Paper No. 10, June 1999).

Lavenex, Sandra, 'Switzerland: Between Intergovernmental Cooperation and Schengen Association', in Marina Caparini and Otwin Marenin (eds.), *Borders and Security Governance: Managing Borders in a Globalised World* (Münster: LIT Verlag, 2006), pp. 233–51.

Lawrence, Shira, 'Anti-Infiltration Bill Passes into Law', ARDC, 11 January 2012 http://www.ardc-israel.org/en/article/anti-infiltration-bill-passes-law

Legomsky, Stephen, 'Secondary Refugee Movements and the Return of Asylum Seekers to Third Countries: The Meaning of Effective Protection' (2003) 15 *International Journal of Refugee Law* 567–677.

Legomsky, Stephen and Rodriguez, Cristina, *Immigration and Refugee Law and Policy* (5th edn, New York: Foundation Press, 2009).

Legrand, Pierre, 'European Legal Systems Are Not Converging' (1996) 45 *International and Comparative Law Quarterly* 52–81.

Leinwand, Donna, 'States enter debate on sharia law: are bans like Oklahoma's necessary, constitutional, anti-Islamic?', *USA Today*, 9 December 2010, p. A3.

Lenaerts, Koen, 'The Contribution of the European Court of Justice to the Area of Freedom, Security and Justice' (2010) 59 *International and Comparative Law Quarterly* 255–301.

Linos, Katerina, 'Diffusion through Democracy' (2011) 55 *American Journal of Political Science* 678–95.

    'When Do Policy Innovations Spread? Lessons for Advocates of Lesson-Drawing' (2006) 119 *Harvard Law Review* 1467–87.

Loescher, Gil, *The UNHCR and World Politics: A Perilous Path* (Oxford: Oxford University Press, 2001).

Lorié, Anouk, 'Dangers await Africans seeking asylum in Israel', *Time Magazine*, 11 December 2009 http://www.time.com/time/world/article/0,8599,1946861,00.html

McAdam, Jane, 'Australian Complementary Protection: A Step-By-Step Approach' (2011) 33 *Sydney Law Review* 687–734.

    Complementary Protection in International Refugee Law (Oxford: Oxford University Press, 2007).

    'Explainer: the facts about the Malaysian solution and Australia's international obligations', *Conversation*, 16 June 2011 http://theconversation.edu.au/explainer-the-facts-about-the-malaysian-solution-and-australias-international-obligations-1861

    'Interpretation of the 1951 Convention', in Andreas Zimmermann (ed.), *The 1951 Convention relating to the Status of Refugees and Its 1967 Protocol: A Commentary* (Oxford: Oxford University Press, 2011), pp. 75–116.

    Submission No. 21 to Senate Standing Committee on Legal and Constitutional Affairs, *Inquiry into the Migration Amendment (Complementary Protection) Bill 2009* (28 September 2009).

    Submission No. 35 to Senate Select Committee, *Inquiry into Ministerial Discretion in Migration Matters* (23 September 2003).

McCrudden, Christopher, 'A Common Law of Human Rights?: Transnational Judicial Conversations on Constitutional Rights' (2000) 20 *Oxford Journal of Legal Studies* 499–532.

McDonald, Clint, 'Danger on the US–Mexico border', *Washington Post*, 31 March 2011 http://www.washingtonpost.com/opinions/danger-on-the-us-mexico-border/2011/03/30/AFQp4KCC_story.html

Macklin, Audrey, 'Disappearing Refugees: Reflections on the Canada–US Safe Third Country Agreement' (2005) 36 *Columbia Human Rights Law Review* 365–426.

Mahnig, Hans (ed.), *Histoire de la politique de migration, d'asile et d'intégration en Suisse depuis 1948* (Zurich: Seismo, 2005).

Mahnig, Hans and Cattacin, Sandro, 'La transformation de la constellation politique internationale', in Hans Mahnig (ed.), *Histoire de la politique de migration, d'asile et d'intégration en Suisse depuis 1948* (Zurich: Seismo, 2005), pp. 405–15.

Maiani, Francesco, 'Fitting EU Asylum Standards in the Dublin Equation: Recent Case Law, Legislative Reforms, and the Position of Dublin "Associates"' (2010) 2/10 *ASYL* 9–19.

'La définition de réfugié entre Genève, Bruxelles et Berne – différences, tensions, ressemblances', in UNHCR and Schweizerische Flüchtlingshilfe (eds.), *Schweizer Asylrecht, EU-Standards und internationales Flüchtlingsrecht, eine Vergleichsstudie/Droit d'asile Suisse, normes de l'UE et droit international des réfugiés, une étude comparative* (Berne: Stämpfli Verlag, 2009), pp. 19–66.

Maiani, Francesco and Vevstad, Vigdis, 'Reflection Note on the Evaluation of the Dublin System and on the Dublin III Proposal' (European Parliament, Directorate-General of Internal Policies, Policy Department C, Citizens Rights and Constitutional Affairs, PE 410.690, March 2009).

Manners, Ian, 'Normative Power Europe: A Contradiction in Terms?' (2002) 40 *Journal of Common Market Studies* 235–58.

Markesinis, Basil (Sir) and Fedtke, Jörg, *Judicial Recourse to Foreign Law: A New Source of Inspiration?* (London: University College London and Austin: University of Texas: 2006).

Martens, Jonathan, 'Moving Freely on the African Continent: The Experiences of ECOWAS and SADC with Free Movement Protocols', in Ryszard Cholewinski and Richard Perruchoud (eds.), *International Migration Law: Developing Paradigms and Key Challenges* (The Hague: TMC Asser Press, 2007), pp. 349–61.

Martin, David A. (ed.), *The New Asylum-Seekers: Refugee Law in the 1980s* (Leiden: Martinus Nijhoff, 1988).

'Reforming Asylum Adjudication', *Report to the Administrative Conference of the United States*, May 1989.

Martin, David A., Aleinikoff, T. Alexander, Motomura, Hiroshi and Fullerton, Maryellen, *Forced Migration: Law and Policy* (St Paul, MN: Thomson/West Publishing, 2007).

Marx, Reinhard, 'The Criteria of Applying the "Internal Flight Alternative" Test in National Refugee Status Determination Procedures' (2002) 14 *International Journal of Refugee Law* 179–218.

Mathew, Penelope, Submission No. 34 to Senate Legal and Constitutional Committee, *Inquiry into the Migration Legislation Amendment (Further Border Protection Measures) Bill* 2002.

Mathew, Penelope and ANU Law Students for Social Justice Society, Submission No. 204 to Senate Legal and Constitutional Committee, *Inquiry into the Administration and Operation of the Migration Act 1958* (9 August 2005) http://www.aph.gov.au/Parliamentary_Business/Committees/Senate_Com mittees?url=legcon_ctte/completed_inquiries/2004-07/migration/submissi ons/sub204.pdf

Mattli, Walter, *The Logic of Regional Integration: Europe and Beyond* (Cambridge: Cambridge University Press, 1999).

'Mexico Declaration and Plan of Action to Strengthen the International Protection of Refugees in Latin America' (2005) 17 *International Journal of Refugee Law* 802–17.

Meyer, John, Frank, David, Hironaka, Ann, Schofer, Evan and Tuma, Nancy, 'The Structuring of a World Environmental Regime, 1870–1990' (1997) 51 *International Organization* 623–51.

'Migration experts discuss the global dilemma of an estimated 22 million refugees', *Breakfast*, ABC Radio (21 May 2003).

Migration Policy Institute, 'European Migration' http://www.migrationpolicy. org/Europe/

Milner, James, *Refugees, the State and the Politics of Asylum in Africa* (London: Palgrave Macmillan, 2009).

Mole, Nuala, *Asylum and the European Convention on Human Rights* (4th edn, Strasbourg: Council of Europe Publishing, 2007).

Moniem, Dallia, 'Torture in the desert', *Africa Review*, 2 March 2012 http://www. africareview.com/Special+Reports/Torture+in+the+desert/-/979182/1357 834/-/fnqhl3/-/index.html

Moreno-Lax, Violeta, 'Dismantling the Dublin System: *MSS* v. *Belgium and Greece*' (2012) 14 *European Journal of Migration and Law* 1–31.

  '*Hirsi Jamaa and Others* v. *Italy* or the Strasbourg Court versus Extraterritorial Migration Control?' (2012) 12 *Human Rights Law Review* 574–98.

  'Seeking Asylum in the Mediterranean: Against a Fragmentary Reading of EU Member States' Obligations Accruing at Sea' (2011) 23 *International Journal of Refugee Law* 174–220.

Motomura, Hiroshi, 2012 Immigration Law Professors Workshop, 14 March 2012 (on file with Maryellen Fullerton).

Mouffe, Chantal, 'Carl Schmitt and the Paradox of Liberal Democracy', in David Dyzenhaus (ed.), *Law as Politics: Carl Schmitt's Critique of Liberalism* (Durham: Duke University Press, 1998), pp. 159–76.

MTI, 'Canada Vows to Continue Deporting Hungarian Asylum Seekers', *Politics.
hu*, 15 October 2012 http://www.politics.hu/20121015/canada-vows-to-
continue-deporting-hungarian-asylum-seekers/

Murillo González, Juan Carlos, 'El derecho de asilo y la protección de refugiados
en el continente americano', in UNHCR, *La protección internacional de
refugiados en las Américas* (Quito: Mantis, 2011), pp. 51–74.

'Principios básicos y posibles respuesta programáticas', in OAS Comisión
Especial de Asuntos Migratorios, *Memoria: Migración extracontinental en
las Américas* (6 April 2010), pp. 19–23.

Musalo, Karen, Moore, Jennifer and Boswell, Richard A., *Refugee Law and Policy:
A Comparative and International Approach* (4th edn, Durham, NC:
Carolina Academic Press, 2011).

Natan, Gilad, *National Programme to Meet the Problem of Infiltrators and Asylum
Seekers Entering Israel across the Egyptian Border* (The Knesset, Research
and Information Center, 25 January 2011).

Nelken, David, 'Puzzling Out Legal Cultures: A Comment on Blankenburg', in
David Nelken (ed.), *Comparing Legal Cultures* (Aldershot: Ashgate, 1997),
pp. 58–88.

New South Wales Young Lawyers, Submission No. 198 to Senate Legal and
Constitutional Committee, *Inquiry into the Administration and Operation
of the Migration Act 1958* (9 August 2005).

Nicholson, Frances, 'Challenges to Forging a Common European Asylum System
in Line with International Obligations', in Steve Peers and Nicola Rogers
(eds.), *EU Immigration and Asylum Law: Text and Commentary* (Leiden
and Boston: Martinus Nijhoff, 2006), pp. 505–38.

Niemann, Arne, 'Explaining Visa, Asylum and Immigration Policy Treaty
Revision: Insights from a Revised Neofunctionalist Framework'
(Constitutionalism Web-Papers ConWEB No.1/2006) http://www.qub.ac.
uk/schools/SchoolofPoliticsInternationalStudiesandPhilosophy/FileStore/
ConWEBFiles/Filetoupload,38372,en.pdf

Noll, Gregor, *Negotiating Asylum: The EU Acquis, Extraterritorial Protection and
the Common Market of Deflection* (The Hague: Martinus Nijhoff, 2000).

'Visions of the Exceptional: Legal and Theoretical Issues Raised by Transit
Processing Centres and Protection Zones' (2003) 5 *European Journal of
Migration and Law* 303–41.

Noll, Gregor and Vedsted-Hansen, Jens, 'Non-Communitarians: Refugee and
Asylum Policies', in P. Alston (ed.), *The EU and Human Rights* (Oxford:
Oxford University Press, 1999), pp. 359–410.

North, Anthony M. and Chia, Joyce, 'Towards Convergence in the Interpretation of the
Refugee Convention: A Proposal for the Establishment of an International
Judicial Commission for Refugees', in Jane McAdam (ed.), *Forced Migration,
Human Rights and Security* (Oxford: Hart, 2008), pp. 225–62.

Okoth-Obbo, George, 'Thirty Years On: A Legal Review of the 1969 OAU Convention Governing the Specific Aspects of Refugee Problems in Africa' (2001) 20 *Refugee Survey Quarterly* 79–138.

O'Nions, Helen, 'Slippery citizenship', working draft (September 2012) (on file with Audrey Macklin).

Organisation suisse d'aide aux réfugiés, *La Suisse finit elle aussi par accorder l'asile aux victimes de persécutions non-étatiques* (Communiqué de presse, Berne, 15 June 2006).

  Manuel de la procédure d'asile et de renvoi (Berne, Stuttgart, Vienna: Haupt, 2009).

Oucho, John and Crush, Jonathan, 'Contra Free Movement: South Africa and the SADC Migration Protocols' (2001) 48 *Africa Today* 139–57.

Paley, Maya, *Surviving in Limbo: Community Formation among Sudanese and Eritrean Asylum Seekers in Israel* (ASSAF, June 2011) http://www.assaf.org.il/en/refugees/refugees-israel

  Surviving in Limbo: Lived Experiences among Sudanese and Eritrean Asylum Seekers in Israel (ASSAF, June 2011) http://www.assaf.org.il/en/refugees/refugees-israel

Pardo, Sharon and Peters, Joel, *Uneasy Neighbours: Israel and the European Union* (Lanham, MD: Lexington Books, 2009).

Parini, Lorena, *La politique d'asile en Suisse: Une perspective systémique* (Paris: L'Harmattan, 1997).

Parini, Lorena and Gianni, Matteo, 'Enjeux et modifications de la politique d'asile en Suisse de 1956 à nos jours', in Hans Mahnig (ed.), *Histoire de la politique de migration, d'asile et d'intégration en Suisse depuis 1948* (Zurich: Seismo, 2005), pp. 189–252.

Paz, Yonathan, 'Ordered Disorder: African Asylum Seekers in Israel and Discursive Challenges to an Emerging Refugee Regime' (UNHCR, New Issues in Refugee Research, Research Paper No. 205, March 2011).

Peers, Steve and Rogers, Nicola (eds.), *EU Immigration and Asylum Law: Text and Commentary* (Dordrecht: Martinus Nijhoff, 2006).

Perry, Avi, 'Solving Israel's African Refugee Crisis' (2010) 51 *Virginia Journal of International Law* 157–84.

Piguet, Etienne, *L'immigration en Suisse* (Lausanne: Presses polytechniques et universitaires romands, 2004).

Piovesan, Flávia and Jubilut, Liliana Lyra, 'Regional Developments: Americas', in Andreas Zimmermann (ed.), *The 1951 Convention relating to the Status of Refugees and Its 1967 Protocol* (Oxford: Oxford University Press, 2011), pp. 205–24.

Plender, Richard and Mole, Nuala, 'Beyond the Geneva Convention: Constructing a *De Facto* Right of Asylum from International Human Rights Instruments', in Frances Nicholson and Patrick Twomey (eds.), *Refugee Rights and Realities:*

Evolving International Concepts and Regimes (Cambridge: Cambridge University Press, 1999), pp. 81–105.

'PM's immigration bill could violate refugee rights', *New Middle East News*, 19 March 2012.

Proussalidis, Daniel, 'Tories push through crackdown on refugees', *Toronto Sun*, 24 April 2012 http://www.torontosun.com/2012/04/24/tories-push-through-crackdown-on-refugees

Public Interest Advocacy Centre, Submission No. 2 to Senate Legal and Constitutional Legislation Committee, *Inquiry into the Provisions of the Migration Legislation Amendment (Identification and Authentication) Bill 2003* (1 September 2003).

Quan, Douglas, 'Experts say security reasons may keep Tamils in detention', *Vancouver Sun*, 6 September 2012. http://www.vancouversun.com/news/Experts+security+reasons+keep+Tamils+detention/3486992/story.html

Ramirez, Francisco and Meyer, John, 'Comparative Education: The Social Construction of the Modern World System' (1980) 6 *Annual Review of Sociology* 369–99.

Ramseyer, Paul André, 'Switzerland and Europe: Between the EC, the CSCE and Neutrality', in Bo Huldt and Atis Leijņš (eds.), *Neutrals in Europe* (Stockholm: Swedish Institute of International Affairs, 1989), pp. 17–26.

Red Cross/EU Office, 'Position paper on the Right to Access to International Protection', Brussels, 17 November 2011.

Refugee Council of Australia, '2010 High Priorities List: Asylum Policy Issues' (20 October 2010) http://www.refugeecouncil.org.au/docs/current/2010_Asylum_priorities.pdf

  Submission No. 12 to the Senate Legal and Constitutional Legislation Committee, *Inquiry into the Provisions of the Migration Legislation Amendment (Procedural Fairness) Bill 2002* (April 2002).

Refugee Council (UK), 'Unsafe Havens, Unworkable Solutions' (Position Paper, June 2003).

'Refugee expert says Australia/Malaysia swap illegal', *ABC News*, 10 June 2011 http://www.abc.net.au/worldtoday/content/2011/s3240886.htm

Refugees' Rights Forum (Hotline for Migrant Workers), 'Asylum Seekers and Refugees in Israel: August 2009 Update', 20 August 2009 http://www.acri.org.il/pdf/refugees0809en.pdf

Refugees' Rights Forum, Letter to Members of the Knesset: Infiltration, 4 June 2008.

  Policy Paper: The Detention of Asylum Seekers and Refugees, June 2008.

Rehaag, Sean, '2011 Refugee Claim Data and IRB Member Recognition Rates: Outcomes by Country and Board Member' (4.table_.xls) (12 March 2012) http://ccrweb.ca/en/2011-refugee-claim-data

Riaño, Yvonne and Wastl-Walter, Doris, 'Historical Shifts in Asylum Policies in Switzerland: Between Humanitarian Values and the Protection of National Identity' (2006) 27 *Refugee Watch* 1–18.

Risse, Thomas, 'Ideas Do Not Float Freely: Transnational Coalitions, Domestic Structures, and the End of the Cold War' (1994) 48 *International Organization* 165–214.

Risse, Thomas, Ropp, Steven and Sikkink, Kathryn, *The Power of Human Rights: International Norms and Domestic Change* (Cambridge: Cambridge University Press, 1999).

Roldán León, Johanna, 'El registro ampliado de refugiados en la frontera norte del Ecuador: un proyecto pionero en la protección internacional de refugiados en la región' in UNHCR, *La protección internacional de refugiados en las Américas* (Quito: Mantis, 2011), pp. 75–88.

Rutinwa, Bonaventure, 'The End of Asylum: The Changing Nature of Refugee Policies in Africa' (2002) 21 *Refugee Survey Quarterly* 12–41.

Safrin, Sabrina, 'The Unexceptionalism of US Exceptionalism' (2008) 41 *Vanderbilt Journal of Transnational Law* 1307–54.

Salter, Mark B. and Mutlu, Can E., 'The "Next Generation" Visa: Belt and Braces or the Emperor's New Clothes?' (Centre for European Policy Studies Paper on Liberty and Security in Europe, October 2011).

Sandholtz, Wayne and Stiles, Kendall, *International Norms and Cycles of Change* (Oxford: Oxford University Press, 2009).

Schmidt, Paul, Immigration Judge (former BIA Chairman, 1995–2001), 7 May 2012 (on file with Maryellen Fullerton).

Schmitter, Philippe C., 'Three Neo-Functional Hypotheses about International Integration' (1969) 23 *International Organization* 161–6.

Schreier, Tal, 'An Evaluation of South Africa's Application of the OAU Refugee Definition' (2008) 25 *Refuge* 53–63.

Schwok, René, (ed.), *Switzerland–European Union: An Impossible Membership?* (Brussels: Peter Lang, 2009).

'Switzerland's Approximation of Its Legislation to the EU *Acquis*: Specificities, Lessons and Paradoxes' (2007) 9 *European Journal of Law Reform* 449–65.

Schwok, René and Levrat, Nicolas, 'Switzerland's Relations with the EU after the Adoption of the Seven Bilateral Agreements' (2001) 6 *European Foreign Affairs Review* 335–54.

Sharpe, Marina, 'The 1969 African Refugee Convention: Innovations, Misconceptions, and Omissions' (2012) 58 *McGill Law Journal* 95–147.

'Organization of African Unity and African Union Engagement with Refugee Protection: 1963 to 2011' (2013) 21 *African Journal of International and Comparative Law* (forthcoming).

Sherwood, Harriet, 'Eritrean refugees trapped by security fence at Israeli–Egyptian border', *Guardian*, 5 September 2012 http://www.guardian.co.uk/world/2012/sep/05/eritrean-refugees-at-israeli-egyptian-border

Silver, Charlotte, 'Tel Aviv no haven for asylum seekers', *Al Jazeera*, 23 February 2012 http://www.aljazeera.com/indepth/opinion/2012/02/2012215161243752551.html

Skran, Claudena, *Refugees in Inter-War Europe: The Emergence of a Regime* (Oxford: Oxford University Press, 1995).

Slaughter, Anne-Marie, 'A Global Community of Courts' (2003) 44 *Harvard International Law Journal* 191–219.

'Global Government Networks, Global Information Agencies, and Disaggregated Democracy' (2003) 24 *Michigan Journal of International Law* 1041–75.

A New World Order (Princeton: Princeton University Press, 2004).

'Sovereignty and Power in a Networked World Order' (2004) 40 *Stanford Journal of International Law* 283–327.

Slaughter, Anne-Marie and Burke-White, William, 'The Future of International Law Is Domestic (or, The European Way of Law)' (2006) 47 *Harvard International Law Journal* 327–52.

Stein, Eric, 'Lawyers, Judges, and the Making of a Transnational Constitution' (1981) 75 *American Journal of International Law* 1–27.

Stevens, Dallal, *UK Asylum Law and Policy: Historical and Contemporary Perspectives* (London: Sweet & Maxwell, 2004).

Stoeva, Preslava, *New Norms and Knowledge in World Politics* (Abingdon, Oxon.: Routledge, 2010).

Storey, Hugo, 'The Advanced Refugee Law Workshop Experience: An IARLJ Perspective' (2003) 15 *International Journal of Refugee Law* 422–9.

'EU Refugee Qualification Directive: A Brave New World?' (2008) 20 *International Journal of Refugee Law* 1–49.

'The Internal Flight Alternative Test: The Jurisprudence Re-Examined' (1998) 10 *International Journal of Refugee Law* 499–532.

Submission by seventeen refugee law academics to the Expert Panel on Asylum Seekers (July 2012) http://www.gtcentre.unsw.edu.au/sites/gtcentre.unsw.edu.au/files/expert_panel_11_7_12.pdf

Taylor, Savitri, 'Protection Elsewhere/Nowhere' (2006) 18 *International Journal of Refugee Law* 283–312.

'Regional Cooperation and the Malaysian Solution' *Inside Story*, 9 May 2011 http://inside.org.au/regional-cooperation-and-the-malaysian-solution/

Teubner, Gunther, 'Legal Irritants: Good Faith in British Law or How Unifying Law Ends up in New Divergences' (1998) 61 *Modern Law Review* 11–32.

Thielemann, Eiko and El-Enany, Nadine, 'Beyond Fortress Europe? How European Cooperation Has Strengthened Refugee Protection', Paper presented at European Union Studies Association's 11th Biennial International Conference, Los Angeles, 23–25 April 2009.

'Common Laws, Diverse Outcomes: Can EU Asylum Initiatives Lead to More Effective Refugee Protection?', Paper prepared for the European Union Studies Association's 12th Biennial International Conference, Boston, 3–5 March 2011 http://www.euce.org/eusa/2011/papers/1a_thielemann.pdf

'Refugee Protection as a Collective Action Problem: Is the EU Shirking Its Responsibilities?' (2010) 19 *European Security* 209–29.

'Tories sweeping immigration reforms target influx of claims from Roma gypsies', *National Post* (16 February 2012) http://news.nationalpost.com/2012/02/16/conservatives-to-announce-further-barriers-to-deter-bogus-refugee-claimants-report/

Tóth, Judit, 'The Incomprehensible Flow of Roma Asylum-Seekers from the Czech Republic and Hungary to Canada' (Centre for European Policy Studies Paper on Liberty and Security in Europe, November 2010).

Tsurkov, Elizabeth, 'Knesset passes bill on prolonged detention of refugees without trial', *972 Magazine*, 10 January 2012 http://972mag.com/knesset-passes-con troversial-bill-on-prolonged-detention-of-asylum-seekers/32487

Tuepker, Anais, 'On the Threshold of Africa: OAU and UN Definition in South African Asylum Practice' (2002) 15 *Journal of Refugee Studies* 409–23.

Türk, Volker, 'Non-State Agents of Persecution', in Vincent Chetail and Vera Gowlland-Debbas (eds.), *Switzerland and the International Protection of Refugees /La Suisse et la protection internationale des réfugiés* (The Hague, London, New York: Kluwer Law International, 2002), pp. 95–109.

Türk, Volker and Nicholson, Frances, 'Refugee protection in international law: an overall perspective', in Erika Feller, Volker Türk and Frances Nicholson (eds.), *Refugee Protection in International Law: UNHCR's Global Consultations on International Protection* (Cambridge: Cambridge University Press, 2003), pp. 3–45.

Turner, Jennifer, 'Liberian Refugees: A Test of the 1969 OAU Convention Governing the Specific Aspects of Refugee Problems in Africa' (1994) 8 *Georgetown Immigration Law Journal* 281–301.

Twining, William, 'Diffusion of Law: A Global Perspective' (2004) 49 *Journal of Legal Pluralism* 1–45.

Globalisation and Legal Theory (Cambridge: Cambridge University Press, 2000).

'Normative and Legal Pluralism: A Global Perspective' (2010) 20 *Duke Journal of Comparative & International Law* 473–517.

'Social Science and Diffusion of Law' (2005) 32 *Journal of Law and Society* 203–40.

Uçarer, Emek M., 'Guarding the Borders of the European Union: Paths, Portals, and Prerogatives', in Sandra Lavenex and Emek M. Uçarer (eds.), *Migration and the Externalities of European Integration* (Lanham, MD: Lexington Books, 2003), pp. 15–32.

Vahl, Marius and Grolimund, Nina, *Integration without Membership: Switzerland's Bilateral Agreements with the European Union* (Brussels: Centre for European Policy Studies, 2007).

Van Garderen, Jacob and Ebenstein, Julie, 'Regional Developments: Africa' in Andreas Zimmermann (ed.), *The 1951 Convention relating to the Status of Refugees and Its 1967 Protocol* (Oxford: Oxford University Press, 2011), pp. 185–204.

Victorian Bar, Submission No. 4 to Senate Legal and Constitutional Legislation Committee, *Inquiry into the Provisions of the Migration Legislation Amendment (Identification and Authentication) Bill 2003* (3 September 2003).

Vierdag, E. W., 'The Country of "First Asylum": Some European Aspects', in David A. Martin (ed.), *The New Asylum Seekers: Refugee Law in the 1980s* (Dordrecht: Martinus Nijhoff, 1988).

Von Gunten, Christina, '*Die Staatlichkeit Verfolgung – eine Voraussetzung der Anerkennung als Flüchtling?*' (2001) 1/01 *ASYL* 22–35.

Ward, Kim, 'Navigation Guide: Regional Protection Zones and Transit Processing Centres' (Information Centre about Asylum and Refugees in the UK, November 2004).

Watt, Nicholas, 'The Guardian profile: Lynton Crosby', *Guardian*, 28 January 2005 http://www.guardian.co.uk/politics/2005/jan/28/uk.conservatives

Weinberg, Lisa Laurel, *Senegal Legal Aid Assessment* (Dakar: WARIPNET, 2008).

Wendt, Alexander, *Social Theory of International Politics* (Cambridge: Cambridge University Press, 1999).

Werenfels, Samuel, *Der Begriff des Flüchtlings im schweizerischen Asylrecht* (Berne: Peter Lang, 1987).

Westhead, Rick, 'Why the Roma are fleeing Hungary and why Canada is shunning them', *The Star.com*, 13 October 2012 http://www.thestar.com/news/world/article/1270708-roma-in-hungary-feel-persecuted-but-they-have-nowhere-to-turn

Wildhaber, Luzius, 'Swiss Neutrality: Legal Base and Historical Background', in Bo Huldt and Atis Leijņš (eds.), *Neutrals in Europe* (Stockholm: Swedish Institute of International Affairs, 1989), pp. 3–15.

Wilsher, Daniel, 'Non-State Actors and the Definition of a Refugee in the United Kingdom: Protection, Accountability or Culpability?' (2003) 15 *International Journal of Refugee Law* 68–112.

Wood, Tamara and McAdam, Jane, 'Australian Asylum Policy All at Sea: An Analysis of *Plaintiff M70/2011 v. Minister for Immigration and Citizenship* and the Australia–Malaysia Arrangement' (2012) 61 *International and Comparative Law Quarterly* 274–300.

Wouters, Kees, *International Legal Standards for the Protection from Refoulement* (Antwerp: Intersentia, 2009).

Zabludovsky, Karla, 'Mexico: bodies found on bridge', *New York Times*, 15 September 2012, p. A8.

'Photographers found dead in Mexico', *New York Times*, 4 May 2012, p. A12.

'Police find 49 bodies by a highway in Mexico', *New York Times*, 14 May 2012, p. A4.

Zard, Monette, 'African Union', in Matthew Gibney and Randall Hansen (eds.), *Immigration and Asylum: From 1900 to the Present* (Santa Barbara: ABC-CLIO, 2005), pp. 5–8.

INDEX